S/

D

Analog Integrated Circuits

Analog Integrated Circuits

Edwin W. Greeneich
Associate Professor
Department of Electrical Engineering
Arizona State University

CHAPMAN & HALL

International Thomson Publishing

New York • Albany • Bonn • Boston • Cincinnati • Detroit • London • Madrid • Melbourne
Mexico City • Pacific Grove • Paris • San Francisco • Singapore • Tokyo • Toronto • Washington

Cover design: Trudi Gershenov
Cover photo: © 1997 PhotoDisc, Inc
Copyright © 1997 by Chapman & Hall

Printed in the United States of America

For more information, contact:

Chapman & Hall
115 Fifth Avenue
New York, NY 10003

Chapman & Hall
2-6 Boundary Row
London SE1 8HN
England

Thomas Nelson Australia
102 Dodds Street
South Melbourne, 3205
Victoria, Australia

Chapman & Hall GmbH
Postfach 100 263
D-69442 Weinheim
Germany

International Thomson Editores
Campos Eliseos 385, Piso 7
Col. Polanco
11560 Mexico D. F.
Mexico

International Thomson Publishing - Japan
Hirakawacho-cho Kyowa Building, 3F
1-2-1 Hirakawacho-cho
Chiyoda-ku, 102 Tokyo
Japan

International Thomson Publishing Asia
221 Henderson Road #05-10
Henderson Building
Singapore 0315

1 2 3 4 5 6 7 8 9 10 XXX 01 00 99 98 97 96

Library of Congress Cataloging-in-Publication Data

Greeneich, Edwin W., 1941-
    Analog integrated circuits / Edwin W. Greeneich.
            p.   cm.
    Includes index.
    ISBN 0-412-08521-6 (alk. paper)
    1. Linear integrated circuits.   . Title.
TK7874.G715   1996   I
621.3815--dc20   96-26747
                                                            CIP

To order this or any other Chapman & Hall book, please contact **International Thomson Publishing, 7625 Empire Drive, Florence, KY 41042.** Phone: (606) 525-6600 or 1-800-842-3636. Fax: (606) 525-7778. e-mail: order@chaphall.com.

For a complete listing of Chapman & Hall's titles, send your request to **Chapman & Hall, Dept. BC, 115 Fifth Avenue, New York, NY 10003.**

CONTENTS

PREFACE

Analog Integrated Circuits deals with the design and analysis of modern analog circuits using integrated bipolar and field-effect transistor technologies. This book is suitable as a text for a one-semester course for senior level or first-year graduate students as well as a reference work for practicing engineers. Advanced students will also find the text useful in that some of the material presented here is not covered in many first courses on analog circuits. Included in this is an extensive coverage of feedback amplifiers, current-mode circuits, and translinear circuits. Suitable background would be fundamental courses in electronic circuits and semiconductor devices.

This book contains numerous examples, many of which include commercial analog circuits. End-of-chapter problems are given, many illustrating practical circuits.

Chapter 1 discuses the models commonly used to represent devices used in modern analog integrated circuits. Presented are models for bipolar junction transistors, junction diodes, junction field-effect transistors, and metal-oxide-semiconductor field-effect transistors. Both large-signal and small-signal models are developed as well as their implementation in the SPICE circuit-simulation program.

The basic building blocks used in a large variety of analog circuits are analyzed in Chapter 2; these consist of current sources, dc level-shift stages, single-transistor gain stages, two-transistor gain stages, and output stages. Both bipolar and field-effect transistor implementations are presented.

Chapter 3 deals with operational amplifier circuits. The four basic op-amp circuits are analyzed: (1) voltage-feedback amplifiers, (2) current-feedback amplifiers, (3) current-differencing amplifiers, and (4) transconductance amplifiers. Selected applications are also presented.

In Chapter 4 feedback amplifiers are discussed. A detailed analysis procedure for various feedback configurations is developed and numerous examples of feedback circuits are presented. Stability considerations and methods for compensation of feedback amplifiers are also discussed.

   Chapter 5 deals with translinear circuits; these are circuits that exploit the
linear relationship between the transconductance of a transistor and either its
current or voltage. Applications of translinear circuits include implementation
of analog functions and generation of trigonometric functions. These circuits
find use in communications, signal processing, and control systems.

Chapter 1

Models for Integrated-Circuit Devices

In the analysis, design and simulation of integrated circuits, models are used to represent the electrical behavior of the devices in the circuit. Consequently, the accuracy to which the actual circuit performance is predicted depends directly on the suitability and accuracy of the models used to represent the devices. It is important that the circuit designer understand the limitations and range of applicability of the device models and the approximations used in their derivation.

In this chapter we discuss the models commonly used to represent devices in analog integrated circuits: bipolar junction transistors, junction diodes, junction field-effect transistors, and metal-oxide-semiconductor field-effect transistors. Included will be models as implemented in the circuit simulation program SPICE.

1.1 Bipolar Junction Transistor

A bipolar junction transistor (BJT) is formed with two *pn* junctions in close proximity to each other. Shown in Fig. 1-1 is a cross-sectional view of a typical silicon bipolar transistor structure used in modern integrated circuits. Depicted is an *npn* transistor comprised of a heavily doped (N^+) emitter region, a lighter-doped (N^-) collector region, and an intervening (P) base region. Electrical contact to the base region is provided by the P^+ polysilicon layer, and the P^+ contact enhancement region (which reduces series parasitic base resistance), and contact to the collector region is made through the N^+ buried layer (which reduces the series parasitic collector resistance), the N^- layer, and the N^+ contact enhancement region. Isolation from other devices in the circuit is provided by the insulating silicon dioxide (SiO_2) layer (which completely surrounds the device laterally) and by the *p*-type substrate (which forms a *pn* junction—normally reverse biased—between the collector region and the substrate).

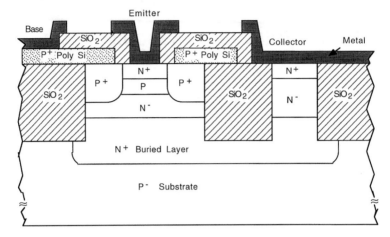

Figure 1-1   Cross-sectional view of an *npn* bipolar integrated-circuit transistor.

The active portion (also termed the intrinsic portion) of the transistor is the vertical $N^+/P/N^-$ layer structure shown beneath the emitter metallization. A one-dimensional representation of this intrinsic device portion is shown in Fig. 1-2(a). Under normal operation, the emitter-base junction is forward biased and the collector-base junction is reverse biased. In this configuration, carriers (electrons for an *npn* transistor) are injected into the base by virtue of the forward bias on the emitter junction. These carriers move by a combination of drift and diffusion through the base to the collector junction, where, due to the reverse bias on this junction, are swept into the collector region, giving rise to a current in the collector. This current, originating in the emitter, is thus controlled predominantly by the emitter-base junction bias and accounts for this structure being an active (transistor) device.

Figure 1-2(b) shows the circuit symbol for an *npn* transistor and the sign convention for voltages and currents. Under normal operation (in which the device is operating in the forward-active region), V_{be} is positive, V_{bc} is negative, and currents flow in the directions depicted in the figure. A one-dimensional representation of the intrinsic portion of a *pnp* transistor is shown in Fig. 1-2(c) and its circuit symbol is illustrated in Fig. 1-2(d). For a *pnp* transistor operating in the forward-active region, V_{be} is negative, V_{bc} is positive, and currents flow in the directions depicted.

Ebers–Moll Static Model

A relatively simple, but yet adequate for many cases, large-signal model for the bipolar transistor is the Ebers–Moll model [1]. It describes the transistor

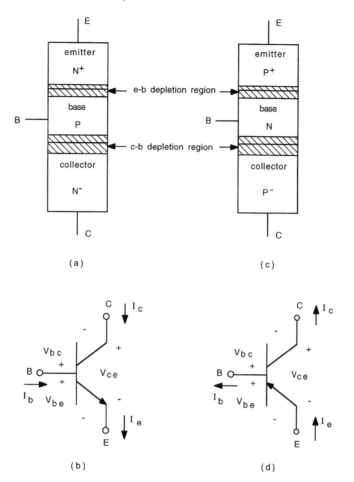

Figure 1-2 (a) One-dimensional representation of the intrinsic portion of an npn transistor structure; (b) *npn* transistor symbol and sign convention; (c) *pnp* transistor structure; (d) *pnp* transistor symbol and sign convention.

currents in terms of the two *pn* junction currents and their respective junction voltages and is illustrated in Fig. 1-3. The emitter-base and collector-base junction currents are given by

$$I_{EF} = I_{ES} \left(e^{qV_{BE}/kT} - 1 \right) \tag{1-1}$$

$$I_{CR} = I_{CS} \left(e^{qV_{BC}/kT} - 1 \right) \tag{1-2}$$

where I_{ES} and I_{CS} are the reverse saturation currents of the emitter-base and collector-base junctions, respectively and kT/q is the thermal voltage.

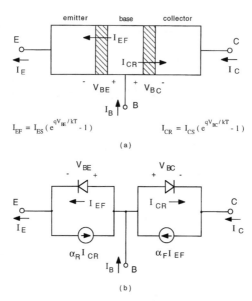

Figure 1-3 (a) Emitter and collector junction currents used in the Ebers–Moll model of the bipolar transistor. (b) Common-base Ebers–Moll static model of an *npn* transistor.

The total collector current (I_C) is comprised of the collector junction current (I_{CR}) and the fraction of the emitter junction current (I_{EF}) reaching the collector. This current arises from the carriers injected from the emitter into the base and their subsequent transport through the base to the collector. This fraction is denoted α_F and represents the ratio of the collector to emitter current when the transistor is operating in the normal (forward-active) mode of operation; that is, with the emitter-base junction forward biased and the collector-base junction reverse biased. Typical values for α_F in modern integrated-circuit transistors are 0.98–0.995. With reference to the circuit model shown in Fig. 1-3(b), the terminal collector current is

$$I_C = \alpha_F I_{EF} - I_{CR} \tag{1-3}$$

Likewise, the total emitter current (I_E) is comprised of the emitter junction current (I_{EF}) and the fraction α_R of the collector junction current reaching the emitter. α_R represents the ratio of the emitter to collector current when the transistor is operating in the inverse (reverse-active) mode of operation (collector-base junction forward biased and emitter-base junction reverse biased). Owing primarily to the large difference in the impurity doping concentrations in the emitter and collector regions of the transistor, α_R is smaller than α_F, with typical values ranging from 0.5 to 0.9. From Fig. 1-3(b),

$$I_E = I_{EF} - \alpha_R I_{CR} \tag{1-4}$$

Applying Kirchoff's current law for the base current ($I_B = I_E - I_C$) gives

$$I_B = (1 - \alpha_F) I_{EF} + (1 - \alpha_R) I_{CR} \tag{1-5}$$

It can be shown from reciprocity conditions applied to the emitter and collector junctions [2] that

$$\alpha_F I_{ES} = \alpha_R I_{CS} = I_S \tag{1-6}$$

where I_S the saturation current of the BJT and is given as

$$I_S = \frac{q D_B n_i^2 A_E}{Q_B} \tag{1-7}$$

D_B is the diffusion constant for minority carriers in the base (electrons for an *npn*, holes for a *pnp*), n_i is the intrinsic carrier concentration of the semiconductor, A_E is the area of the emitter-base junction, and Q_B is the number of majority carrier charges per unit area in the base (holes for an *npn*, electrons for a *pnp*). Typical values for I_S in an integrated-circuit transistor range from about 10^{-17} A for a small-geometry, low-current device to 10^{-15} A for a large device such as might be used in the output stage where large currents are required.

Using Eq. (1-6) in Eqs. (1-3) and (1-4) gives for the Ebers–Moll equations:

$$I_C = I_S (e^{q V_{BE}/kT} - 1) - \frac{I_S}{\alpha_R} (e^{q V_{BC}/kT} - 1) \tag{1-8}$$

$$I_E = \frac{I_S}{\alpha_F} (e^{q V_{BE}/kT} - 1) - I_S (e^{q V_{BC}/kT} - 1) \tag{1-9}$$

These equations describe the large-signal behavior of the bipolar transistor and, as such, there is no restriction on either the magnitude or polarity of the junction voltages. They can thus be used to describe transistor operation in four regions of operation:

(i) Forward-active. Here, the emitter-base junction is forward biased (V_{BE} positive for an *npn*, negative for a *pnp*) and the collector-base junction is reverse biased (V_{BC} negative for an *npn*, positive for a *pnp*). If the reverse bias on the collector junction is at least several kT/q in magnitude, then the *exp* $(q V_{BC}/kT)$ terms in Eqs. (1-8) and (1-9) are much smaller than -1 and can be neglected. This gives for forward-active region:

$$I_C = I_S (e^{q V_{BE}/kT} - 1) + \frac{I_S}{\alpha_R} \tag{1-10}$$

$$I_E = \frac{I_S}{\alpha_F} (e^{q V_{BE}/kT} - 1) + I_S \tag{1-11}$$

Equation (1-11) can be used in Eq. (1-10) to express the collector current in terms of the emitter current:

$$I_C = \alpha_F I_E + I_{CO} \tag{1-12}$$

where

$$I_{CO} = \frac{I_S(1 - \alpha_F \alpha_R)}{\alpha_R} \tag{1-13}$$

I_{CO} is the collector current obtained with the emitter open circuited ($I_E = 0$). At room temperature (27°C), I_{CO} is small (typically in the range of 10^{-13} A–10^{-10} A) and can usually be neglected. However, for silicon, I_{CO} doubles for about every 8°C increase in temperature and so may not be negligible at high temperatures.

Normally in the forward-active mode the base-emitter bias is at least several kT/q in value so that $\exp(qV_{BE}/kT)$ is $\gg 1$. Neglecting the -1 and I_S terms in Eqs. (1-10) and (1-11) gives

$$I_C \approx I_S e^{qV_{BE}/kT} \tag{1-14}$$

and

$$I_E \approx \frac{I_S}{\alpha_F} e^{qV_{BE}/kT} \tag{1-15}$$

as commonly used expressions for the collector and emitter currents.

(ii) Reverse-active. In this region, the emitter-base junction is reverse biased and the collector-base junction is forward biased, which results in carriers being injected from the collector region (which now acts like and emitter) into the base where they transport through the base and are collected by the reverse bias on the emitter (which now acts like a collector). The transistor is operating in an inverse mode and the directions of the emitter and collector currents are now reversed from that depicted in Fig. 1-2.

For $|V_{BE}| \ll -kT/q$, $|V_{BE}| \gg kT/q$, and neglecting the reverse bias leakage current, we have from Eqs. (1-8) and (1-9)

$$I_C \approx -\frac{I_S}{\alpha_R} e^{qV_{BC}/kT} \tag{1-16}$$

$$I_E \approx -I_S e^{qV_{BC}/kT} \tag{1-17}$$

(iii) Saturation. Here, both junctions are forward biased and hence both are injecting carriers into the base. Each junction acts both as an emitter and collector, and the net behavior can be described by a superposition of forward-active and reverse-active modes.

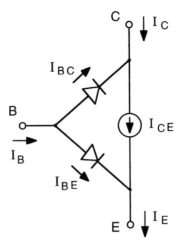

$$I_{BE} = \frac{I_S}{\beta_F}(e^{qV_{BE}/kT} - 1), \quad I_{BC} = \frac{I_S}{\beta_R}(e^{qV_{BC}/kT} - 1), \quad I_{CE} = I_S\frac{I_S}{\beta_F}(e^{qV_{BE}/kT} - e^{qV_{BC}/kT}),$$

Figure 1-4 Common-emitter Ebers–Moll static model of an *npn* transistor.

For $|V_{BE}| \gg kT/q$ and $|V_{BC}| \gg kT/q$, again neglecting the reverse leakage current,

$$I_C \approx I_S e^{qV_{BE}/kT} - \frac{I_S}{\alpha_R} e^{qV_{BC}/kT} \tag{1-18}$$

$$I_E \approx \frac{I_S}{\alpha_F} e^{qV_{BE}/kT} - I_S e^{qV_{BC}/kT} \tag{1-19}$$

I_C and I_E may both be positive or negative, depending on which junction injects more heavily. The base current is always positive (flowing into the base for an *npn* transistor and flowing out of the base for a *pnp* transistor) because it is supplying carriers to the base for injection back into the emitter and collector regions due to the forward bias on each junction.

(iv) Cutoff. In this region, both junctions are reverse biased and the only currents that flow are those which comprise the small reverse leakage currents of the two junctions. For For $|V_{BE}| \ll -kT/q$ and $|V_{BC}| \ll -kT/q$,

$$I_C \approx -I_S(1 - 1/\alpha_R) \tag{1-20}$$

$$I_E \approx -I_S(1/\alpha_F - 1) \tag{1-21}$$

A common-emitter configuration of the Ebers–Moll model is shown in Fig. 1-4. This form is used in many circuit simulation programs (e.g., SPICE [3]) to model the large-signal static characteristics of bipolar junction transistors. From the model, the terminal currents are

$$I_C = I_S(e^{qV_{BE}/kT} - 1) - I_S\left(1 + \frac{1}{\beta_R}\right)(e^{qV_{BC}/kT} - 1) \tag{1-22}$$

$$I_E = I_S\left(1 + \frac{1}{\beta_F}\right)(e^{qV_{BE}/kT} - 1) - I_S(e^{qV_{BC}/kT} - 1) \tag{1-23}$$

$$I_B = \frac{I_S}{\beta_F}(e^{qV_{BE}/kT} - 1) + \frac{I_S}{\beta_R}(e^{qV_{BC}/kT} - 1) \tag{1-24}$$

β_F is the forward common-emitter current gain, I_C/I_B at $V_{BC} = 0$, and is related to the forward common-base current gain α_F as

$$\beta_F = \frac{\alpha_F}{1 - \alpha_F} \tag{1-25}$$

β_R is the reverse common-emitter current gain, $-I_E/I_B$ at $V_{BE} = 0$ and is related to the reverse common-base current gain α_R as

$$\beta_R = \frac{\alpha_R}{1 - \alpha_R} \tag{1-26}$$

Figure 1-5 shows simulated I_C–V_{CE} characteristics of an *npn* transistor using Eqs. (1-22) and (1-24), illustrating the behavior in the four regions of operation. Note that in the saturation region, V_{CE} is small. A bipolar transistor operating in this region is often modeled by assuming a constant voltage, $V_{CE}(\text{sat})$, typically 0.1–0.2 V in value, to represent the saturation condition.

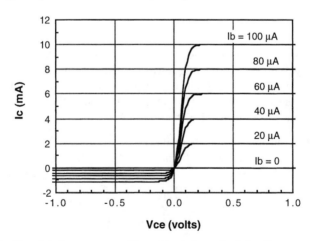

Figure 1-5 Simulated common-emitter output characteristics for an *npn* transistor at 27° C. Device parameters are $I_S = 2 \times 10^{-16}$ A, $\beta_F = 100$, and $\beta_R = 10$.

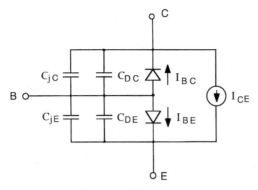

Figure 1-6 Common-emitter Ebers–Moll large-signal model of an *npn* transistor.

Ebers–Moll Dynamic Model

Charge storage in the bipolar transistor is modeled by adding capacitances to the equivalent circuit. These capacitances model the charges associated with the junction depletion regions and the neutral regions of the device. Figure 1-6 shows the large-signal common-emitter Ebers–Moll model with these capacitances added. C_{jE} and C_{jC} represent the space-charge capacitances of the emitter-base junction and collector-base junction depletion regions, respectively. They vary in accordance with the bias voltage applied to the junction and can be adequately modeled for reverse and small forward bias as

$$C_{jE}(V_{BE}) = \frac{C_{jE}(0)}{(1 - V_{BE}/\phi_E)^{m_E}} \tag{1-27}$$

$$C_{jC}(V_{BC}) = \frac{C_{jC}(0)}{(1 - V_{BC}/\phi_C)^{m_C}} \tag{1-28}$$

$C_{jE}(0)$ and $C_{jC}(0)$ are the values of the emitter-base and collector-base junction capacitances at zero bias ($V_{BE} = 0$ or $V_{BC} = 0$), ϕ_E and ϕ_C are the emitter-base and collector-base junction barrier potentials, and m_E and m_C are the emitter-base and collector-base junction gradient factors. For a uniformly doped step junction, m is $\frac{1}{2}$, whereas for a linearly graded junction, m is $\frac{1}{3}$. In practice, actual junctions will have a value for m between these values, the specific value dependent on the particular impurity dopant concentration profile. It is common to choose either $\frac{1}{2}$ or $\frac{1}{3}$ to represent a given junction, the choice being made based on whether the junction doping profile appears closer to a step grade or to a linear grade. In SPICE [4], if the Ebers–Moll model is used, the value for m is fixed at $\frac{1}{3}$.

Equations (1-27) and (1-28) are written for an *npn* transistor, where V_{BE} and V_{BC} are negative for reverse bias. For a *pnp* transistor, use V_{EB} and V_{CB} in Eqs. (1-27) and (1-28), respectively.

To prevent infinite values for the junction capacitances at forward voltages equal to the junction barrier potentials, SPICE limits the forward bias for which Eqs. (1-27) and (1-28) are used to $F_C \phi_E$ and $F_C \phi_C$, where F_C is a factor between 0 and 1 (SPICE default = 0.5). For forward biases larger than these values, the junction capacitances are modeled by a linear extrapolation:

$$C_{jE}(V_{BE}) = \frac{C_{jE}(0)}{(1 - F_C)^{1 + m_E}} \left(1 - F_C(1 + m_E) + \frac{m_E V_{BE}}{\phi_E} \right) \text{ for } V_{BE} \geq F_C \phi_E \quad (1\text{-}29)$$

$$C_{jC}(V_{BC}) = \frac{C_{jC}(0)}{(1 - F_C)^{1 + mc}} \left(1 - F_C(1 + m_C) + \frac{m_C V_{BC}}{\phi_C} \right) \text{ for } V_{BC} \geq F_C \phi_C \quad (1\text{-}30)$$

Charge storage due to the mobile carriers injected into the neutral regions of the transistor are modeled by the diffusion capacitances C_{DE} and C_{DC}. C_{DE} represents the capacitance associated with injection at the emitter junction and C_{DC} represents the capacitance associated with injection at the collector junction. They are given as

$$C_{DE}(V_{BE}) = \tau_F \frac{q I_S}{kT} e^{q V_{BE}/kT} \quad (1\text{-}31)$$

$$C_{DC}(V_{BC}) = \tau_R \frac{q I_S}{kT} e^{q V_{BC}/kT} \quad (1\text{-}32)$$

where τ_F is the forward transit time across the neutral base region from emitter to collector, and τ_R is the reverse transit time across the neutral base region from collector to emitter. Under reverse bias, the diffusion capacitance is small compared to the junction capacitance and is usually neglected.

Base-Width Modulation

As depicted in Fig. 1-5 the Ebers–Moll model gives a constant collector current with respect to V_{CE} for a transistor operating in the forward-active or reverse-active regions. In practice, the collector current is seen to increase with increasing collector–emitter voltage, as illustrated in Fig. 1-7 for forward-active bias. This increase in collector current is a result of a change in the neutral base width with collector junction bias. An increase in the reverse bias on the collector junction increases the width of the collector-base depletion region, which, in turn, causes the width of the neutral base region to decrease. The effect of this base-width modulation on the collector current (called the

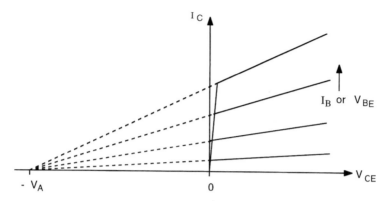

Figure 1-7   Common-emitter output characteristics illustrating the effects of base-width modulation (Early effect) on output conductance.

Early effect [5]) can be seen from Eqs. (1-7) and (1-14), which combine to give

$$I_C = \frac{qD_B n_i^2 A_E}{Q_B} e^{qV_{BE}/kT} \tag{1-33}$$

for the collector current in the forward-active region. Recall that Q_B is the number of majority carrier charges per unit area in the base and is equal to the volume density of this charge times the width of the neutral base region. A reduction in base-width reduces Q_B and thereby increases I_C.

For modeling purposes, a linear fit to the output characteristics is often made. The extrapolated curves then intersect the negative V_{CE} axis at a point which is defined as the Early voltage, V_A, as shown in Fig. 1-7. Using this parameter, the slope of the collector current–voltage characteristics is given by

$$\frac{\partial I_C}{\partial V_{CE}} = \frac{I_C(0)}{V_A} \tag{1-34}$$

where $I_C(0)$ is the value of the collector current at $V_{CE} = 0$, given by Eq. (1-14). It should be remarked that a similar effect occurs for a transistor operated in the reverse-active mode. Here, the base width is modulated by the reverse bias on the emitter-base junction, and the increase in current with collector voltage is characterized by the reverse *Early voltage*, V_B. The corresponding model parameters in SPICE for the forward Early voltage and the reverse Early voltage are VAF and VAR, respectively.

Equation (1-34) defines the output conductance which can be incorporated into the large-signal model for the forward-active region, shown in Fig. 1-8 for both common-emitter and common-base configurations. In Fig. 1-8,

$$R_O = \frac{V_A}{I_C(0)} = \frac{V_A}{I_s e^{qV_{BE}/kT}} \tag{1-35}$$

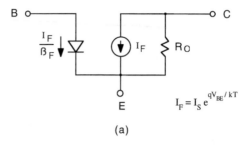

(a)

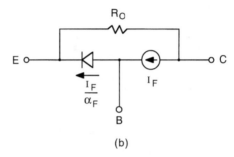

(b)

Figure 1-8 (a) **Large-signal static common-emitter model for forward-active region; (b) common-base model.**

The collector current is

$$I_C = I_F + \frac{V_{CE}}{R_O} = I_S e^{qV_{BE}/kT}\left(1 + \frac{V_{CE}}{V_A}\right) \tag{1-36}$$

EXAMPLE. Figure 1-9(a) shows a simple common-emitter amplifier circuit, driven by a current of $5\,\mu A$. Determine the collector current I_C and the output voltage V_o. The transistor parameters are $I_S = 5 \times 10^{-16}$ A, $\beta_F = 100$, and $V_A = 50$ V.

From Eq. (1-36) and the model depicted in Fig. 1-8(a),

$$I_C = \beta_F I_B (1 + V_{CE}/V_A)$$

where from the circuit

$$V_{CE} = V_o = V_{CC} - I_C R_C$$

which combined with the previous equation gives

$$I_C = \frac{\beta_F I_B (1 + V_{CC}/V_A)}{1 + \beta_F I_B R_C/V_A} = \frac{(100)(5 \times 10^{-6})(1 + 15/50)}{1 + (100)(5 \times 10^{-6})(10 \times 10^{3})/50} = 591\,\mu A$$

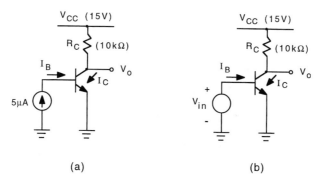

(a) (b)

Figure 1-9 Example common-emitter amplifier circuit: (a) current driven; (b) voltage driven.

and

$$V_o = 15 - (0.591\,\text{mA})(10\,\text{k}\Omega) = 9.09\,\text{V}$$

Figure 1-9(b) shows the same amplifier circuit driven by a voltage source. Determine and sketch (a) I_B as a function of the input, V_{in}, for V_{in} ranging from 0 to 1 V and (b) V_o as a function of V_{in}. Take room temperature, $kT/q = 26\,\text{mV}$. Here, $V_{BE} = V_{in}$, so

$$I_B = \frac{I_S}{\beta_F}e^{qV_{in}/kT} = \frac{5\times10^{-16}}{100}e^{V_{in}/0.026} = 5\times10^{-18}\,e^{V_{in}/0.026}\,\text{A}$$

This result is plotted in Fig. 1-10(a). Note the steep increase in base current with base-emitter voltage for V_{BE} beyond about 0.7 V. This is, of course, due to the exponential current–voltage characteristic. As an approximation to the circuit model, the base-emitter voltage is often taken to be constant for a transistor operating in the active region. For a silicon bipolar transistor operating at room temperature this voltage, denoted $V_{BE}\,(\text{on})$, is typically in the range of 0.7–0.8 V. For the voltage drive (b),

$$I_C = I_S e^{qV_{in}/kT}\left(1 + \frac{V_o}{V_A}\right)$$

which combined with $V_o = V_{CC} - I_C R_C$ gives

$$V_o = \frac{15 - (5\times10^{-16})(10\times10^3)\,e^{V_{in}/0.026}}{1 + (5\times10^{-16})(10\times10^3)\,e^{V_{in}/0.026}/50} = \frac{15 - (5\times10^{-12})\,e^{V_{in}/0.026}}{1 + (1\times10^{-13})\,e^{V_{in}/0.026}}$$

This result is plotted in Fig. 1-10(b) for the portion of the curve labeled "forward-active region." At V_{in} equal to approximately 0.75 V the transistor enters the saturation region (both emitter and collector junctions are forward-biased)

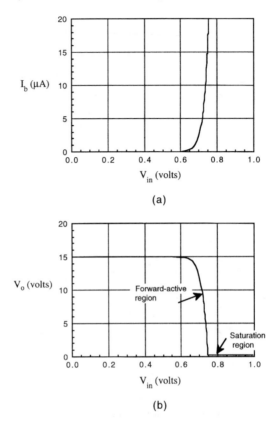

Figure 1-10 (a) Base current and (b) output voltage as a function of V_{in} for example common-emitter amplifier circuit.

and the collector-to-emitter voltage, V_{CE} (and hence V_o in this example), saturates at a small value, typically 0.1–0.2 V, as illustrated in the figure. Also note that for V_{in} less than about 0.6 V the output remains high (at V_{CC}), even though the transistor is still operating in the forward-active region. This is because the collector current at these base-emitter voltages is small such that $I_C R_C \ll V_{CC}$.

Small-Signal Models of Bipolar Junction Transistors

In some applications, the magnitudes of the signals in a circuit are small compared to the bias voltages and currents. In these situations, linear circuit models for the device may be used to determine the circuit response to these small signals. The advantage of doing this is that now a linear circuit is to be analyzed instead of a nonlinear circuit.

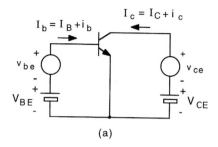

(a)

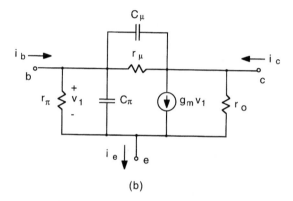

(b)

Figure 1-11 **(a) Decomposition of transistor currents and voltages into dc and small-signal components. (b) Common-emitter small-signal equivalent circuit model.**

Figure 1-11(a) illustrates the decomposition of transistor currents and voltages into dc (quiescent) and small-signal components. Base drive to the transistor consists of the dc bias voltage V_{BE} connected in series with the signal voltage v_{be}, giving a total base-emitter voltage $V_{be} = V_{BE} + v_{be}$ and a corresponding total base current $I_b = I_B + i_b$. The convention followed here is to represent dc quantities by uppercase symbols and subscripts, and small-signal quantities by lowercase symbols and subscripts and total quantities by uppercase symbols and lowercase subscripts.

A common-emitter small-signal equivalent circuit model for a bipolar transistor operating in the forward-active region is shown in Fig. 1-11(b). Its parameters are determined as follows:

Using Eq. (1-36),

$$g_m = \frac{dI_c}{dV_{be}}\bigg|_{v_{be}=0} = \frac{qI_s}{kT}e^{qV_{BE}/kT}\left(1 + \frac{V_{CE}}{V_A}\right) = \frac{qI_C}{kT} \tag{1-37}$$

g_m the transconductance and its value is seen to depend linearly on the collector dc bias current.

Figure 1-8(a) and Eq. (1-37) can be used to determine the variation in base current with base-emitter voltage.

$$g_\pi = \left.\frac{dI_b}{dV_{be}}\right|_{v_{be}=0} = \frac{d(I_F/\beta_F)}{dV_{be}} \approx \frac{1}{\beta_F}\frac{dI_c}{dV_{be}} = \frac{g_m}{\beta_F} \tag{1-38}$$

The approximation here is that β_F remains constant for small-signal variations in V_{be}, which is generally true. Hence, the small-signal base resistance is

$$r_\pi = \frac{1}{g_\pi} = \frac{\beta_F}{g_m} \tag{1-39}$$

The small-signal output resistance r_o results from the variation in collector current with collector bias voltage (Early effect). Using Eq. (1-36),

$$\frac{1}{r_o} = g_o = \left.\frac{dI_c}{dV_{ce}}\right|_{v_{ce}=0} = \frac{I_S e^{qV_{BE}/kT}}{V_A} = \frac{I_C}{V_A} \tag{1-40}$$

r_μ models the variation in base current with collector bias voltage:

$$\frac{1}{r_\mu} = g_\mu = \left.\frac{dI_b}{dV_{ce}}\right|_{v_{ce}=0} = \frac{d(I_F/\beta_F)}{dV_{ce}} \approx \frac{1}{\beta_F}\frac{dI_c}{dV_{ce}} = \frac{1}{\beta_F r_o} \tag{1-41}$$

r_μ is typically a very large resistance and in most cases is neglected in the small-signal model.

The capacitance C_π is the diffusion capacitance C_{DE} in parallel with the emitter-base junction capacitance C_{jE}:

$$C_\pi = \tau_F \frac{qI_S}{kT} e^{qV_{BE}/kT} + C_{jE}(V_{BE}) = g_m\tau_F + C_{jE}(V_{BE}) \tag{1-42}$$

With a reverse-biased base-collector junction, the diffusion capacitance C_{DC} is negligibly small, so the capacitance C_μ, is just the base-collector junction capacitance

$$C_\mu = C_{jC}(V_{BC}) \tag{1-43}$$

Generally, the diffusion capacitance is much larger than the junction space-charge capacitance so that C_π is usually much larger than C_μ.

An alternate form of the common-emitter small-signal model is the common-base configuration illustrated in Fig. 1-12. Here, the input is applied to the emitter and the output is taken at the collector. In application to a circuit in which a transistor is connected in a common-base configuration, this form of the model is often more convenient to analyze. Either form of the model is valid, however, and may be used irrespective of the particular circuit

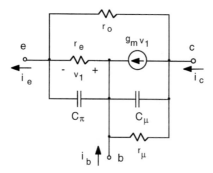

Figure 1-12   Common-base small-signal equivalent circuit model.

configuration. With reference to Fig. 1-11, the small-signal emitter current is

$$i_e = \left(\frac{1}{r_\pi} + g_m\right) v_1 + \frac{v_{ce}}{r_o} + sC_\pi v_1 \qquad (1\text{-}44)$$

From Fig. 1-12,

$$i_e = \frac{v_1}{r_e} + \frac{v_{ce}}{r_o} + sC_\pi v_1 \qquad (1\text{-}45)$$

Equating Eqs. (1-44) and (1-45) gives the value of the small-signal emitter resistance

$$r_e = \frac{1}{g_m + \dfrac{1}{r_\pi}} = \frac{1}{g_m(1 + 1/\beta_F)}) = \frac{\alpha_F}{g_m} \qquad (1\text{-}46)$$

Parasitic Elements in Integrated-Circuit Bipolar Transistors

The fabrication process for integrated circuit transistors introduces other circuit elements (parasitics) in addition to those associated with the intrinsic portion of the device. Figure 1-13 illustrates the origin of these parasitic elements for an *npn* transistor. Table 1-1 identifies each element.

A simplified model which combines the principal parasitic elements affecting circuit performance is illustrated in Fig. 1-14. With reference to Fig. 1-13, $r_E = R_E^+$, $r_B = R_B^+ + R_B$, $r_C = R_{C1} + R_{BL} + R_{C2} + R_C^+$. In addition, C_{BC}^+ and C_{BC}^b can be combined with C_{jC}. Typical values for the parasitic resistances in an integrated circuit BJT range from a few ohms for r_E to a few hundred ohms for r_B and r_C. The ohmic emitter resistance r_E is often neglected; r_B and r_C can be

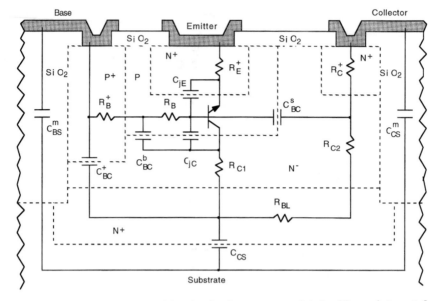

Figure 1-13   Principal parasitic circuit elements associated with an integrated-circuit BJT.

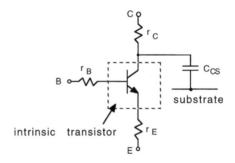

Figure 1-14   Simplified equivalent circuit which retains the principal parasitic elements.

neglected if they are small in relation to the other resistances in the base circuit and collector circuit, respectively.

Transistor Cutoff Frequency

A useful figure-of-merit to characterize the frequency performance of a bipolar transistor is the cutoff frequency, f_T, which is defined as the frequency at which the common-emitter small-signal short-circuit current gain is equal to unity. A

Table 1-1 Parasitic Elements for an Integrated-Circuit BJT

Element	Description
R_B	Ohmic base resistance of the active transistor
R_B^+	Resistance of the extrinsic base region
R_{C1}	Ohmic collector resistance of the active transistor
R_{BL}	Lateral resistance of the buried layer
R_{C2}	Vertical resistance of the extrinsic collector region
R_C^+	Resistance of the collector contact region
R_E^+	Ohmic emitter resistance of the active transistor
C_{BC}^b	Bottom wall junction capacitance of the extrinsic base-collector region
C_{BC}^s	Side-wall junction capacitance of the extrinsic base-collector region
C_{BC}^+	Junction capacitance of the base contact and extrinsic collector region
C_{BC}^m	Base metallization-substrate capacitance
C_{CS}	Buried layer-substrate capacitance
C_{CS}^m	Collector metallization-substrate capacitance
C_{jC}	Collector-base junction capacitance of the active transistor
C_{jE}	Emitter-base junction capacitance of the active transistor

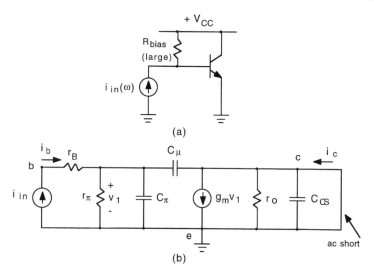

(a)

(b)

Figure 1-15 **(a) Circuit for determining the common-emitter cutoff frequency f_T. (b) Small-signal equivalent circuit, neglecting r_E, r_C, r_μ, and R_{bias}.**

circuit used to determine this cutoff frequency is shown in Fig. 1-15(a) and the corresponding small-signal equivalent circuit is shown in Fig. 1-15(b). From Fig. 1-15(b), the small-signal current gain [denoted $\beta\,(j\omega)$] is found to be

$$\frac{i_c}{i_b}(j\omega) = \beta\,(j\omega) = \frac{g_m r_\pi (1 - j\omega\,C_\mu/g_m)}{1 + j\omega\,r_\pi(C_\pi + C_\mu)} \qquad (1\text{-}47)$$

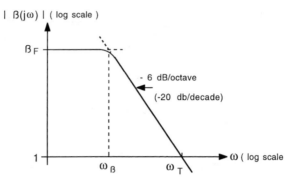

Figure 1-16   Magnitude of the small-signal short-circuit current gain versus frequency.

At low frequencies, $\beta\,(j\omega) \to g_m\, r_\pi = \beta_F$. Because C_π is usually much larger than C_μ, the second term in the numerator of Eq. (1-47) (which represents the feed-forward current in C_μ,) is small and can be neglected. Thus,

$$\beta\,(j\omega) \approx \frac{\beta_F}{1 + j\omega\, r_\pi\,(C_\pi + C_\mu)} \tag{1-48}$$

The variation in the magnitude of the small-signal current gain with frequency is illustrated in Fig. 1-16. The corner frequency ω_β is the frequency at which $|\beta\,(j\omega)|$ is down by 3 dB $(1/\sqrt{2})$ from the low-frequency value β_F. From Eq. (1-48),

$$\omega_\beta = \frac{1}{\beta_F}\frac{g_m}{C_\pi + C_\mu} \tag{1-49}$$

At high frequencies, where $\beta\,(j\omega)$ approaches unity, the 1 in the denominator of Eq. (1-48) can be neglected and

$$\beta\,(j\omega) \approx \frac{g_m}{j\omega\,(C_\pi + C_\mu)} \tag{1-50}$$

which has unity magnitude at

$$\omega = \omega_T = \frac{g_m}{C_\pi + C_\mu} = \beta_F\,\omega_\beta \tag{1-51}$$

and the cutoff frequency is

$$f_T = \frac{1}{2\pi}\frac{g_m}{C_\pi + C_\mu} \tag{1-52}$$

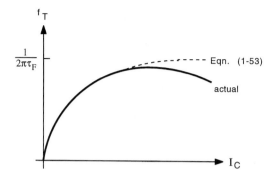

Figure 1-17 Variation in f_T with collector current.

Using Eqs. (1-37) and (1-42),

$$f_T = \frac{1}{2\pi}\left[\cfrac{1}{\cfrac{kT}{qI_C}(C_{jE} + C_{jC}) + \tau_F}\right] \tag{1-53}$$

The cutoff frequency is seen to increase with collector current at low currents due to the increased charge and discharge rates of C_{jE} and C_μ. At high currents, f_T is dominated by the base transit time τ_F and according to Eq. (1-53) approaches a constant value $1/2\pi\tau_F$. In practice, the neutral base width of a bipolar transistor widens at high currents (Kirk effect [6]), causing an increase in τ_F with current and a subsequent fall-off in f_T at high currents. This behavior is illustrated in Fig. 1-17.

EXAMPLE. A bipolar transistor has a cutoff frequency of 4 GHz, measured at a collector current of 1 mA. It is used in an amplifier circuit at 500 µA. Determine (a) the elements of the common-emitter small-signal equivalent circuit of Fig. 1-11(b) and (b) the transistor cutoff frequency. The transistor has the following parameters: $\beta_F = 150$, $V_A = 100$ V, $C_{jE} = 0.2$ pF and $C_{jC} = 0.1$ pF. Take room temperature $kT/q = 26$ mV.

Unknown is the forward transit time τ_F. Using Eq. (1-53) for the known value of f_T at $I_C = 1$ mA,

$$\tau_F = \frac{1}{2\pi f_T} - \frac{kT}{qI_C}(C_{jE} + C_{jC})$$

yielding

$$\tau_F = \frac{1}{(2\pi)(4 \times 10^9)} - \frac{26\,\mathrm{mV}}{1\,\mathrm{mA}}(0.2 + 0.1) \times 10^{-12}\,\mathrm{F} = 32\,\mathrm{ps}$$

(a) From Eq. (1-37) the transconductance at $I_C = 500\,\mu A$ is

$$g_m = \frac{qI_C}{kT} = \frac{0.5\,mA/V}{0.026\,V} = 19.2\,mA/V$$

The small-signal base resistance from Eq. (1-39) is

$$r_\pi = \frac{\beta_F}{g_m} = \frac{150}{19.2\,mA/V} = 7.81\,k\Omega$$

The output resistance from Eq. (1-40) is

$$r_o = \frac{V_A}{I_C} = \frac{100\,V}{0.5\,mA} = 200\,k\Omega$$

and from Eq. (1-41), the collector-base resistance is

$$r_\mu = \beta_F r_o = (150)(200\,k\Omega) = 30\,M\Omega$$

From Eq. (1-42), the small-signal base-emitter capacitance is

$$C_\pi = g_m \tau_F + C_{jE} = (19.2 \times 10^{-3}\,A/V)(32 \times 10^{12}\,s) + 0.2 \times 10^{-12}\,F$$

$$= 8.14 \times 10^{-13}\,F = 0.814\,pF$$

and, finally, from Eq. (1-42), the small-signal collector-base capacitance is

$$C_\mu = C_{jC} = 0.1\,pF$$

(b) The new cutoff frequency from Eq. (1-52) is

$$f_T = \frac{g_m}{2\pi(C_\pi + C_\mu)} = \frac{19.2\,mA/V}{(2\pi)(0.814 + 0.1)\,pF} = 3.34\,GHz$$

1.2 Junction Diode

Any of the *pn* junctions that comprise the bipolar transistor structure may be used as an integrated-circuit junction diode: the base-emitter junction, the base-collector junction, and the collector-substrate junction all produce viable diodes, each with differing characteristics [7]. The most common diode structure for analog integrated circuits is produced by connecting the base and collector terminals of an *npn* transistor, as illustrated in Fig. 1-18(a). There are good reasons for fabricating diodes in this form: With the base and collector shorted, $V_{BC} = 0$; from Eq. (1-8), we have for the diode

$$I_D = I_S(e^{qV_D/kT} - 1) \tag{1-54}$$

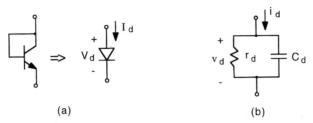

(a)   (b)

Figure 1-18   (a) Integrated-circuit junction diode formed from an *npn* transistor. (b) Small-signal equivalent circuit.

The diodes are fabricated concurrently with the *npn* transistors, and thus they both have identical reverse saturation currents (I_S), except as scaled by their respective emitter areas [see Eq. (1-7)]. Hence, for example, if an equal-area diode and bipolar transistor are connected in a circuit in which V_D and V_{BE} are equal, then the diode current and the collector current of the transistor will be the same (neglecting transistor base current and Early effect). This behavior (as we shall see later) can be quite useful in analog circuits.

The small-signal equivalent circuit of the junction diode is shown in Fig. 1-18(b). Directly from the small-signal bipolar transistor model (Fig. 1-12) we have

$$r_d = r_e \| r_o \approx \frac{1}{g_m} \tag{1-55}$$

and

$$C_d = C_\pi \tag{1-56}$$

1.3   Junction Field-Effect Transistor

A junction field-effect transistor (JFET) is a device whose operation results from the modulation of a conducting channel by a voltage applied to a gate control electrode. Unlike the bipolar transistor where current transport involves both majority and minority carriers, current transport in the JFET is by majority carriers only; hence, it is termed a unipolar device. Shown in Fig. 1-19 is a cross-sectional view of an integrated-circuit *p*-channel junction field-effect transistor. The active region of the device consists of the thin *p*-type layer bounded on top and bottom by *n*-type regions, forming two *pn* junctions between the gate (top and bottom) and the channel (*P* region). The two heavily doped P^+ regions provide ohmic contacts to the source and drain ends of the conducting channel.

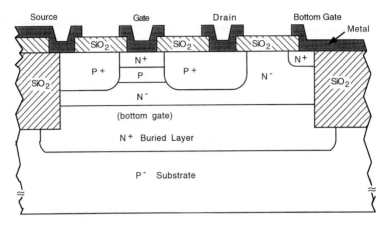

Figure 1-19   Cross-sectional view of an integrated-circuit *p*-channel junction field-effect transistor.

Device Characteristics

Figure 1-20 illustrates the active region of the *p*-channel JFET with normal biases applied. The thickness of the depletion region surrounding the gate-channel *pn* junction is determined by the voltage across the junction, in this case being a function of the gate-source bias (V_{GS}) and the drain-source bias (V_{DS}). V_{GS} is normally positive and V_{DS} is negative, resulting in a reverse-biased gate junction. This produces essentially zero gate current—just a small reverse-bias junction leakage current. The undepleted portion of the *p*-type layer provides

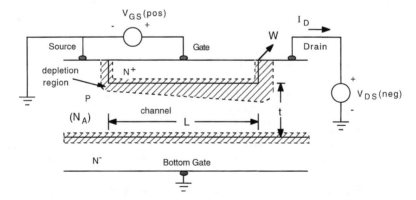

Figure 1-20   Active region of a *p*-channel JFET with normal biases applied. The reverse bias on the gate-channel junction is largest at the drain end of the channel and smallest at the source end, resulting in a variation in the thickness of the conducting channel region.

the conducting channel, whose thickness (and hence its conductance) is controlled by both V_{GS} and V_{DS}. Drain current I_D flows out of the drain terminal.

With reference to Fig. 1-20, several operating points are worthy of note: As V_{GS} is increased, the thickness of the depletion layer increases, narrowing the conducting channel. At a sufficiently large value of V_{DS} the depletion layer will extend completely through the channel to the bottom-gate pn junction. Because V_{DS} is negative, the reverse voltage across the gate-channel junction is smallest at the source end of the channel and is largest at the drain end of the channel. Thus, if the channel is depleted at the source end, then the entire channel region will be depleted (pinched off) and no conduction will occur. The transistor will be turned off. For the p-channel device depicted in Fig. 1-20, this occurs at a gate-source voltage of

$$V_{GS} = \frac{qN_A t^2}{2\varepsilon_s} - \phi_i = V_P \qquad (1\text{-}57)$$

where N_A is the doping concentration of the p-type channel (assumed constant), t is the thickness of the P layer, ε_s is the dielectric permittivity of the semiconductor, and ϕ_i is the barrier potential of the gate-channel junction. Also assumed in this calculation is that the doping concentration of the N^+ gate region is much greater than that of the P-channel, so that the depletion layer at the top gate appears mostly on the p-side of the junction. In addition, with the P-channel doping concentration larger than the N^- bottom gate, the depletion layer thickness on the p-side of bottom gate junction is negligibly small. This voltage [Eq. (1-57)] is denoted the pinch-off voltage V_P, and represents the gate-source voltage at which the device is cut off. When $V_{DS} = V_{GS} - V_P$, the depletion region of the top gate extends through the channel to the bottom gate just at the drain end of the channel, resulting in the channel being pinched off at that point. This voltage is denoted the saturation voltage

$$V_{Dsat} = V_{GS} - V_P \qquad (1\text{-}58)$$

For V_{DS} less than V_{Dsat} the drain current in the JFET is controlled by both V_{GS} and V_{DS}; for V_{DS} greater than $V_{DS}(\text{sat})$, the drain current is relatively independent of V_{DS} and depends mainly on V_{GS}. To keep the gate-channel junction reverse biased, the maximum gate-source voltage is zero and thus the maximum drain current occurs for $V_{GS} = 0$. At $V_{DS} = V_{Dsat}$, this maximum current is denoted I_{DSS} and for a uniformly doped channel region is given by

$$I_{DSS} = G_0 \left[V_P - \frac{2}{3} \frac{(V_P + \phi_i)^{3/2} - \phi_i^{3/2}}{(V_P - \phi_i)^{1/2}} \right] \qquad (1\text{-}59)$$

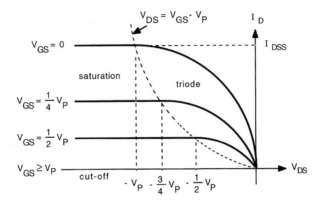

Figure 1-21   Idealized *I–V* characteristics of a *p*-channel JFET.

where

$$G_0 = \frac{q\mu_p N_A tW}{L} \tag{1-60}$$

and represents the conductance of the complete undepleted channel.

Figure 1-21 shows the idealized $I - V$ characteristics of a p-channel JFET, illustrating the three regions of operation: cutoff, saturation, and triode. For a detailed analysis of the JFET, the reader is referred to one of the many references in the literature, such as Refs. 2 and 8. A simple quadratic model [9] has been found to adequately describe the characteristics of JFET devices, independent of their particular doping profile.

In the triode region, the drain current is approximated by

$$I_D = I_{DSS}\left[2\left(1 - \frac{V_{GS}}{V_P}\right)\left(-\frac{V_{DS}}{V_P}\right) - \left(-\frac{V_{DS}}{V_P}\right)^2\right] \tag{1-61}$$

for $V_{DS} > V_{GS} - V_P$.

In the saturation region, the drain current is approximated by

$$I_D = I_{DSS}\left(1 - \frac{V_{GS}}{V_P}\right)^2 \tag{1-62}$$

for $V_{DS} \leq V_{GS} - V_P$.

Actual JFET devices operated in the saturation region do not show a constant drain current – drain voltage characteristic, as depicted in Fig. 1-21, but rather I_D is seen to increase with increasing V_{DS}. This behavior is brought about by a decrease in the effective channel length resulting from the increased gate-drain depletion region for $|V_{DS}| > |V_{Dsat}|$. This channel-length modulation with

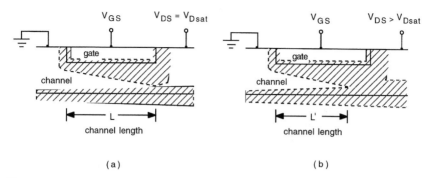

(a)   (b)

Figure 1-22   Illustration of channel length modulation in a JFET. (a) At $V_{DS} = V_{Dsat}$, the channel is pinched off just at the drain end of the channel. (b) For $V_{DS} > V_{Dsat}$, the channel pinch-off point moves back toward the source, resulting in an effective channel length L' that is less than the geometrical channel length L.

drain voltage is illustrated in Fig. 1-22 and is analogous to the base-width modulation (Early effect) in a bipolar transistor. Figure 1-23 illustrates the actual characteristics for a p-channel JFET. The slope in the drain current characteristics are characterized by the Early effect voltage V_A, and for operation in the saturation region, the drain current is approximated by

$$I_D = I_{DSS}\left(1 - \frac{V_{GS}}{V_P}\right)^2\left(1 - \frac{V_{DS}}{V_A}\right) \qquad (1\text{-}63)$$

For FET devices, it is common practice to use the channel-length modulation parameter λ in place of the Early voltage. For a p-channel JFET, $\lambda = -1/V_A$,

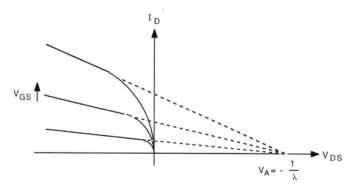

Figure 1-23   Actual characteristics of a p-channel JFET illustrating the effects of channel-length modulation. The finite slope in the drain current is characterized by the Early voltage V_A.

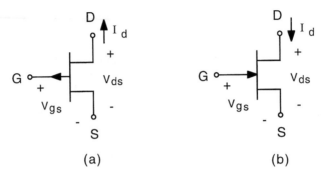

Figure 1-24   Circuit symbols and sign conventions for (a) *p*-channel and (b) *n*-channel JFET.

and the drain current characteristics in the saturation region are thus expressed as

$$I_D = I_{\mathrm{DSS}} \left(1 - \frac{V_{\mathrm{GS}}}{V_P} \right)^2 (1 + \lambda V_{\mathrm{DS}}) \qquad (1\text{-}64)$$

Figure 1-24 shows the circuit symbols and sign conventions for *p*-channel and *n*-channel JFETs. For an *n*-channel JFET, the pinch-off voltage is negative and the parameter λ is positive; in normal operation, the gate-source voltage is negative, the drain-source voltage is positive, and current flows into the drain terminal. Thus, Eqs. (1-61) and (1-64) may be used to model the *n*-channel characteristics provided $V_{\mathrm{DS}} < V_{\mathrm{GS}} - V_P$ for operation in the triode region and $V_{\mathrm{DS}} \geq V_{\mathrm{GS}} - V_P$ for operation in the saturation region.

Large-Signal Model

The large-signal static model of an *n*-channel JFET is shown in Fig. 1-25. With negative gate voltage, the gate-source and gate-drain *pn* junctions are reverse biased, resulting in negligible gate current and $I_D \approx I_{\mathrm{DS}}$. In the SPICE simulation program, the large-signal static drain current is modeled as

$$I_{\mathrm{DS}} = \begin{cases} 0 & \text{for } V_{\mathrm{GS}} - V_{T0} < 0 \\ \beta V_{\mathrm{DS}} [2 (V_{\mathrm{GS}} - V_{T0}) - V_{\mathrm{DS}}] (1 + \lambda V_{\mathrm{DS}}) & \text{for } V_{\mathrm{GS}} - V_{T0} > V_{\mathrm{DS}} > 0 \qquad (1\text{-}65) \\ \beta (V_{\mathrm{GS}} - V_{T0})^2 (1 + \lambda V_{\mathrm{DS}}) & \text{for } V_{\mathrm{DS}} \geq V_{\mathrm{GS}} - V_{T0} > 0 \end{cases}$$

where V_{T0} (threshold parameter) $= V_P$ and is taken as negative for both *p*- and *n*-channel JFETs. The parameter β is given as

$$\beta = \frac{I_{\mathrm{DSS}}}{V_P^2} \qquad (1\text{-}66)$$

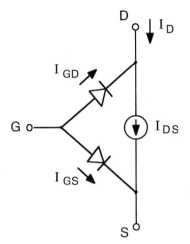

$$I_{GD} = I_S (e^{qV_{GD}/kT} - 1), \quad I_{GS} = I_S (e^{qV_{GS}/kT} - 1)$$

$$I_{DS} = \begin{cases} 0 & \text{for } V_{GS} \le V_P \\ I_{DSS} [2(1-V_{GS}/V_P)(-V_{DS}/V_P)-(V_{DS}/V_P)^2]) & \text{for } V_{GS}-V_P > V_{DS} > 0 \\ I_{DSS} (1-V_{GS}/V_P)^2 (1+\lambda V_{DS}) & \text{for } V_{DS} \ge V_{GS} - V_P \end{cases}$$

Figure 1-25   Large-signal static model of an *n*-channel JFET.

It may be readily shown that the two forms given in Eqs. (1-64) and (1-65) for operation in the saturation region are equivalent. The SPICE model adds the channel-length modulation term $(1 + \lambda V_{DS})$ to the characteristic for operation in the triode region to avoid a discontinuity in the drain current at $V_{DS} = V_{GS} - V_{T0}$. In practice, of course, there is no channel-length modulation in this region; the error, however, is small.

EXAMPLE. Figure 1-26 shows a simple common-source JFET circuit. Determine the drain current I_D and the output voltage V_O. The transistor parameters are $V_P = -5\,\text{V}$, $I_{DSS} = 1.5\,\text{mA}$, and $\lambda = 0.03\,\text{V}^{-1}$.

Not known is the operating region of the device. $V_{GS} = -2\,\text{V} > V_P$, so the JFET is not turned off. It is, therefore, operating in either the triode or saturation region. We will assume initially that it is in saturation and see if the results are consistent with that assumption.

From Eq. (1-64)

$$I_D = I_{DSS} (1 - V_{GS}/V_P)^2 (1 + \lambda V_O)$$

where from the circuit

$$V_O = V_{DD} - I_D R_D$$

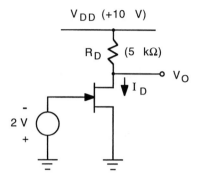

Figure 1-26   Example common-source JFET circuit.

yielding

$$I_D = I_{\text{DSS}}(1 - V_{\text{GS}}/V_P)^2[1 + \lambda(V_{\text{DD}} - I_D R_D)]$$

Solving for I_D gives

$$I_D = \frac{I_{\text{DSS}}(1 - V_{\text{GS}}/V_P)^2(1 + \lambda V_{\text{DD}})}{1 + \lambda I_{\text{DSS}}R_D(1 - V_{\text{GS}}/V_P)^2} = \frac{(1.5)(1 - 2/5)^2[1 + (0.03)(10)]}{1 + (0.03)(1.5)(5)(1 - 2/5)^2} = 0.649\,\text{mA}$$

and

$$V_O = 10 - (0.649)(5) = 6.75\,\text{V}$$

Here, $V_{\text{DS}} = V_O = 6.75\,\text{V} > V_{\text{GS}} - V_P = 3\,\text{V}$, so the device is operating in the saturation region.

EXERCISE. Determine the value for R_D in the previous example for which the JFET just enters the triode region. (*Ans.* 11.9 kΩ)

Large-Signal Dynamic Model of the JFET

Charge storage in the JFET is modeled by the space-charge capacitances associated with the gate junction. With the gate junction reverse biased, the diffusion capacitance is negligibly small and can be neglected. Figure 1-27 shows the large-signal dynamic model of an n-channel JFET. The capacitances C_{GS} and C_{GD} are the capacitances associated with the gate-source and gate-drain junctions and are modeled as

$$C_{\text{GS}}(V_{\text{GS}}) = \frac{C_{\text{GS}}(0)}{(1 - V_{\text{GS}}/\phi_i)^m} \tag{1-67}$$

$$C_{\text{GD}}(V_{\text{GD}}) = \frac{C_{\text{GD}}(0)}{(1 - V_{\text{GD}}/\phi_i)^m} \tag{1-68}$$

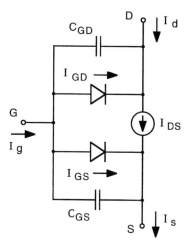

Figure 1-27   Large-signal dynamic model of an *n*-channel JFET.

where $C_{GS}(0)$ and $C_{GD}(0)$ are the zero-bias values of the gate-source and gate-drain junction capacitances, respectively, and m is the junction grading coefficient. In SPICE, m is set to 0.5 and cannot be changed.

For a *p*-channel JFET model, reverse the two diodes and the current source, reverse the directions of the terminal currents in Fig. 1-27, and change the signs in the denominators of Eqs. (1-67) and (1-68) from minus to plus.

Small-Signal Model of the JFET

Figure 1-28 shows the small-signal equivalent circuit for a JFET operating either in the triode or saturation region. The transconductance is found from Eqs. (1-61) and (1-64):

$$g_m = \frac{dI_d}{dV_{gs}}\bigg|_{v_{gs}=0} = \begin{cases} \dfrac{2I_{DSS}}{V_P^2}\,V_{DS} & \text{for } V_{DS} < V_{GS} - V_P \\[3mm] -\dfrac{2I_{DSS}}{V_P}\left(1 - \dfrac{V_{GS}}{V_P}\right)(1 + \lambda V_{DS}) & \text{for } V_{DS} \geq V_{GS} - V_P \end{cases} \tag{1-69}$$

The small-signal output resistance is determined using Eqs. (1-61) and (1-64):

$$\frac{1}{r_o} = g_o = \frac{dI_d}{dV_{ds}}\bigg|_{v_{ds}=0} = \begin{cases} \dfrac{2I_{DSS}}{V_P}\left(\dfrac{V_{GS}}{V_P} - \dfrac{V_{DS}}{V_P} - 1\right) & \text{for } V_{DS} < V_{GS} - V_P \\[3mm] \lambda I_{DSS}\left(1 - \dfrac{V_{GS}}{V_P}\right)^2 & \text{for } V_{DS} \geq V_{GS} - V_P \end{cases} \tag{1-70}$$

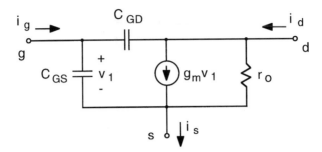

Figure 1-28   Small-signal equivalent circuit model for a JFET.

If $\lambda V_{DS} \ll 1$, the output resistance in saturation may be approximated as

$$r_o \approx \frac{1}{\lambda I_D} \tag{1-71}$$

The values of C_{GS} and C_{GD} are determined from Eqs. (1-67) and (1-68), evaluated at the dc operating point.

Parasitic Elements in Integrated-Circuit JFETs

The principal parasitic elements associated with integrated-circuit junction field-effect transistors are the ohmic resistances of the source and drain contact regions, denoted r_S and r_D, respectively, and the junction capacitances associated with the bottom gate. Figure 1-29 illustrates the origin of these parasitic

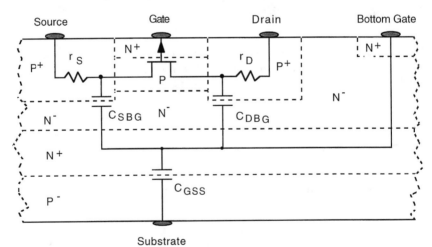

Figure 1-29   Principal parasitic circuit elements associated with an integrated-circuit JEFT.

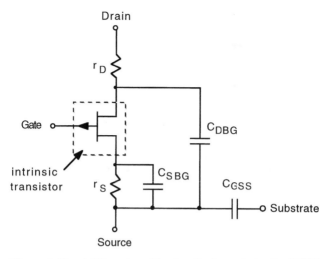

Figure 1-30 Adding parasitic circuit elements to the JFET.

elements for a *p*-channel JFET: C_{SBG} is the capacitance between the source and bottom gate, C_{DBG} is the capacitance between the drain and bottom gate, and C_{GSS} is the capacitance between the bottom gate and substrate.

In practice, only the top gate is driven, which gives the highest frequency response [10]. The bottom gate can either be connected to a separate dc bias voltage or connected directly to the source terminal; for the latter, the JFET including the parasitic elements can be represented as shown in Fig. 1-30.

Transistor Cutoff Frequency

The unity-gain cutoff frequency f_T for a JFET is calculated in a fashion similar to that for the bipolar transistor. The small-signal equivalent circuit for this analysis is given as shown in Fig. 1-31, from which the current gain is found to be

$$\frac{i_d}{i_g}(j\omega) = \frac{g_m - j\omega\, C_{GD}}{j\omega\,(C_{GS} + C_{GD})} \approx \frac{g_m}{j\omega\,(C_{GS} + C_{GD})} \tag{1-72}$$

where in the last term the feed-forward current in C_{GD} has been neglected in relation to g_m. From Eq. (1-72), the unity-gain frequency is found to be

$$f_T = \frac{g_m}{2\pi\,(C_{GS} + C_{GD})} \tag{1-73}$$

EXAMPLE. Determine the cutoff frequency for an *n*-channel JFET operating at $I_D = 1\,\text{mA}$ and $V_{DS} = 5\,\text{V}$. The device parameters are $I_{DSS} = 1.5\,\text{mA}$, $V_P = -3\,\text{V}$,

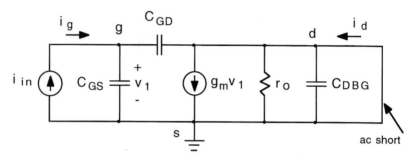

Figure 1-31 **Small-signal circuit for determining cutoff frequency f_T of the JFET. The parasitic source and drain resistances, r_S and r_D, are normally small compared to $1/g_m$ and are neglected here.**

$\lambda = 0.02\,\text{V}^{-1}$, $C_{GS}(0) = 0.25\,\text{pF}$, and $C_{GD}(0) = 0.1\,\text{pF}$. For this device, $\phi_i = 0.8\,\text{V}$ and $m = \frac{1}{3}$.

From Eq. (1-64), the gate-source voltage, assuming operation in the saturation region, is

$$V_{GS} = V_P\left(1 - \sqrt{\frac{I_D}{I_{DSS}(1 + \lambda V_{DS})}}\right) = -3\left(1 - \sqrt{\frac{1}{1.5\,(1 + 0.02 \times 5)}}\right) = -0.665\,\text{V}$$

Here, $V_{DS} = 5\,\text{V} > V_{GS} - V_P = 2.34\,\text{V}$, so the JFET is in saturation.

From Eq. (1-69), the transconductance is

$$g_m = -\frac{2I_{DSS}}{V_P}\left(1 - \frac{V_{GS}}{V_P}\right) = -\frac{(2)(1.5\,\text{mA})}{-3\,\text{V}}\left(1 - \frac{0.665}{3}\right)^{1/3} = 0.778\,\text{mA/V}$$

From Eq. (1-67), the gate-source capacitance at $V_{GS} = -0.665\,\text{V}$ is

$$C_{GS} = \frac{C_{GS}(0)}{(1 - V_{GS}/\phi_i)^m} = \frac{0.25\,\text{pF}}{(1 + 0.665/0.8)^{1/3}} = 0.204\,\text{pF}$$

The gate-drain voltage is

$$V_{GD} = V_{GS} - V_{DS} = -0.665\,\text{V} - 5\,\text{V} = -5.665\,\text{V}$$

Using Eq. (1-68), the gate-drain capacitance is

$$C_{GD} = \frac{C_{GD}(0)}{(1 - V_{GD}/\phi_i)^m} = \frac{0.1\,\text{pF}}{(1 + 5.665/0.8)^{1/3}} = 0.0498\,\text{pF}$$

The cutoff frequency from Eq. (1-73) is

$$f_T = \frac{g_m}{2\pi(C_{GS} + C_{GD})} = \frac{0.778 \times 10^{-3}}{(2)(\pi)(0.204 + 0.0498) \times 10^{-3}} = 488\,\text{MHz}$$

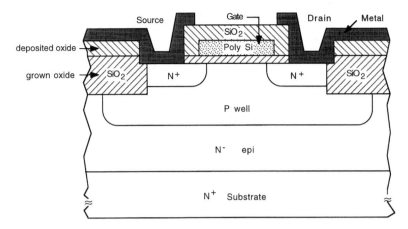

Figure 1-32   Cross-sectional view of an *n*-channel MOS integrated-circuit transistor.

1.4   Metal-Oxide-Semiconductor Field-Effect Transistor

In the metal-oxide-semiconductor field-effect transistor (MOSFET), the gate control electrode is physically separated from the conducting channel by a thin insulating dielectric layer. The voltage applied to the gate electrode modulates the concentration of mobile carriers in the channel and hence its conductance. Like the JFET, the MOSFET is also a unipolar device. Shown in Fig. 1-32 is a cross-sectional view of an integrated-circuit *n*-channel MOS transistor. This structure, as with most modern MOSFETs, utilizes a polysilicon layer as the gate electrode in place of a metal layer; they are still referred to as metal-oxide-semiconductor (MOS) transistors, however. A thin (typically 30 – 80 nm thick) silicon dioxide layer separates the gate from the channel region, which extends laterally between the N^+ source and drain contact regions.

Device Characteristics

Figure 1-33 illustrates the active region of the *n*-channel MOSFET with normal biases applied. With zero voltage applied to the gate, there is no conducting channel between the N^+ source and drain regions;[*] the device acts like two back-to-back *pn* junctions and only a small reverse-leakage current flows from

---

[*] There is a class of MOSFET devices in which a conducting channel exists even in the absence of an applied gate voltage. These are called depletion-mode devices and a negative gate voltage (positive for *p*-channel devices) is required to turn them off.

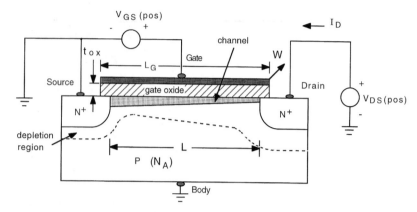

Figure 1-33   Active region of an *n*-channel MOSFET with normal bias applied.

source to drain. The gate-oxide-semiconductor sandwich acts like a parallel-plate capacitor; with a positive gate voltage V_{GS} applied to the structure, negative charge is induced in the top surface region of the semiconductor beneath the gate oxide. If the gate voltage is large enough, this induced electron concentration will exceed the background hole concentration of the *p*-type semiconductor, creating an *n*-type region (inversion layer) at the surface, and there is now a complete *n*-type conducting channel between source and drain. The gate voltage required to create the inversion layer is termed the threshold voltage V_{TH}; for V_{GS} less than V_{TH}, no conducting channel exists and the device is turned off.

In normal practice, the semiconductor body (substrate) is connected to the source. In some applications, however, the body is connected to separate bias voltage. This bias changes the semiconductor channel potential and hence the charge that is induced by the gate. The effect on the threshold voltage is related to the body-source voltage V_{BS} and is modeled as

$$V_{TH} = V_{TO} + \gamma(\sqrt{2\phi_P - V_{BS}} - \sqrt{2\phi_P}) \tag{1-74}$$

where V_{TO} is the threshold voltage for $V_{BS} = 0$. The parameter γ is given as

$$\gamma = \frac{\sqrt{2\varepsilon_s q N_A}}{C'_{OX}} \tag{1-75}$$

C'_{OX} is the capacitance per unit area of the gate-oxide region, given by

$$C'_{OX} = \frac{\varepsilon_{OX}}{t_{OX}} \tag{1-76}$$

where ε_{OX} is the dielectric permittivity of the oxide and t_{OX} is its thickness. ϕ_P is the Fermi potential of the semiconductor, given by

$$\phi_P = \frac{kT}{q} \ln\left(\frac{N_A}{n_i}\right) \tag{1-77}$$

With $V_{GS} > V_{TH}$, a conducting channel exists and the drain current I_D increases with increasing drain voltage V_{DS}. As V_{DS} is increased, the potential in the channel increases, being largest at the drain end of the channel. When $V_{DS} = V_{GS} - V_{TH}$, the voltage across the gate oxide at the drain ($V_{GD} = V_{GS} - V_{DS}$) is no longer large enough to create the n-type inversion layer and the channel is pinched off at that point. This value of drain voltage, denoted V_{Dsat}, is given by

$$V_{Dsat} = V_{GS} - V_{TH} \tag{1-78}$$

and the corresponding drain current, denoted I_{Dsat}, is given by

$$V_{Dsat} = \frac{\mu_n C'_{OX} W}{2L} (V_{GS} - V_{TH})^2 \tag{1-79}$$

where μ_n is the electron mobility in the channel, and W and L are the channel width and length dimensions, respectively (as illustrated in Fig. 1-33).

For values of V_{DS} less than V_{Dsat}, the drain current is well approximated by

$$I_D = \frac{\mu_n C'_{OX} W}{L} \left(V_{GS} - V_{TH} - \frac{1}{2} V_{DS}\right) V_{DS} \tag{1-80}$$

for $V_{DS} < V_{GS} - V_{TH}$ and describes operation in the triode region [11]. Note that the drain current is proportional to the channel width – channel length ratio W/L; this is analogous to the variation in collector current with emitter area A_E in a bipolar transistor.

For V_{DS} larger than V_{Dsat}, the device is operating in the saturation region and the current is given by

$$I_D = \frac{\mu_n C'_{OX} W}{2L} (V_{GS} - V_{TH})^2 (1 + \lambda V_{DS}) \tag{1-81}$$

for $V_{DS} \geq V_{GS} - V_{TH}$. In Eq. (1-81) we have included the channel-length modulation parameter λ, which models the narrowing of the inversion channel length as V_{DS} is increased beyond V_{Dsat}. Figure 1-34 illustrates the $I–V$ characteristics for an n-channel MOSFET. In a p-channel MOSFET, V_{TH} is negative (positive for a depletion-mode device), V_{GS} and V_{DS} are negative, and current flows out of the drain. Figure 1-35 illustrates the circuit symbols and sign conventions for n-channel and p-channel MOSFETs.

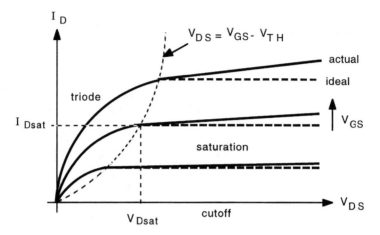

Figure 1-34 *I – V* characteristics of an n-channel MOSFET. Actual devices show a finite output conductance in the saturation region, characterized by the channel-length modulation parameter λ.

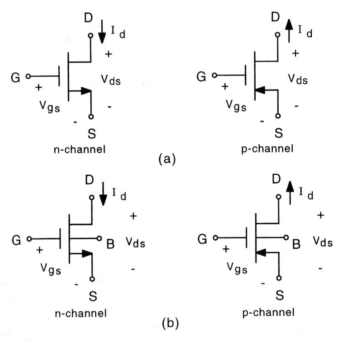

Figure 1-35   Circuit symbols and sign conventions for *n*-channel and *p*-channel MOS transistors. (a) Normal symbols for body connected to source. (b) Symbols for separate body connection.

In the SPICE simulation program, the drain current is modeled as

$$I_D = \begin{cases} KP \dfrac{W}{L - 2X_{jl}}\left(V_{GS} - V_{TH} - \dfrac{1}{2}V_{DS}\right)V_{DS}(1 + \lambda V_{DS}) & \text{for } V_{GS} - V_{TH} > V_{DS} > 0 \\[2ex] \dfrac{KP}{2}\dfrac{W}{L - 2X_{jl}}(V_{GS} - V_{TH})^2(1 + \lambda V_{DS}) & \text{for } V_{DS} \geq V_{GS} - V_{TH} > 0 \end{cases}$$

$$(1\text{-}82)$$

KP is the transconductance parameter and is equal to $\mu_n C'_{OX}$. X_{jl} is the distance by which the gate electrode overlaps the source and drain regions ($2X_{jl} = L_G - L$ in Fig. 1-33), and L is the gate length (labeled L_G in Fig. 1-33). The threshold voltage V_{TH} is modeled after Eq. (1-74) using the zero-bias threshold voltage parameter V_{T0} and the body-effect parameter γ. Alternately, in place of γ, the channel mobility μ_n (μ_p for the p-channel), oxide thickness t_{OX}, and channel doping concentration N_A (N_D for the p-channel) may be used as model parameters.

EXAMPLE. An NMOS transistor is to be used as a "linear resistor" (Fig. 1-36). Find the gate bias V_{bias} to give a maximum nonlinearity in the resistance characteristic of 5% at $V_D = 1$ V and determine the resulting resistance value. The transistor parameters are $V_{TH} = 2$ V and $\mu_n C'_{OX} W/L = 100 \, \mu A/V^2$.

In a region where V_{DS} is small relative to $V_{GS} - V_{TH}$, the $I_D - V_{DS}$ characteristic is nearly linear, given approximately from Eq. (1-80) as

$$I_D = \mu_n C'_{OX}\frac{W}{L}(V_{GS} - V_{TH})V_{DS}$$

Linearity will be characterized by the fractional deviation in current between the ideal resistance characteristic and the actual drain current at $V_D = 1$ V, as illustrated in Fig. 1-36. This gives

$$\left.\frac{\Delta I_D}{I_D}\right|_{V_D = 1\,V} = \frac{\mu_n C'_{OX}\dfrac{W}{2L}V_D^2}{\mu_n C'_{OX}\dfrac{W}{L}\left(V_{bias} - V_{TH} - \dfrac{1}{2}V_D\right)V_D} = \frac{V_D}{2\left(V_{bias} - V_{TH} - \dfrac{1}{2}V_D\right)} = 0.05$$

Solving for the required gate bias yields

$$V_{bias} = 10.5 + V_{TH} = 12.5 \, V$$

and the corresponding resistance is

$$R = \frac{1}{\mu_n C'_{OX}\dfrac{W}{L}(V_{bias} - V_{TH})} = \frac{1}{(100 \times 10^{-6}\,A/V^2)(10.5\,V)} = 952 \, \Omega$$

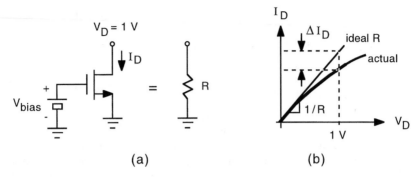

(a)   (b)

Figure 1-36   (a) Linear resistor example. (b) Ideal versus actual characteristic.

MOSFET Capacitance

There are numerous capacitances associated with the MOSFET structure; the origin of these capacitances is illustrated in Fig. 1-37. The total gate-to-source capacitance C_{GS} is comprised of

$$C_{GS} = C_{GS}^I + C_{GS}^O \tag{1-83}$$

where C_{GS}^I is the gate-oxide capacitance associated with the source region of the intrinsic transistor structure and is modeled as [12]

$$C_{GS}^I = \begin{cases} C_{OX}' WL \left\{ 1 - \left[\dfrac{V_{GS} - V_{TH} - V_{DS}}{2\,(V_{GS} - V_{TH})m V_{DS}} \right]^2 \right\} & \text{triode region} \\ \dfrac{2}{3} C_{OX}' WL & \text{saturation region} \end{cases} \tag{1-84}$$

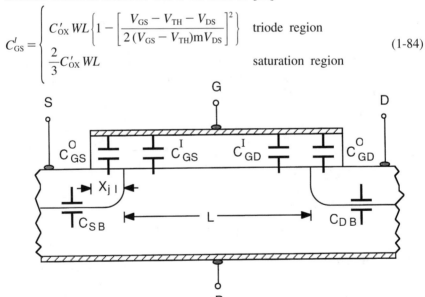

Figure 1-37   Origin of principal capacitances associated with a MOSFET.

C_{GS}^{O} is the parasitic capacitance resulting from the overlap of the gate and source and is given by

$$C_{GS}^{O} = C_{OX}' W X_{jl} \qquad (1\text{-}85)$$

In SPICE, the gate-to-source per unit-length capacitance C_{GSO} is used, so

$$C_{GS}^{O} = C_{GSO} W \qquad (1\text{-}86)$$

where

$$C_{GSO} = C_{OX}' L \qquad (1\text{-}87)$$

The total gate-to-drain capacitance C_{GD} is comprised of

$$C_{GD} = C_{GD}^{I} + C_{GD}^{O} \qquad (1\text{-}88)$$

where C_{GD}^{I} is the gate-oxide capacitance associated with the drain region of the intrinsic transistor structure and is modeled as [12]

$$C_{GD}^{I} = \begin{cases} C_{OX}' W L \left\{ 1 - \left[\dfrac{V_{GS} - V_{TH}}{2\,(V_{GS} - V_{TH}) - V_{DS}} \right]^{2} \right\} & \text{triode region} \\[4mm] \approx 0 & \text{saturation region} \end{cases} \qquad (1\text{-}89)$$

C_{GD}^{O} is the parasitic capacitance resulting from the overlap of the gate and drain and is given as

$$C_{GD}^{O} = C_{OX}' W X_{jl} \qquad (1\text{-}90)$$

In SPICE, the gate-to-source per unit-length capacitance C_{GDO} parameter is used, giving

$$C_{GD}^{O} = C_{GDO} W \qquad (1\text{-}91)$$

where

$$C_{GDO} = C_{OX}' L \qquad (1\text{-}92)$$

C_{SB} and C_{DB} represent the *pn* junction capacitances formed between the source and body (substrate), and the drain and body regions, respectively. They can be modeled as

$$C_{SB}(V_{SB}) = \frac{C_{SB}(0)}{(1 + V_{SB}/\phi_i)^{1/2}} \qquad (1\text{-}93)$$

and

$$C_{DB}(V_{DB}) = \frac{C_{DB}(0)}{(1 + V_{DB}/\phi_i)^{1/2}} \qquad (1\text{-}94)$$

where $C_{SB}(0)$ and $C_{DB}(0)$ are the zero-bias capacitances of the source-body and drain-body *pn* junctions, respectively.

Included in the SPICE model is the capacitance between the gate and body formed by the overlap of the gate oxide beyond the intrinsic region in the width (W) dimension. This parasitic capacitance is modeled as

$$C_{GB} = C_{GBO}L \tag{1-95}$$

where C_{GBO} is the gate-body (substrate) overlap (beyond W) capacitance per unit length. This capacitance is normally quite small compared to the other parasitic capacitances and is neglected here.

Small-Signal Model of the MOSFET

Figure 1-38 shows the small-signal equivalent circuit for a MOSFET operating either in the triode or saturation region. The transconductance is found from Eqs. (1-80) and (1-81):

$$g_m = \frac{dI_d}{dV_{gs}}\bigg|_{v_{gs}=0} = \begin{cases} \dfrac{\mu_n C'_{OX} W}{L} V_{DS} & \text{for } V_{DS} < V_{GS} - V_{TH} \\[2ex] \dfrac{\mu_n C'_{OX} W}{L} (V_{GS} - V_{TH})(1 + \lambda V_{DS}) & \text{for } V_{DS} \geq V_{GS} - V_{TH} \end{cases} \tag{1-96}$$

In the saturation region, the transconductance can be expressed in terms of the drain current as

$$g_m = \frac{2I_D}{V_{GS} - V_{TH}} \approx \sqrt{2\mu_n C'_{OX} \frac{W}{L} I_D} \tag{1-97}$$

where we have made use of Eq. (1-81) and assumed that $\lambda V_{DS} \ll 1$. Note that the transconductance is proportional to the square root of the drain current; contrast

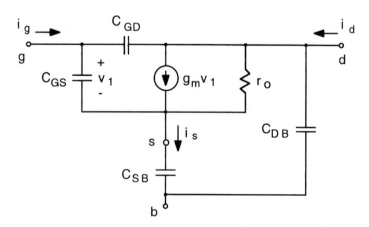

Figure 1-38   Small-signal equivalent circuit for a MOSFET.

this with the bipolar transistor in which g_m is linearly proportional to the collector current—see Eq. (1-37).

The small-signal output resistance is determined from Eqs. (1-80) and (1-81):

$$\frac{1}{r_o} = g_o = \left.\frac{dI_d}{dV_{Ds}}\right|_{v_{ds}=0} = \begin{cases} \dfrac{\mu_n C'_{OX} W}{L}(V_{GS} - V_{TH} - V_{DS}) & \text{for } V_{DS} < V_{GS} - V_{TH} \\[2ex] \lambda I_D & \text{for } V_{DS} \geq V_{GS} - V_{TH} \end{cases}$$

$$(1\text{-}98)$$

The values of C_{GS} C_{GD}, C_{SB}, and C_{DB} are determined from Eqs. (1-83), (1-88), (1-93) and (1-94), respectively, evaluated at the dc operating point.

Transistor Cutoff Frequency

The unity-gain cutoff frequency f_T for the MOSFET is similar to that for the JFET:

$$f_T = \frac{g_m}{2\pi(C_{GS} + C_{GD})} \tag{1-99}$$

Using Eq. (1-96) for g_m in the saturation region (and assuming $\lambda V_{DS} \ll 1$), f_T can be expressed as

$$f_T = \frac{\mu_n(V_{GS} - V_{TH})}{4\pi L^2\left(\dfrac{1}{3} + \dfrac{X_{jl}}{L}\right)} \quad \text{for } V_{DS} \geq V_{GS} - V_{TH} \tag{1-100}$$

where Eqs. (1-83) – (1-85) and Eqs. (1-88) – (1-90) have been used for the capacitances C_{GS} and C_{GD}. Equation (1-100) indicates that the high-frequency behavior of a MOSFET varies as the square of the channel length L; a fabrication process that reduces the channel length has a significant effect on device, and hence circuit speed.

EXAMPLE. A MOSFET with a channel length L of $3\,\mu\text{m}$ has a unity-gain cutoff frequency f_T of $800\,\text{MHz}$. A new fabrication process allows the channel length to be reduced to $2\,\mu\text{m}$. Determine the new cutoff frequency, assuming that X_{jl} remains at $1\,\mu\text{m}$.

From Eq. (1-100)

$$\frac{f_T(2\,\mu\text{m})}{f_T(3\,\mu\text{m})} = \frac{(3\,\mu\text{m})^2\left(\dfrac{1}{3} + \dfrac{1}{3}\right)}{(2\,\mu\text{m})^2\left(\dfrac{1}{3} + \dfrac{1}{2}\right)} = 1.8$$

giving

$$f_T = (1.8)(800\,\text{MHz}) = 1.44\,\text{GHz}$$

Problems

For all problems assume room temperature, $kT/q = 26\,\text{mV}$.

1.1 (a) Using the Ebers – Moll model for a transistor operating in the saturation region, show that

$$V_{\text{CE (sat)}} = \frac{kT}{q} \ln \left(\frac{\dfrac{1}{\alpha_R} + \dfrac{1}{\beta_R} \dfrac{I_C}{I_B}}{1 - \dfrac{1}{\beta_F} \dfrac{I_C}{I_B}} \right)$$

(b) What is $V_{\text{CE (sat)}}$ for $I_C \rightarrow 0$?

(c) At a constant base current I_B, what is I_C for $V_{\text{CE (sat)}} \rightarrow 0$?

1.2 Determine the elements of the common-emitter small-signal equivalent circuit of a bipolar transistor used in a circuit with $V_{\text{BE}} = 0.75\,\text{V}$ and $V_{\text{CE}} = 2.5\,\text{V}$. The transistor has the following parameters: $I_S = 2 \times 10^{-16}\,\text{A}$, $\beta_F = 75$, $V_A = 100\,\text{V}$, $\tau_F = 20\,\text{ps}$, $C_{\text{jE}}(0) = 0.15\,\text{pF}$, and $C_{\text{jC}}(0) = 0.2\,\text{pF}$. Assume that the value of C_{jE} at 0.75 V forward bias is twice its zero-bias value. Take $\phi_C = 0.7\,\text{V}$ and $m_C = \frac{1}{3}$.

1.3 For the transistor in Problem 1.2, determine and sketch a plot (using log scales) of the magnitude of the common-emitter small-signal current gain as a function of frequency from 1 MHz to 10 GHz.

1.4 Using the common-base small-signal equivalent circuit (Fig. 1-12), find the frequency ω_α at which the short-circuit common-base current gain $(i_c/i_e)(j\omega)$ is down by 3 dB from the low-frequency value α_F. Neglect the output resistance r_o.

1.5 Figure 1-39 illustrates two ways of implementing a two-diode string using *npn* transistors. Derive the forward-bias *I–V* characteristic for the two configurations, assuming identical transistors and that $\beta_F \gg 1$. At a constant forward-bias current, which diode string has the largest voltage drop V?

1.6 An *n*-channel JFET has the following data, measured in saturation:

$$I_D(V_{\text{GS}} = -2\,\text{V}, V_{\text{DS}} = 5\,\text{V}) = 275\,\mu\text{A}$$

$$I_D(V_{\text{GS}} = -2\,\text{V}, V_{\text{DS}} = 10\,\text{V}) = 300\,\mu\text{A}$$

$$I_D(V_{\text{GS}} = 0, V_{\text{DS}} = 10\,\text{V}) = 1.2\,\mu\text{A}.$$

Determine the parameters V_P, I_{DSS} and λ for the JFET.

1.7 Repeat the example given in Fig. 1-26 for $R_D = 15\,\text{k}\Omega$.

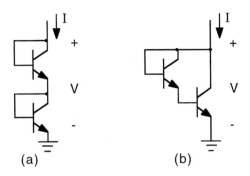

Figure 1-39   Two-diode interconnections for Problem 1.5.

1.8 Show that the transconductance of a JFET in saturation is proportional to the square root of I_D.

1.9 Determine I_D and V_O in the circuit of Fig. 1-40. The JFET parameters are $V_P = -4\,\text{V}$, $I_{DSS} = 2\,\text{mA}$, and $\lambda = 0$.

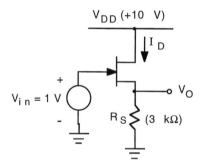

Figure 1-40   Circuit for Problem 1.9.

1.10 A p-channel JFET is to be used as a "pinched resistor" in an integrated circuit. In this application, the gate and source of the JFET are connected together and the device functions as a two-terminal nonlinear resistive element. (a) Use Eq. (1-61) to derive the resistance R_D as a function of V_{DS}. (b) Using $I_{DSS} = 500\,\mu\text{A}$ and $V_P = 4\,\text{V}$, determine and sketch a plot of R_D versus V_{DS} for V_{DS} ranging from 0 to $-5\,\text{V}$. What is the range of V_{DS} such that the nonlinearity in resistance does not exceed 10%?

1.11 Determine I_D and V_O in the circuit of Fig. 1-41. The MOSFET parameters are $\mu_p C'_{OX} W/L = 200\,\mu\text{A}/\text{V}^2$, $V_{TH} = -2\,\text{V}$, and $\lambda = -0.02\,\text{V}^{-1}$.

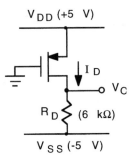

Figure 1-41   Circuit for Problem 1.11.

1.12 An n-channel MOSFET has the following parameters: $W = 12\,\mu m$, $L = 1.5\,\mu m$, $X_{jl} = 0.5\,\mu m$, $C'_{OX} = 5 \times 10^{-8}\,F/cm^2$, $V_{TH} = 1\,V$, $\lambda = 0.04\,V^{-1}$, and $C_{DB(0)} = 0.1\,pF$.
Determine and sketch the small-signal equivalent circuit for this transistor used in a circuit with $V_{GS} = 2.5\,V$, $V_{DS} = 3\,V$, and $V_{SB} = 0$. Take $\mu_n = 600\,cm^2/$V-s and $\phi_i = 0.8\,V$.

1.13 A useful figure-of-merit for a transistor which relates its gain and bias current is the transconductance /current ratio g_m/I. (a) Determine this fig-ure-of-merit for a bipolar transistor (operating in the forward-active re-gion) g_m/I_C and for a MOSFET (operating in the saturation region) g_m/I_D. Compare the two at room temperature, taking $V_{GS} - V_{TH} = 1\,V$ for the MOS-FET. (b) An n-channel MOSFET is to be designed to give the same transconductance as a BJT, both operating at a current of 1 mA. Deter-mine the channel width W required to achieve this transconductance; the fabrication process gives $L = 1.5\,\mu m$ and $t_{OX} = 60\,nm$. Take $\mu_n = 600\,cm^2/$V-s and $\varepsilon_{OX} = 3.45 \times 10^{-13}\,F/cm$. Is this a realistic size for a modern integrated-circuit device?

1.14 Determine the $I-V$ characteristic for each of the two MOSFET "diode" connections illustrated in Fig. 1-42. The two NMOS transistors in Fig. 1-42(a) are identical and both the NMOS and PMOS transistors are enhancement mode devices. Use $\beta_n = \mu_n C'_{OX} W_n/L_n$ and V_{TH} to represent the NMOS transistors, and $\beta_p = \mu_p C'_{OX} W_p/L_p$ and $V_{Tp} = V_{TH}$ to represent the PMOS transistor. For each ot the two configurations sketch the $I-V$ characteristic for $V > 0$.

1.15 The induced charge per unit area in the channel of a MOSFET is given by

$$Q'_{CH}(x) = C'_{OX}[V_{GS} - V_{TH} - V(x)]$$

where $V(x)$ is the channel potential equal to zero at the source end ($x = 0$)

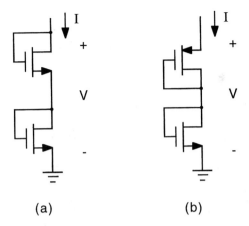

Figure 1-42   (a) Series NMOS and (b) series PMOS and NMOS for Problem 1.14.

and equal to V_{DS} at the drain end $(x = L)$. The channel potential as a function of position is related to I_D and Q'_{CH} as

$$dV = \frac{I_D}{W \mu_n Q'_{CH}(x)} dx$$

The total charge stored in the channel is

$$Q_{CH} = w \int_0^L Q'_{CH}(x) dx$$

Using

$$C'_{GS} = \frac{dQ_{CH}}{dV_{GS}}$$

show that the gate-to-source capacitance in saturation given in Eq. (1-84) results.

Hint: In saturation, take $V_{DS} = V_{GS} - V_{TH}$ and use Eq. (1-79) for I_D.

References

1. J.J Ebers and J.L. Moll, "Large-Signal Behavior of Junction Transistors," *Proc. IRE*, 42, 1761 (1954).

2. R.S. Muller and T.I. Kamins, *Device Electronics for Integrated Circuits*, 2nd ed., Wiley, New York, 1986.

3. P. Antognetti and G. Massobrio (eds.), *Semiconductor Device Modeling with SPICE*, McGraw-Hill, New York, 1988.

4. L.W. Nagel, "SPICE2: A Computer Program to Simulate Semiconductor Circuits," *Electronics Research Laboratory Report No. ERL-M520*, University of California, Berkeley, 1975.

5. J.M. Early, "Effects of Space-Charge Layer Widening in Junction Transistors," *Proc. IRE*, 40, 1401 (1952).

6. C.T. Kirk, "A Theory of Transistor Cut-Off Frequency (f_t) Falloff at High Currents," *IEEE Trans. Electron Devices*, ED-9, 164–174 (1962).

7. H.C. Lin, "Diode Operation of a Transistor in Functional Blocks," *IEEE Trans. Electron Devices*, ED-10, 189–194 (1963).

8. P.R. Gray and R.G. Meyer, *Analysis and Design of Analog Integrated Circuits*, 3rd ed., Wiley, New York, 1993, Chap. 1.

9. R.D. Middlebrook and I. Richer, "Limits on the Power-Law Exponent for Field-Effect Transistor Transfer Characteristics," *Solid-State Electron.*, 6, 542–544 (1963).

10. L.K. Nanver and E.J.G. Goudena, "Design Considerations for Integrated High-Frequency p-Channel JFET's," *IEEE Trans. Electron Devices*, ED-35, 1924–1933 (1988).

11. D.K. Ferry, L.A. Akers, and E.W. Greeneich, *Ultra Large Scale Integrated Microelectronics*, Prentice-Hall, Englewood Cliffs, NJ, 1988, Chap. 2.

12. J.E. Meyer, "MOS Models and Circuit Simulation," *RCA Rev.*, 32 (1971).

Chapter 2

Analog Integrated-Circuit Blocks

A typical analog integrated circuit is composed of several pieces of circuitry, each of which performs a specific circuit function contributing to the overall operation of the circuit. These basic circuit building blocks are common to a large variety of analog circuits and it is convenient to consider them individually. Figure 2-1 shows a two-stage operational amplifier circuit (Op-Amp) and illustrates the individual building blocks that make up the circuit.

In this chapter, many of the circuit blocks commonly found in analog integrated circuits are discussed: current sources, dc level-shift stages, gain stages, and output stages.

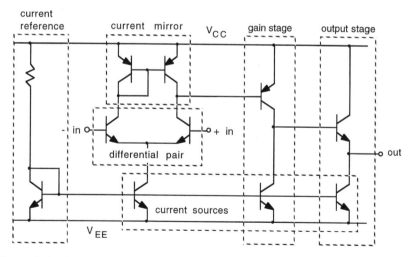

Figure 2-1 A two-stage operational amplifier circuit illustrating its component circuit blocks.

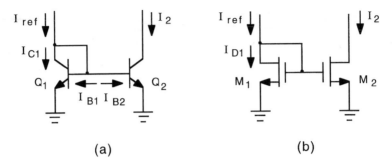

Figure 2-2   Basic current mirror (a) using BJTs and (b) using MOSFETs.

2.1 Current Sources

Current sources provide currents that are relatively constant and independent of device parameters and voltage; they can also be made relatively independent of temperature and power-supply variations as well. In analog circuits, current sources are used for dc biasing and as load elements in amplifier stages. In a current-source circuit, a reference current in one branch is reproduced or mirrored in another branch; hence, these circuits are also called *current mirrors.*

Basic Current Mirror

Figure 2-2(a) shows the basic current mirror fashioned with bipolar transistors. In the circuit, both transistors have the same base-emitter voltage. Thus, if the transistors are identical and the output transistor Q_2 is operating in the forward-active region, then the collector currents of the two transistors will be equal (neglecting Early effect) and the output current I_2 will be approximately equal to the reference current I_{ref}. For each transistor, operating in forward active, we have from Eq. (1-36)

$$I_C = I_S e^{qV_{BE}/kT}(1 + V_{CE}/V_A) \qquad (2\text{-}1)$$

The transistor saturation current I_S is proportional to emitter area [see Eq. (1-7)]. In an integrated-circuit process, the two transistors (and others) are fabricated simultaneously and, hence, will have identical values of I_S, except as scaled by their respective emitter areas (designer specified); they will also have other closely matched device parameters, such as current gain β_F and Early voltage V_A. In the current mirror, we have for Q_1 and Q_2 at equal V_{BE},

$$\frac{I_{C1}}{A_1(1 + V_{BE}/V_A)} = \frac{I_{C2}}{A_2(1 + V_{CE2}/V_A)} \qquad (2\text{-}2)$$

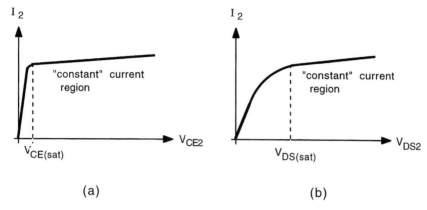

Figure 2-3 **Output current characteristics of (a) the BJT current and (b) the MOSFET current mirror of Fig. 2-1.**

where A_1 and A_2 are the emitter areas of Q_1 and Q_2, respectively. In the circuit,

$$I_{\text{ref}} = I_{C1} + I_{B1} + I_{B2} = I_{C1} + \frac{I_{C1}}{\beta_F} + \frac{I_{C2}}{\beta_F} \approx I_{C1} + \frac{I_{C1}}{\beta_F} + \frac{A_2}{A_1}\frac{I_{C1}}{\beta_F} = I_{C1}\left[1 + \frac{1}{\beta_F}\left(1 + \frac{A_2}{A_1}\right)\right]$$

(2-3)

which used in Eq. (2-2) gives for the output of the current source

$$I_2 = \frac{A_2}{A_1}I_{\text{ref}}\left(\frac{1}{1 + \dfrac{1}{\beta_F}\left(1 + \dfrac{A_2}{A_1}\right)}\right)\left(\frac{1 + V_{\text{CE2}}/V_A}{1 + V_{\text{BE}}/V_A}\right)$$

(2-4)

If $\beta_F \gg 1$ and $V_A \gg V_{\text{CE}}$, then Eq. (2-4) reduces to

$$I_2 \approx \frac{A_2}{A_1}I_{\text{ref}}$$

(2-5)

The output characteristic of the basic BJT current mirror are illustrated in Fig. 2-3(a).

EXAMPLE. Find the output current at $V_O = 10\,\text{V}$ of the simple current source shown in Fig. 2-4. Except for emitter areas, the transistors are identical with $\beta_F = 100$ and $V_A = 50\,\text{V}$. $A_2 = \frac{1}{2}A_1$. Take $V_{\text{BE}} = V_{\text{BE(on)}} = 0.7\,\text{V}$. Repeat the calculation if base current and the Early effect are neglected.

From the circuit,

$$I_{\text{ref}} = \frac{V_{\text{CC}} - V_{\text{BE(on)}}}{R} = \frac{15\,\text{V} - 0.7\,\text{V}}{10\,\text{k}\Omega} = 1.43\,\text{mA}$$

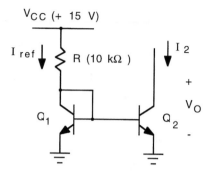

Figure 2-4   Simple current-source example.

Using Eq. (2-4),

$$I_2 = \frac{1}{2}(1.43\,\text{mA})\left(\frac{1}{1+\left(\dfrac{1}{100}\right)\left(1+\dfrac{1}{2}\right)}\right)\left(\frac{1+10/50}{1+0.7/50}\right) = 834\,\mu\text{A}$$

Neglecting I_B and V_A,

$$I_2 = \frac{A_2}{A_1}I_{\text{ref}} = \frac{1}{2}(1.43\,\text{mA}) = 715\,\mu\text{A}$$

EXERCISE. In the above example, determine the actual base-emitter voltage V_{BE}. Take $I_{S1} = 5 \times 10^{-16}$ A at room temperature. What is the value of I_{ref} at the actual value of V_{BE}? (*Ans*: $V_{\text{BE}} = 0.745\,\text{V}, I_{\text{ref}} = 1.426\,\text{mA}$)

Multiple current sources may be fashioned using a single reference, such as illustrated in Fig. 2-5. The output current of an individual source (neglecting base current and Early effect) is given as

$$I_j \approx \frac{A_j}{A_1}I_{\text{ref}} \tag{2-6}$$

where $j = 2, 3, \cdots, N$,

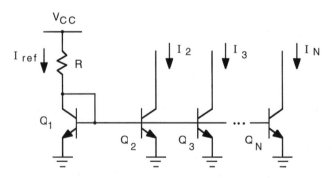

Figure 2-5   Multiple current sources using a single reference.

This technique is commonly used in analog circuits where several bias currents are required—see Fig. 2-1 for example. As additional current-source transistors are added, however, additional base current must be supplied by the reference current, which detracts from the reference transistor's collector current I_{C1}. This can lead to significant error, especially for low-beta transistors. The use of base-current compensation—to be discussed later in this section—can reduce this error.

For the MOS version of the current mirror [Fig. 2-2(b)], the drain current in saturation is given by Eq. (1-81):

$$I_D = \frac{\mu_n C'_{ox} W}{2L} (V_{GS} - V_{TH})^2 (1 + \lambda V_{DS}) \qquad (2\text{-}7)$$

Here, $I_{ref} = I_{D1}$, which when combined with Eq. (2-7), yields

$$I_2 = \frac{(W/L)_2}{(W/L)_1} I_{ref} \left(\frac{1 + \lambda V_{DS2}}{1 + \lambda V_{GS}} \right) \qquad (2\text{-}8)$$

In the MOS current mirror, the output current scales with the channel width-to-channel length ratios W/L of the transistors. Normally, the channel length L is fixed for a given fabrication process and the channel width dimension W is varied.

EXAMPLE. Determine the output current at $V_O = 5$ V for the current source given in Fig. 2-6. The transistors have the following parameters: $\mu_n C'_{ox} = 20\,\mu\text{A/V}^2$, $V_{TH} = 1$ V, $\lambda = 0.02$ V^{-1}, $(W/L)_1 = 10$, and $(W/L)_2 = 15$.

From the circuit,

$$I_{ref} = \frac{V_{DD} - V_{GS}}{R}$$

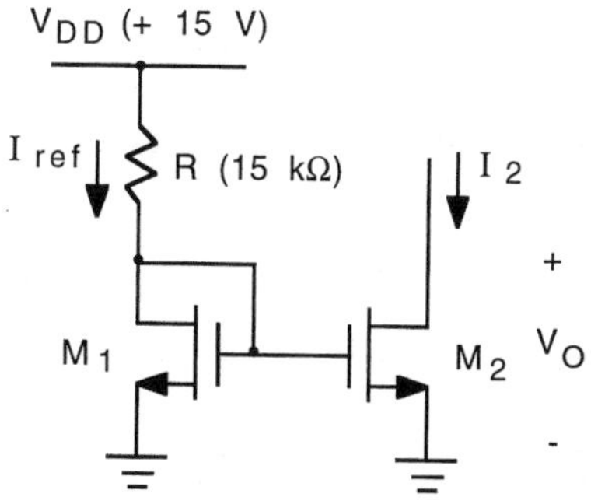

Figure 2-6 MOS current-source example.

The gate-to-source voltage is found using Eq.(1-79):

$$V_{GS} = V_{TH} + \sqrt{\frac{2I_{ref}}{\mu_n C'_{ox}(W/L)_1}}$$

which combined with the previous equation yields a quadratic equation in I_{ref}:

$$I_{ref}^2 - \left[2\left(\frac{V_{DD} - V_{TH}}{R}\right) + \frac{2}{\mu_n C'_{ox}(W/L)_1 R^2}\right]I_{ref} + \left(\frac{V_{DD} - V_{TH}}{R}\right)^2 = 0$$

Substituting for the device and circuit parameters gives

$$I_{ref}^2 - 1.9114 I_{ref} + 0.8711 = 0$$

which yields

$$I_{ref} = 0.750 \text{ mA}$$

The corresponding gate-to-source voltage is

$$V_{GS} = 1\text{ V} + \sqrt{\frac{(2)(0.75\text{ mA})}{(0.02\text{ mA/V}^2)(10)}} = 3.74\text{ V}$$

Using Eq. (2-7),

$$I_2 = \frac{15}{10}(0.750\text{ mA})\left(\frac{1 + (0.02)(5)}{1 + (0.02)(3.74)}\right) = 1.15\text{ mA}$$

Base-Current Compensated Current Mirror

A primary source of error in the basic current mirror of Fig. 2-2(a) arises from the finite base currents, which results in I_{C1} differing from I_{ref}—by a factor of $[1 + (1 + A_2/A_1)/\beta_F]$. In high-beta transistors (say 100 or greater), this difference is small; however, with smaller gain devices (such as with lateral *pnp* transistors), the difference can be significant. The base-current error can be reduced by adding current gain to the reference transistor Q_1, as illustrated in Fig. 2-7. The difference between I_{ref} and I_{C1} is now equal to the base current of Q_3, which is less than $I_{B1} + I_{B2}$. Assuming identical transistors, except for emitter areas, we have

$$I_{ref} = I_{C1} + I_{B3} = I_{C1} + \frac{I_{E3}}{\beta_F + 1} = I_{C1} + \frac{I_{B1}}{\beta_F + 1} + \frac{I_{B2}}{\beta_F + 1} \qquad (2\text{-}9)$$

With $I_C = \beta_F I_B$ and, neglecting the Early effect, $I_{C2} \approx (A_2/A_1)I_{C1}$, this leads to

$$I_{ref} = I_{C1}\left[1 + \frac{1}{\beta_F(\beta_F + 1)}\left(1 + \frac{A_2}{A_1}\right)\right] \qquad (2\text{-}10)$$

giving a factor of $\beta_F + 1$ improvement in the base-current error.

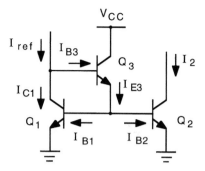

Figure 2-7 Base-current compensated current mirror.

The collector currents of the reference and output transistors scale as

$$\frac{I_{C1}}{A_1(1 + 2V_{BE}/V_A)} = \frac{I_{C2}}{A_2(1 + V_{CE2}/V_A)} \tag{2-11}$$

which combined with Eq. (2-9) gives

$$I_2 = \frac{A_2}{A_1} I_{ref} \left(\frac{1}{1 + \dfrac{1}{\beta_F^2 + \beta_F}\left(1 + \dfrac{A_2}{A_1}\right)} \right) \left(\frac{1 + V_{CE2}/V_A}{1 + 2V_{BE}/V_A} \right) \tag{2-12}$$

For a reasonably large value of beta, the base-current terms can be neglected, giving

$$I_2 \approx \frac{A_2}{A_1} I_{ref} \left(\frac{1 + V_{CE2}/V_A}{1 + 2V_{BE}/V_A} \right) \tag{2-13}$$

Cascode Current Source

A second source of error in current sources arises from the finite output resistance of the current-source transistors, which results in a variation in output current with voltage, as depicted in Fig. 2-3; this variation in current with voltage is characterized by the effective output resistance of the current source R_o. In the simple current source using the basic current mirror, this output resistance is simply the output resistance r_o of the transistors. Several modifications to the basic current mirror can provide current sources with increased output resistance; one example is the *cascode current source*, illustrated in Fig. 2-8 for bipolar transistors. In this circuit, Q_3 and Q_4 form a basic current mirror, and a second mirror stage consisting of Q_1 and Q_2 is added in series. In this connection, Q_2 and Q_4 form a common-base : common-emmiter cascode pair;

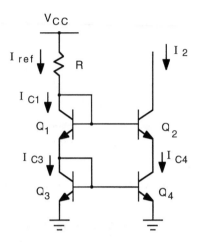

Figure 2-8   Cascode current source.

diode-connected Q_1 provides a V_{BE} level shift to ensure that Q_4 remains in the foward-active region.

With reference to Fig. 2-8, assuming identical transistors,

$$I_{C1} = \frac{I_{ref}}{1 + 2/\beta_F} \tag{2-14}$$

and, neglecting the Early effect,

$$I_{C3} = \frac{I_{E1}}{1 + 2/\beta_F} = I_{C4} \tag{2-15}$$

Using

$$I_C = \frac{\beta_F}{\beta_F + 1} I_E \tag{2-16}$$

leads to

$$I_2 = I_{ref} \frac{1}{1 + \dfrac{4}{\beta_F}\left(1 + \dfrac{1}{\beta_F}\right)} \approx I_{ref} \frac{1}{1 + 4/\beta_F} \tag{2-17}$$

which shows a factor-of-2 improvement in beta sensitivity over the simple current source.

The output resistance R_o of the cascode current source is calculated from its small-signal equivalent circuit, shown in Fig. 2-9. In this calculation, a small-signal test current i_x is applied to the output port of the current source and the

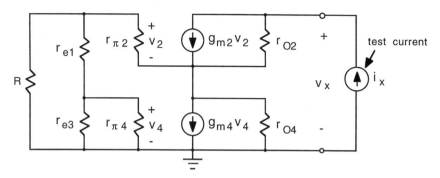

Figure 2-9 **Small-signal equivalent circuit of the cascode current source for calculating output resistance.**

resulting response v_x is measured; the ratio of the two v_x/i_x then gives R_o.[*] With reference to Fig. 2-9, several points are worthy of note: The current in r_{o4} is small relative to the current $g_{m4} v_4$ and, because r_{o4} is not connected to the output, will be neglected; the reference current resistance R is usually much larger than the emitter resistance r_e and will be neglected; $r_{\pi4}$, which is in parallel with r_{e3}, is the larger of the two by a factor of $\beta_F + 1$ and can be neglected; all four collector currents are approximately equal; thus, $r_{e1} \approx r_{e3}$, both denoted r_e, and $g_{m2} \approx g_{m4}$, both denoted g_m. With these approximations, the simplified equivalent circuit in Fig. 2-10 results.

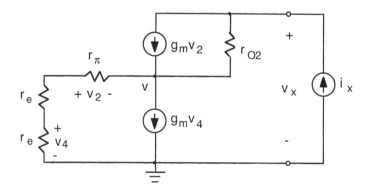

Figure 2-10 **Simplified circuit of Fig. 2-9.**

---

[*] An equally valid method is to use a test voltage v_x and measure the response current i_x.

Summing the currents at the node connecting the emitter of Q_2 and the collector of Q_4 gives

$$i_x = g_m v_4 + \frac{v}{r_\pi + 2r_e} \approx g_m v_4 + \frac{v}{r_\pi} = g_m \left(v_4 + \frac{v}{\beta_F} \right) \tag{2-18}$$

where in the second expression we have assumed $r_\pi \gg 2r_e$.

The current in r_{o2} is $i_x - g_m v_2$, giving

$$v_x = (i_x - g_m v_2) r_{o2} + v \tag{2-19}$$

Because $r_\pi \approx \beta_F r_e$, $v_4 \approx -v_2/\beta_F$ and $v_2 \approx -v$. This, combined with Eqs. (2-18) and (2-19) gives

$$v_x = i_x \left[\left(1 + \frac{\beta_F}{2} \right) r_{o2} + \frac{\beta_F}{2g_m} \right] \tag{2-20}$$

The last term on the right-hand side of Eq. (2-20) is $r_\pi/2$, which is much smaller than $\beta_F r_{o2}/2$, and is neglected; also $\beta_F/2 \gg 1$, yielding

$$R_o = \frac{v_x}{i_x} \approx \frac{\beta_F}{2} r_{o2} \tag{2-21}$$

The output resistance of the cascode current source is thus a factor of $\beta_F/2$ greater than that of the simple current source.

Wilson Current Source

Another current source that achieves a high output resistance is the Wilson current source [1], illustrated in Fig. 2-11. In this configuration, the diode-connected reference transistor Q_3 operates as a negative feedback element in the

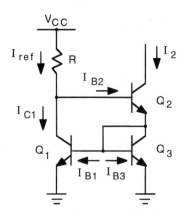

Figure 2-11   Wilson current source.

output circuit of the source, which tends to stabilize the output current I_2 to I_{ref}. To see this, suppose that the output voltage of the source is raised, causing I_2 to increase; this, in turn, increases I_{C3} and thereby V_{BE3}, causing I_{C1} to increase. This increase in I_{C1} subtracts from I_{ref}, causing I_{B2} to decrease, thereby decreasing I_{C2}. The output current thus remains nearly constant, giving a high output resistance. A small-signal analysis of the circuit gives an output resistance of

$$R_o \approx \frac{\beta_F}{2} r_{o2} \qquad (2\text{-}22)$$

similar to the result obtained for the cascode current source.

The Wilson current source also has low-beta sensitivity. From the circuit,

$$I_2 = I_{ref} + I_{B1} + I_{B3} - 2I_{B2} \approx I_{ref} \qquad (2\text{-}23)$$

which shows a high degree of base-current cancellation. A detailed analysis, assuming identical transistors and taking $V_A = \infty$, gives

$$I_2 = I_{ref}\left(1 - \frac{2}{\beta_F^2 + 2\beta_F + 2}\right) \approx I_{ref}\left(1 - \frac{2}{\beta_F^2}\right) \qquad (2\text{-}24)$$

for $\beta_F \gg 1$. This gives a factor-of-β_F improvement over the basic current source.

EXAMPLE. Determine the current and output resistance of the Wilson current source of Fig. 2-11 with $V_{CC} = 18$ V and $R = 10 \, k\Omega$. The transistors are identical with $\beta_F = 100$ and $V_A = 75$ V. Take $V_{BE(on)} = 0.7$ V.

The reference current is

$$I_{ref} = \frac{V_{CC} - 2V_{BE(on)}}{R} = \frac{18 \text{ V} - (2)(0.7 \text{ V})}{10 \, k\Omega} = 1.660 \, mA$$

Using Eq. (2-24),

$$I_2 = (1.66 \, mA)\left[1 - 2/(100)^2\right] = 1.6597 \, mA$$

Using Eq. (1-40),

$$r_{o2} = \frac{V_A}{I_{C2}} = \frac{75 \text{ V}}{1.6597 \, mA} = 45.19 \, k\Omega$$

giving

$$R_o = \frac{100}{2}(45.19 \, k\Omega) = 2.26 \, M\Omega$$

In the Wilson current source of Fig. 2-11, $V_{CE1} = 2V_{BE}$, whereas $V_{CE3} = V_{BE}$; this difference in collector-emitter voltages gives a slight mismatch in collector currents due to the finite output resistance of the transistors. The two collector voltages can be equalized by adding a diode-connected transistor in the reference

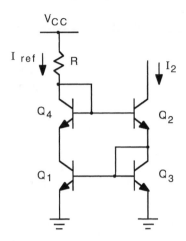

Figure 2-12   Improved Wilson current source. With this circuit, $V_{CE1} = V_{CE3}$, so a precise match between I_{C1} and I_{C3} is obtained.

side of the current source, as illustrated in Fig. 2-12. With this arrangement, I_{C1} and I_{C3} are made equal and, neglecting the output resistance of Q_2, I_2 is exactly equal to I_{ref}.

Both versions of the Wilson current source can be implemented in MOS technology as well; Fig. 2-13(a) illustrates an NMOS Wilson current mirror and Fig. 2-13(b) illustrates the improved current mirror with NMOS transistors. A small-signal analysis of either circuit gives for the output resistance

$$R_o \approx \left[1 + (1 + g_{m1} r_{o1}) \frac{g_{m2}}{g_{m3}} \right] r_{o2} \qquad (2\text{-}25)$$

For identical transistors, this reduces to $R_o \approx (2 + g_{m1} r_{o1}) r_{o2}$.

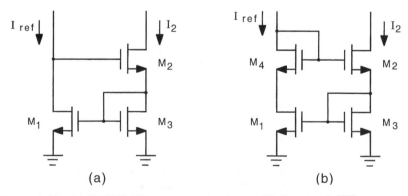

Figure 2-13   (a) NMOS Wilson current mirror. (b) Improved Wilson current mirror using NMOS.

One drawback to the MOS Wilson current source is the minimum output voltage required to keep both M_2 and M_3 operating in the saturation region; for identical transistors, this minimum voltage is equal to $2V_{GS} - V_{TH}$. In some applications, this can severely limit the dynamic range of the current source, especially with low power-supply voltages.

Resistor-Ratioed Current Source

An additional method by which currents can be scaled is to place resistors in the emitter legs of the basic current source; such an arrangement, illustrated in Fig. 2-14, is called a *resistor-ratioed current source*. The voltage dropped across each of the resistors leads to differing base-emitter voltages for the transistors and, hence, differing collector currents. With reference to Fig. 2-14, summing the voltages around the base-emitter loop, neglecting base currents, gives

$$V_{BE1} + I_{ref}R_1 - I_2 R_2 - V_{BE2} = 0 \tag{2-26}$$

where, assuming $V_A = \infty$,

$$V_{BE1,2} = \frac{kT}{q} \ln\left(\frac{I_{C1,2}}{I_{S1,2}}\right) \tag{2-27}$$

Substituting Eq. (2-27) into Eq. (2-26) and rearranging leads to

$$I_2 = \frac{R_1}{R_2} I_{ref} \left[1 + \frac{\frac{kT}{q} \ln\left(\frac{A_2}{A_1} \frac{I_{ref}}{I_2}\right)}{I_{ref} R_1} \right] \tag{2-28}$$

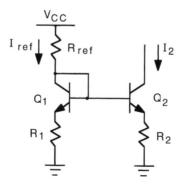

Figure 2-14 Resistor-ratioed current source.

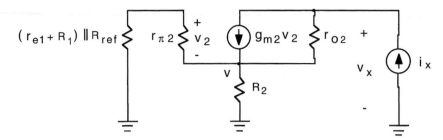

Figure 2-15   Circuit for calculation of output resistance.

The reference current is determined from

$$I_{ref} = \frac{V_{CC} - V_{BE1}}{R_{ref} + R_1}$$

(2-29)

If the voltage drop across R_1 is made large—say, on the order of V_{BE}—then the second term inside the square brackets of Eq. (2-28) is negligibly small relative to the first term and the currents become related by the ratio of the two resistor values:

$$I_2 \approx \frac{R_1}{R_2} I_{ref}$$

(2-30)

which, to first order, is independent of temperature. Also, if Q_1 and Q_2 are scaled such that $A_2/A_1 = I_2/I_{ref}$, then the logarithmic term is zero and Eq. (2-30) results.

The resistor R_2 in the emitter of Q_2 provides negative feedback and thereby raises the output resistance of the current source. The small-signal equivalent circuit for calculating the output resistance is shown in Fig. 2-15. Summing the currents at the emitter node of Q_2 gives

$$i_x = \frac{v}{R_2} + \frac{v}{(r_{e1} + R_1)\|R_{ref} + r_{\pi 2}}$$

(2-31)

where $(r_{e1} + R_1)\|R_{ref}$ denotes the parallel combination of resistances $r_{e1} + R_1$ and R_{ref}. Assuming that the ratio of the two currents I_2 and I_{ref} are within a factor of 10 or so, then r_{e1} is small relative to $r_{\pi 2}$ and can be neglected in Eq. (2-31). This gives

$$v \approx \frac{(R_1\|R_{ref} + r_{\pi 2}) R_2}{R_1\|R_{ref} + R_2 + r_{\pi 2}} i_x$$

(2-32)

and

$$v_2 = -\frac{r_{\pi 2} R_2}{R_1\|R_{ref} + R_2 + r_{\pi 2}} i_x$$

(2-33)

Summing the voltages around the output loop gives

$$v_x = (i_x - g_{m2} v_2) r_{o2} + v \tag{2-34}$$

and using Eqs. (2-32) and (2-33) yields

$$v_x = \left(i_x + \frac{\beta_F R_2}{R_1 \| R_{\text{ref}} + R_2 + r_{\pi2}} i_x \right) r_{o2} + \frac{(R_1 \| R_{\text{ref}} + r_{\pi2}) R_2}{R_1 \| R_{\text{ref}} + R_2 + r_{\pi2}} i_x \tag{2-35}$$

If $\beta_F r_{o2} \gg (R_1 \| R_{\text{ref}} + r_{\pi2})$, then the second term on the right-hand side of Eq. (2-35) is negligibly small, yielding

$$R_o \approx \left(1 + \frac{\beta_F R_2}{R_1 \| R_{\text{ref}} + R_2 + r_{\pi2}} \right) r_{o2} \tag{2-36}$$

EXAMPLE. Find the output current and output resistance of the resistor-ratioed current source of Fig. 2-14 with $V_{CC} = 10\,\text{V}$, $R_1 = 1\,\text{k}\Omega$, $R_2 = 4\,\text{k}\Omega$, and $R_{\text{ref}} = 10\,\text{k}\Omega$. Take for the transistors, $\beta_F = 100$, $V_A = 75\,\text{V}$, $I_{S1} = 5 \times 10^{-16}\,\text{A}$, $I_{S2} = 2.5 \times 10^{-16}\,\text{A}$, and $A_1 = 2A_2$.

Equation (2-28) is transcendental and will be solved iteratively for I_2. I_{ref} is not known until V_{BE1} is determined; V_{BE1} will be assumed initially to be equal to 0.7 V and this value will be used to determine an initial value for I_{ref}, which, in turn, is used in Eq. (2-28) to determine an initial value for I_2; from this value, an updated value for V_{BE1} is determined and the procedure is repeated until a converged solution is obtained. Fortunately, the non linearity in Eq. (2-8) is logarithmic and so two or three iterations are usually sufficient to achieve a converged solution of adequate accuracy. Using Eq. (2-29),

$$I_{\text{ref}} \approx \frac{10\,\text{V} - 0.7\,\text{V}}{10\,\text{k}\Omega + 1\,\text{k}\Omega} = 0.8455\,\text{mA}$$

which, used in Eq. (2-28), gives an initial value for I_2 of 215.7 μA. Using this value in Eq. (2-27), gives

$$V_{BE2} = 0.026 \ln \left(\frac{215.7 \times 10^{-6}}{2.5 \times 10^{-16}} \right) \text{V} = 0.715\,\text{V}$$

which is used in Eq. (2-26) to obtain an updated value for V_{BE1}:

$$V_{BE1} = V_{BE2} + I_2 R_2 - I_{\text{ref}} R_1 = 0.715\,\text{V} + (0.2157\,\text{mA})(4\,\text{k}\Omega) - (0.8455\,\text{mA})(1\,\text{k}\Omega)$$
$$= 0.732\,\text{V}$$

This value is used in Eq. (2-29) to obtain a new value for I_{ref} of 0.8425 mA. A second iteration cycle is sufficient, giving the final values:

$$I_{\text{ref}} = 0.8426\,\text{mA}, \qquad I_2 = 215.0\,\mu\text{A}$$
$$V_{BE1} = 0.732\,\text{V}, \qquad V_{BE2} = 0.714\,\text{V}$$

The ratio of I_2 to I_{ref} is

$$\frac{I_2}{I_{\text{ref}}} = \frac{0.2150\,\text{mA}}{0.8426\,\text{mA}} = 0.2552$$

which is close to the value of 0.25 predicted by Eq. (2-30).
For the output resistance,

$$r_{o2} = \frac{V_{A2}}{I_2} = \frac{75\,\text{V}}{0.215\,\text{mA}} = 348.8\,\text{k}\Omega$$

and

$$r_{\pi 2} = \frac{\beta_F}{g_{m2}} = \frac{100}{0.215\,\text{mA}/0.026\,\text{V}} = 12.1\,\text{k}\Omega$$

which, combined in Eq. (2-36), gives

$$R_o = \left(1 + \frac{(100)\,(4\,\text{k}\Omega)}{(10\,\text{k}\Omega\|(1\,\text{k}\Omega) + 4\,\text{k}\Omega + 12.1\,\text{k}\Omega}\right)(348.8\,\text{k}\Omega) = 8.55\,\text{M}\Omega$$

Widlar Current Source

Figure 2-16 shows a special case of the resistor-ratioed current source in which the resistor in the emitter leg of Q_1 is omitted. This configuration, called the Widlar current source [2], is useful in providing very low output currents, but without a commensurately low reference current, which would require a large (and therefore impractical) reference resistance. Setting R_1 equal to zero in Eq. (2-28) gives for the output current of the Widlar current source;

$$I_2 = \frac{kT}{qR_2}\ln\left(\frac{A_2}{A_1}\frac{I_{\text{ref}}}{I_2}\right) \tag{2-37}$$

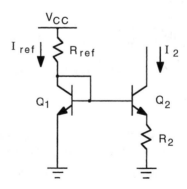

Figure 2-16   Widlar current source.

where

$$I_{\text{ref}} = \frac{V_{\text{CC}} - V_{\text{BE1}}}{R_{\text{ref}}} \tag{2-38}$$

Likewise, setting $R_1 = 0$ in the anaiysis previously carried out for the resistor-ratioed current source gives for the output resistance of the Widlar current source:

$$R_o = \left(1 + \frac{\beta_F R_2}{r_{e1} \| R_{\text{ref}} + R_2 + r_{\pi2}}\right) r_{o2} \approx \left(\frac{1 + g_{m2} R_2}{1 + g_{m2} R_2 / \beta_F}\right) r_{o2} \tag{2-39}$$

where in the second equation we have neglected r_{e1} in comparison with $r_{\pi2}$ and assumed that $\beta_F \gg 1$. Further, if $g_{m2} R_2 \ll \beta_F$, then

$$R_o = (1 + g_{m2} R_2) r_{o2} \tag{2-40}$$

2.2 DC Level-Shift Stages

In integrated circuits, large-value capacitors are impractical, and as a result, successive stages in a circuit are dc coupled. DC level-shift stages are used to provide voltage-level compatibility between the output of one stage and the input of the next stage to which it is connected. There are a variety of techniques available to accomplish the required level shift; some of the more commonly used ones are discussed briefly in this section.

V_{BE} Voltage Shift Stages

The base-emitter voltage of a forward-biased bipolar transistor can provide a convenient, well-controlled voltage-level shift. Figure 2-17 illustrates some commonly used level-shift stages based on the V_{BE} drop. In Fig. 2-17(a), an emitter follower stage provides a single V_{BE}-level shift:

$$V_2 = V_1 - V_{\text{BE1}} \tag{2-41}$$

where

$$V_{\text{BE1}} = \frac{kT}{q} \ln\left(\frac{I_O}{I_{S1}}\right) \tag{2-42}$$

An added benefit of this stage is the relatively high input resistance provided by the emitter follower which reduces the loading at the output of the previous stage to which it connects; most level-shift stages employ an emitter follower (or source follower with MOS transistors) buffer as part of the level-shift circuit.

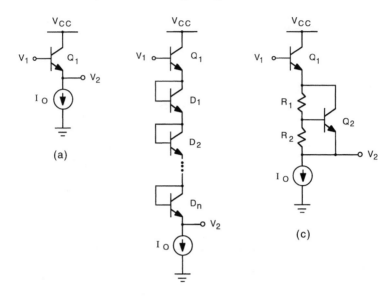

Figure 2-17   DC level-shift stages using the base-emitter voltage drop: (a) single V_{BE} emitter follower; (b) multiple V_{BE} diode string; (c) V_{BE} multiplier.

Multiple diode-connected transistors can be used to provide level shifts larger than V_{BE}. In Fig. 2-17(b),

$$V_2 = V_1 - (n + 1) V_{BE} \qquad (2\text{-}43)$$

where it is assumed that the n diode-connected transistors are idential to the emitter follower transistor Q_1. As each diode requires a separate isolation region in its fabrication, the diode string level-shift circuit can require sizable chip area if several diodes are used. Additionally, a silicon *pn* junction shows a negative voltage–temperature coefficient of about 2 mV per degree Kelvin; the diode string will have an overall temperature coefficient of approximately $2(n + 1)$ mV/°K, which can represent a significant temperature dependence if many diodes are used.

An alternative to multiple series diodes is the V_{BE} multiplier stage, illustrated in Fig. 2-17(c). The current in R_2 is equal to V_{BE2}/R_2 and, neglecting base current, is the same current in R_1, giving

$$V_2 = V_1 - V_{BE1} - V_{BE2}(1 + R_1/R_2) \qquad (2\text{-}44)$$

If the currents in R_1 and R_2 are small relative to I_{C2}, then $V_{BE1} \approx V_{BE2}$, giving

$$V_2 \approx V_1 - (2 + R_1/R_2) V_{BE} \qquad (2\text{-}45)$$

for the level shift.

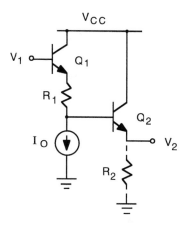

Figure 2-18 Level-shift stage using cascade emitter follower.

Cascade Emitter Follower Level-Shift Stage

Figure 2-18 shows a level-shift stage comprised of two emitter followers connected in cascade. From the circuit, neglecting base currents,

$$V_2 = V_1 - V_{BE1} - I_O R_1 - V_{BE2} \qquad (2\text{-}46)$$

If the output is connected to a high-impedance point, then the emitter current of Q_2 will be low, causing Q_2 to operate in a region where it exhibits low current gain β_F. A resistance (R_2) connected in the emitter leg of Q_2 will raise its emitter current; choosing a value of R_2 to give $I_{E2} = I_O$ produces $V_{BE1} = V_{BE2}$ and, for identical transitors, yields

$$V_2 = V_1 - 2V_{BE} - I_O R_1 \qquad (2\text{-}47)$$

where

$$V_{BE} = \frac{kT}{q} \ln\left(\frac{I_O}{I_S}\right) \qquad (2\text{-}48)$$

Composite npn–pnp Level-Shift Stage

Both *npn* and *pnp* transistors can be combined to form level-shift circuits [3]. Figure 2-19 shows a commonly used stage. With approximately equal base-emitter voltages for Q_1 and Q_2, the voltage at node a is equal to V_1, and the current in R_1 is $(V_{CC} - V_1)/R_1$, which equals $I_{C1} + I_{E2}$; neglecting base currents, $I_{C1} = I_O$ and $I_{E2} = I_2$. The level-shifted voltage V_2 is equal to $I_2 R_2$, which yields

$$V_2 = \frac{R_2}{R_1}(V_{CC} - V_1) - I_O R_2 \qquad (2\text{-}49)$$

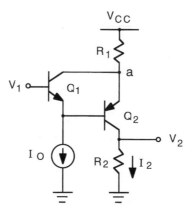

Figure 2-19 Level-shift stage using composite *npn–pnp*.

This level-shift stage has a nonunity voltage gain ($A_V = -R_2/R_1$) unless R_1 and R_2 are made equal. If R_2 is eliminated, the circuit becomes a voltage-controlled current source with

$$I_2 = \frac{V_{CC} - V_1}{R_1} - I_O \tag{2-50}$$

MOS Level-Shift Stages

Figure 2-20 shows two commonly used level-shift stages using NMOS transistors. Transistor M_1 operates as a source follower and M_2 provides the bias current. The level shift is equal to V_{GS1}, and as long as $V_1 \le (V_{DD} + V_{TH})$, M_1 operates in the saturation region. Using Eq. (1-81), neglecting channel-length modulation ($\lambda = 0$), we have for the circuit of Fig. 2-20(a):

$$V_2 = \frac{V_1}{1 + \sqrt{\dfrac{(W/L)_2}{(W/L)_1}}} - V_{TH}\left(\frac{1 - \sqrt{\dfrac{(W/L)_2}{(W/L)_1}}}{1 + \sqrt{\dfrac{(W/L)_2}{(W/L)_1}}}\right) \tag{2-51}$$

For $(W/L)_2 \ll (W/L)_1$, the radical terms in Eq. (2-51) are negligible and the level shift is approximately

$$V_2 = V_1 - V_{TH} \tag{2-52}$$

For the special case in which $(W/L)_1 = (W/L)_2$, the circuit functions as a voltage divider with

$$V_2 = \frac{1}{2}V_1 \tag{2-53}$$

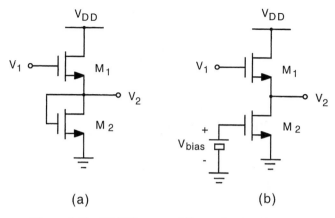

Figure 2-20   NMOS source follower level-shift stages.

In the circuit of Fig. 2-20(b), M_2 is in saturation provided

$$V_{bias} \leq \frac{V_1}{1 + \sqrt{\dfrac{(W/L)_2}{(W/L)_1}}} + \frac{\sqrt{\dfrac{(W/L)_2}{(W/L)_1}}}{1 + \sqrt{\dfrac{(W/L)_2}{(W/L)_1}}} V_{TH} \qquad (2\text{-}54)$$

and the level shift is

$$V_2 = V_1 - \left(1 - \sqrt{\frac{(W/L)_2}{(W/L)_1}}\right) V_{TH} - \sqrt{\frac{(W/L)_2}{(W/L)_1}} V_{bias} \qquad (2\text{-}55)$$

For $(W/L)_1 = (W/L)_2$,

$$V_2 = V_1 - V_{bias} \qquad (2\text{-}56)$$

2.3 Single-Transistor Gain Stages

Single transistors, combined with either resistive or active loads, produce the simplest circuits which can provide useful amplification in analog circuits. Although more complex circuits can provide improved characteristics, these basic single-transistor gain stages are utilized in certain portions of many analog integrated circuits. The three singie-transistor configurations utilizing bipolar and fieid-effect transistors are briefiy discussed in this section, each of which has a particular set of input resistance, output resistance, and gain characteristics.

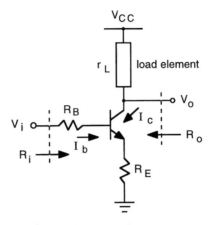

Figure 2-21   Common-emitter gain stage with resistances added in the base and emitter legs. R_i and R_o represent the small-signal equivalent input and output resistances, respectively. r_L is the smal-signal equivalent resistance of the load element.

Common-Emitter Gain Stages

A common-emitter (CE) stage, illustrated in Fig. 2-21, provides voltage gain and exhibits both high input and output resistances. In this configuration, the input is applied to the base and the output is taken at the collector. The resistance R_E added in the emitter leg produces emitter degeneration [4]. In actuality, this resistance causes negative feedback for the common-emitter transistor; the input voltage to the transistor (V_{be}) is reduced from the input signal (V_i) by the voltage drop across R_E, which is proportional to the output current (I_C). As a result, both the input resistance and output resistance of the stage are increased by the feedback; correspondingly, the voltage gain is reduced. The resistance R_B added in the base leg represents the output resistance of the signal source (V_i) driving the stage.

For the transistor operating in the forward-active region, we have for the collector current

$$I_c = I_S e^{qV_{be}/kT}\left(1 + \frac{V_{ce}}{V_A}\right) \tag{2-57}$$

or, in terms of base current,

$$I_c = \beta_F I_b\left(1 + \frac{V_{ce}}{V_A}\right) \tag{2-58}$$

where

$$I_b = \frac{V_i - V_{be}}{R_B + (\beta_F + 1)R_E} \tag{2-59}$$

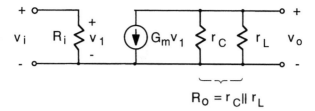

$$R_o = r_c \| r_L$$

Figure 2-22 Small-signal two-port equivalent circuit of the common-emitter gain stage.

and

$$V_{be} = \frac{kT}{q} \ln \left(\frac{I_c}{I_S} \right) = \frac{kT}{q} \ln \left(\frac{\beta_F I_b}{I_S} \right) \tag{2-60}$$

Substituting Eq. (2-59) into Eq. (2-58) yields

$$I_c = \frac{\beta_F (V_i - V_{be})}{R_B + (\beta_F + 1) R_E} \left(1 + \frac{V_{ce}}{V_A} \right) \tag{2-61}$$

The two-port equivalent circuit shown in Fig. 2-22 may be used to represent the small-signal behavior of the common-emitter stage. The small-signal input resistance R_i can be obtained directly from Eq. (2-59):

$$R_i = \frac{dV_i}{dI_b} = \frac{dV_{be}}{dI_b} + R_B + (\beta_F + 1) R_E \tag{2-62}$$

Using $I_c = \beta_F I_b$, noting that $dV_{be}/dI_c = 1/g_m$ and that $\beta_F = g_m r_\pi$, we obtain

$$R_i = R_B + r_\pi + (\beta_F + 1) R_E \tag{2-63}$$

which, for $\beta_F \gg 1$, can be written as

$$R_i \approx R_B + r_\pi (1 + g_m R_E) \tag{2-64}$$

The small-signal equivalent transconductance can be obtained from Eq. (2-61); assuming that $V_A \gg V_{ce}$,

$$\frac{1}{G_m} = \frac{dV_i}{dI_c} = \frac{dV_{be}}{dI_c} + \frac{R_B + (\beta_F + 1) R_E}{\beta_F} \tag{2-65}$$

which evaluates to

$$G_m = \frac{g_m}{1 + \dfrac{R_B}{r_\pi} + \dfrac{(\beta_F + 1) R_E}{r_\pi}} \tag{2-66}$$

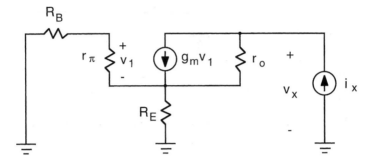

Figure 2-23   Small-signal equivalent circuit of CE stage for calculation of output resistance.

which, for $\beta_F \gg 1$, can be expressed as

$$G_m \approx \frac{g_m}{1 + \dfrac{R_B}{r_\pi} + g_m R_E} \tag{2-67}$$

The output resistance r_C seen looking into the collector of the CE transistor is evaluated from the small-signal test circuit shown in Fig. 2-23; this circuit is the same as that used to evaluate the output resistance of the resistor-ratioed current source (Fig. 2-15) with $(r_{e1} + R_1) \| R_{ref} = R_B$ and $R_2 = R_E$. From Eq. (2-36)

$$r_C = \left(1 + \frac{\beta_F R_E}{R_B + R_E + r_\pi}\right) r_o \tag{2-68}$$

where r_o is the small-signal output resistance of the transistor, given by V_A/I_C. The total small-signal output resistance is

$$R_o = r_C \| r_L \tag{2-69}$$

Common-Emitter Gain Stage with Resistive Load

A common-emitter gain stage utilizing a fixed resistance as a load element is shown in Fig. 2-24. Here, $V_o = V_{CC} - I_c R_C$ and $V_{ce} = V_o$. Using this, with $R_E = 0$, in Eq. (2-61), the large-signal voltage transfer relation is obtained:

$$V_o = \frac{V_{CC} - \beta_F (V_i - V_{be}) \dfrac{R_C}{R_B}}{1 + \dfrac{\beta_F (V_i - V_{be}) R_C}{V_A R_B}} \tag{2-70}$$

This relationship holds for the transistor operating in the forward-active region. If we take the base-emitter voltage to be a constant $V_{BE(on)}$ for the active region,

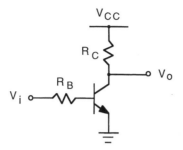

Figure 2-24 Common-emitter gain stage with resistive load.

then for $V_i < V_{BE(on)}$, the transistor is off and the output voltage is at V_{CC}. As V_i increases, V_o (and hence the collector voltage V_c) decreases; when V_{bc} becomes positive, the transistor enters the saturation region, giving $V_o = V_{CE(sat)}$. This occurs at an input voltage

$$V_{i(sat)} = V_{BE(on)} + \frac{V_{CC} - V_{CE(sat)}}{1 + V_{CE(sat)}/V_A} \left(\frac{R_B}{\beta_F R_C} \right) \tag{2-71}$$

Because $V_A \gg V_{CE(sat)}$, Eq. (2-71) simplifies to

$$V_{i(sat)} = V_{BE(on)} + (V_{CC} - V_{CE(sat)}) \frac{R_B}{\beta_F R_C} \tag{2-72}$$

The large-signal voltage transfer characteristic for the CE stage is sketched in Fig. 2-25. The characteristic in the active region is linear for $V_A = \infty$.

The small-signal voltage gain of the resistive-loaded CE stage is calculated from Fig. 2-22:

$$A_v = \frac{v_o}{v_i} = -G_m R_o \tag{2-73}$$

where, with R_E set to zero in Eq. (2-66), the equivalent transconductance is

$$G_m = \frac{g_m}{1 + R_B/r_\pi} \tag{2-74}$$

and from Eq. (2-69),

$$R_o = r_o \| R_C \tag{2-75}$$

which combine to give

$$A_v = -\frac{g_m (r_o \| R_C)}{1 + R_B/r_\pi} \tag{2-76}$$

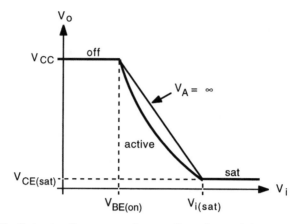

Figure 2-25   Output voltage versus input voltage for resistive-loaded CE stage.

EXAMPLE. Determine the small-signal voltage gain at room temperature of the CE amplifier in Fig. 2-24. In the circuit, $R_B = 1\,k\Omega$, $R_C = 10\,k\Omega$, and the transistor is biased at $I_C = 500\,\mu A$. The transistor parameters are $\beta_F = 100$ and $V_A = 75\,V$.

The transistor transconductance is

$$g_m = \frac{qI_C}{kT} = \frac{0.500\,mA}{0.026\,V} = 19.2\,mA/V$$

The transistor output resistance is

$$r_o = \frac{V_A}{I_C} = \frac{75\,V}{0.500\,mA} = 150\,k\Omega$$

and the transistor input resistance is

$$r_\pi = \frac{\beta_F}{g_m} = \frac{100}{19.2\,mA/V} = 5.21\,k\Omega$$

Using Eq. (2-76), the voltage gain is

$$A_v = -\frac{19.2\,mA/V}{1 + (1\,k\Omega/5.21\,k\Omega)}\frac{(150\,k\Omega)(10\,k\Omega)}{150\,k\Omega + 10\,k\Omega} = -151$$

Common-Emitter Gain Stage with Active Load

From a practical sense, the voltage gain of the resistive-loaded gain stage is limited by the load resistor, R_C in the circuit of Fig. 2-24. Large gains require

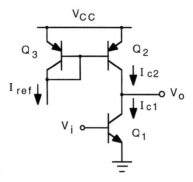

Figure 2-26   Common-emitter gain stage with active load.

large resistance values, which, in turn, require a sizable chip area. The output resistance of a transistor can be utilized as an effective load element, replacing a fixed resistive load. Figure 2-26 shows a common-emitter gain stage with an active load provided by a *pnp* current-source transistor, Q_2; the effective load resistance is r_{o2}, which when combined with the output resistance r_{o1} of the CE transistor Q_1 provides a high overall output resistance for the stage.

For the collector current of transistor Q_1 in Fig. 2-26,

$$I_{c1} = I_{S1}\, e^{qV_i/kT}\left(1 + \frac{V_o}{V_{A1}}\right) \tag{2-77}$$

Assuming that the two *pnp* transistors, Q_2 and Q_3, are identical and noting that $V_{be2} = V_{be3}$, we have

$$\frac{I_{c2}}{1 + \dfrac{V_{ec2}}{V_{A2}}} = \frac{I_{c3}}{1 + \dfrac{V_{ec3}}{V_{A3}}} \tag{2-78}$$

where the *pnp* Early voltages, V_{A2} and V_{A3}, are taken as positive quantities. Now, $V_{ec2} = V_{CC} - V_o$ and $V_{ec3} = V_{eb3}$. Neglecting base current, we have $I_{c3} = I_{ref}$, and assuming that $V_{A3} \gg V_{eb3}$, Eq. (2-78) becomes approximately

$$I_{c2} \approx I_{ref}\left(1 + \frac{V_{CC} - V_o}{V_{A2}}\right) \tag{2-79}$$

Equating I_{c1} and I_{c2}, and solving for the output voltage gives

$$V_o = \frac{V_{CC} + V_{A2}\left(1 - \dfrac{I_{S1}}{I_{ref}}\, e^{qV_i/kT}\right)}{1 + \dfrac{V_{A2}}{V_{A1}}\dfrac{I_{S1}}{I_{ref}}\, e^{qV_i/kT}} \tag{2-80}$$

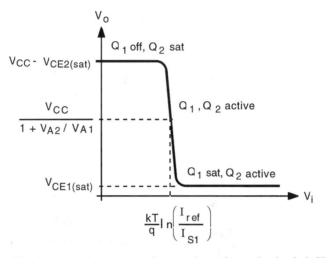

Figure 2-27   Output voltage versus input voltage for active-loaded CE stage.

The voltage transfer characteristic is sketched in Fig. 2-27. At low input voltage (V_i less than about 0.7 V), Q_1 is off and Q_2 is saturated (albeit at very low current), and $V_o = V_{CC} - V_{CE2(sat)}$. At high input voltage, Q_1 is saturated, Q_2 is active, and $V_o = V_{CE1(sat)}$. At $I_{c1} = I_{ref}$, which occurs at an input voltage of

$$V_i = \frac{kT}{q} \ln \left(\frac{I_{ref}}{I_{S1}} \right) \tag{2-81}$$

the output voltage is

$$V_o = \frac{V_{CC}}{1 + V_{A2}/V_{A1}} \tag{2-82}$$

If the *npn* and *pnp* Early voltages are equal, then at this operating point, $V_o = V_{CC}/2$.

The small-signal voltage gain with no load connected to the output can be obtained by differentiating Eq. (2-80):

$$A_v = \frac{dV_o}{dV_i} = -\frac{q}{kT} \frac{V_{A1} V_{A2}}{V_{A1} + V_{A2} (I_{S1}/I_{ref}) e^{qV_i/kT}} \times$$

$$\left[\frac{I_{S1}}{I_{ref}} e^{qV_i/kT} + \frac{V_{CC} + V_{A2} 1 - (I_{S1}/I_{ref}) e^{qV_i/kT})}{V_{A1} + V_{A2}(I_{S1}/I_{ref} e^{qV_i/kT}} \right] \tag{2-83}$$

At $I_{S1} \exp{(qV_i/kT)} = I_{\mathrm{ref}}$, Eq. (2-83) simplifies to

$$A_v = -\frac{q}{kT}\frac{V_{A1}\,V_{A2}}{V_{A1} + V_{A2}}\left(1 + \frac{V_{CC}}{V_{A1} + V_{A2}}\right) \qquad (2\text{-}84)$$

The second term inside the brackets of Eq. (2-84) is normally $\ll 1$; this gives

$$A_v \approx -\frac{q}{kT}\left(\frac{V_{A1}\,V_{A2}}{V_{A1} + V_{A2}}\right) \qquad (2\text{-}85)$$

Using the relatonship $V_A = I_C\,r_o$, Eq. (2-85) can be recast as

$$A_v = -g_m(r_{o1}\|r_{o2}) \qquad (2\text{-}86)$$

which is identical to the voltage gain obtained from a small-signal analysis of the circuit in Fig. 2-26.

As an example of the potentially large voltage gain obtainable with the active-loaded gain stage, consider the CE stage with $V_{A1} = V_{A2} = 100\,\mathrm{V}$. At room temperature, Eq. (2-85) calculates to

$$A_v = -\frac{1}{0.026\,\mathrm{V}}\left(\frac{(100\,\mathrm{V})\,(100\,\mathrm{V})}{100\,\mathrm{V} + 100\,\mathrm{V}}\right) = -1923$$

Common-Source Gain Stage with Resistive Load

Figure 2-28(a) shows a common-source (CS) gain stage using NMOS transistors. Here, a "diode"-connected transistor (M_2) is used as a nonlinear resistive element, which eliminates the additional process steps required to fabricate separate integrated-circuit resistors. The voltage transfer characteristic is sketched in Fig. 2-28(b). For $V_i < V_{\mathrm{TH}}$, transistor M_1 is off, transistor M_2 is in saturation (at negligibly small current), and the output voltage is at $V_{DD} - V_{\mathrm{TH}}$. As V_i is increased above V_{TH}, M_1 turns on, operating intially in the saturation region; M_2 operates always in saturation. Because M_2 presents a relatively low value of effective load resistance to the CS transistor M_1, the effects of channel-length modulation can be neglected; in this region of operation,

$$I_{d1} \approx \frac{\mu_n\,C'_{\mathrm{ox}}}{2}\left(\frac{W}{L}\right)_1 (V_i - V_{\mathrm{TH}})^2 \qquad (2\text{-}87)$$

and

$$I_{d2} \approx \frac{\mu_n\,C'_{\mathrm{ox}}}{2}\left(\frac{W}{L}\right)_2 (V_{DD} - V_o - V_{\mathrm{TH}})^2 \qquad (2\text{-}88)$$

Equating I_{d1} and I_{d2} yields

$$V_o = V_{DD} - V_{\mathrm{TH}} - \sqrt{\frac{(W/L)_1}{(W/L)_2}}\,(V_i - V_{\mathrm{TH}}) \qquad (2\text{-}89)$$

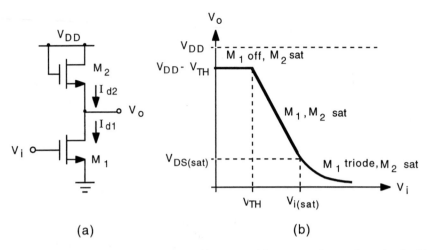

(a)   (b)

Figure 2-28 (a) **Common-source gain stage with saturated transistor load. (b) Output voltage versus input voltage.**

The output voltage is seen to vary linearly with the input voltage; the approximate small-signal voltage gain can be obtained from the slope of this characteristic:

$$A_v = \frac{dV_o}{dV_i} = -\sqrt{\frac{(W/L)_1}{(W/L)_2}} \qquad (2\text{-}90)$$

Thus, for a voltage gain greater than unity, $(W/L)_1$ must be made larger than $(W/L)_2$; usually, M_1 is made with a short channel length (L) and a wide channel width (W), and M_2 is made with a long channel length and a narrow channel width. In practice, constraints on chip area limit gains to about 10.

At larger input voltage, M_2 comes out of saturation and enters the triode region. This occurs at,

$$V_i = V_{i(\text{sat})} = \frac{V_{DD} + \sqrt{\dfrac{(W/L)_1}{(W/L)_2}}\, V_{TH}}{1 + \sqrt{\dfrac{(W/L)_1}{(W/L)_2}}} \qquad (2\text{-}91)$$

and the corresponding output voitage

$$V_o = V_{o(\text{sat})} = \frac{V_{DD} - V_{TH}}{1 + \sqrt{\dfrac{(W/L)_1}{(W/L)_2}}} \qquad (2\text{-}92)$$

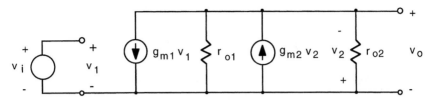

Figure 2-29   Small-signal equivalent circuit of the common-source gain stage.

The small-signal equivalent of the common-source gain NMOS gain stage is shown in Fig. 2-29. Summing the currents at the output node gives

$$g_{m1} v_i + g_{m2} v_o + \frac{v_o}{r_{o1}} + \frac{v_o}{r_{o2}} = 0 \tag{2-93}$$

which evaluates to

$$A_v = \frac{v_o}{v_i} = -\frac{g_{m1}}{g_{m2} + 1/r_{o1} + 1/r_{o2}} \tag{2-94}$$

Normally, $g_m \gg 1/r_o$, in which case Eq. (2-94) reduces to

$$A_v \approx -\frac{g_{m1}}{g_{m2}} \tag{2-95}$$

which, using Eq. (1-96), can be easily shown to be identical to Eq. (2-90).
The small-signal output resistance of this gain stage is

$$R_o = \frac{1}{g_{m2} + 1/r_{o1} + \dfrac{1}{r_{o2}}} \approx \frac{1}{g_{m2}} \tag{2-96}$$

EXAMPLE. Determine the small-signal voltage gain and output resistance of the CS amplifier in Fig. 2-28. In the circuit, $V_{DD} = 10$ V and the transistors are biased at $V_o = 5$ V. The NMOS parameters are $\mu_n C_{ox}' = 20\ \mu\text{A}/\text{V}^2$, $V_{TH} = 1$ V, $(W/L)_1 = 60$, and $(W/L)_2 = 1$. The transistor output resistances may be neglected.

Using Eq. (2-90), the small-signal voltage gain is

$$A_v = -\sqrt{\frac{60}{1}} = -7.75$$

From Eq. (1-96), the transconductance of M_2 is

$$g_{m2} = \mu_n C_{ox}' \left(\frac{W}{L}\right)_2 (V_{DD} - V_O - V_{TH}) = (20\ \mu\text{A}/\text{V}^2)(1)(10 - 5 - 1)\,\text{V} = 80\ \mu\text{A}/\text{V}$$

The output resistance from Eq. (2-96) is

$$R_o = \frac{1}{80 \times 10^{-6}\,\text{A/V}} = 12.5\,\text{k}\Omega$$

Common-Source Gain Stage with Active Load

The MOS equivalent of the active-loaded common-emitter gain stage depicted in Fig. 2-26 is shown in Fig. 2-30(a), in which the PMOS current source transistor M_2 provides the active load for the NMOS common-source transistor M_1. Here, as with the bipolar counterpart, the high output resistance of the load and gain transistors—when they are operating in the saturation region—combine to give the stage large gain. The voltage transfer characteristic of the active-loaded common-source stage is sketched in Fig. 2-30(b). For V_i less than V_{TN}, the threshold voltage of the NMOS transistor, M_1 is off and M_2 is operating in the triode region (at essentially zero current and zero voltage drop V_{ds}); the output voltage in this region is at V_{DD}. As V_i is increased beyond V_{TN}, M_1 begins to conduct and the output falls; in this region, M_1 operates in saturation and M_2 remains in the triode region. When the output reaches $V_{DD} - V_{SG3} - V_{TP}$, where V_{TP} is the threshold voltage of the PMOS transistors, M_2 enters the saturation region [identified as point 1 in Fig. 2-30(b)]. In this region of maximum gain, the drain current of M_1 is given as

$$I_{d1} = \frac{\mu_n C'_{ox}}{2}\left(\frac{W}{L}\right)_1 (V_i - V_{TN})^2 (1 + \lambda_1 V_o) \tag{2-97}$$

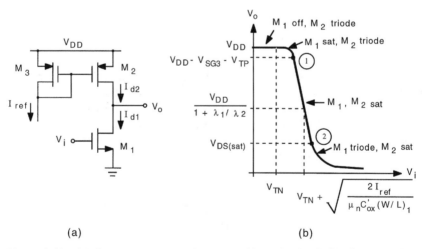

(a)   (b)

Figure 2-30 **(a) Common-source gain stage with active load. (b) Output voltage versus input voltage.**

The PMOS current mirror currents are related as

$$\frac{I_{d2}}{1 + \lambda_2 V_{sd2}} = \frac{I_{d3}}{1 + \lambda_3 V_{sd3}} \tag{2-98}$$

Now, $I_{d3} = I_{ref}$, $V_{sd2} = V_{DD} - V_o$, and $V_{sd3} = V_{sg3} \ll 1/\lambda_3$, which used in Eq. (2-98) gives

$$I_{d2} \approx I_{ref} [1 + \lambda_2 (V_{DD} - V_o)] \tag{2-99}$$

Equating I_{d1} and I_{d2}, and solving for the output voltage results in

$$V_o = \frac{V_{DD} + \dfrac{1}{\lambda_2}\left[1 - \dfrac{\mu_n C'_{ox}}{2I_{ref}}\left(\dfrac{W}{L}\right)_1 (V_i - V_{TN})^2\right]}{1 + \dfrac{\lambda_1}{\lambda_2}\dfrac{\mu_n C'_{ox}}{2I_{ref}}\left(\dfrac{W}{L}\right)_1 (V_i - V_{TN})^2} \tag{2-100}$$

At

$$\frac{\mu_n C'_{ox}}{2}\left(\frac{W}{L}\right)_1 (V_i - V_{TN})^2 = I_{ref} \tag{2-101}$$

the output voltage is

$$V_o = \frac{V_{DD}}{1 + \lambda_1/\lambda_2} \tag{2-102}$$

which occurs at an input voltage

$$V_i = V_{TN} + \sqrt{\frac{2I_{ref}}{\mu_n C'_{ox} (W/L)_1}} \tag{2-103}$$

As V_i is increased further, M_1 comes out of saturation and enters the triode region [labeled point 2 in Fig. 2-30(b)]. The normal range of operation on this gain stage is between points 1 and 2 where both the gain and load transistors are operating in saturation

The small-signal voltage gain with no load attached to the output can be obtained by differentiating Eq. (2-100):

$$A_v = \frac{dV_o}{dV_i} = -\frac{(\mu_n C'_{ox}/I_{ref})(W/L)_1 (V_i - V_{TN})}{\lambda_2 + \lambda_1 (\mu_n C'_{ox}/2I_{ref})(W/L)_1 (V_i - V_{TN})^2} \times$$

$$\left\{1 + \frac{\lambda_1 \lambda_2 V_{DD} + \lambda_1 [1 - (\mu_n C'_{ox}/2I_{ref})(W/L)_1 (V_i - V_{TN})^2]}{\lambda_2 + \lambda_1 (\mu_n C'_{ox}/2I_{ref})(W/L)_1 (V_i - V_{TN})^2}\right\} \tag{2-104}$$

At

$$\frac{\mu_n C'_{ox}}{2} (W/L)_1 (V_i - V_{TN})^2 = I_{ref}$$

which is at an operating point where $I_{d1} \approx I_{ref}$, Eq. (2-104) simplifies to

$$A_v = - \frac{(\mu_n C'_{ox}/I_{ref})(W/L)_1 (V_i - V_{TN})}{\lambda_1 + \lambda_2} \left[1 + \frac{\lambda_1 \lambda_2 V_{DD}}{\lambda_1 + \lambda_2}\right] \qquad (2\text{-}105)$$

The second term inside the square brackets of Eq. (2-105) is normally $\ll 1$ and can be neglected. This gives

$$A_v \approx - \frac{\mu_n C'_{ox} (W/L)_1 (V_i - V_{TN})}{I_{ref}(\lambda_1 + \lambda_2)} \qquad (2\text{-}106)$$

The numerator on the right-hand side of Eq. (2-106) is equal to the transconductance g_{m1} of transistor M_1. Using Eq. (1-98) to relate the output resistance of transistors M_1 and M_2 to the operating current I_{ref} and their respective channel-length modulation parameters λ, Eq. (2-106) can be expressed as

$$A_v = - g_{m1} \left(\frac{1}{r_{o1}} + \frac{1}{r_{o2}}\right)^{-1} = - g_{m1} (r_{o1} \| r_{o2}) \qquad (2\text{-}107)$$

which is identical to the result obtained from a small-signal analysis of the circuit in Fig. 2-30(a). The corresponding small-signal output resistance is

$$R_o = r_{o1} \| r_{o2} \qquad (2\text{-}108)$$

Common-Collector (Emitter Follower) Gain Stage

A common-collector (CC) stage with a resistive load is illustrated in Fig. 2-31(a). This configuration in which the input is applied to the base and the output is taken at the emitter is also referred to as an *emitter follower*. This stage does not exhibit voltage gain—it does have current gain—but finds application primarily as a buffer circuit owing to its high input resistance and low output resistance. Unlike the common-emitter configuration in which the load resistance is connected only to the output circuit, in the common-collector configuration the load resistance is common to both the input and output circuit. For this reason, both the input and output resistances of the stage depend on the value of the load resistance (and on the value of the input source resistance R_B as well). From Fig. 2-31(a) the output voltage is

$$V_o = V_i - I_b R_B - V_{be} \qquad (2\text{-}109)$$

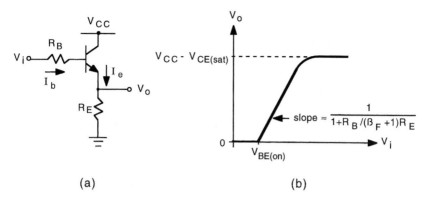

Figure 2-31 **(a) Common-collector (emitter follower) stage. (b) Voltage transfer characteristic.**

where for $V_i \geq 0$, the transistor is operating in the forward-active region, giving

$$I_b = \frac{V_i - V_{be}}{R_B + (\beta_F + 1) R_E} \tag{2-110}$$

with

$$V_{be} = \frac{kT}{q} \ln\left(\frac{I_c}{I_S}\right) = \frac{kT}{q} \ln\left(\frac{V_o}{I_S(1 + 1/\beta_F) R_E}\right) \tag{2-111}$$

Substituting Eqs. (2-110) and (2-111) into Eq. (2-109) yields the transfer characteristic

$$V_o + \frac{kT}{q}\left(\frac{1}{1 + \dfrac{R_B}{(\beta_F + 1) R_E}}\right) \ln\left(\frac{V_o}{I_S(1 + 1/\beta_F) R_E}\right) = \left(\frac{1}{1 + \dfrac{R_B}{(\beta_F + 1) R_E}}\right) V_i \tag{2-112}$$

It should be remarked that for small values of the input V_{be} will be small, resulting in a small collector current and a near zero output voltage. As an approximation, we assume the transistor to essentially be turned off until V_i reaches $V_{BE(on)}$. The voltage transfer characteristic is sketched in Fig. 2-31(b). For small and moderate values of V_o, the logarithmic term in Eq. (2-112) is small and the characteristic is nearly linear with a slope of approximately

$$\frac{dV_o}{dV_i} \approx \frac{1}{1 + \dfrac{R_B}{(\beta_F + 1) R_E}} \tag{2-113}$$

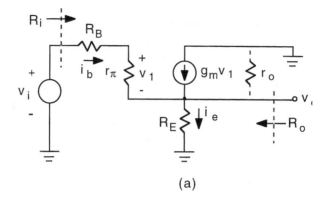

(a)

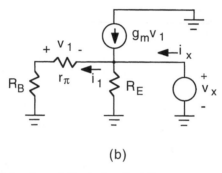

(b)

Figure 2-32 (a) **Small-signal equivalent circuit of the common-collector (emitter follower) configuration.** (b) **Circuit for calculating the small-signal output resistance.**

which approaches unity gain for small values of R_B and/or large values of R_E. The upper limit on the output is reached when the transistor enters the saturation region, giving $V_o(\text{max}) = V_{CC} - V_{CE(\text{sat})}$.

Figure 2-32(a) shows the small-signal equivalent circuit of the common-collector stage from which the input resistance and voltage gain are calculated. The transistor output resistance r_o is in parallel with R_E and as, normally, $r_o \gg R_E$, it is neglected. From the circuit

$$v_i = i_b(R_B + r_\pi) + v_o \qquad (2\text{-}114)$$

where

$$v_o = i_e R_E = (i_b + g_m v_1) R_E \qquad (2\text{-}115)$$

and

$$v_1 = i_b r_\pi \qquad (2\text{-}116)$$

which combine to give

$$v_i = i_b (R_B + r_\pi) + i_b (R_E + g_m r_\pi R_E) \tag{2-117}$$

The small-signal output resistance, noting that $g_m r_\pi = \beta_F$, is

$$R_i = \frac{v_i}{i_b} = R_B + r_\pi + (\beta_F + 1) R_E \tag{2-118}$$

For $\beta_F \gg 1$, this is approximately

$$R_i \approx R_B + r_\pi (1 + g_m R_E) \tag{2-119}$$

From Eq. (2-115) the output voltage can be written as

$$v_o = (\beta_F + 1) i_b R_E \tag{2-120}$$

which, when combined with Eq. (2-118), gives the small-signal voltage gain

$$A_v = \frac{v_o}{v_i} = \frac{1}{1 + \dfrac{R_B + r_\pi}{(\beta_F + 1) R_E}} \tag{2-121}$$

The voltage gain is less than unity; however, if $(\beta_F + 1) R_E \gg R_B + r_\pi$, the gain can be close to unity.

The circuit for calculating the small-signal output resistance is shown in Fig. 2-32(b). Here, it is more convenient to use a test voltage v_x and calculate the resulting current response i_x. Summing the currents at the emitter node gives

$$g_m v_1 + i_x = \frac{v_x}{R_E} + i_1 \tag{2-122}$$

where

$$i_1 = \frac{v_x}{R_B + r_\pi} \tag{2-123}$$

and

$$v_1 = -i_1 r_\pi \tag{2-124}$$

Combining Eqs. (2-123) and (2-124) into Eq. (2-122) gives the output resistance

$$R_o = \frac{v_x}{i_x} = R_E \left\| \left(\frac{R_B + r_\pi}{\beta_F + 1} \right) \right. \tag{2-125}$$

The two-port equivalent circuit shown in Fig. 2-33 can be used to represent the small-signal behavior of the common-collector (emitter follower) stage, where R_i, A_v, and R_o are given by Eqs. (2-118), (2-121), and (2-125), respect-

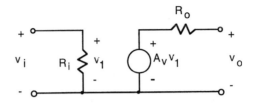

Figure 2-33 Small-signal two-port equivalent circuit of the common-collector (emitter follower) stage.

ively. Because the voltage gain of the emitter follower is usually close to unity, the dependent voltage-source form of the two-port equivalent circuit is more appropriate than the equivalent G_m form, shown in Fig. 2-22.

EXAMPLE. Determine the input resistance, output resistance, and voltage gain of the emitter follower stage in Fig. 2-31. In the circuit, $R_B = 1\,\text{k}\Omega$, $R_E = 2\,\text{k}\Omega$, and the transistor is biased such that $V_O = 1\,\text{V}$. Assume room temperature and take $\beta_F = 100$.

The dc collector bias current is

$$I_C = \left(\frac{\beta_F}{\beta_F + 1}\right)\left(\frac{V_O}{R_E}\right) = \left(\frac{100}{101}\right)\left(\frac{1\,\text{V}}{2\,\text{k}\Omega}\right) = 0.495\,\text{mA}$$

$$r_\pi = \frac{kT}{qI_C}\beta_F = \left(\frac{0.026\,\text{V}}{0.495\,\text{mA}}\right)(100) = 5.25\,\text{k}\Omega$$

The input resistance is from Eq. (2-118):

$$R_i = 1\,\text{k}\Omega + 5.25\,\text{k}\Omega + (101)(2\,\text{k}\Omega) = 208\,\text{k}\Omega$$

The output resistance is from Eq. (2-125):

$$R_o = (2\,\text{k}\Omega)\left\|\left(\frac{1\,\text{k}\Omega + 5.25\,\text{k}\Omega}{101}\right) = 60.0\,\Omega\right.$$

The voltage gain is from Eq. (2-121):

$$A_v = \frac{1}{1 + \dfrac{1\,\text{k}\Omega + 5.25\,\text{k}\Omega}{(101)(2\,\text{k}\Omega)}} = 0.970$$

EXERCISE. For the previous example, determine the input bias voltage required to give a dc operating point of $V_O = 1\,\text{V}$. Take for the transistor $I_S = 2 \times 10^{-16}\,\text{A}$. (*Ans.* 1.75 V)

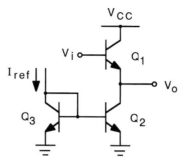

Figure 2-34   Emitter follower stage with active load.

Emitter Follower Stage with Active Load

The linear range of the common-collector (emitter follower) stage can be extended by using an active load in place of a resistive load. In Fig. 2-34, Q_2 and Q_3 comprise a current source which sets the emitter bias current of the emitter follower transistor Q_1. This fixes the base-emitter voltage of Q_1 to a constant value and

$$V_o = V_i - V_{be1} \qquad (2\text{-}126)$$

where

$$V_{be1} = \frac{kT}{q} \ln\left(\frac{I_{c1}}{I_{S1}}\right) \approx \frac{kT}{q} \ln\left(\frac{I_{e1}}{I_{S1}}\right) \qquad (2\text{-}127)$$

Using $I_{e1} = I_{c2}$ and taking $I_{c2} \approx I_{ref}$, the transfer characteristic becomes

$$V_o \approx V_i - \frac{kT}{q} \ln\left(\frac{I_{ref}}{I_{S1}}\right) \qquad (2\text{-}128)$$

The linear range extends over the region in which both Q_1 and Q_2 are operating in the forward-active region; this range is $V_{CE(sat)} < V_o < V_{CC} - V_{CE(sat)}$.

Common-Drain (Source Follower) Gain Stage

Like its bipolar counterpart, the common-drain (source follower) configuration finds primary application as a buffer circuit. Figure 2-35(a) shows a source follower stage with a resistive load. The output voltage is given by

$$V_o = I_d R_S \qquad (2\text{-}129)$$

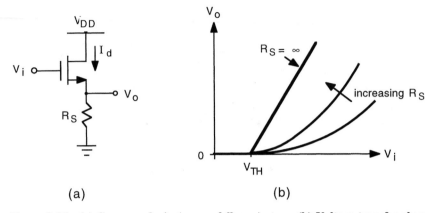

(a)   (b)

Figure 2-35   (a) Common-drain (source follower) stage. (b) Voltage transfer characteristic.

where, for $V_{TH} < V_i \leq V_{DD} + V_{TH}$, the transistor is operating in saturation with a drain current (neglecting λ) given by

$$I_d = \frac{\mu_n C_{ox}'}{2}\left(\frac{W}{L}\right)(V_i - V_o - V_{TH})^2 \tag{2-130}$$

Substituting Eq. (2-129) into Eq. (2-130) and solving the resulting quadratic equation for the output voltage yields

$$V_o = V_i - V_{TH} + \frac{1}{\mu_n C_{ox}'\left(\dfrac{W}{L}\right)R_S}\left[1 - \sqrt{1 + 2\mu_n C_{ox}'\left(\frac{W}{L}\right)R_S(V_i - V_{TH})}\,\right]$$

$$\tag{2-131}$$

This characteristic is sketched in Fig. 2-35(b). For very large values of R_S, the characteristic is nearly linear with a slope of unity.

A small-signal analysis of the source follower circuit [Fig. 2-35(a)] yields a voltage gain of

$$A_v = \frac{v_o}{v_i} = \frac{1}{1 + \dfrac{1}{g_m R_S}} \tag{2-132}$$

an input resistance

$$R_i = \infty \tag{2-133}$$

and an output resistance

$$R_o = \frac{1}{g_m}\bigg\| R_S \tag{2-134}$$

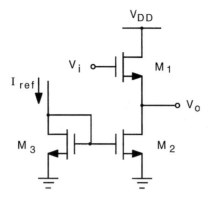

Figure 2-36 Source follower with active load.

Source Follower Stage with Active Load

The linearity of the common-drain (source follower) stage may be improved by current-source biasing. Figure 2-36 shows a source follower circuit with an active load. The current source, consisting of M_2 and M_3, sets the bias current in M_1 and hence its gate-source voltage. For the circuit,

$$V_o = V_i - V_{gs1} \qquad (2\text{-}135)$$

where, noting that $I_{d1} = I_{d2} = I_{ref}$,

$$V_{gs1} = V_{TH} + \sqrt{\frac{2I_{ref}}{\mu_n C'_{ox} (W/L)_1}} \qquad (2\text{-}136)$$

Common-Base Gain Stages

A common-base (CB) stage, illustrated in Fig. 2-37, provides voltage gain and exhibits a low input resistance and a high output resistance. In this configuration, the input is applied to the emitter and the output is taken at the collector. The resistance R_E represents the output resistance of the driving source and the resistance R_B added in the base leg produces base degeneration (in the same fashion as the emitter degeneration resistance in the common-emitter stage). Unlike the CE stage, however, in which the driving source supplies an input base current, the input current to the CB stage is a much higher emitter current. For this reason, the common-base configuration is not as widely employed as the common-emitter configuration; it does have a couple of features which make it attractive in certain applications: (1) The base-collector capacitance ($C\mu$) in a CE configuration provides negative feedback from the output to the

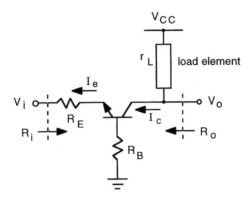

Figure 2-37   Common-base gain stage with resistances added in the emitter and base legs. R_i **and** R_o **represent the small-signal input and output resistances, respectively.** r_L **is the small-signal equivalent resistance of the load element.**

input; the feedback is enhanced by the gain of the stage (the Miller effect [5]), resulting in a much degraded frequency response. In the CB configuration, this capacitance appears at the output only, resulting in a much higher frequency response. (2) The reverse-bias breakdown voltage between collector and base is considerably higher than that between collector and emitter [6]; with the same transistor, the CB configuration can provide higher output voltages, which may be required in some high-voltage applications.

For the transistor operating in the forward-active region (which requires V_i to be negative), we have for the collector current in terms of the input emitter current

$$I_c = \frac{I_e(1 + V_{ce}/V_A)}{\dfrac{1}{\alpha_F} + \dfrac{V_{ce}}{V_A}} \qquad (2\text{-}137)$$

where

$$I_e = -\frac{V_i + V_{be}}{R_E + R_B/(\beta_F + 1)} \qquad (2\text{-}138)$$

and

$$V_{be} = \frac{kT}{q} \ln\left(\frac{\alpha_F I_e}{I_S}\right) \qquad (2\text{-}139)$$

Substituting Eq. (2-138) into Eq. (2-137) yields

$$I_c = -\frac{(V_i + V_{be})}{R_E + R_B/(\beta_F + 1)} \frac{1 + V_{ce}/V_A}{1/\alpha_F + V_{ce}/V_A} \qquad (2\text{-}140)$$

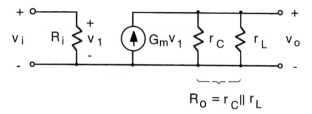

Figure 2-38 **Small-signal two-port equivalent circuit of the common-base gain stage.**

The unilateral two-port equivalent circuit shown in Fig. 2-38 may be used to represent the small-signal behavior of the common-base stage; note the direction of the collector current source relative to that in the CE two-port equivalent circuit of Fig. 2-22. The small-signal input resistance R_i can be obtained directly from Eq. (2-138):

$$R_i = -\frac{dV_i}{dI_e} = R_E + \frac{R_B}{\beta_F + 1} + \frac{dV_{be}}{dI_e} \qquad (2\text{-}141)$$

Using $I_c = \alpha_F I_e$, noting that $\alpha_F/g_m = r_e$, results in

$$R_i = R_E + r_e + \frac{R_B}{\beta_F + 1} \qquad (2\text{-}142)$$

The small-signal equivalent transconductance can be obtained from Eq. (2-140); assuming that $V_A \gg V_{ce}$,

$$\frac{1}{G_m} = -\frac{dV_i}{dI_c} = \frac{R_E + R_B/(\beta_F + 1)}{\alpha_F} + \frac{dV_{be}}{dI_c} \qquad (2\text{-}143)$$

which evaluates to

$$G_m = \frac{g_m}{1 + R_E/r_e + R_B/(\beta_F + 1)\,r_e} \qquad (2\text{-}144)$$

The output resistance r_C seen looking into the collector of the CB transistor is evaluated from the small-signal test circuit shown in Fig. 2-39; the common-base equivalent circuit (Fig. 1-12) is used to model the transistor with the collector current source being expressed in terms of the current i_1 in r_e. The voltage v_x is equal to the voltage drop across r_o plus the voltage drop across R_E:

$$v_x = (i_x - \alpha_F i_i)\,r_o + [i_x + (1 - \alpha_F)\,i_1]\,R_E = i_x(r_o + R_E) + i_1[(1 - \alpha_F)R_E - \alpha_F r_o]$$

$$\approx (i_x - \alpha_F i_1)\,r_o \qquad (2\text{-}145)$$

for $r_o \gg R_E$.

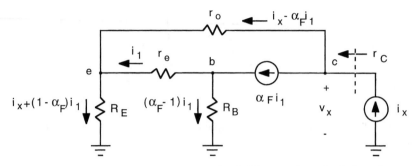

Figure 2-39 **Small-signal equivalent circuit of CB stage for calculation of output resistance.**

The current i_1 is

$$i_1 = \frac{v_b - v_e}{r_e} = \frac{(\alpha_F - 1) i_1 R_B - [i_x + (1 + \alpha_F) i_1] R_E}{r_e} \qquad (2\text{-}146)$$

which, substituted into Eq. (2-145) gives

$$r_C = \frac{v_x}{i_x} = \left[1 + \frac{\alpha_F R_E}{r_e + (1 - \alpha_F)(R_B + R_E)} \right] r_o \qquad (2\text{-}147)$$

which can be expressed alternately as

$$r_C = \left(1 + \frac{R_E}{1/g_m + (R_B + R_E)/\beta_F} \right) r_o \qquad (2\text{-}148)$$

Note, that for R_E large,

$$r_C \rightarrow (\beta_F + 1) r_o \qquad (2\text{-}149)$$

The total small-signal output resistance is

$$R_o = r_C \| r_L \qquad (2\text{-}150)$$

Common-Base Gain Stage with Resistive Load

A common-base gain stage utilizing a fixed resistive load is shown in Fig. 2-40(a) and the voltage transfer characteristic is sketched in Fig. 2-40(b). For $V_i > - V_{BE(on)}$, the transistor is off and the output is at V_{CC}. As V_i is increased negatively beyond this point the transistor conducts, operating initially in the active region, and the output falls. When V_o becomes negative, the base-collector junction is forward biased and the transistor enters the saturation region; in this region, the output saturates at $- V_{BC(on)}$, where $V_{BC(on)}$ is the

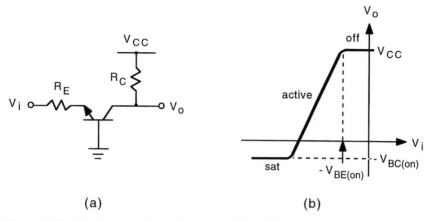

(a)   (b)

Figurz 2-40 **(a) Common-base gain stage with resistive load. (b) Voltage transfer characteristic.**

"turn-on" voltage of the base collector junction (about 0.5 V for a silicon integrated-circuit BJT).

Taking the base-emitter voltage to be a constant $V_{BE(on)}$ for operation in the active region and setting $R_B = 0$, we have from Eq. (2-140)

$$I_c = -\frac{\alpha_F(V_i + V_{BE(on)})}{R_E}\left(1 + \frac{V_{ce}}{V_A}\right) \tag{2-151}$$

where

$$V_{ce} = V_c - V_e = V_o + V_{BE(on)} \tag{2-152}$$

Substituting $I_c = (V_{CC} - V_o)/R_C$ and Eq. (2-152) into Eq. (2-151) and solving for the output voltage gives

$$V_o = \frac{V_{CC} + \alpha_F(V_i + V_{BE(on)})\dfrac{R_C}{R_E}\left(1 + \dfrac{V_{BE(on)}}{V_A}\right)}{1 - \dfrac{\alpha_F(V_i + V_{BE(on)})R_C}{V_A R_E}} \tag{2-153}$$

For negligible Early effect (large V_A), Eq. (2-153) simplifies to

$$V_o \approx V_{CC} + \alpha_F(V_i + V_{BE(on)})\frac{R_C}{R_E} \tag{2-154}$$

The small-signal voltage gain of the CB stage in Fig. 2-39(a) is

$$A_v = \frac{v_o}{v_i} = G_m R_o \tag{2-155}$$

where, setting $R_B = 0$ in Eq. (2-144),

$$G_m = \frac{g_m}{1 + R_E / r_e} = \frac{g_m}{1 + g_m R_E / \alpha_F} \approx \frac{g_m}{1 + g_m R_E} \qquad (2\text{-}156)$$

and

$$R_o = r_C \parallel R_C \qquad (2\text{-}157)$$

where, from Eq. (2-148),

$$r_C = \left(1 + \frac{R_E}{1/g_m + R_E/\beta_F}\right) r_o = \left(1 + \frac{g_m R_E}{1 + g_m R_E/\beta_F}\right) r_o \qquad (2\text{-}158)$$

The small-signal input resistance is, from Eq. (2-142),

$$R_i = R_E + r_e = R_E + \frac{\alpha_F}{g_m} \qquad (2\text{-}159)$$

EXAMPLE. Determine the input resistance, output resistance, and small-signal voltage gain at room temperature of the CB amplifier in Fig. 2-40 (a). In the circuit, $R_E = 100\,\Omega$, $R_C = 10\,\text{k}\Omega$, and the transistor is biased at $I_C = 500\,\mu\text{A}$. The transistor parameters are $\beta_F = 100$ and $V_A = 75\,\text{V}$.

The transistor transconductance $g_m = 19.2\,\text{mA/V}$ and the transistor output resistance $r_o = 150\,\text{k}\Omega$. The small-signal emitter resistance is

$$r_e = \frac{\alpha_F}{g_m} = \frac{\beta_F}{(\beta_F + 1)\,g_m} = \frac{100}{(101)\,(19.2 \times 10^{-3}\,\text{A/V})} = 51.6\,\Omega$$

The input resistance is from Eq. (2-159)

$$R_i = 100\,\Omega + 51.6\,\Omega = 151.6\,\Omega$$

The resistance seen looking into the collector is from Eqn. (2-158)

$$r_C = \left(1 + \frac{(19.2\,\text{mA/V})\,(0.1\,\text{k}\Omega)}{1 + \dfrac{(19.2\,\text{mA/V})\,(0.1\,\text{k}\Omega)}{100}}\right) 150\,\text{k}\Omega = 433\,\text{k}\Omega$$

which is negligible with respect to R_C; so the output resistance is

$$R_o \approx R_C = 10\,\text{k}\Omega$$

The effective transconductance is from Eq. (2-156)

$$G_m = \frac{19.2\,\text{mA/V}}{1 + (19.2\,\text{mA/V})\,(0.1\,\text{k}\Omega)} = 6.58\,\text{mA/V}$$

Using Eq. (2-155), the voltage gain is

$$A_v = (6.58\,\text{mA/V})\,(10\,\text{k}\Omega) = 65.8$$

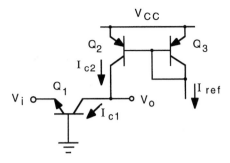

Figure 2-41   Common-base stage with active load.

Common-Base Stage with Active Load

A common-base gain stage utilizing an active load is shown in Fig. 2-41. Like the active-loaded common-emitter stage, this configuration also has a high output resistance, resulting in high gain; the input resistance, however, is low—a factor of $\beta_F + 1$ lower than with an equivalent CE stage. The collector current of Q_1 is

$$I_{c1} = I_{S1} e^{-qV_i/kT}\left(1 + \frac{V_o - V_i}{V_{A1}}\right)$$ (2-160)

The collector current I_{c2} of the current source transistor is given by Eq. (2-79), which, equated with I_{c1} and solved for the output voltage, yields

$$V_o = \frac{V_{CC} + V_{A2}\left[1 + \left(\frac{V_i}{V_{A1}} - 1\right)\frac{I_{S1}}{I_{\text{ref}}}e^{-qV_i/kT}\right]}{1 + \frac{V_{A2}}{V_{A1}}\frac{I_{S1}}{I_{\text{ref}}}e^{-qV_i/kT}}$$ (2-161)

Except for the negative input voltage, this result is similar to that obtained for the active-loaded CE stage [see Eq. (2-80)].

The small-signal voltage gain is

$$A_v = \frac{v_o}{v_i} = g_{m1}(r_{o1}\|r_{o2})$$ (2-162)

The input resistance is

$$R_i = r_{e1}$$ (2-163)

and the output resistance is

$$R_o = r_{o1}\|r_{o2}$$ (2-164)

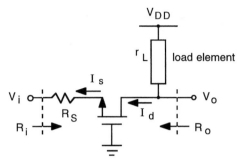

Figure 2-42 Common-gate gain stage. R_i and R_o represent the small-signal input and output resistances, respectively.

Common-Gate Gain Stage

Figure 2-42 shows a common-gate stage fashioned with NMOS, which functions very similarly to the common-base stage. For the transistor operating in the saturation region ($V_i < -V_{TH} - I_S R_S$ and $V_o \geq -V_{TH}$), the drain current is given as

$$I_d = \frac{\mu_n C'_{ox}}{2} \left(\frac{W}{L}\right) (V_{gs} - V_{TH})^2 (1 + \lambda V_{ds}) \qquad (2\text{-}165)$$

where

$$V_{gs} = -V_i - I_S R_S \qquad (2\text{-}166)$$

and

$$V_{ds} = V_o - V_i - I_S R_S \qquad (2\text{-}167)$$

Substituting Eqs. (2-166) and (2-167) into Eq. (2-165) yields

$$I_d = \frac{\mu_n C'_{ox}}{2} \left(\frac{W}{L}\right) (-V_i - V_{TH} - I_d R_S)^2 [1 + \lambda (V_o - V_i - I_d R_S)] \quad (2\text{-}168)$$

The two-port equivalent circuit of Fig. 2-38 also applies for the common-gate stage. The small-signal input resistance R_i can be obtained directly from Eq. (2-166):

$$R_i = -\frac{dV_i}{dI_s} = R_S + \frac{dV_{gs}}{dI_s} = R_S + \frac{dV_{gs}}{dI_d} \qquad (2\text{-}169)$$

Noting that dI_d/dV_{gs} is the transistor transconductance g_m gives

$$R_i = R_S + \frac{1}{g_m} \qquad (2\text{-}170)$$

The small-signal equivalent transconductance G_m can be obtained from Eq. (2-168); assuming that $\lambda V_{ds} \ll 1$,

$$G_m = -\frac{dI_d}{dV_i} = -\mu_n C'_{ox}\left(\frac{W}{L}\right)(-V_i - V_{TH} - I_d R_S)\left(-1 - R_S\frac{dI_d}{dV_i}\right) \quad (2\text{-}171)$$

The first term on the right-hand side of Eq. (2-171) is g_m and the last fraction is R_i^{-1}. This yields

$$G_m = \frac{g_m}{1 + g_m R_S} \quad (2\text{-}172)$$

It is easily shown that the small-signal output resistance R_o is

$$R_o = [(1 + g_m R_S) r_o + R_S] \, \| \, r_L \approx [(1 + g_m R_S) r_o] \, \| \, r_L \quad (2\text{-}173)$$

for $g_m r_o \gg 1$.

2.4 Two-Transistor Gain Stages

Gain stages comprised of two interconnected transistors are widely used in many analog integrated circuits. Like single-transistor stages, each configuration has a unique set of characteristics. Three commonly used two-transistor configurations are discussed in this section: (1) cascode, (2) cascade, and (3) differential pair.

Cascode Configuration

The cascode configuration consists of a common-emitter (common-source) –common-base (common-gate) interconnection, illustrated with bipolar transistors in Fig. 2-43(a). The gain of this stage is provided by the CE transistor Q_1. Q_2, connected in a CB configuration, serves to reduce the feedback from the output to the input that occurs at high frequency through the collector-base capacitance C_μ; there is no Miller effect associated with Q_2 because its base is at ac ground potential, and the Miller effect associated with Q_1 is minimal because the output impedance at its collector is low (r_{e2}). Thus, the cascode stage can have large bandwidth along with high gain.

In Fig. 2-43(a) $I_{c2} = \alpha_{F2} I_{c1}$, and the transconductance for the two-port small-signal equivalent circuit representation in Fig. 2-43(b) is

$$G_m = \alpha_{F2} g_{m1} \approx g_{m1} \quad (2\text{-}174)$$

The input resistance is

$$R_i = r_{\pi 1} \quad (2\text{-}175)$$

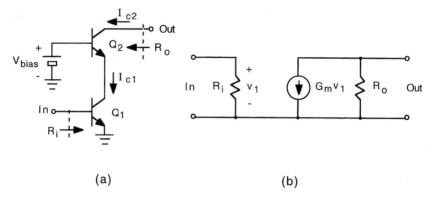

(a)   (b)

Figure 2-43 (a) **Cascode gain stage using BJTs.** (b) **Two-port small-signal equivalent circuit.**

For the output resistance, we recognize that the output resistance of Q_1 (r_{o1}) is in series with the emitter of Q_2; thus, Eq. (2-158) applies with "R_E" = r_{o1}:

$$R_o = \left(1 + \frac{g_{m2}\, r_{o1}}{1 + g_{m2}\, r_{o1}/\beta_{F2}}\right) r_{o2} \qquad (2\text{-}176)$$

Because $g_{m2}\, r_{o1}$ is usually $\gg \beta_{F2}$, Eq. (2-176) reduces to

$$R_o \approx \beta_{F2}\, r_{o2} \qquad (2\text{-}177)$$

The input resistance of the cascode stage can be increased by employing an emitter follower at the input, as illustrated in Fig. 2-44; this configuration is used at the input stage of some wideband amplifiers, such as in the CA 3040. An optional bias source (or resistance) may be used at the emitter of Q_1 to raise its operating current; without it, Q_1 may operate in a region where its current gain β_F is low, reducing its input resistance. From the circuit,

$$V_i = V_{be1} + V_{be2} \qquad (2\text{-}178)$$

and the small-signal input resistance is determined as

$$R_i = \frac{dV_i}{dI_{b1}} = \frac{dV_{be1}}{dI_{b1}} + \frac{dV_{be2}}{dI_{b1}} = \beta_{F1}\frac{dV_{be1}}{dI_{c1}} + \frac{dI_{c2}}{dI_{b1}}\frac{dV_{be2}}{dI_{c2}} \qquad (2\text{-}179)$$

Now,

$$I_{c2} = \beta_{F2}I_{b2} = \beta_{F2}(I_{e1} - I_{bias}) = \beta_{F2}[(\beta_{F1} + 1)I_{b1} - I_{bias}] \qquad (2\text{-}180)$$

so $dI_{c2}/dI_{b1} = \beta_{F2}(\beta_{F1} + 1)$ and

$$R_i = \frac{\beta_{F1}}{g_{m1}} + (\beta_{F1} + 1)\frac{\beta_{F2}}{g_{m2}} = \ddot{r}_{\pi1} + (\beta_{F1} + 1)\, r_{\pi2} \qquad (2\text{-}181)$$

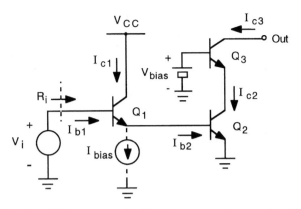

Figure 2-44 Emitter follower cascode. The bias current source for Q_1 is optional.

For $I_{bias} = 0$,

$$I_{c2} = \frac{\beta_{F2}(\beta_{F1} + 1)}{\beta_{F1}} I_{c1} \tag{2-182}$$

which for identical transistors ($\beta_{F1} = \beta_{F2}$) gives $r_{\pi 1} = (\beta_F + 1)r_{\pi 2}$, and Eq. (2-181) becomes

$$R_i = 2r_{\pi 1} \tag{2-183}$$

The effective transconductance of the emitter follower cascode is found from

$$\frac{1}{G_m} = \frac{dV_i}{dI_{c3}} = \frac{dV_{be1}}{dI_{c3}} + \frac{dV_{be2}}{dI_{c3}} = \frac{dV_{be1}}{dI_{c1}}\frac{dI_{c1}}{dI_{c3}} + \frac{dV_{be2}}{dI_{c2}}\frac{dI_{c2}}{dI_{c3}} \tag{2-184}$$

Neglecting base currents, we have $dI_{c2} \approx dI_{c3}$ and $dI_{c1} \approx dI_{b2} = dI_{c2}/\beta_{F2} \approx dI_{c3}/\beta_{F2}$. Noting that $dV_{be}/dI_c = 1/g_m$, Eq. (2-184) becomes

$$G_m = \frac{g_{m1}g_{m2}}{g_{m1} + g_{m2}/\beta_{F2}} \tag{2-185}$$

For $I_{bias} = 0$, $g_{m2} \approx \beta_{F2}g_{m1}$ and

$$G_m \approx \frac{g_{m2}}{2} \tag{2-186}$$

The small-signal output resistance R_o remains the same as given in Eq. (2-177).

The cascode gain stage fashioned with field-effect transistors is illustrated in Fig. 2-45. In the JFET version [Fig. 2-45(b)], the input voltage is negative and V_{bias} is set such that V_{GS2} is negative. Here, $R_i \approx \infty$. Because $I_{d1} = I_{d2}$, the two-port equivalent transconductance [Fig. 2-43(b)] is

$$G_m = g_{m1} \tag{2-187}$$

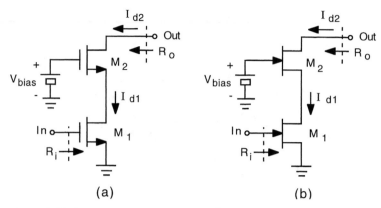

Figure 2-45 Cascode gain stage using FETs: (a) MOSFETS; (b) JFETs.

The output resistance is determined from Eq. (2-173) by setting $"R_S" = r_{o1}$ and $r_L = \infty$, giving

$$R_o = (1 + g_{m2}r_{o1})r_{o2} + r_{o1} \approx (1 + g_{m2}r_{o1})r_{o2} \qquad (2\text{-}188)$$

for $g_{m2}r_{o2} \gg 1$.

Cascade Configuration

The cascade configuration consists of an input common-collector (emitter follower) transistor interconnected with either a common-emitter transistor or a second common-collector transistor; in both configurations, the input emitter follower transistor is employed to increase current gain and input resistance. The common-collector–common-emitter (CC–CE) cascade configuration is shown in Fig. 2-46. As with the cascade configuration, an optional bias source (or resistor) may be used to set the operating current of the input transistor. An alternate form of the CC–CE cascade is shown in Fig. 2-46(b); this is the so-called *Darlington* configuration, in which both collectors are tied together. In the Darlington, both transistors can be fabricated within the same isolation region, which results in a smaller chip area than would be required with the normal cascade configuration [Fig. 2-46(a)] in which separate isolation regions would be required for the two transistors. The Darlington configuration, however, has a much poorer frequency response due to the Miller effect of Q_1 whose collector is now connected to the output; the Darlington is thus limited to relatively low-frequency applications.

The small-signal input resistance of the CC–CE cascade is the same as the emitter follower cascade:

$$R_i = r_{\pi1} + (\beta_{F1} + 1)r_{\pi2} \qquad (2\text{-}189)$$

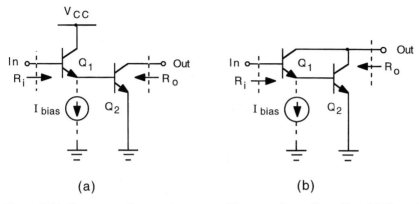

Figure 2-46 Common-collector–common-emitter cascade configuration. (a) Normal connection with output taken at the collector of Q_2. (b) Darlington connection with the collectors of Q_1 and Q_2 tied together.

The small-signal output resistance for the cascade configuration in Fig. 2-46(a) is

$$R_o = r_{o2} \qquad (2\text{-}190)$$

The output resistance of the Darlington configuration in Fig. 2-46(b) is slightly less than this [Eq. (2-190)] due to r_{o1}, which is now connected to the output circuit.

The small-signal equivalent transconductance for the configuration in Fig. 2-46(a) is calculated from

$$\frac{1}{G_m} = \frac{dV_i}{dI_{c2}} \qquad (2\text{-}191)$$

Using Eq. (2-178) and noting that $I_{c2} \approx \beta_{F2} I_{c1}$, we obtain

$$G_m = \frac{g_{m1} g_{m2}}{g_{m1} + g_{m2}/\beta_{F2}} \qquad (2\text{-}192)$$

The transcoductance for the Darlington configuration [Fig. 2-46(b)] is determined from

$$\frac{1}{G_m} = \frac{dV_i}{dI_{\text{out}}} = \frac{dV_i}{d(I_{c1} + I_{c2})} \qquad (2\text{-}193)$$

If $\beta_{F2} \gg 1$, this gives the same result as in Eq. (2-192).

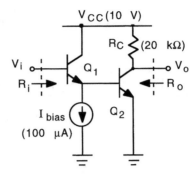

Figure 2-47 CC–CE cascade amplifier example.

EXAMPLE. Determine the small-signal input resistance, output resistance, and the voltage gain of the CC–CE cascade amplifier shown in Fig. 2-47. Transistor Q_2 is biased at $V_O = 5$ V. The transistor parameters are $\beta_F = 100$ and $V_A = 50$ V.

The collector current of Q_2 is

$$I_{C2} = \frac{V_{CC} - V_O}{R_C} = \frac{10\,\text{V} - 5\,\text{V}}{20\,\text{k}\Omega} = 250\,\mu\text{A}$$

Its transconductance is

$$g_{m2} = \frac{qI_{C2}}{kT} = \frac{0.250\,\text{mA}}{0.026\,\text{V}} = 9.62\,\text{mA/V}$$

and

$$r_{\pi 2} = \frac{\beta_{F2}}{g_{m2}} = \frac{100}{9.62\,\text{mA/V}} = 10.4\,\text{k}\Omega$$

The collector current of Q_1 is

$$I_{C1} = \frac{\beta_{F1}}{\beta_{F1} + 1} I_{E1} = \frac{\beta_{F1}}{\beta_{F1} + 1}(I_{\text{bias}} + I_{B1}) = \frac{\beta_{F1}}{\beta_{F1} + 1}\left(I_{\text{bias}} + \frac{I_{C2}}{\beta_{F2}}\right)$$

$$= \frac{100}{101}\left(100\,\mu\text{A} + \frac{250\,\mu\text{A}}{100}\right) = 101\,\mu\text{A}$$

Its transconductance is

$$g_{m1} = \frac{0.101\,\text{mA}}{0.026\,\text{V}} = 3.88\,\text{mA/V}$$

and

$$r_{\pi 1} = \frac{100}{3.88\,\text{mA}/\text{V}} = 25.8\,\text{k}\Omega$$

The input resistance, calculated from Eq. (2-181), is

$$R_i = 25.8\,\text{k}\Omega + (101)(10.4\,\text{k}\Omega) = 1.08\,\text{M}\Omega$$

The output resistance of Q_2 is

$$r_{o2} = \frac{V_{A2}}{I_{C2}} = \frac{50\,\text{V}}{0.250\,\text{mA}} = 200\,\text{k}\Omega$$

and the output resistance is

$$R_o = R_C \| r_{o2} = (20\,\text{k}\Omega) \| (200\,\text{k}\Omega) = 18.2\,\text{k}\Omega$$

Using Eq. (2-185), the transconductance of the amplifier is

$$G_m = \frac{(3.88\,\text{mA}/\text{V})(9.62\,\text{mA}/\text{V})}{3.88\,\text{mA}/\text{V} + (9.62\,\text{mA}/\text{V})/100} = 9.39\,\text{mA}/\text{V}$$

The voltage gain is

$$A_v = -G_m R_o = -(9.39\,\text{mA}/\text{V})(18.2\,\text{k}\Omega) = -171$$

The common-collector–common-collector (CC–CC) cascade configuration is shown in Fig. 2-48. This configuration is used primarily as a buffer stage

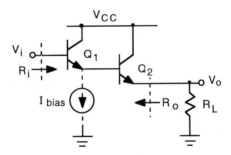

Figure 2-48 Common-collector–common-collector (CC–CC) cascade configuration.

which provides increased input resistance over a single common-collector (emitter follower) stage. The small-signal equivalent circuit of the CC–CC cascade is shown in Fig. 2-49(a): The output resistance of transistor Q_1 is neglected because it is not connected to the output; likewise, the output resistance of Q_2 is neglected because it is connected to a low-resistance point,

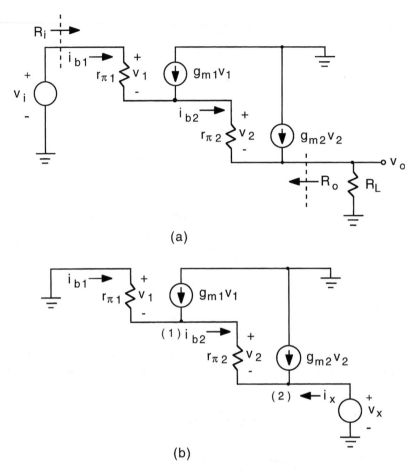

(a)

(b)

Figure 2-49 (a)   **Small-signal equivalent circuit of the CC–CC cascade. (b) Circuit for calculating the small-signal output resistance.**

the emitter of Q_2. With reference to Fig. 2-49(a): the voltage at the emitter of Q_1 is $v_2 + v_o$, so the base current of Q_1 is

$$i_{b1} = \frac{v_i - v_2 - v_o}{r_{\pi 1}} \qquad (2\text{-}194)$$

where

$$v_2 = (g_{m1} v_1 + i_{b1}) r_{\pi 2} \qquad (2\text{-}195)$$

and

$$v_o = \left(g_{m2} v_2 + \frac{v_2}{r_{\pi 2}} \right) R_L = \frac{(\beta_{F2} + 1) R_L}{r_{\pi 2}} v_2 \qquad (2\text{-}196)$$

which combined with $v_1 = i_{b1} r_{\pi 1}$ yields

$$i_{b1} = \frac{v_i}{r_{\pi 1} + (\beta_{F1} + 1) r_{\pi 2} + (\beta_{F1} + 1)(\beta_{F2} + 1) R_L} \qquad (2\text{-}197)$$

which gives the input resistance

$$R_i = \frac{v_i}{i_{b1}} = r_{\pi 1} + (\beta_{F1} + 1)[r_{\pi 2} + (\beta_{F2} + 1) R_L] \qquad (2\text{-}198)$$

For $I_{\text{bias}} = 0$ and identical transistors, the input resistance becomes

$$R_i = 2r_{\pi 1} + (\beta_F + 1)^2 R_L \qquad (2\text{-}199)$$

Substituting $v_1 = i_{b1} r_{\pi 1}$ and Eq. (2-195) into Eq. (2-196) yields

$$v_o = (\beta_{F1} + 1)(\beta_{F2} + 1) i_{b1} R_L \qquad (2\text{-}200)$$

which, using Eq. (2-197), gives the voltage gain

$$A_v = \frac{v_o}{v_i} = \frac{1}{1 + \dfrac{r_{\pi 2}}{(\beta_{F2} + 1) R_L} + \dfrac{r_{\pi 1}}{(\beta_{F1} + 1)(\beta_{F2} + 1) R_L}} \qquad (2\text{-}201)$$

which for identical transistors and $I_{\text{bias}} = 0$ becomes

$$A_v = \frac{1}{1 + \dfrac{2r_{\pi 1}}{(\beta_F + 1)^2 R_L}} \qquad (2\text{-}202)$$

Figure 2-49(b) shows the circuit for calculating the output resistance of the CC–CC cascade. In normal application, the load R_L represents the input resistance of the next stage and so it is not included as part of the output resistance of the CC–CC stage (the total resistance at the output is $R_o \| R_L$). Summing the currents at node (1),

$$g_{m1} v_1 + i_{b1} - i_{b2} = 0 \qquad (2\text{-}203)$$

where

$$v_1 = i_{b1} r_{\pi 1} \qquad (2\text{-}204)$$

$$i_{b1} = -\frac{v_2 + v_x}{r_{\pi 1}} \qquad (2\text{-}205)$$

and

$$i_{b2} = \frac{v_2}{r_{\pi 2}} \tag{2-206}$$

which combine to give

$$v_2 = -\frac{(\beta_{F1} + 1)\, r_{\pi 2}}{r_{\pi 1} + (\beta_{F1} + 1)\, r_{\pi 2}}\, v_x \tag{2-207}$$

Summing the currents at node (2),

$$g_{m2}\, v_2 + i_{b2} + i_x = 0 \tag{2-208}$$

which, using Eqs. (2-206) and (2-207), gives

$$i_x = \frac{(\beta_{F1} + 1)(\beta_{F2} + 1)}{r_{\pi 1} + (\beta_{F1} + 1)\, r_{\pi 2}}\, v_x \tag{2-209}$$

The output resistance is

$$R_o = \frac{v_x}{i_x} = \frac{r_{\pi 2}}{\beta_{F2} + 1} + \frac{r_{\pi 1}}{(\beta_{F1} + 1)(\beta_{F2} + 1)} \tag{2-210}$$

which for $I_{bias} = 0$ and identical transistors becomes

$$R_o = \frac{2 r_{\pi 1}}{(\beta_F + 1)^2} \tag{2-211}$$

The input and output resistances of the CC–CC cascade can also be simply obtained using the results of the single emitter follower, Fig. 2-31(a). Consider the node connecting the emitter of Q_1 and the base of Q_2. Looking into the base of Q_2 at this node, we see a resistance of $r_{\pi 2} + (\beta_{F2} + 1) R_L$. This resistance at the emitter of Q_1 corresponds to the resistance "R_E" in Fig. 2-31(a), giving an input resistance

$$R_i = r_{\pi 1} + (\beta_{F1} + 1)\, "R_E" \tag{2-212}$$

which is identical to Eq. (2-198). Looking back into the emitter of Q_1, we see a resistance of $r_{\pi 1}/(\beta_{F1} + 1)$. This resistance at the base of Q_2 corresponds to the resistance "R_B" in Fig. 2-31(a), giving an output resistance

$$R_o = \frac{"R_B" + r_{\pi 2}}{\beta_{F2} + 1} \tag{2-213}$$

which is identical to Eq. (2-210).

As seen, two-transistor cascades using bipolar transistors provide increased input resistance and current gain over their single-transistor counterparts. Because the input resistance of field-effect transistors is very high (nearly infi-

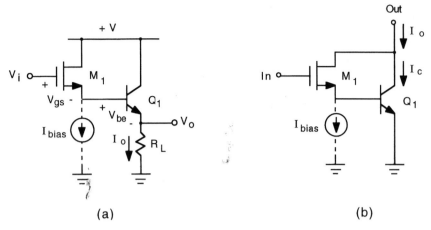

(a) (b)

Figure 2-50 BiCMOS cascades: (a) Common-drain–common-collector configuration; (b) Darlington configuration.

nite), two-transistor cascade configurations are rarely used in all FET circuits. However, in circuits fabricated with both BJTs and MOSFETs (termed Bi-CMOS) or BJTs and JFETs (termed BiFET) several mixed two-transistor cascade configurations find useful application. Figure 2-50 shows two Bi-CMOS cascades: (a) a common-drain–common-collector (CD–CC) configuration; (b) a Darlington configuration. The CD–CC configuration in Fig. 2-50(a) is used as a unity-gain buffer circuit with infinite input resistance. From the circuit,

$$V_i = V_{gs} + V_{be} + V_o = V_{gs} + V_{be} + I_o R_L \qquad (2\text{-}214)$$

The small-signal effective transconductance G_m, calculated from Eq. (2-214) is

$$G_m = \frac{dI_o}{dV_i} = \frac{(\beta_F + 1)\, g_m^{FET}\, g_m^{BJT}}{g_m^{BJT} + \beta_F g_m^{FET} + (\beta_F + 1)\, g_m^{FET}\, g_m^{BJT} R_L} \qquad (2\text{-}215)$$

which, combined with the load resistance, gives the small-signal voltage gain

$$A_v = \frac{v_o}{v_i} = G_m R_L = \left(1 + \frac{1}{(\beta_F + 1)\, g_m^{FET} R_L} + \frac{r_\pi}{(\beta_F + 1)\, R_L}\right)^{-1} \qquad (2\text{-}216)$$

The BiCMOS Darlington configuration in Fig. 2-50(b) can provide a large voltage gain with infinte input resistance. The small-signal effective transcon-

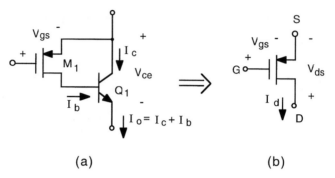

Figure 2-51 **(a) PMOS–*npn* BJT cascade. (b) Composite equivalent.**

ductance is calculated in a fashion similar to that for the all bipolar version [Fig. 2-46 (b)], giving

$$G_m = \frac{dV_i}{dI_o} \approx \frac{dV_i}{dI_c} = \frac{g_m^{FET} g_m^{BJT}}{g_m^{FET} + \frac{g_m^{BJT}}{\beta_F}} \tag{2-217}$$

The small-signal resistance seen looking into the drain of M_1 is $(1 + g_m^{FET} r_\pi) r_o^{FET}$ [see Eq. (2-158) with $\beta_F = \infty$] and the resistance seen looking into the collector of Q_1 is r_o^{BJT}. Thus, the small-signal resistance at the output of the BiCMOS Darlington stage is

$$R_o = (1 + g_m^{FET} r_\pi) r_o^{FET} \parallel r_o^{BJT} \tag{2-218}$$

The PMOS–*npn* BJT cascade shown in Fig. 2-51(a) has interesting characteristics [7, 8]. The base current in Q_1 is set by the drain current in M_1, which is determined by the input applied across the gate and source. The output current is

$$I_o = I_c + I_b \tag{2-219}$$

where for Q_1 operating in the forward-active region

$$I_c = \beta_F I_b \left(1 + \frac{V_{ce}}{V_A}\right) \tag{2-220}$$

and for M_1 operating in saturation

$$I_b = \frac{\mu_p C_{ox}'}{2} \left(\frac{W}{L}\right) (V_{gs} - V_{TH})^2 (1 + \lambda V_{sd}) \tag{2-221}$$

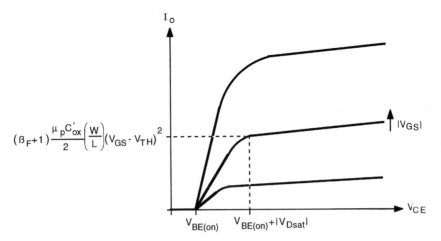

Figure 2-52   Output characteristics of the PMOS–*npn* BJT cascade.

Substituting Eqs. (2-220) and (2-221), with $V_{sd} = V_{ce} - V_{be} \approx V_{ce}$, into Eq. (2-219), and neglecting the cross-product term containing λ/V_A gives approximately

$$I_o \approx (\beta_F + 1)\frac{\mu_p C'_{ox}}{2}\left(\frac{W}{L}\right)(V_{gs} - V_{TH})^2\left(1 + \frac{V_{ce}}{V_{Aeff}}\right) \qquad (2\text{-}222)$$

where

$$V_{Aeff} = \frac{V_A}{1 + \lambda V_A} \qquad (2\text{-}223)$$

The output current thus appears to be that of the PMOS device multiplied by a factor of $\beta_F + 1$. The composite equivalent shown in Fig. 2-51(b) may be used to represent the PMOS–*npn* BJT cascade. This equivalent can be viewed as a PMOS transistor with an effective W/L ratio that is $(\beta_F + 1)$ times larger than the actual PMOS device in the cascade. This equivalence must not be taken too literally, however; Figure 2-52 shows the output characteristics of the PMOS–*npn* BJT cascade, showing an offset of $V_{BE(On)}$ in the output voltage characteristic.

The small-signal equivalent transconductance of the composite (for M_1 in saturation and Q_1 in the forward-active region) is

$$G_m = (\beta_F + 1)\, g_m^{FET} \qquad (2\text{-}224)$$

and the output resistance is

$$R_o = r_o^{FET} \,\|\, r_o^{BJT} \qquad (2\text{-}225)$$

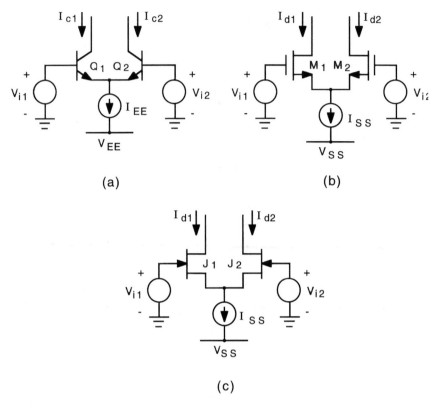

Figure 2-53   Differential-pair configuration: (a) using BJTs; (b) using MOSFETs; (c) using JFETs.

Differential Pair Configuration

Differential-pair gain stages are used widely in many monolithic analog circuits: operational amplifiers, comparators, and voltage regulators, to name a few. The basic differential pair, illustrated in Fig. 2-53, consists of two emitter-coupled (source-coupled) transistors with inputs applied to each base (gate) and outputs taken at either or both collectors (drains). A current source is commonly used to bias the common-emitter (source) node, although a resistor can also be used (with degraded amplifier characteristics). The symmetry between the two branches of the differential pair provides for balanced operation of the circuit in which inputs applied differentially are amplified and those applied in common (to both inputs) are rejected [9]. In this section, we present the characteristics of the differential-pair configuration using both bipolar and field-effect transistors.

Bipolar Differential Pair.

Consider the BJT differential pair shown in Fig. 2-53(a). The biasing current source, I_{EE}, is assumed initially to be ideal—the effects of a finite output resistance of the actual current source will be considered later. Summing the currents at the common-emitter node, and assuming identical transistors, we have

$$I_{e1} + I_{e2} = \frac{I_{c1}}{\alpha_F} + \frac{I_{c2}}{\alpha_F} = I_{EE} \qquad (2\text{-}226)$$

where, neglecting the Early effect,

$$I_{c1} = I_S e^{qV_{be1}/kT}, \qquad I_{c2} = I_S e^{qV_{be2}/kT} \qquad (2\text{-}227)$$

Summing the voltages around the base-emitter loop of the two transistors gives

$$-V_{i1} + V_{be1} - V_{be2} + V_{i2} = 0 \qquad (2\text{-}228)$$

or

$$V_{be1} - V_{be2} = V_{i1} - V_{i2} \equiv V_{id} \qquad (2\text{-}229)$$

where V_{id} denotes the difference of the two inputs, the *differential input voltage*. The two collector currents thus scale as

$$\frac{I_{c1}}{I_{c2}} = e^{q(V_{be1} - V_{be2})/kT} = e^{qV_{id}/kT} \qquad (2\text{-}230)$$

which, combined with Eq. (2-226) gives

$$I_{c1} = \frac{\alpha_F I_{EE}}{1 + e^{-qV_{id}/kT}}, \qquad I_{c2} = \frac{\alpha_F I_{EE}}{1 + e^{qV_{id}/kT}} \qquad (2\text{-}231)$$

The collector currents (normalized to $\alpha_F I_{EE}$) are plotted as a function of the differential input voltage (normalized to kT/q) in Fig. 2-54. Note that for $|V_{id}|$ equal to about $4kT/q$ (approximately 100 mV at room temperature), one transistor is essentially off and the other conducts the full bias current I_{EE}. The differential output current, $I_o = I_{c1} - I_{c2}$, is

$$I_o = \alpha_F I_{EE} \left(\frac{1}{1 + e^{-qV_{id}/kT}} - \frac{1}{1 + e^{qV_{id}/kT}} \right) \qquad (2\text{-}232)$$

which can be manipulated to be expressed in the following form:

$$I_o = \alpha_F I_{EE} \tanh\left(\frac{qV_{id}}{2kT} \right) \qquad (2\text{-}233)$$

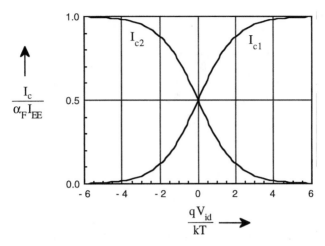

Figure 2-54 Collector currents as a function of differential input voltage for the bipolar differential pair.

The slope of the I_o–V_{id} characteristic represents the effective differential transconductance:

$$G_{md} = \frac{dI_o}{dV_{id}} = \frac{q\alpha_F I_{EE}}{2kT} \text{sech}^2\left(\frac{qV_{id}}{2kT}\right) \tag{2-234}$$

which is a maximum at V_{id} near zero:

$$\left.\frac{dI_o}{dV_{id}}\right|_{V_{id}=0} = \frac{q\alpha_F I_{EE}}{2kT} = \frac{qI_{CQ}}{kT} = g_m \tag{2-235}$$

where I_{CQ} represents the quiescent collector current of either transistor. The maximum effective differential transconductance of the differential pair is thus equal to the transistor transconductance.

MOSFET Differential Pair.

For the MOSFET differential pair [Fig. 2-53(b)], summing the currents at the common-source node gives

$$I_{s1} + I_{s2} = I_{d1} + I_{d2} = I_{SS} \tag{2-236}$$

where, for operation in the saturation region, assuming identical transistors and neglecting channel-length modulation,

$$I_{d1} = \frac{\mu_n C'_{ox}}{2}\left(\frac{W}{L}\right)(V_{gs1} - V_{TH})^2, \qquad I_{d2} = \frac{\mu_n C'_{ox}}{2}\left(\frac{W}{L}\right)(V_{gs2} - V_{TH})^2 \tag{2-237}$$

Summing the voltages around the gate-source loop gives

$$V_{gs1} - V_{gs2} = V_{i1} - V_{i2} \equiv V_{id} \qquad (2\text{-}238)$$

which, using Eq. (2-237) yields

$$\sqrt{\frac{2I_{d1}}{\mu_n C'_{ox}(W/L)}} - \sqrt{\frac{2I_{d2}}{\mu_n C'_{ox}(W/L)}} = V_{id} \qquad (2\text{-}239)$$

Combining Eqs. (2-236) and (2-239) and solving the resulting quadratic equation gives the drain currents as a function of the differential input voltage:

$$I_{d1} = \frac{I_{SS}}{2} + \frac{\mu_n C'_{ox}}{4}\left(\frac{W}{L}\right)V_{id}\sqrt{\frac{4I_{SS}}{\mu_n C'_{ox}(W/L)} - V_{id}^2} \qquad (2\text{-}240)$$

and

$$I_{d2} = \frac{I_{SS}}{2} - \frac{\mu_n C'_{ox}}{4}\left(\frac{W}{L}\right)V_{id}\sqrt{\frac{4I_{SS}}{\mu_n C'_{ox}(W/L)} - V_{id}^2} \qquad (2\text{-}241)$$

The maximum drain current that either transistor can have is I_{SS} and occurs when V_{id} is large enough such that one transistor is off and the other is conducting the full bias current. Using Eq. (2-239), the range in V_{id} for which Eqs. (2-240) and (2-241) remain valid is

$$-\sqrt{\frac{2I_{SS}}{\mu_n C'_{ox}(W/L)}} < V_{id} < \sqrt{\frac{2I_{SS}}{\mu_n C'_{ox}(W/L)}} \qquad (2\text{-}242)$$

Unlike the bipolar differential pair in which the input voltage range depends only on temperature, the input range for the MOSFET differential pair depends on device geometry as well as bias current; typical input ranges are from 1 to 3 V. Taking the differential output current $I_o = I_{d1} - I_{d2}$, we have

$$I_o = \frac{\mu_n C'_{ox}}{2}\left(\frac{W}{L}\right)V_{id}\sqrt{\frac{4I_{SS}}{\mu_n C'_{ox}(W/L)} - V_{id}^2} \qquad (2\text{-}243)$$

The output current (normalized to I_{SS}) is plotted as a function of the differential input voltage [normalized to $\sqrt{2I_{SS}/\mu_n C'_{ox}(W/L)}$] in Fig. 2-55. The effective differential transconductance of the MOSFET pair is

$$G_{md} = \frac{dI_o}{dV_{id}} = \frac{\mu_n C'_{ox}}{2}\left(\frac{W}{L}\right)\sqrt{\frac{4I_{SS}}{\mu_n C'_{ox}(W/L)} - V_{id}^2}\left[1 - \frac{V_{id}^2}{\dfrac{4I_{SS}}{\mu_n C'_{ox}(W/L)} - V_{id}^2}\right] \qquad (2\text{-}244)$$

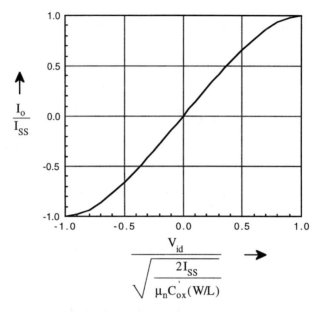

Figure 2-55 Output current as a function of differential input voltage for a MOSFET differential pair.

which is a maximum at V_{id} near zero:

$$\left.\frac{dI_o}{dV_{id}}\right|_{V_{id}=0} = \sqrt{\mu_n C'_{ox} (W/L) I_{SS}} = g_m \qquad (2\text{-}245)$$

Like the bipolar differential pair, the maximum effective differential transconductance of the MOSFET differential pair is equal to the quiescent transconductance of the transistor.

JFET Differential Pair.

Analysis of the JFET differential pair [Fig. 2-53(c)] proceeds in a fashion similar to the MOSFET pair. Using Eq. (1-62) for the drain current in saturation, the currents are found as

$$I_{d1} = \frac{I_{SS}}{2} + \frac{I_{DSS}}{2V_P^2} V_{id} \sqrt{\frac{2I_{SS} V_P^2}{I_{DSS}} - V_{id}^2} \qquad (2\text{-}246)$$

and

$$I_{d2} = \frac{I_{SS}}{2} - \frac{I_{DSS}}{2V_P^2} V_{id} \sqrt{\frac{2I_{SS} V_P^2}{I_{DSS}} - V_{id}^2} \qquad (2\text{-}247)$$

The maximum drain current of either JFET in the pair is I_{DSS}; the resulting differential input voltage range is

$$\sqrt{\frac{I_{SS}}{I_{DSS}}}\,V_P < V_{id} < -\sqrt{\frac{I_{SS}}{I_{DSS}}}\,V_P \tag{2-248}$$

The differential output current $I_o = I_{d1} - I_{d2}$ is

$$I_o = \frac{I_{DSS}}{V_P^2}\,V_{id}\sqrt{\frac{2I_{SS}\,V_P^2}{I_{DSS}} - V_{id}^2} \tag{2-249}$$

The variation in current with input voltage is similar in form to the MOSFET result and a plot of the JFET differential-pair transfer characteristic looks similar to Fig. 2-55. The maximum effective differential transconductance of the JFET pair is

$$G_{md}(\text{max}) = \left.\frac{dI_o}{dV_{id}}\right|_{V_{id}=0} = -\frac{I_{DSS}}{V_P}\sqrt{\frac{2I_{SS}}{I_{DSS}}} \tag{2-250}$$

which again is equal to the pair transistor quiescent transconductance.

Resistor Load

A resistive-loaded differential gain stage using bipolar transistors is illustrated in Fig. 2-56. The current source transistor Q_3 provides the bias current for the differential pair. The output voltages are given by

$$V_{o1} = V_{CC} - I_{c1}R_C \tag{2-251}$$

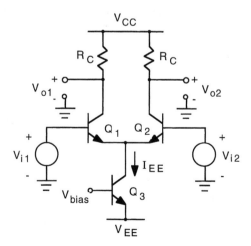

Figure 2-56 Resistive-loaded differential pair using BJTs.

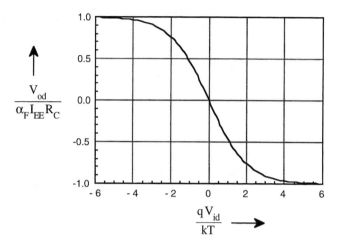

Figure 2-57 Differential output voltage as a function of differential input voltage for the resistive-loaded bipolar differential pair.

and

$$V_{o2} = V_{CC} - I_{c2} R_C \tag{2-252}$$

Using Eq. (2-233), the differential output voltage is

$$V_{od} = V_{o1} - V_{o2} = -I_o R_C = \alpha_F I_{EE} R_C \tanh\left(\frac{-qV_{id}}{2kT}\right) \tag{2-253}$$

which is plotted (in normalized form) in Fig. 2-57. Note that V_{od} is zero when V_{id} is zero; this allows differential gain stages to be directly cascaded together without introducing dc offset voltages, and thereby not requiring dc level shifting.

The range in input voltage over which the transfer characteristic in Fig. 2-57 is approximately linear is limited to about $V_{id} \approx \pm kT/q$. This linear range can be extended by adding resistors in the emitter legs of the differential pair, as illustrated in Fig. 2-58. This causes emitter degeneration and the "linear" range is thereby increased by the voltage drop across the two resistors of $I_{EE} R_E$; the voltage gain of the differential pair is, of course, reduced. Summing the voltages around the base-emitter loop in Fig. 2-58 gives

$$-V_{i1} + V_{be1} + I_{e1} R_E - I_{e2} R_2 - V_{be2} + V_{i2} = 0 \tag{2-254}$$

For $I_{EE} R_E \gg kT/q$, the difference in the two base-emitter voltages will be small compared to the $I_e R_E$ voltage drops allowing V_{be1} and V_{be2} to be taken as approximately equal in Eq. (2-254). Thus,

$$(I_{e1} - I_{e2}) R_E \approx V_{i1} - V_{i2} \equiv V_{id} \tag{2-255}$$

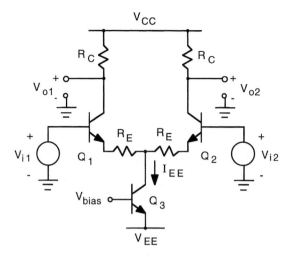

Figure 2-58 **Bipolar differential pair with emitter degeneration resistors.**

Using Eq. (2-255), combined with Eq. (2-226), gives for the collector currents

$$I_{c1} = \frac{\alpha_F I_{EE}}{2} + \frac{\alpha_F V_{id}}{2R_E}, \qquad I_{c2} = \frac{\alpha_F I_{EE}}{2} - \frac{\alpha_F V_{id}}{2R_E} \qquad (2\text{-}256)$$

from which

$$V_{od} = - \frac{\alpha_F R_C}{R_E} V_{id} \qquad (2\text{-}257)$$

which is valid for $V_{id} < I_{EE} R_E$. The differential voltage gain in this case is determined by the ratio of the collector-load and emitter-degeneration resistances, independent of the bias current of the pair.

The symmetry of the differential amplifier configuration allows the small-signal response to be determined by splitting the amplifier into two equivalent circuits, each of which is simpler than the original circuit. To do so, we decompose the small-signal input voltages, v_{i1} and v_{i2}, into two components: differential and common; the total response is then given by the superposition of the *differential-mode* and *common-mode* responses. With this in mind, we define

$$v_{id} \equiv v_{i1} - v_{i2} \qquad (2\text{-}258)$$

as the *difference* of the inputs, representing the differential-mode component, and

$$v_{ic} \equiv \frac{v_{i1} + v_{i2}}{2} \qquad (2\text{-}259)$$

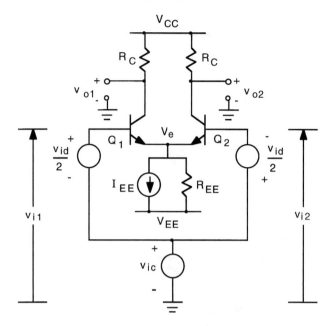

Figure 2-59 Differential pair with small-signal differential-mode and common-mode inputs.

as the *average* of the inputs, representing the common-mode component. With these definitions, the inputs are comprised of

$$v_{i1} = \frac{v_{id}}{2} + v_{ic} \qquad (2\text{-}260)$$

and

$$v_{i2} = -\frac{v_{id}}{2} + v_{ic} \qquad (2\text{-}261)$$

This is illustrated for the differential amplifier shown in Fig. 2-59, where the current biasing transistor is represented by a current source I_{EE} and a resistance R_{EE}, representing the output resistance of the current source transistor. v_{id} is the desired signal applied differentially at the input. v_{ic} represents a signal that is applied in common to both inputs, usually arising from noise or other extraneous signals that enter the amplifier circuit; a measure of the performance of a differential amplifier is the degree by which common-mode input signals are rejected compared to the degree by which differential-mode input signals are amplified.

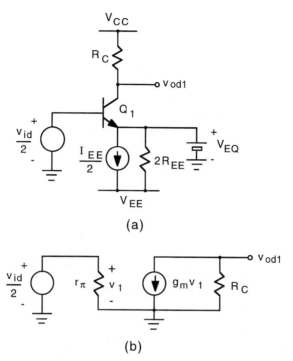

(a)

(b)

Figure 2-60 (a) Differential-mode half-circuit. (b) Small-signal equivalent circuit.

Consider first the circuit with only small-signal differential inputs applied: input $+v_{id}/2$ applied to Q_1 and input $-v_{id}/2$ applied to Q_2. As v_{id} goes positive the emitter current of Q_1 will increase by a small amount above its quiescent value (of approximately $I_{EE}/2$), whereas the emitter current of Q_2 will decrease below its quiescent value by the same amount. As a result, the potential V_e at the common emitter node will remain constant and equal to its quiescent value, denoted V_{EQ}; as far as the differential response is concerned, the common emitter node potential can be set to V_{EQ} (approximately -0.7 V in value) without any change in circuit response. The resulting circuit can be split into two halves, each half (called the differential-mode half-circuit) representing the circuit that describes the response to a differential input voltage. Figure 2-60(a) shows the differential-mode half-circuit for Q_1. The corresponding small-signal equivalent circuit is given in Fig. 2-60(b). From the circuit, the small-signal differential output voltage at the collector of Q_1 is

$$v_{od1} = -g_m R_C \frac{v_{id}}{2} \qquad (2\text{-}262)$$

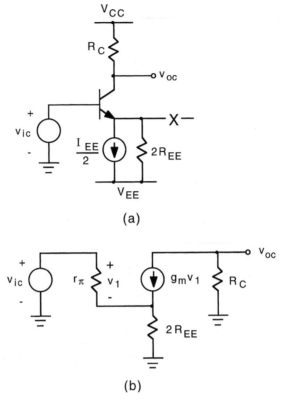

Figure 2-61   **(a) Common-mode half-circuit. (b) Small-signal equivalent circuit.**

The right-hand side of the differential pair is identical except for the opposite input polarity; the corresponding output at the collector of Q_2 is

$$v_{od2} = g_m R_C \frac{v_{id}}{2}$$ (2-263)

The differential-mode voltage gain is then

$$A_{vd} = \frac{v_{od1} - v_{od2}}{v_{id}} = -g_m R_C$$ (2-264)

   Consider now the circuit with only a common-mode input. With v_{ic} applied to both inputs, each side conducts equally and the circuit can be split into two halves without altering the response. The common-mode half-circuit is shown in Fig. 2-61(a), and the corresponding small-signal equivalent circuit is illustrated in Fig. 2-61(b). From the circuit, the small-signal common-mode output voltage is

$$v_{oc} = -g_m R_C v_1 \qquad (2\text{-}265)$$

where

$$v_1 = \frac{r_\pi}{r_\pi + 2(\beta_F + 1)R_{EE}} v_{ic} \qquad (2\text{-}266)$$

which substituted into Eq. (2-265) gives the common-mode voltage gain

$$A_{vc} = \frac{v_{oc}}{v_{ic}} = -\frac{g_m r_\pi R_C}{r_\pi + 2(\beta_F + 1)R_{EE}} = -\frac{g_m R_C}{1 + 2g_m R_{EE}(1 + 1/\beta_F)} \qquad (2\text{-}267)$$

The common-mode rejection ratio (CMRR) characterizes the degree to which common-mode inputs are amplified in comparison to differential-mode inputs:

$$\text{CMRR} \equiv \frac{A_{vd}}{A_{vc}} \qquad (2\text{-}268)$$

For the resistive-loaded bipolar differential pair of Fig. 2-56, we have

$$\text{CMRR} = 1 + 2g_m R_{EE}\left(1 + \frac{1}{\beta_F}\right) \qquad (2\text{-}269)$$

Alternately, because $I_{EQ} = I_{EE}/2$, Eq. (2-269) can be expressed as

$$\text{CMRR} = 1 + \frac{q I_{EE} R_{EE}}{kT} = 1 + \frac{q V_{A3}}{kT} \qquad (2\text{-}270)$$

Using a biasing current source with a high output resistance will increase the common-mode rejection ratio.

The input resistance of the differential pair can be characterized by the response to differential and common-mode inputs. The differential input resistance R_{id} is the resistance seen between the two inputs with only a differential input applied. By inspection of Fig. 2-60(b) the input resistance at Q_1 is

$$\frac{R_{id}}{2} = r_\pi \qquad (2\text{-}271)$$

and similarly for the input at Q_2, giving

$$R_{id} = 2r_\pi \qquad (2\text{-}272)$$

The common-mode input resistance R_{ic} is the resistance at one input with only a common-mode input applied. From Fig. 2-61(b) the input resistance is

$$R_{ic} = r_\pi + 2(\beta_F + 1)R_{EE} \qquad (2\text{-}273)$$

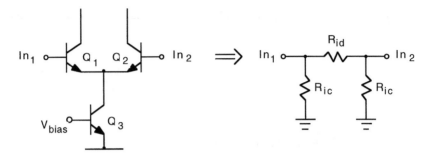

Figure 2-62   Equivalent circuit for the input resistance of the bipolar differential pair.

The input resistance of the differential pair can be represented by the equivalent circuit illustrated in Fig. 2-62.

EXAMPLE. Determine the differential-mode and common-mode voltage gains, the common-mode rejection ratio, the differential input resistance, and the common-mode input resistance of the differential amplifier shown in Fig. 2-63. Assume room temperature and take $V_{BE(on)} = 0.7$ V. The transistor parameters are $\beta_F = 100$ and $V_A = 75$ V. The output resistance of transistors Q_1 and Q_2 can be neglected in comparison with the $10 - k\Omega$ load resistors.

The reference current for Q_4 is

$$I_{ref} = \frac{V_{CC} - V_{EE} - V_{BE4}}{R_{ref}} = \frac{30\,V - 0.7\,V}{40\,k\Omega} = 0.733\,mA$$

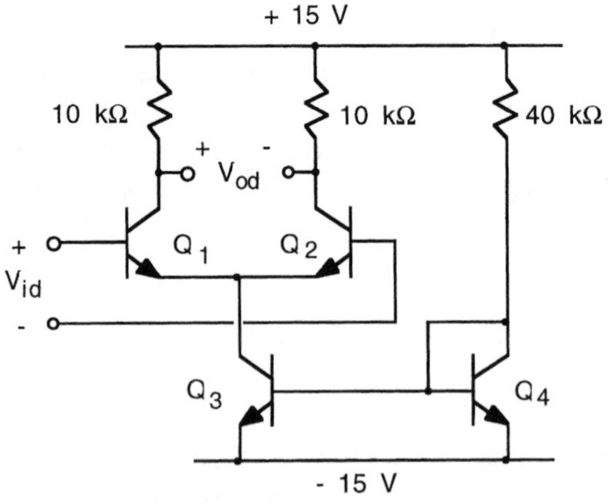

Figure 2-63   Example differential amplifier circuit.

The biasing current is

$$I_{EE} = I_{ref}\left(1 + \frac{V_{CE3}}{V_A}\right) = 0.733\,\text{mA}\left(1 + \frac{14.3\,\text{V}}{75\,\text{V}}\right) = 0.873\,\text{mA}$$

The current source transistor output resistance is

$$R_{EE} = \frac{V_A}{I_{EE}} = \frac{75\,\text{V}}{0.873\,\text{mA}} = 85.9\,\text{k}\Omega$$

The quiescent collector current for the differential pair transistors is

$$I_{CQ} = \frac{\alpha_F I_{EE}}{2} = \frac{(100)(0.873\,\text{mA})}{(2)(101)} = 0.432\,\text{mA}$$

The transistor transconductance is

$$g_m = \frac{qI_{CQ}}{kT} = \frac{0.432\,\text{mA}}{0.026\,\text{V}} = 16.6\,\text{mA/V}$$

and the transistor input resistance is

$$r_\pi = \frac{\beta_F}{g_m} = \frac{100}{16.6\,\text{mA/V}} = 6.02\,\text{k}\Omega$$

The differential voltage gain, using Eq. (2-264), is

$$A_{vd} = -(16.6\,\text{mA/V})(10\,\text{k}\Omega) = -166$$

The common-mode voltage gain, using Eq. (2-267), is

$$A_{vc} = -\frac{(16.6\,\text{mA/V})(10\,\text{k}\Omega)}{1 + (2)(16.6\,\text{mA/V})(85.9\,\text{k}\Omega)(1 + 1/100)} = -0.0576$$

and the common-mode rejection ratio is

$$\text{CMRR} = \frac{A_{vd}}{A_{vc}} = \frac{-166}{-0.0576} = 2882 \text{ or } 69.2\,\text{dB}$$

The differential input resistance, using Eq. (2-272), is

$$R_{id} = (2)(6.02\,\text{k}\Omega) = 12.0\,\text{k}\Omega$$

and the common-mode input resistance, using Eq. (2-273), is

$$R_{ic} = 60.2\,\text{k}\Omega + (2)(101)(85.9\,\text{k}\Omega) = 17.4\,\text{M}\Omega$$

The input resistance of the differential pair may be increased by employing emitter followers at the inputs, such as illustrated in Fig. 2-64. This forms an

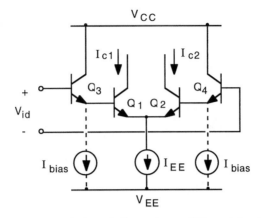

Figure 2-64   Emitter follower input differential pair.

CC–CE cascade configuration for the differential-mode and common-mode half circuits. Using Eq. (2-189), the differential input resistance of Fig. 2-64 is

$$R_{id} = 2\,[r_{\pi 3} + (\beta + 1)\,r_{\pi 1}] \tag{2-274}$$

and using Eq. (2-192), the effective differential transconductance is

$$G_{md} = \frac{g_{m1}\,g_{m3}}{\dfrac{g_{m1}}{\beta_F} + g_{m3}} \tag{2-275}$$

For $I_{bias} = 0$, $I_{c1} \approx \beta_F I_{c3}$, giving

$$G_{md} = \frac{g_{m1}}{2} \tag{2-276}$$

and

$$R_{id} = 4\beta_F\,r_{\pi 1} \tag{2-277}$$

Active Load

A bipolar differential pair with an active load is illustrated in Fig. 2-65. Here, the reference current for Q_3 is set by the collector current of Q_1; under quiescent conditions, $I_{ref} = \alpha_F I_{EE}/2$. This circuit with a large-value load resistance at the output has a large voltage gain, requiring only a small input signal (usually considerably less than kT/q in magnitude) to drive the output to its full operating range. For V_{id} "large" negative, Q_1 is off and Q_2 conducts the full bias current I_{EE}, saturating with the output at approximately $-V_{BC(on)}$. For V_{id} "large" positive, Q_2 is off and Q_1 conducts the full-bias current; Q_4 is saturated (at very

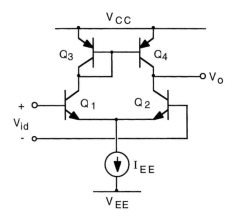

Figure 2-65   Differential pair with active load.

low current) and the output is at $V_{CC} - V_{CE\,(sat)}$. In between, all transistors are operating in the active region. Writing the collector currents for the active region,

$$I_{c1} = I_S^{NPN} e^{qV_{be1}/kT}\left(1 + \frac{V_{ce1}}{V_A^{NPN}}\right)$$

$$I_{c2} = I_S^{NPN} e^{qV_{be2}/kT}\left(1 + \frac{V_{ce2}}{V_A^{NPN}}\right)$$

$$I_{c3} = I_S^{PNP} e^{qV_{eb3}/kT}\left(1 + \frac{V_{ec3}}{V_A^{PNP}}\right)$$

$$I_{c4} = I_S^{PNP} e^{qV_{eb4}/kT}\left(1 + \frac{V_{ec4}}{V_A^{PNP}}\right) \tag{2-278}$$

where we have assumed the *NPN* transistors to be identical, likewise for the *PNP* transistors, and have taken both Early voltages V_A^{NPN} and V_A^{PNP} to be positive quantities. From the circuit,

$$V_{ce1} = V_{CC} - V_{eb3} - V_e$$

where V_e is the potential at the common-emitter node connection of Q_1 and Q_2. Because V_{id} is small, $V_e \approx -V_{be1}$, so

$$V_{ce1} \approx V_{CC} - V_{eb3} + V_{be1} \approx V_{CC}$$

where we have taken V_{eb3} and V_{be1} to be equal because I_{c1} and I_{c3} are approximately equal. For Q_2,

$$V_{ce2} = V_o - V_e \approx V_o + V_{BE\,(on)}$$

where we have approximated V_{be2} by $V_{BE(on)}$. Likewise for Q_3,

$$V_{ec3} = V_{eb3} \approx V_{BE(on)}$$

and for Q_4,

$$V_{ec4} = V_{CC} - V_o$$

Using Eq. (2-278) to express the ratio of the collector currents of the differential-pair transistors, we have

$$\frac{I_{c1}}{I_{c2}} = \frac{1 + V_{CC}/V_A^{NPN}}{1 + (V_o + V_{BE(on)})/V_A^{NPN}} \exp\left(\frac{q(V_{be1} - V_{be2})}{kT}\right)$$

$$= \frac{1 + V_{CC}/V_A^{NPN}}{1 + (V_o + V_{BE(on)})/V_A^{NPN}} e^{qV_{id}/kT} \tag{2-279}$$

$V_{eb3} = V_{eb4}$, so

$$\frac{I_{c3}}{I_{c4}} = \frac{1 + V_{BE(on)}/V_A^{PNP}}{1 + (V_{CC} - V_o)/V_A^{PNP}} \tag{2-280}$$

Now, $I_{c2} = I_{c4}$, and neglecting base currents, $I_{c1} = I_{c3}$. Thus, equating Eqs. (2-279) and (2-280) we have

$$\frac{[1 + (V_o + V_{BE(on)})/V_A^{NPN}][1 + V_{BE(on)}/V_A^{PNP}]}{[1 + (V_{CC} - V_o)/V_A^{PNP}](1 + V_{CC}/V_A^{NPN})} = e^{qV_{id}/kT} \tag{2-281}$$

Taking the natural logarithm of both sides of Eq. (2-281) gives

$$V_{id} = \frac{kT}{q} \ln\left[\frac{[1 + (V_o + V_{BE(on)})/V_A^{NPN}][1 + V_{BE(on)}/V_A^{PNP}]}{[1 + (V_{CC} - V_o)/V_A^{PNP}](1 + V_{CC}/V_A^{NPN})}\right] \tag{2-282}$$

For V_A large with respect to V_{CC}, V_o, and V_{BE}, the factors on the right-hand side of Eq. (2-282) are of the form $1 + x$, where $x \ll 1$. Using the approximation $\ln(1 + x) \approx x$, Eq. (2-282) can be written approximately as

$$V_{id} \approx \frac{kT}{q}\left(\frac{V_o + V_{BE(on)}}{V_A^{NPN}} + \frac{V_{BE(on)}}{V_A^{PNP}} - \frac{V_{CC} - V_o}{V_A^{PNP}} - \frac{V_{CC}}{V_A^{NPN}}\right) \tag{2-283}$$

which solved for V_o yields

$$V_o \approx V_{CC} - V_{BE(on)} + \frac{V_A^{NPN} V_A^{PNP}}{V_A^{NPN} + V_A^{PNP}} \frac{qV_{id}}{kT} \tag{2-284}$$

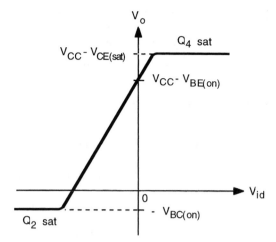

Figure 2-66   Voltage transfer characteristic for the active-loaded differential pair.

The voltage transfer characteristic is sketched in Fig. 2-66. A more detailed analysis of Eq. (2-281) gives for the transfer characteristic [10]

$$V_o \approx V_{CC} - V_{BE\,(on)} + \frac{2V_A^{NPN} V_A^{PNP}}{V_A^{NPN} + V_A^{PNP}} \ \tanh\left(\frac{qV_{id}}{2kT}\right) \tag{2-285}$$

For $V_{id} \ll 2kT$ (which is generally true for the operating range of the active-loaded differential pair), $\tanh(qV_{id}/2kT) \approx qV_{id}/2kT$, giving a result identical to Eq. (2-284).

The slope of the transfer characteristic gives the small-signal voltage gain. Using Eq. (2-284), we obtain

$$\frac{dV_o}{dV_{id}} = \frac{q}{kT} \frac{V_A^{NPN} V_A^{PNP}}{V_A^{NPN} + V_A^{PNP}} \tag{2-286}$$

Noting that $V_A = I_{CQ} r_o \approx I_{EE} r_o / Z$ gives

$$\frac{dV_o}{dV_{id}} = \frac{qI_{CQ}}{kT} \frac{r_o^{NPN} r_o^{PNP}}{r_o^{NPN} + r_o^{PNP}} = g_m (r_o^{NPN} \| r_o^{PNP}) \tag{2-287}$$

A small-signal equivalent circuit for the active-loaded differential pair is shown in Fig. 2-67. The unloaded voltage gain is given by

$$\frac{v_o}{v_{id}} = G_{md} (r_o^{NPN} \| r_o^{PNP}) \tag{2-288}$$

where G_{md} is given by Eq. (2-235) and equals the transconductance g_m of the pair transistors, and the voltage gain is the same as that obtained in Eq. (2-287).

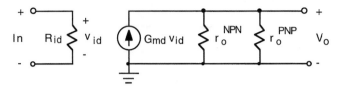

Figure 2-67 Small-signal equivalent circuit for the active-loaded differential pair.

An ideal active-loaded differential pair with perfectly matched transistors has an infinite common-mode rejection ratio. This is illustrated in Fig. 2-68 which shows the small-signal currents resulting from a common-mode input signal; the common-mode collector current of Q_1 is mirrored at the output which combines with collector current of Q_2 to give zero output common-mode

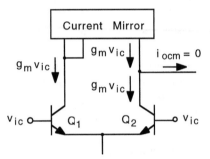

Figure 2-68   Small-signal common-mode currents in the active-loaded differential pair.

current. In practice, there is a small common-mode output resulting from mismatches in transistor characteristics. A small-signal analysis of the circuit in Fig. 2-65 gives the common-mode rejection ratio as [11]

$$\text{CMRR} \approx \frac{g_{m1} g_{m2} (g_{m3} + g_{m4})}{(g_{m3} + g_{m4})(g_{m1}/r_{o2} - g_{m2}/r_{o1}) + \dfrac{1}{R_{EE}}(g_{m1} g_{m4} - g_{m2} g_{m3})} \tag{2-289}$$

which becomes infinite for matched *NPN* and *PNP* pairs.

Figure 2-69 shows a differential pair using NMOS transistors, with a fixed resistance load in Fig. 2-69(a) and with a saturated NMOS load in Fig. 2-69(b). For Fig. 2-69(a), the differential output voltage is

$$V_{od} = (I_{d1} - I_{d2}) R_D = I_o R_D \tag{2-290}$$

which using Eq. (2-243) gives

$$V_{od} = \frac{\mu_n C'_{ox}}{2}\left(\frac{W}{L}\right) R_D V_{id} \sqrt{\frac{4I_{SS}}{\mu_n C'_{ox} (W/L)} - V_{id}^2} \tag{2-291}$$

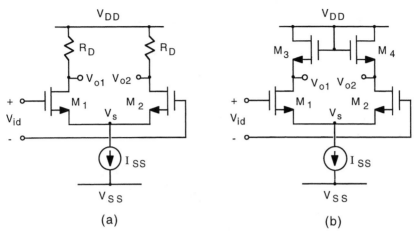

Figure 2-69 NMOS differential pair: (a) fixed resistance load; (b) saturated NMOS load.

The small-signal equivalent circuits of the differential-mode and common-mode half-circuits are shown in Fig. 2-70(a) and 2-70(b), respectively. For the differential-mode response,

$$v_{od1} = -\frac{g_m R_D v_{id}}{2} \tag{2-292}$$

and similarly for v_{od2}, giving

$$A_{vd} = \frac{v_{od}}{v_{id}} = -g_m R_D \tag{2-293}$$

For the common-mode response,

$$A_{vc} = \frac{v_{oc}}{v_{ic}} = -\frac{g_m R_D}{1 + 2g_m R_{SS}} \tag{2-294}$$

The common-mode rejection ratio is

$$\text{CMRR} \frac{A_{vd}}{A_{vc}} = 1 + 2g_m R_{SS} = 1 + 2R_{SS}\sqrt{\mu_n C'_{ox}(W/L) I_{SS}} \tag{2-295}$$

At comparable bias current levels, the transconductance of the MOSFET is considerably less than that of the BJT; thus, the CMRR of the MOS differential pair is smaller than a similar bipolar circuit.

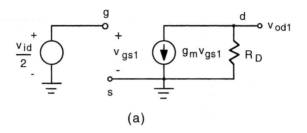

(a)

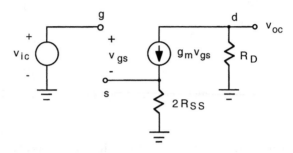

Figure 2-70   Small-signal equivalent circuits for the resistive-loaded NMOS differential pair: (a) differential mode; (b) common mode. The resistance R_{SS} represents the output resistance of the bias current source I_{SS}.

In Fig. 2-69(b), NMOS transistors M_3 and M_4, operating in saturation, provide the load elements for the differential pair transistors, M_1 and M_2. For

$$-\sqrt{\frac{2I_{SS}}{\mu_n C'_{ox}(W/L)_2}} < V_{id} < \sqrt{\frac{2I_{SS}}{\mu_n C'_{ox}(W/L)_1}}$$

both transistors M_1 and M_2 are conducting and operating in saturation. Assuming that all transistors are identical, except for their W/L ratios, we write for the drain currents,

$$I_{d1} = \frac{\mu_n C'_{ox}}{2} \left(\frac{W}{L}\right)_1 (V_{gs1} - V_{TH})^2$$

$$I_{d2} = \frac{\mu_n C'_{ox}}{2} \left(\frac{W}{L}\right)_2 (V_{gs2} - V_{TH})^2$$

$$I_{d3} = \frac{\mu_n C'_{ox}}{2} \left(\frac{W}{L}\right)_3 (V_{DD} - V_{o1} - V_{TH})^2$$

$$I_{d4} = \frac{\mu_n C'_{ox}}{2} \left(\frac{W}{L}\right)_4 (V_{DD} - V_{o2} - V_{TH})^2 \qquad (2\text{-}296)$$

Equating I_{d1} and I_{d3} yields

$$V_{o1} = V_{DD} - V_{TH} - \sqrt{\frac{(W/L)_1}{(W/L)_3}}\,(V_{gs1} - V_{TH}) \qquad (2\text{-}297)$$

and equating I_{d2} and I_{d4} yields

$$V_{o2} = V_{DD} - V_{TH} - \sqrt{\frac{(W/L)_2}{(W/L)_4}}\,(V_{gs2} - V_{TH}) \qquad (2\text{-}298)$$

The differential output voltage is

$$V_{od} = V_{o1} - V_{o2} = -\sqrt{\frac{(W/L)_1}{(W/L)_3}}\,(V_{gs1} - V_{gs2}) = -\sqrt{\frac{(W/L)_1}{(W/L)_3}}\,V_{id} \quad (2\text{-}299)$$

where we have assumed that the channel width-to-length ratios (W/L) of the differential-pair transistors (M_1 and M_2) are equal as are those of the load transistors (M_3 and M_4).

It can be easily shown that the small-signal differential-mode voltage gain is given by

$$A_{vd} = -\frac{g_{m1}}{g_{m3}} = -\sqrt{\frac{(W/L)_1}{(W/L)_3}} \qquad (2\text{-}300)$$

and that the small-signal common-mode voltage gain is

$$A_{cm} = -\frac{g_{m1}}{g_{m3}\,(1 + 2g_{m1}R_{SS})} \qquad (2\text{-}301)$$

The common-mode rejection ratio is

$$\text{CMRR} = 1 + 2g_{m1}R_{SS} = 1 + 2R_{SS}\sqrt{\mu_n C_{ox}'\,(W/L)_1 I_{SS}} \qquad (2\text{-}302)$$

and is identical to that of the resistive-loaded pair.

The active-loaded MOSFET differential pair, shown in Fig. 2-71, operates in a fashion similar to its bipolar counterpart (Fig. 2-65). The unloaded small-signal voltage gain is

$$\frac{v_o}{v_{id}} = g_{m1}\,(r_o^{\text{NMOS}} \| r_o^{\text{PMOS}}) \qquad (2\text{-}303)$$

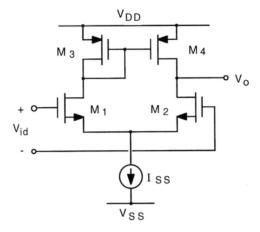

Figure 2-71   CMOS differential pair with active load.

where r_o^{NMOS} and r_o^{PMOS} are the output resistances of the NMOS and PMOS transistors, respectively. The stage exhibits an output resistance of

$$R_o = r_o^{\text{NMOS}} \parallel r_o^{\text{PMOS}} = \frac{2}{I_{SS}(\lambda_N + \lambda_P)} \qquad (2\text{-}304)$$

where λ_N and λ_P are the channel-length modulation parameters of the NMOS and PMOS transistors, respectively. Also, as with the active-loaded bipolar differential pair, the CMOS version has a very high common-mode rejection ratio.

2.5 Output Stages

Output stages are used as an interface to drive an external load connected to the integrated circuit. In this role, the output stage must be able to deliver power to the load with minimal distortion of the signal. It should also not limit the frequency response of the circuit. Figure 2-72 shows the characteristics of an *ideal* output stage. The linear transfer characteristic [Fig. 2-72(b)] produces an undistorted output and the output voltage swing which ranges from the negative power supply (V^-) to the positive power supply (V^+) provides the maximum signal voltage that can be delivered to the load. The idealized output characteristic [Fig. 2-72(d)] shows that the output stage can deliver any amount of current required by the load; this implies a zero output resistance for the stage, which means all of the signal is delivered to the load. An infinite input resistance, as depicted in Fig. 2-72(c), produces no loading of the previous

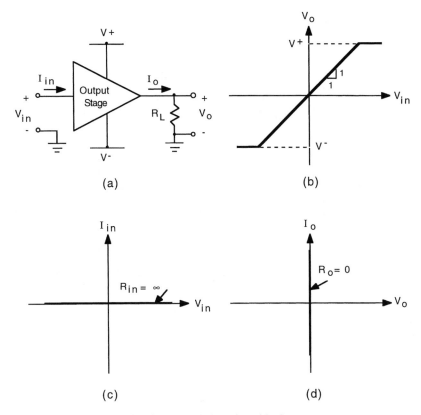

Figure 2-72 Characteristics of an ideal output stage.

stage at the input to the output stage; in an actual output stage, its input resistance should be high.

Emitter Follower and Source Follower Output Stages

The nearly linear transfer characteristic and low output resistance of an emitter follower make it ideal for use in an output stage. Figure 2-73(a) shows an output stage using a single emitter follower. Q_2 is a current-source transistor which provides a bias current I_Q for the emitter of Q_1. This arrangement keeps the bias current out of the load resistance which otherwise would result in significant quiescent standby power being dissipated in the load. From the circuit,

$$V_o = V_{in} - V_{be1} = V_{in} - \frac{kT}{q} \ln\left(\frac{I_{c1}}{I_{S1}}\right) \qquad (2\text{-}305)$$

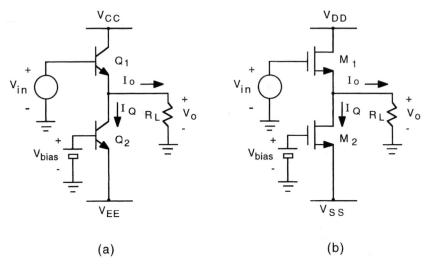

(a)   (b)

Figure 2-73 (a) Emitter follower output stage. (b) Source follower output stage.

where

$$I_{c1} = \alpha_F I_{e1} = \alpha_F (I_Q + I_o) = \alpha_F (I_Q + V_o / R_L) \tag{2-306}$$

which combined with Eq. (2-305) yields

$$V_o + \frac{kT}{q} \ln\left[\frac{\alpha_F (I_Q + V_o / R_L)}{I_{S1}}\right] = V_{in} \tag{2-307}$$

The nonlinearity in this transfer characteristic is logarithmic, so for values of load resistance such that $|V_o / R_L|$ is significantly less than the bias current I_Q, the output is very linear; for even larger values of output current, the nonlinearity is still small, typically on the order of 0.1% or so.

If this output stage is part of an integrated circuit, then the input voltage to the stage will be limited to $V_{EE} < V_{in} < V_{CC}$. Consequently, the maximum *positive* output voltage will be approximately $V_{CC} - V_{BE(on)}$. The maximum negative output voltage depends on the value of the load resistance relative to the bias current. For large values of R_L, the output is limited when Q_2 goes into saturation, giving a maximum negative output voltage of $V_{EE} + V_{CE(sat)}$. When $V_o = -I_Q R_L$, then $I_{e1} = 0$, causing Q_1 to become cutoff. If R_L is less than $(V_{EE} + V_{CE(sat)})/I_Q$ in value, then Q_1 will cutoff before Q_2 goes into saturation, thereby limiting the maximum negative output voltage to $-I_Q R_L$. The voltage transfer characteristic for the emitter follower output stage is sketched in Fig. 2-74, illustrated for two different values of load resistance.

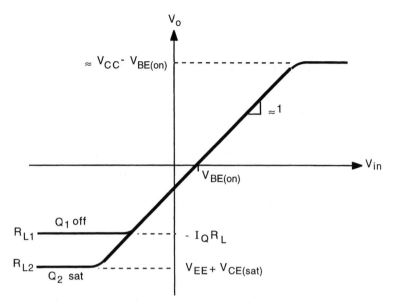

Figure 2-74 **Voltage transfer characteristic for the emitter follower output stage of Fig. 2-73(a) depicting two different values of $R_L (R_{L2} > R_{L1})$.**

This circuit, like all Class A-type stages, suffers from low-power efficiency; this is because the bias current I_Q flows in both Q_1 and Q_2 at zero output, resulting in a standby quiescent power dissipation of $(V_{CC} - V_{EE})I_Q$. The maximum power efficiency is limited to about 25%.

A source follower output stage using MOSFETs is shown in Fig. 2-73(b). For this circuit,

$$V_o = V_{in} - V_{gs1} = V_{in} - V_{TH} - \sqrt{\frac{2I_{d1}}{\mu_n C'_{ox}(W/L)_1}} \tag{2-308}$$

where

$$I_{d1} = I_Q + \frac{V_o}{R_L} \tag{2-309}$$

resulting in

$$V_o + \sqrt{\frac{2(I_Q + V_o/R_L)}{\mu_n C'_{ox}(W/L)_1}} = V_{in} - V_{TH} \tag{2-310}$$

Here, the nonlinearity is square root, resulting in a somewhat less linear transfer characteristic than with a bipolar transistor stage; the transfer characteristic is similar to Fig. 2-74. Again, for small values of R_L, transistor M_1 is cutoff at $V_o = -I_Q R_L$.

Complementary Output Stages

The low-power efficiency of the Class A-type stage can be improved by using complementary devices in a push–pull configuration. Figure 2-75(a) illustrates a complementary output stage using *npn* and *pnp* emitter followers operating in Class AB. The two diode-connected transistors Q_1 and Q_2 provide a $2V_{be}$ voltage drop between the bases of Q_3 and Q_4; at zero output ($V_o = 0$), both output devices are biased slightly on with a quiescent current I_Q. This arrangement eliminates the "dead-band" (and the resulting crossover distortion) in the transfer characteristic that would otherwise occur due to the positive V_{be} required for Q_3 to conduct and the negative V_{be} required for Q_4 to conduct.

Starting from $V_o = 0$, as V_{in} is increased, the voltage at the base of Q_4 is increased, causing Q_4 to conduct less; at the same time, the voltage at the base of Q_3 is increased due to the constant voltage drop across the two forward-biased diodes Q_1 and Q_2, causing Q_3 to conduct more heavily. With increasing input voltage, Q_4 turns off and Q_3 sources the full output current to the load. For a positive output, Q_4 is essentially off and Q_3 is on, giving

$$V_o = V_{in} + V_{eb2} + V_{be1} - V_{be3} \approx V_{in} + V_{BE(on)} \qquad (2\text{-}311)$$

The small-signal input resistance of the output stage for V_o positive is approximately

$$R_{in} \approx \frac{1}{g_{m2}} + \frac{1}{g_{m1}} + r_{\pi3} + (\beta_3 + 1) R_L \qquad (2\text{-}312)$$

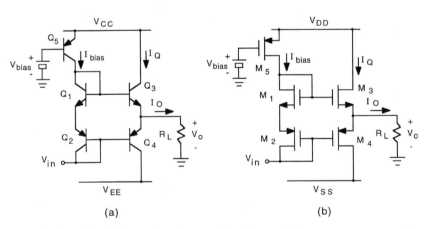

(a)   (b)

Figure 2-75   Class AB complementary output stage with crossover compensation: (a) using BJTs; (b) using MOSFETs.

In the negative direction, as V_{in} is lowered, the voltage at the base of Q_4 is lowered, causing Q_4 to conduct more heavily; at the same time, the voltage at the base of Q_3 is also lowered, causing it to conduct less. With decreasing input voltage, Q_3 turns off and Q_4 sinks the full output current from the load. For a negative output, Q_3 is essentially off and Q_4 is on, giving

$$V_o = V_{in} + V_{eb4} \approx V_{in} + V_{BE(on)} \qquad (2\text{-}313)$$

The input resistance for negative output is approximately

$$R_{in} \approx r_{\pi 4} + (\beta_4 + 1)R_L \qquad (2\text{-}314)$$

The quiescent bias current I_Q can be determined by summing the base-emitter voltages around the loop containing Q_1–Q_4:

$$V_{be1} + V_{be2} = V_{be3} + V_{eb4} \qquad (2\text{-}315)$$

where neglecting base currents gives

$$\frac{kT}{q}\ln\left(\frac{I_{bias}}{I_{S1}}\right) + \frac{kT}{q}\ln\left(\frac{I_{bias}}{I_{S2}}\right) = \frac{kT}{q}\ln\left(\frac{I_Q}{I_{S3}}\right) + \frac{kT}{q}\ln\left(\frac{I_Q}{I_{S4}}\right) \qquad (2\text{-}316)$$

from which

$$I_Q = I_{bias}\sqrt{\frac{I_{S3}I_{S4}}{I_{S1}I_{S2}}} \qquad (2\text{-}317)$$

Figure 2-76 shows an improved output stage using complementary emitter follower transistors for crossover-distortion compensation [12]. Here, $V_o \approx V_{in}$,

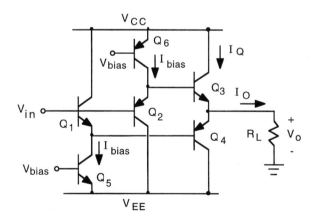

Figure 2-76 Improved Class AB output stage with complementary emitter follower crossover distortion compensation.

resulting in very little offset between input and output. This stage also has a higher input resistance; for V_o positive,

$$R_{in} \approx r_{\pi 2} + (\beta_2 + 1) [r_{\pi 3} + (\beta_3 + 1) R_L] \qquad (2\text{-}318)$$

and for V_o negative,

$$R_{in} \approx r_{\pi 1} + (\beta_1 + 1) [r_{\pi 4} + (\beta_4 + 1) R_L] \qquad (2\text{-}319)$$

A complementary output stage using MOSFETs is shown in Fig. 2-75(b). The two diode-connected MOS transistors M_1 and M_2 provide a $2V_{gs}$ voltage drop for crossover compensation. The stage operates in a fashion similar to the BJT version [Fig. 2-75(a)]. For positive output, M_4 is essentially off and M_3 is on, giving

$$V_o = V_{in} + V_{sg2} + V_{gs1} - V_{gs3} \approx V_{in} + V_{GS(on)} \qquad (2\text{-}320)$$

For negative output, M_3 is off and M_4 is on, giving

$$V_o = V_{in} + V_{sg4} \approx V_{in} + V_{GS(on)} \qquad (2\text{-}321)$$

The quiescent bias current I_Q is determined by summing the gate-source voltages around the loop containing M_1–M_4:

$$V_{gs1} + V_{sg2} = V_{gs3} + V_{sg4} \qquad (2\text{-}322)$$

where, assuming equal threshold voltages and gate-oxide thicknesses for the NMOS transistors and likewise for the PMOS transistors, gives

$$\sqrt{\frac{2I_{bias}}{\mu_n C'_{oxn} (W/L)_1}} + \sqrt{\frac{2I_{bias}}{\mu_p C'_{oxp} (W/L)_2}} = \sqrt{\frac{2I_Q}{\mu_n C'_{oxn} (W/L)_3}} + \sqrt{\frac{2I_Q}{\mu_p C'_{oxp} (W/L)_4}}$$

$$(2\text{-}323)$$

Solving for I_Q,

$$I_Q = I_{bias} \left[\frac{(W/L)_3 (W/L)_4}{(W/L)_1 (W/L)_2} \left(\frac{\sqrt{\mu_n C'_{oxn} (W/L)_1} + \sqrt{\mu_n C'_{oxp} (W/L)_2}}{\sqrt{\mu_n C'_{oxn} (W/L)_3} + \sqrt{\mu_p C'_{oxp} (W/L)_4}} \right)^2 \right] \qquad (2\text{-}324)$$

EXAMPLE. Figure 2-77 shows a class AB BiCMOS output stage in which the PMOS–*npn* composite forms a quasi-complementary device. (a) Determine the quiescent bias current I_Q, and the maximum positive V_o^+ and negative V_o^- output voltages for V_{in} ranging from -15 to -15 V. (b) Simulate the circuit using SPICE to check the results in (a) and give plots of V_o, and I_{C5} and I_{C6} versus V_{in}. The *npn* transistor parameters are $I_S = 2 \times 10^{-17}$ A (1X device) and $\beta_F = 100$. The PMOS transistor parameters are $V_{TH} = -0.8$ V and $\mu_p C'_{ox} = 25 \, \mu\text{A}/\text{V}^2$. Assume room temperature and take $V_{BE(on)} = 0.7$ V and $V_{CE(sat)} = 0.2$ V.

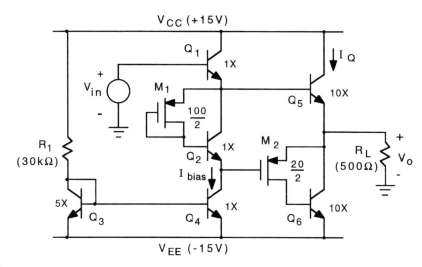

Figure 2-77 **Class AB quasi-complementary BiCMOS output stage.** n_X denotes relative emitter areas of the bipolar transistors; the fractions denote the channel-width and channel-length dimensions W/L (μm) of the PMOS transistors.

(a) Summing the base-emitter and gate-source voltages around the loop containing M_1, Q_2, M_2, and Q_5 gives

$$V_{be2} - V_{be5} = V_{sg2} - V_{sg1}$$

Neglecting base currents, we have $I_{d1} = I_{bias}/\beta_F$ and $I_{d2} = I_Q/\beta_F$, which used in the expression for the source-gate voltages yields

$$\frac{kT}{q} \ln\left(\frac{I_Q}{I_{bias}} \frac{I_{S2}}{I_{S5}}\right) + \sqrt{\frac{2I_Q}{\beta_F \mu_p C'_{ox}(W/L)_2}} = \sqrt{\frac{2I_{bias}}{\beta_F \mu_p C'_{ox}(W/L)_1}} \quad (3\text{-}325)$$

From the circuit, $I_{bias} = I_{ref}(I_{S4}/I_{S3})$, where $I_{ref} = (V_{CC} - V_{EE} - V_{BE(on)})/R_1 = 977\ \mu A$, giving $I_{bias} = 195\ \mu A$. Substituting into Eq. (2-325) provides

$$0.026 \ln\left(\frac{I_Q}{195\ \mu A} \frac{1}{10}\right) + \sqrt{\frac{2I_Q}{(100)(25)(20/2)}} = \sqrt{\frac{(2)(195)}{(100)(25)(100/2)}}$$

which solved numerically gives $I_Q = 175\ \mu A$.

For V_o positive, Q_5 is on and M_2/Q_6 are off, giving $V_o = V_{in} - V_{be1} - V_{be5} \approx V_{in} - 2V_{BE(on)}$. At $V_{in} = +15\ V$, the maximum positive output is then $V_o^+ = 15 - (2)(0.7\ V) = 13.6\ V$. For V_o negative, Q_5 is off and M_2/Q_6 are on. The maximum negative output is reached when Q_4 goes into saturation (as V_{in} is lowered, the collector voltage of Q_4, which is equal to $V_{in} - V_{be1} - V_{sg1} - V_{be2}$, is also lowered, causing Q_4 to saturate when its collector voltage reaches $V_{EE} + V_{CE4(sat)}$). At this point $V_o^- = V_{EE} + V_{CE4\,(sat)} + V_{sg2}$. The source-gate voltage of M_2 is given by

$$V_{sg2} = -V_{TH} + \sqrt{\frac{2I_{d2}}{\mu_p C'_{ox}(W/L)_2}}$$

where $I_{d2} = I_{c2}/\beta_F$ and $I_{c2} \approx -V_o/R_L$, which at maximum negative output is approximately V_{EE}. So $I_{c2} \approx -V_{EE}/R_L = 15\,V/0.5\,k\Omega = 30\,mA$, giving $I_{d2} = 30\,mA/100 = 300\,\mu A$. The source-gate voltage of M_2 is then

$$V_{sg2} = 0.8\,V + \sqrt{\frac{(2)(300)}{(25)(20/2)}}\,V = 2.35\,V$$

and the maximum negative output voltage is $V_o^- = -15\,V + 0.2\,V + 2.35\,V = -12.45\,V$.

(b) A PSPICE program listing for the BiCMOS output stage is as follows:

```
BICMOS.CIR - BiCMOS Output Stage
*
VCC 10 0 15V
VEE 20 0 -15V
VIN 1 0 DC 1.483V (this value gives Vo = 0 )
*
Q1 10 1 2 QN 1
Q2 2 3 4 QN 1
Q3 5 5 20 QN 5
Q4 4 5 20 QN 1
Q5 10 2 7 QN 10
Q6 7 6 20 QN 10
M1 3 3 2 2 MP W = 100U L = 2U
M2 6 4 7 7 MP W = 20U L = 2U
R1 10 5 30K
RL 7 0 500
*
.MODEL QN NPN (BF = 100 IS = 2E − 17A)
.MODEL MP PMOS (VTO = − 0.8V KP = 25U)
.OP
.DC VIN −15 15 0.1
.PLOT DC V(7) IC(Q5) IC(Q6)
.PROBE
.END
```

Plots of V_o, I_{c5}, and I_{c6} versus V_{in} are presented in Fig. 2-78. From the plot, the maximum V_o^+ and V_o^- are about 13.5 and $-12.5\,V$, respectively. The quiescent

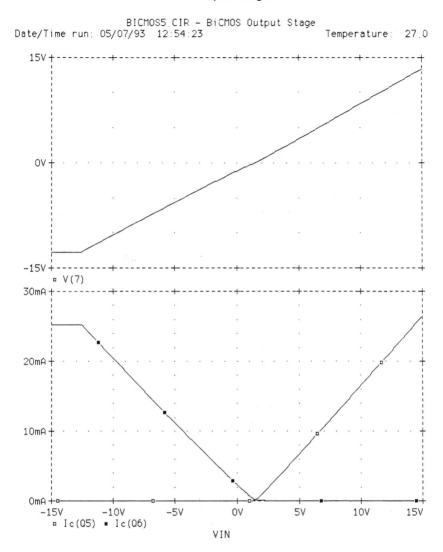

BICMOS5.CIR - BiCMOS Output Stage
Date/Time run: 05/07/93 12:54:23   Temperature: 27.0

Figure 2-78 PSPICE plot of BiCMOS output stage characteristics. Upper curve: V_o versus V_{in}. Lower curves: I_{c5} and I_{c6} versus V_{in}.

currents from the simulation are $I_{c4}\,(I_{bias}) = 193\ \mu A$, $I_{c5} = 171\ \mu A$, and $I_{c6} = 173\ \mu A$, all of which agree well with those calculated by hand.

Problems

For all problems assume room temperature, $kT/q = 26\,\text{mV}$.
Note: Where required, use the following device parameters unless otherwise specified:

NPN: $\beta_F = 100$ $I_S = 2 \times 10^{-16}\,\text{A}$ $V_A = 75\,\text{V}$

PNP: $\beta_F = 50$ $I_S = 5 \times 10^{-17}\,\text{A}$ $V_A = 75\,\text{V}$

NMOS: $W/L = 10$ $\mu_n C'_{ox} = 30\,\mu\text{A}/\text{V}^2$ $V_{TH} = 1\,\text{V}$ $\lambda = 0.02\,\text{V}^{-1}$

PMOS: $W/L = 30$ $\mu_n C'_{ox} = 10\,\mu\text{A}/\text{V}^2$ $V_{TH} = -1\,\text{V}$ $\lambda = 0.02\,\text{V}^{-1}$.

2.1 A resistance added in series with the base of the basic current mirror, Fig. 2-79, can compensate for base current error. Show that if R is chosen such that $R = 2kT/qI_2$, then $I_2 \approx I_{ref}$, neglecting transistor output resistance. *Hint:* You may find the approximation $\ln(1 - x) \approx -x$, for $x \ll 1$, useful.

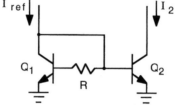

Figure 2-79   Base-current compensation of basic current mirror for Problem 2.1.

2.2 Show that the output resistance of the Wilson current source, Fig. 2-11, is given by Eq. (2-22).

2.3 Show that the output resistance of the NMOS Wilson current mirror, Fig. 2-13(a), is given by Eq. (2-25).

2.4 In the current source of Fig. 2-80, neglecting base currents, show that

$$I_o = \frac{A_3 A_5}{A_1 A_4} I_{ref}$$

where A_i = emitter area.

2.5 Derive an expression for the output current I_2 in the current source of Fig. 2-81. The MOSFETs are identical, except for W/L ratios. neglect channel-length modulation.

2.6 (a) For the improved Wilson current source of Fig. 2-12, show, neglecting the Early effect for Q_2, that $I_2 = I_{ref}$. Do **not** neglect base currents but assume the transistors to be identical.

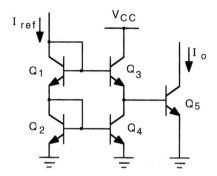

Figure 2-80   Current source for Problem 2.4.

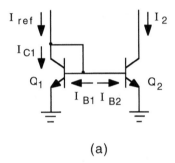

(a)

Figure 2-81   Current source for Problem 2.5.

(b) Simulate this circuit using SPICE (or equivalent circuit simulator) to show a plot of I_2 versus V_{C2} (the collector voltage of Q_2) for V_{C2} ranging from 0 to 10 V. From your results, determine the output resistance of the current source and compare with that calculated using Eq. (2-22). Take for the circuit, $V_{CC} = 10$ V and $R = 10$ kΩ. *Note:* Because of the high output resistance of this circuit, you will need to reduce the tolerance in the SPICE program to get an accurate simulation. To do so, add the following statement in your SPICE file: **.OPTIONS RELTOL = .00001**

2.7 Find the output current and output resistance for the Widlar current source of Fig. 2-16. The transistors are identical. Circuit parameters: $V_{CC} = 10$ V, $R_{ref} = 20$ kΩ, and $R_2 = 1$ kΩ.

2.8 Find the output current I_2 and the output resistance of the current source shown in Fig. 2-82. The *pnp* transistors are identical except for their emitter areas, as indicated.

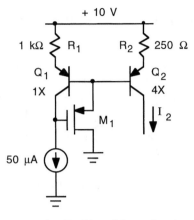

Figure 2-82   Current source for Problem 2.8. n_X denotes relative emitter areas.

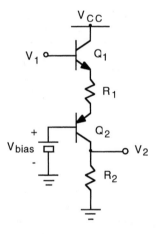

Figure 2-83 Level-shift circuit for Problem 2.9.

2.9 Find V_2 relative to V_1 for the *npn–pnp* level-shift stage of Fig. 2-83. You may neglect base currents and take $V_{be} = V_{BE\,(on)}$.

2.10 Neglecting base current, show that for the V_{BE} multiplier circuit of Fig. 2-84,

$$R_o = \frac{dV_o}{dI_o} = \frac{R_1 + R_2}{1 + g_m R_2} \approx \frac{V_o}{V_{BE}} \frac{kT}{qI_c} \quad \text{for } g_m R_2 \gg 1.$$

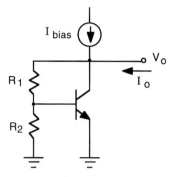

Figure 2-84 V_{BE} **multiplier circuit for Problem 2.10.**

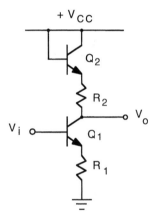

Figure 2-85 Inverting amplifier circuit for Problem 2.11.

2.11 (a) Derive an expression for the voltage transfer characteristic (V_o versus V_i) of the inverting amplifier circuit of Fig. 2-85. Base current may be neglected.
(b) Sketch the transfer characteristic for V_i ranging from 0 to $+ V_{CC}$.
(c) This circuit can be used as a unity-gain inverting amplifier for proper values of R_1 and R_2. Determine this relation.

2.12 Derive an expression that gives the large-signal transfer characteristic (V_o as a function of V_i) for the common-emitter gain stage of Fig. 2-24 with $R_B = 0$. Do **not** neglect the Early effect; use the Early voltage V_A in your analysis. What does the characteristic become for $V_A \to \infty$?

2.13 Figure 2-86 shows a common-emitter amplifier with diode biasing. Taking $V_{be} = V_{BE(on)}$, determine an expression for the output voltage V_o, assuming

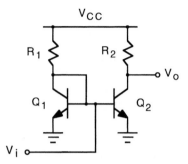

Figure 2-86 Diode-biased common-emitter gain stage for Problem 2.13.

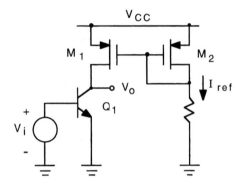

Figure 2-87 Active-loaded common-emitter gain stage for Problem 2.14.

transistor Q_2 is operating in the forward-active mode. The transistors are identical. What does V_o become for $R_1 = 2R_2$?

2.14 Derive an expression giving V_o as a function of V_i for the PMOS active-loaded common-emitter amplifier circuit of Fig. 2-87. Use V_A and λ to characterize the Early effects in Q_1 and M_1, respectively. Transistors M_1 and M_2 are identical.

2.15 The emitter follower stage of Fig. 2-31 is biased at $V_i = V_{CC}/2$. Determine the output voltage V_o, the small-signal input resistance, output resistance, and voltage gain. Take for the circuit, $V_{CC} = 10\,\mathrm{V}$, $R_B = 500\,\Omega$, and $R_E = 1\,\mathrm{k}\Omega$. You may take $V_{be} \approx V_{BE(on)} = 0.7\,\mathrm{V}$.

2.16 Verify that the small-signal output resistance of the common-gate gain stage of Fig. 2-42 is given by Eq. (2-173).

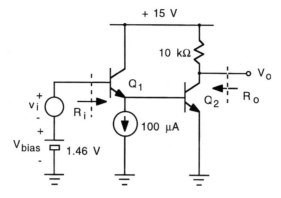

Figure 2-88 Cascade amplifier circuit for Problem 2.17.

2.17 For the cascade amplifier in Fig. 2-88 determine the quiescent (@ $v_i = 0$) output voltage V_O, the small-signal input resistance R_i, output resistance R_o, and the voltage gain v_o/v_i. Neglect the Early effect for Q_1, but not for Q_2.

2.18 Determine the quiescent (@ $v_i = 0$) collector current in Q_1, drain current in M_1, output voltage V_O, and the small-signal voltage gain v_o/v_i for the BiCMOS Darlington stage shown in Fig. 2-89. Take $V_{be} = V_{BE\,(on)} = 0.7\,V$ for Q_1.

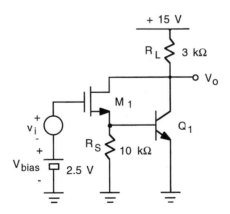

Figure 2-89 BiCMOS Darlington stage for Problem 2.18.

2.19 The μA 701 cascode amplifier circuit is shown in Fig. 2-90.
(a) Find the dc collector currents in the transistors and the output voltage V_O. Base currents may be neglected. Refer to Problem 2.13 for inspiration.

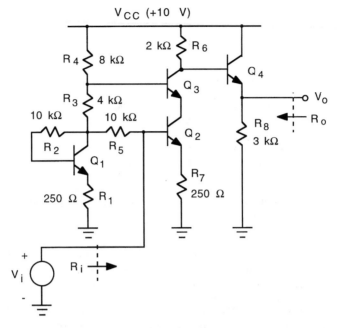

Figure 2-90   Cascode amplifier for Problem 2.19.

(b) Determine the small-signal input and output resistance, and the voltage gain v_o/v_i for the amplifier.

2.20 For the emitter follower common-base cascode circuit of Fig. 2-91 determine the small-signal input resistance R_i, output resistance R_o, and the

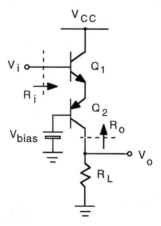

Figure 2-91   Emitter follower common-base cascode circuit for Problem 2.20.

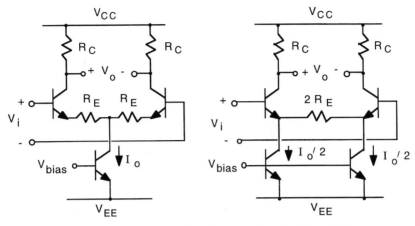

Figure 2-92   Differential gain stages for Problem 2.23.

effective transconductance G_m, expressing each in terms of the small-signal device parameters r_π, r_e, r_o, and g_m, as appropriate.

2.21 Carry out the analysis for the drain currents in a JFET differential pair leading to Eqs. (2-246) and (2-247).

2.22 Consider the resistive-loaded differential pair circuit of Fig. 2-56 in which the output resistances (r_o) of transistors Q_1 and Q_2 are not neglected. (a) Show that the differential-mode voltage gain becomes

$$A_{vd} = -\frac{g_m R_C}{1 + I_{EE} R_C/2V_A}$$

assuming $\beta_F \gg 1$.
(b) Show that the corresponding common-mode rejection ratio becomes

$$\text{CMRR} = \frac{1 + qV_A/kT}{1 + I_{EE} R_C/2V_A}$$

here it is assumed that $\beta_F r_o \gg R_C$.

2.23 Show that the two differential gain stages in Fig. 2-92 are equivalent. Consider both the differential-mode and common-mode response. Assume that the output resistances of the current source transistors are much larger than R_E.

2.24 (a) Show for the single-ended amplifier of Fig. 2-93 that $v_o = (-A_{vd} + A_{vc})v_i/2$. Neglect the output resistances of the differential-pair transistors.

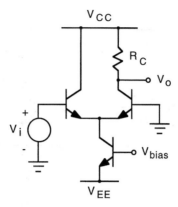

Figure 2-93   Single-ended differential-pair amplifier for Problem 2.24.

(b) Show that the maximum voltage gain (v_o/v_i) is equal to qV_{CC}/kT. Under what conditions is this maximum gain reached?

2.25 Consider the resistive-loaded differential amplifier of Fig. 2-56 in which a resistance R_B is added in each base. Determine the small-signal differential-mode and common-mode voltage gains and the common-mode rejection ratio.

2.26 Design an NMOS differential amplifier using saturated loads as in Fig. 2-69(b). The amplifier is to have a differential voltage gain of 5 and a minimum input signal range of $\pm 1\,\mathrm{V}$. Prescribed are $+6\,\mathrm{V}$ and $-6\,\mathrm{V}$ power supplies. For your design you will need to specify the channel dimensions of transistors M_1–M_4 and the value of the bias current I_{SS}. The fabrication process gives $\mu_n C_{ox}' = 30\,\mu\mathrm{A/V}^2$ and a minimum channel dimension of $1.2\,\mu\mathrm{m}$. You should use the smallest-sized devices that will meet the design specifications. *Note:* You will need to consider the conditions required to ensure transistors M_1 and M_2 remain operating in saturation throughout the input signal range.

2.27 (a) Determine the differential-mode and common-mode voltage gains, the common-mode rejection ratio, and the differential-mode and common-mode input resistances of Fig. 2-58 with $R_C = 10\,\mathrm{k\Omega}$, $R_E = 250\,\Omega$, and $I_{EE} = 500\,\mu\mathrm{A}$. Neglect V_A for Q_1 and Q_2, but not for Q_3. Compare the value of A_{vd} with that evaluated using Eq. (2-257), explaining any discrepancy.
(b) Determine the range in common-mode input voltage over which transistors Q_1–Q_3 remain active with $V_{CC} = +10\,\mathrm{V}$ and $V_{EE} = -10\,\mathrm{V}$. Take $V_{BE\,(on)} = 0.7\,\mathrm{V}$ and $V_{CE\,(sat)} = 0.2\,\mathrm{V}$.

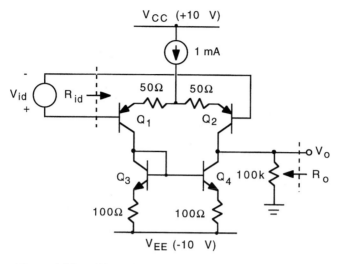

Figure 2-94 Differential amplifier circuit for Problem 2.29.

2.28 Consider the active-loaded differential pair of Fig. 2-65 with a load resistance R_L connected to the output. Show that, neglecting transistor base currents and Early effect, the voltage transfer characteristic is given by

$$V_o = I_{EE} R_L \ \tanh\left(\frac{qV_{id}}{2kT}\right).$$

2.29 Determine the differential input resistance R_{id}, the output resistance R_o, and the small-signal voltage gain v_o/v_i for the differential amplifier of Fig. 2-94. Do **not** neglect the output resistances of the transistors. Check your results by circuit simulation using SPICE.

2.30 The circuit shown in Fig. 2-95 is a current mirror with gain. Determine an expression giving I_2 in terms of I_{ref} and V_d. Neglect the Early effect.

2.31 Figure 2-96 shows two versions of a BiCMOS differential gain stage. For version (a) show that the small-signal voltage gain (neglecting base currents) is given by

$$\frac{v_o}{v_{id}} = \frac{qV_A}{kT(1 + \lambda V_A)}$$

where for version (b),

$$\frac{v_o}{v_{id}} = \frac{2V_A}{1 + \lambda V_A} \sqrt{\frac{\mu_n C'_{ox}(W/L)}{I_{SS}}}$$

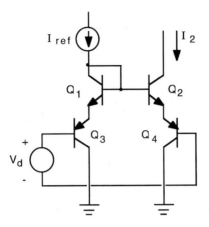

Figure 2-95   Circuit for Problem 2.30.

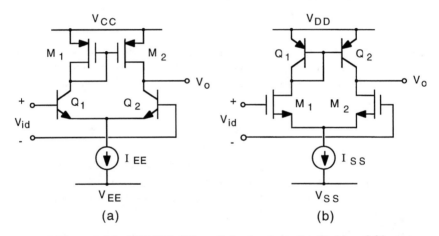

Figure 2-96   BiCMOS differential gain stages for Problem 2.31.

Using the transistor parameters given at the beginning of the problem section, calculate the voltage gains of the two stages. Take $I_{SS} = 300\,\mu A$.

2.32 Consider the emitter follower output stage of Fig. 2-73(a). The linearity in the transfer characteristic can be calculated as $V_o/(V_{in} - V_{BE(on)})$.
(a) Taking

$$V_{BE(on)} = \frac{kT}{q}\,\ln\!\left(\frac{\alpha_F I_Q}{I_{S1}}\right)$$

show that this leads to

$$\text{Linearity} = \frac{1}{1 + \dfrac{kT}{qV_o}\ln\left(1 + \dfrac{V_o}{I_Q R_L}\right)}$$

(b) Consider the circuit in which $V_{CC} = 12\,\text{V}$, $V_{EE} = -12\,\text{V}$, and $I_Q = 20\,\text{mA}$. Calculate the linearity at the maximum output that can occur without clipping of the signal for (i) $R_L = 500\,\Omega$ and (ii) $R_L = 5\,\text{k}\Omega$.

2.33 In a fashion similar to that carried out in Problem 2.32, show that the linearity in the source follower output stage of Fig. 2-73(b) may be expressed as

$$\text{Linearity} = \frac{1}{1 + \dfrac{1}{V_o}\sqrt{\dfrac{2I_Q}{\mu_n C'_{ox}(W/L)_1}}\left[\sqrt{1 + \dfrac{V_o}{I_Q R_L}} - 1\right]}$$

where

$$V_{GS(on)} = V_{TH} + \sqrt{\dfrac{2I_Q}{\mu_n C'_{ox}(W/L)_1}}$$

Calculate the linearity for the same circuit parameters as the emitter follower stage. Take $W/L = 300$ for the MOSFETs.

2.34 For the output stage shown in Fig. 2-97 determine and carefully sketch (including breakpoints, axis intercepts, slopes, etc.) the transfer characteristic V_{out} versus V_{in} for V_{in} ranging from -6 to $+6\,\text{V}$. You may neglect base currents and take $|V_{BE(on)}| = 0.7\,\text{V}$ and $|V_{CE(sat)}| = 0.2\,\text{V}$.

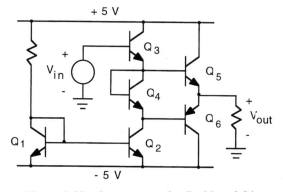

Figure 2-97   Output stage for Problem 2.34.

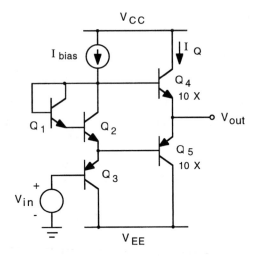

Figure 2-98   741 op amp output stage for Problem 2.35. Transistors Q_4 and Q_5 are identical to their *npn* and *pnp* counterparts, but have 10 times the emitter areas.

2.35 A simplified schematic of the 741 op amp output stage is shown in Fig. 2-98.

(a) Show that at $V_o = 0$, the quiescent bias current of the output transistors is given approximately by

$$I_Q = I_{bias}\sqrt{\frac{I_{S4}I_{S5}}{\beta_{F2}I_{S1}I_{S2}}}$$

(b) What is the maximum value for I_{bias} if the quiescent power dissipation in the output stage is limited to 12 mW? Take $V_{CC} = 15\,V$ and $V_{EE} = -15\,V$.

(c) Assuming $V_{EE} < V_{in} < V_{CC}$, sketch the transfer characteristic V_{out} verses V_{in} for V_{in} ranging from $-15\,V$ to $+15\,V$ Assume $V_{BE\,(on)} = 0.7\,V$.

2.36 A simplified schematic of the 1530 op amp output stage is shown in Fig. 2-99.

(a) Describe qualitatively the operation of the circuit, including the maximum and minimum values for V_o.

(b) Determine the quiescent collector current I_Q and the corresponding input voltage V_{iQ} at $V_o = 0$

(c) Determine the small-signal voltage gain v_o/v_i for V_i near V_{iQ}. Neglect V_A.

(d) Simulate the circuit using SPICE to verify your analysis. Show a plot of V_o versus V_i.

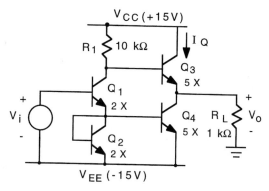

Figure 2-99 1530 op amp output stage for Problem 2.36 *n*X denotes relative emitter areas.

2.37 Repeat the example of Fig. 2-77 using the modified BiCMOS output stage shown in Fig. 2-100. Explain any differences found with this circuit compared to the example circuit.

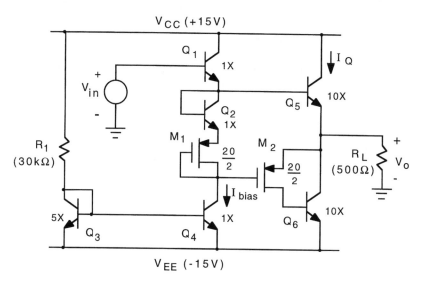

Figure 2-100   Class AB BiCMOS output stage for Problem 2-37. n_X denotes relative emitter areas of the bipolar transistors; the fractions denote the channel-width and channel-length dimensional W/L (μm), respectively, the PMOS transistor.

References

1. G.R. Wilson, "A Monolithic Junction FET-NPN Operational Amplifier," *IEEE J. Solid State Circuits, SC-3*, 341–348 (1968).

2. R.J. Widlar, "Some Circuit Design Techniques for Linear Integrated Circuits," *IEEE Trans. Circuit Theory, CT-12*, pp. 586–590 (1965).

3. A.B. Grebene, *Bipolar and MOS Analog Integrated Circuit Design*, Wiley, New York, 1984, Chap. 4.

4. P.R. Gray and R.G. Meyer, *Analysis and Design of Analog Integrated Circuits*, 3rd ed., Wiley, New York, 1993, p. 215.

5. A.S. Sedra and K.C. Smith, *Microelectronic Circuits*, 2nd ed., Holt, Rinehart and Winston, New York, 1987, Chaps. 2 and 7.

6. A.S. Grove, *Physics and Technology of Semiconductor Devices*, Wiley, New York, 1967, pp. 230–233.

7. K. Tsugaru, Y. Sugimoto, M. Noda, and T. Ito, "A Single-Power-Supply 10-b Video BiCMOS Sample-and-Hold IC," *IEEE J. Solid State Circuits, 25*, 653–659 (1990).

8. P.R. Gray and R.G. Meyer, *Analysis and Design of Analog Integrated Circuits*, 3rd ed., Wiley, New York, 1993, p. 399.

9. L.J. Giacoletto, *Differential Amplifiers*, Wiley, New York, 1970, p. 5.

10. P.R. Gray and R.G. Meyer, *Analysis and Design of Analog Integrated Circuits*, 3rd ed., Wiley, New York, 1993, pp. 299–301.

11. Y.S. Choi, *BiCMOS Operational Amplifier Design*, Ph.D. Dissertation, Arizona State University, 1993, p. 37.

12. K. Fukahori, Y. Nishikawa, and A.R. Hamade, "A High Precision Micropower Operational Amplifier," *IEEE J. Solid State Circuits, SC-14* (1979).

Chapter 3

Operational Amplifiers

An operational amplifier (op-amp) is essentially a differential-input high-gain direct-coupled analog circuit that is used to amplify the difference of two input signals, either voltage or current. Originally, op-amps were very high-gain voltage amplifiers which utilized negative feedback to perform mathematical *operations* on analog signals, hence the name operational amplifier. In recent years, a variety of operational amplifier circuits have evolved with differing behavioral characteristics.

In this chapter, four basic op-amp circuit types are discussed: (1) voltage-feedback amplifiers, (2) current-feedback amplifiers, (3) current-differencing amplifiers, and (4) transconductance amplifiers.

3.1 Voltage-Feedback Amplifiers

Nearly all operational amplifiers operate with feedback, wherein a portion of the output signal is fed back to the inverting input of the amplifier. In a voltage-feedback amplifier, a fraction of the output voltage is combined (out of phase) with the input voltage signal applied to the amplifier. This feedback combined with the forward open-loop voltage gain of the amplifier sets the overall closed-loop response of the amplifier. Figure 3-1 shows an idealized model for a voltage-feedback amplifier. The transfer characteristics of most operational amplifiers can be well approximated by a single-pole response, usually a result of compensation (to be discussed in Chapter 4). For the open-loop voltage gain, we have

$$a(j\omega) = \frac{a_o}{1 + j(\omega/\omega_o)} \tag{3-1}$$

where ω_o is the frequency at which the open-loop gain is down by 3 dB from the gain (a_o) at low frequency (-3 dB frequency).

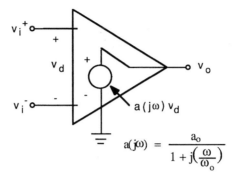

Figure 3-1   Idealized model for a voltage-feedback amplifier.

A noninverting amplifier configuration is shown in Fig. 3-2. Resistors R_1 and R_2 form a voltage divider to feed a fraction of the output voltage back to the inverting input of the amplifier; for negligible amplifier input currents, the feedback signal is $v_{fb} = v_o R_1/(R_1 + R_2)$, which combined at the input gives

$$v_d = v_{in} - \frac{R_1}{R_1 + R_2} v_o \tag{3-2}$$

The closed-loop voltage gain is then

$$\frac{v_o}{v_{in}} \equiv A_v(j\omega) = \frac{a(j\omega)}{1 + a(j\omega) R_1/(R_1 + R_2)} = \frac{a(j\omega)}{1 + T(j\omega)} \tag{3-3}$$

As expressed on the right-hand side of Eq. (3-3) the closed-loop gain is determined by the loop gain $T(j\omega)$, which is equal to the product of the forward open-loop gain of the amplifier $a(j\omega)$ and the voltage-feedback factor $f = v_{fb}/v_o = R_1/(R_1 + R_2)$. Using Eq. (3-1) for the open-loop gain of the amplifier in Eq. (3-3) yields

$$A_v(j\omega) = \frac{1 + R_2/R_1}{1 + j(\omega/\omega_a)} = \frac{A_{vo}}{1 + j(\omega/\omega_a)} \tag{3-4}$$

where A_{vo} is the low-frequency closed-loop voltage gain $(1 + R_2/R_1)$, and ω_a is the frequency at which the closed-loop gain is down by 3 dB and is given by

$$\omega_a = \frac{a_o \omega_o}{A_{vo}} = \frac{\omega_T}{A_{vo}} \tag{3-5}$$

The product of the open-loop gain and 3-dB bandwidth $a_o \omega_o$ represents the unity-gain frequency ω_T. The gain-versus-frequency characteristics of the voltage-feedback amplifier are sketched in Fig. 3-2. Note the gain-bandwidth trade-off: $A_{vo} f_{-3dB} = f_T$.

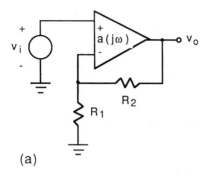

(a)

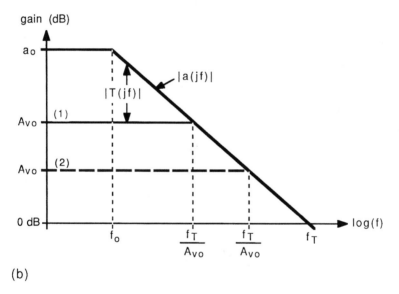

(b)

Figure 3-2   (a) Noninverting amplifier. (b) Gain-versus-frequency characteristics.

Single-Stage Op-Amp

A single-stage operational amplifier consists of a differential-input gain stage and a unity-gain output stage. These simple amplifier circuits are used primarily for high-frequency (but relatively low-gain) amplifiers and for some low-cost multiamplifier integrated-circuit chips (e.g., quad op-amps). Figure 3-3 shows a model of a single-stage op-amp. Compensation is applied at the output

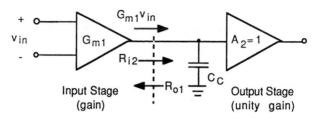

Figure 3-3   Model of a single-stage op-amp.

of the input gain stage and is assumed to dominate the frequency response of the amplifier. The low-frequency open-loop gain is

$$a_o = G_{m1}(R_{o1}||R_{i2}) \tag{3-6}$$

where G_{m1} is the effective transconductance of the input stage, R_{o1} is the output resistance of the input stage and R_{i2} is the input resistance of the output stage. The open-loop -3-dB frequency is

$$\omega_o = \frac{1}{(R_{o1}||R_{i2})C_C} \tag{3-7}$$

and the open-loop unity-gain frequency is

$$\omega_T = \frac{G_{m1}}{C_C} \tag{3-8}$$

A simple single-stage operational-amplifier circuit is shown in Fig. 3-4. For the input stage,

$$G_{m1} = \frac{qI_1}{2kT} \tag{3-9}$$

and

$$R_{o1} = r_{o2}||r_{o4} = \frac{2}{I_1}\left(\frac{V_A^{NPN} V_A^{PNP}}{V_A^{NPN} + V_A^{PNP}}\right) \tag{3-10}$$

The intrinsic voltage gain of the input stage is

$$G_{m1}R_{o1} = \frac{V_A(\text{eff})}{kT/q} \tag{3-11}$$

where

$$V_A(\text{eff}) = \frac{V_A^{NPN} V_A^{PNP}}{V_A^{NPN} + V_A^{PNP}} \tag{3-12}$$

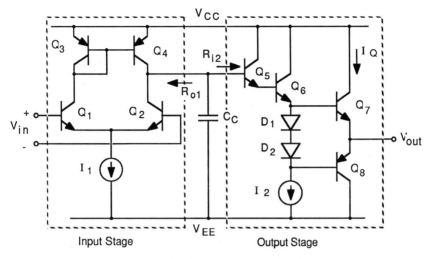

Figure 3-4 Simple single-stage operational amplifier.

The voltage gain of the input stage is thus determined by the ratio of the effective Early voltage of the input stage transistors to the thermal voltage. Assuming a worst-case condition with a short circuit at the output, the input resistance of the output stage is

$$R_{i2} = 2r_{\pi 5} + \beta_5 \beta_6 (r_{\pi 7}) \| (2r_d + r_{\pi 8}) \tag{3-13}$$

where r_d is the small-signal resistance of diodes D_1 and D_2. Assuming equal *NPN* current gains for transistors Q_5 and Q_6, Eq. (3-13) can be expressed as

$$R_{i2} = \beta_{NPN}^2 \frac{kT}{qI_Q} \left[\frac{I_Q}{I_2} + \beta_{NPN} \left\| \left(\frac{I_Q}{I_2} + \beta_{PNP} \right) \right. \right] \tag{3-14}$$

Normally, the quiescent bias current (I_Q) in the output transistors is of the same order as the bias current I_2. Thus,

$$R_{i2} \approx \beta_{NPN}^3 \frac{kT}{qI_Q} \left(\frac{1}{1 + \dfrac{\beta_{NPN}}{\beta_{PNP}}} \right) \tag{3-15}$$

and is typically much larger than the output resistance of the input stage (R_{o1}). The voltage gain of the output stage is approximately unity, giving for the overall low-frequency open-loop gain of the amplifier:

$$a_o \approx \frac{V_A \,(\text{eff})}{kT/q} \tag{3-16}$$

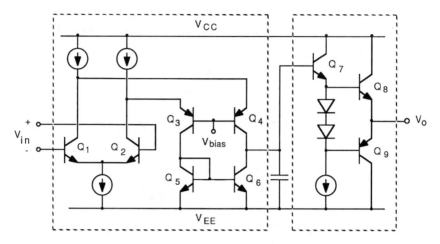

Figure 3-5   Simplified schematic of the HA-2500 single-stage op-amp.

As an example, if the *NPN* and *PNP* Early voltages are 100 V each, then at room temperature, $a_o = 50$ V/0.025 V = 2000 (or 66 dB).

A simplified schematic of the HA-2500 single-stage operational amplifier is shown in Fig. 3-5. In the input stage, the cascode connections of Q_1–Q_4 and Q_2–Q_3 form a folded-cascode differential amplifier. This configuration gives a higher bandwidth than a simple differential pair due to the reduced Miller capacitance effect on the input stage.

Two-Stage Op-Amp

The most common operational amplifier is the two-stage configuration. As illustrated in Fig. 3-6, the two-stage op-amp consists of two gain stages and an output stage. As such, these amplifiers have higher gain than single-stage

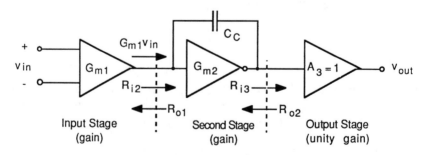

Figure 3-6   Model of a two-stage op-amp.

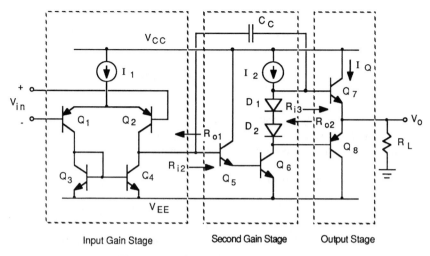

Figure 3-7   Simple two-stage op-amp.

op-amps, but they have larger phase shift, requiring additional compensation to ensure stability. The low-frequency open-loop gain is

$$a_o = G_{m1}(R_{o1}||R_{i2})G_{m2}(R_{o2}||R_{i3}) \qquad (3\text{-}17)$$

where G_{m1} and G_{m2} are the effective transconductance of the input and second gain stages, respectively, R_{o1} and R_{o2} are the output resistance of the input and second gain stages, respectively, and R_{i2} and R_{i2} are the input resistance of the second gain and output stages, respectively.

A simple two-stage operational-amplifier circuit is shown in Fig. 3-7. For the input stage, G_{m1} and R_{o1} are the same as given in Eqs. (3-9) and (3-10), respectively. For the second gain stage

$$G_{m2} = \frac{g_{m6}}{2} = \frac{qI_2}{2kT} \qquad (3\text{-}18)$$

$$R_{i2} = 2r_{\pi5} = \frac{2\beta_{NPN}^2}{g_{m6}} = \frac{2\beta_{NPN}^2 kT}{qI_2} \qquad (3\text{-}19)$$

and

$$R_{o2} = \begin{cases} (2r_d + r_{o6})||r_{oI2}, & V_o \text{ positive} \\ r_{o6}||(2r_d + r_{oI2}), & V_o \text{ negative} \end{cases} \qquad (3\text{-}20)$$

where r_d is the small-signal diode resistance of diodes D_1 and D_2, and r_{oI2} is the output resistance of the bias current source I_2. In Eq. (3-18), we have assumed equal current gains for transistors Q_5 and Q_6. For positive output, transistor Q_7 is on, whereas for negative output, transistor Q_8 is on. Thus, the input resistance of the output stage is given by

$$R_{i3} = \begin{cases} r_{\pi7} + \beta_{NPN} R_L, & V_o \text{ positive} \\ r_{\pi8} + \beta_{PNP} R_L, & V_o \text{ negative} \end{cases} \qquad (3\text{-}21)$$

Because the *PNP* beta is usually smaller than the *NPN* beta, the second equation for R_{i3} represents the worst-case loading on the second gain stage. In addition, R_{o2} will normally be much larger than R_{i3}.

High-Frequency Characteristics

A first-order ac circuit model to analyze the high-frequency characteristics of the two-stage op-amp depicted in Fig. 3-7 is shown in Fig. 3-8 [1]; in this model it is assumed that the compensation capacitance C_C dominates the response of the amplifier. The input stage provides a small-signal drive current of $g_m v_i$ to the second gain stage, which, at high frequencies flows mainly through C_C. The high gain of the second stage places its input at near ac ground potential, giving an output voltage of

$$v_o \approx \frac{g_m v_i}{s C_C} \qquad (3\text{-}22)$$

The open-loop unity-gain frequency is then

$$\omega_T = 2\pi f_T = \frac{g_m}{C_C} \qquad (3\text{-}23)$$

where g_m is given by $q I_1 / 2kT$.

In practice, the value of C_C is chosen such that ω_T is less than or equal to the dominant open-loop pole frequency of the uncompensated amplifier; this

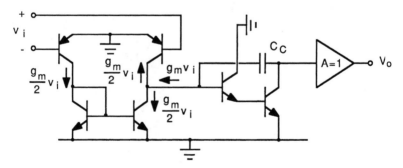

Figure 3-8   First-order ac circuit model to characterize small-signal frequency response.

forces the phase response to be dominated by the compensation capacitance, providing amplifier stability (to be discussed in Chapter 4). For most general-purpose operational amplifiers, C_C will range in value from about 20 to 50 pF. As an example, at room temperature with $I_1 = 20\,\mu A$ and $C_C = 25\,pF$,

$$f_T = \frac{qI_1}{4\pi kTC_C} = \frac{20 \times 10^{-6}}{(4\pi)(0.026)(25 \times 10^{-12})} = 2.45\,\text{MHz} \qquad (3\text{-}24)$$

Slew Rate

The *slew rate* is a parameter used to characterize the rate at which the output voltage of an operational amplifier can change; it is usually expressed in volts per microsecond and is determined as the maximum rate of change in output voltage for a large-signal step input. In practice, for op-amps whose frequency response is dominated by the compensation capacitance, the slew rate is limited by the maximum rate that the compensation capacitance can be charged or discharged. Figure 3-9 shows a simplified model to calculate the slew rate for a two-stage op-amp [1]. As depicted in the figure, for a large positive step input, Q_2 will turn off and Q_1 will conduct the full input stage bias current, I_1. This current, flowing into the reference transistor Q_3, is mirrored in Q_4, giving a maximum output current $I_o = I_1$ to charge C_C: $C_C dV_o/dt = I_1$. The slew rate is thus determined by

$$\text{S.R.} = \frac{I_1}{C_C} \qquad (3\text{-}25)$$

Relating the transconductance of the input stage transistors to I_1, the slew rate can be expressed in terms of the open-loop unity-gain frequency, Eq. (3-23):

$$\text{S.R.} = \frac{I_1}{g_m}\omega_T = \frac{2kT}{q}\omega_T \qquad (3\text{-}26)$$

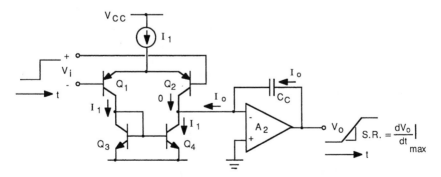

Figure 3-9   Simplified model to calculate slew rate.

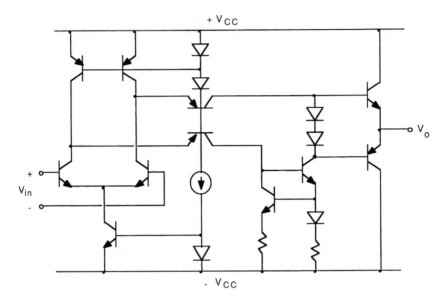

Figure 3-10   Simplified schematic of LM-6365 high-speed operational amplifier.

The slew rate (for the case of a simple bipolar input stage) is thus independent of the input stage bias current; the increase in transconductance accompanying an increase in bias current produces a higher amplifier gain, which requires a larger compensation capacitance to set ω_T. For the example above with $I_1 = 20\,\mu\text{A}$ and $C_C = 25\,\text{pF}$, the slew rate is 0.8 V/μs. Careful design with high-frequency transistors can produce high-performance amplifiers with improved slew rate. A simplified schematic of the LM-6365 high-speed operational amplifier is shown in Fig. 3-10. It boasts an f_T of 725 MHz and a slew rate of 300 V/μs.

As expressed by Eq. (3-26), the slew rate for a given f_T is determined by the I_1/g_m ratio of the input stage, which for the simple bipolar circuit of the type depicted in Fig. 3-9, is fixed at $2kT/q$; altering the circuit to increase the I_1/g_m ratio can improve the slew rate. One method is to use emitter degeneration to reduce the transconductance of the input stage, illustrated in Fig. 3-11. Here, the transconductance of the input stage is reduced by a factor of $1 + g_m R_E$, giving an increased slew rate of

$$\text{S.R.} = \left(\frac{2kT}{q} + I_1 R_E\right)\omega_T \tag{3-27}$$

In the example above with $I_1 = 20\,\mu\text{A}$ and $R_E = 20\,\text{k}\Omega$, the slew rate would increase from 0.8 V/μs to about 7 V/μs. The physical reason for the increase

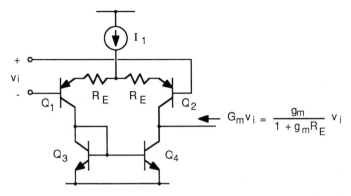

Figure 3-11   Reduction of input stage transconductance using emitter degeneration.

is that with emitter degeneration the gain of the input stage is reduced, lowering the overall open-loop gain of the amplifier, thereby requiring a smaller value of compensation capacitance C_C. The input stage bias current is the same; therefore, as indicated by Eq. (3-25), the slew rate increases. The drawback to using emitter degeneration is that mismatches in the resistor values produce a dc input offset voltage.

Another method to increase the I_1/g_m ratio is to use field-effect transistors in the input stage, such as illustrated in Fig. 3-12 with p-channel JFETs. At a given bias current, the transconductance of a field-effect transistor is much less than that of a bipolar transistor, increasing the slew rate by a factor of perhaps 10–30 for a typical FET device. A disadvantage is the increased input offset voltage with field-effect transistors over bipolar transistors.

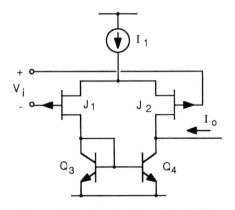

Figure 3-12   Input stage using JFETs.

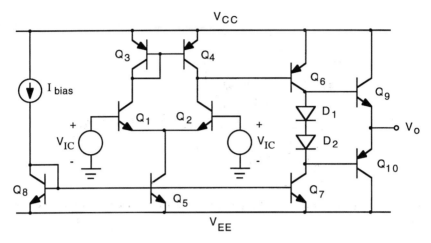

Figure 3-13   Operational-amplifier circuit illustrating common-mode input range.

Common-Mode Input Range

The common-mode input range is the maximum range in dc voltage that can be applied simultaneously to both inputs without causing the op-amp to cease operating normally. This range is an important parameter because it represents the maximum dc levels of signals that may be applied to the amplifier inputs; as such, a wide common-mode input range is desirable. The limits in input range are reached when one or more of the transistors in the amplifier no longer operate in the active region, usually in the input stage.

As an example, consider the operational-amplifier circuit shown in Fig. 3-13. The lower limit on V_{IC} is reached when current source transistor Q_5 saturates:

$$V_{IC}^- = V_{BE1,2} + V_{CE5} + V_{EE} \approx V_{BE(on)} + V_{CE(sat)} + V_{EE} \qquad (3\text{-}28)$$

The upper limit on V_{IC} is reached when differential-pair transistor Q_2 saturates:

$$V_{IC}^+ = V_{CC} - V_{EB6} - V_{CE2} + V_{BE2} \approx V_{CC} - V_{CE(sat)} \qquad (3\text{-}29)$$

Thus, for this example, the common-mode input range is from about 1 V above the V_{EE} supply to about 0.1 V below the V_{CC} supply. This common-mode range is usually adequate when power supply voltages are relatively large; for operational amplifiers operated from low supply voltages (say, 1–2 V), this range may pose some limitations in certain applications. There are modifications to the input stage which can extend this common-mode input range [2].

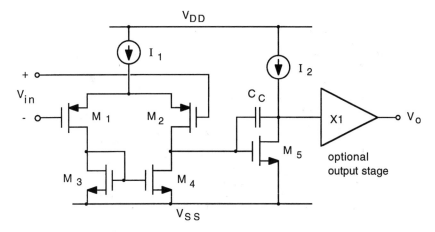

Figure 3-14   Simple two-stage CMOS op-amp.

Two-Stage CMOS Op-Amp

A simple two-stage operational amplifier implemented in CMOS technology is shown in Fig. 3-14 [3]. Transistors M_1–M_4 comprise an active-loaded differential-pair input stage, and M_5, with an active load provided by I_2, is a common-source second gain stage. For applications with light external loads, the amplifier does not use an output stage. The low-frequency, open-circuit, open-loop voltage gain is

$$a_o = G_{m1} R_{o1} G_{m2} R_{o2} \tag{3-30}$$

with

$$G_{m1} = g_{m1} = \sqrt{\mu_p C'_{ox} (W/L)_1 I_1} \tag{3-31}$$

$$R_{o1} = r_{o2} \| r_{o4} = \frac{2}{I_1} \left(\frac{1}{\lambda_N + \lambda_P} \right) \tag{3-32}$$

$$G_{m2} = g_{m5} = \sqrt{2 \mu_n C'_{ox} (W/L)_5 I_2} \tag{3-33}$$

and

$$R_{o2} = r_{o5} \| r_{oI2} \tag{3-34}$$

where r_{oI2} is the output resistance of the second stage bias current source I_2. Owing to the smaller transconductances, the CMOS op-amp will have a lower gain than its bipolar counterpart operating at the same bias current.

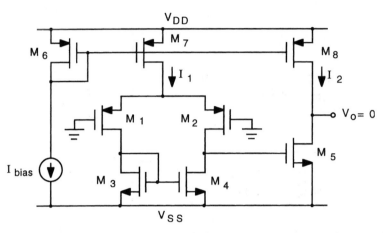

Figure 3-15   Two-stage CMOS op-amp illustrating offset constraints. (From Ref. 3)

The slew rate of the CMOS amplifier is

$$\text{S.R.} = \frac{I_1}{g_{m1}} \omega_T = \sqrt{\frac{I_1}{\mu} C'_{\text{ox}} (W/L)_1} \cdot \omega_T \tag{3-35}$$

Because of the lower g_m/I ratio for MOSFET devices, the CMOS amplifier generally has a higher slew rate than a comparable bipolar amplifier.

As discussed in Ref. 3, the relatively low gain per stage of the CMOS operational amplifier results in the input-referred dc offset voltage being heavily dependent on both the differential input stage and the second gain stage, unlike the bipolar amplifier in which the much higher gain per stage results in the input offset voltage being determined primarily by the gain of the input stage alone. Consequently, design constraints are placed on the relative channel-width–channel-length (W/L) dimensions of the transistors in the CMOS amplifier. In the two-stage CMOS op-amp shown in Fig. 3-15, we desire $V_o = 0$ with the inputs grounded. In the input stage, $I_{D4} = I_{D3} = I_1/2$, and assuming matched transistors, we have, therefore, $V_{DS4} = V_{DS3} = V_{GS3}$; thus, $V_{GS5} = V_{GS4}$, which using Eq. (1-81) leads to

$$\frac{I_{D4}}{(W/L)_4 (1 + \lambda_N V_{DS4})} = \frac{I_{D5}}{(W/L)_5 (1 + \lambda_N V_{DS5})} \tag{3-36}$$

where

$$V_{DS4} \approx V_{TN} + \sqrt{\frac{I_1}{\mu_n C'_{\text{ox}} (W/L)_4}}$$

and

$$V_{DS5} = -V_{SS}$$

Now $V_{GS7} = V_{GS8}$, which, noting that $I_{D7} = 2I_{D4}$ and $I_{D8} = I_{D5}$, gives

$$\frac{2I_{D4}}{(W/L)_7 (1 + \lambda_P V_{SD7})} = \frac{I_{D5}}{(W/L)_8 (1 + \lambda_P V_{SD8})} \tag{3-37}$$

where

$$V_{SD7} = V_{DD} - V_{SG2} \approx V_{DD} + V_{TP} - \sqrt{\frac{I_1}{\mu_P C'_{ox} (W/L)_2}}$$

and

$$V_{SD8} = V_{DD}$$

Combining Eqs. (3-36) and (3-37), the zero offset voltage constraint is

$$\frac{\left(\dfrac{W}{L}\right)_5 (1 - \lambda_N V_{SS})}{\left(\dfrac{W}{L}\right)_4 \left[1 + \lambda_N \left(V_{TN} + \sqrt{\dfrac{I_1}{\mu_n C'_{ox} (W/L)_4}}\right)\right]} =$$

$$\frac{2\left(\dfrac{W}{L}\right)_8 (1 + \lambda_P V_{DD})}{\left(\dfrac{W}{L}\right)_7 \left[1 + \lambda_P \left(V_{DD} + V_{TP} - \sqrt{\dfrac{I_1}{\mu_p C'_{ox} (W/L)_7}}\right)\right]} \tag{3-38}$$

In practice, the channel lengths (L) of the NMOS and PMOS transistors are held fixed, and the channel widths (W) are scaled to fit the constraint requirements.

EXAMPLE. Determine the required channel width (W) of transistor M_5 to achieve zero offset in the amplifier shown in Fig. 3-15 in which $V_{DD} = 10\,V$, $V_{SS} = -10\,V$, and $I_{bias} = 50\,\mu A$. For the transistors, $\mu_n C'_{ox} = 30\,\mu A/V^2$, $V_{TN} = 1\,V$, $\lambda_N = 0.02\,V^{-1}$, $\mu_p C'_{ox} = 10\,\mu A/V^2$, $V_{TP} = -1\,V$, and $\lambda_P = 0.02\,V^{-1}$. The channel lengths (L) are all $2\,\mu m$; the channel widths are $W_{1,2,3,4,6,7} = 20\,\mu m$ and $W_8 = 40\,\mu m$.

The first- and second-stage bias currents are

$$I_1 = \frac{(W/L)_7 (1 + \lambda_P V_{SD7})}{(W/L)_6 (1 + \lambda_P V_{SD6})} I_{bias} \quad \text{and} \quad I_2 = \frac{(W/L)_8 (1 + \lambda_P V_{SD8})}{(W/L)_6 (1 + \lambda_P V_{SD6})} I_{bias}$$

respectively, with

$$V_{SD6} = V_{SG6} \approx -V_{TP} + \sqrt{\frac{2I_{bias}}{\mu_p C'_{ox}(W/L)_6}} = 2\ V$$

$$V_{SD7} = V_{DD} - V_{SG2} \approx V_{DD} + V_{TP} - \sqrt{\frac{\frac{(W/L)_7}{(W/L)_6}\frac{I_{bias}}{2}}{\mu_p C'_{ox}\left(\frac{W}{L}\right)_2}} = 8.29\ V$$

$$V_{SD8} = V_{DD} = 10\ V$$

This gives $I_1 = 56.0\ \mu A$ and $I_2 = 115\ \mu A$. Now,

$$V_{DS4} \approx V_{TN} + \sqrt{\frac{I_1}{\mu_n C'_{ox}(W/L)_4}} = 1.43\ V$$

Using Eq. (3-38), the offset constraint on M_5 is

$$\left(\frac{W}{L}\right)_5 = \frac{(2)(40/2)[1+(0.02)(10)](20/2)[1+(0.02)(1.43)]}{(20/2)[1+(0.02)(8.29)][1-(0.02)(-10)]} = 35.27$$

Thus, $W_5 = 35.27 \times 2\ \mu m = 70.54\ \mu m$.

3.2 Current-Feedback Amplifiers

In a current-feedback amplifier, a fraction of the output current is combined at the inverting input to the amplifier. These current-mode circuits can provide larger closed-loop bandwidths and higher slewing rates than their voltage-mode (i.e., voltage-feedback amplifier) counterparts [4]. Figure 3-16 shows an

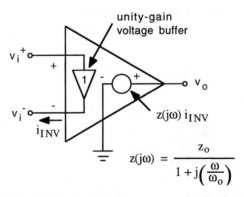

Figure 3-16   Idealized model for a current-feedback amplifier.

idealized model for a current-feedback amplifier. The amplifier contains a unity-gain voltage buffer between the inverting and noninverting inputs, causing the voltage at the input nodes to be equal. For an ideal current-feedback amplifier, the input impedance at the inverting input is zero and the input impedance at the noninverting input is infinite. At the output is a current-controlled voltage source in which the output voltage is proportional to the inverting input current i_{INV} through the *transimpedance* parameter $z(j\omega)$. Again, as a result of compensation in the amplifier, the transimpedance can be well approximated by a single-pole response of the form

$$z(j\omega) = \frac{z_o}{1 + j(\omega/\omega_o)} \tag{3-39}$$

where ω_o is the frequency at which the transimpedance is down by 3 dB from its value (z_o) at low frequency. In general, z_o will be high in value.

A noninverting amplifier configuration is shown in Fig. 3-17. Current is fed back from the output through R_2 to the inverting input of the amplifier; due to the unity-gain buffer between the two inputs, the voltage at the noninverting input is equal to v_{in}, and the feedback current is then $(v_o - v_{in})/R_2$, which, combined at the input, gives

$$i_{INV} = \frac{v_{in}}{R_1} - \frac{v_o - v_{in}}{R_2} = \left(1 + \frac{R_2}{R_1}\right)\frac{v_{in}}{R_2 + z(j\omega)} \tag{3-40}$$

The closed-loop voltage gain is then

$$\frac{v_o}{v_{in}} \equiv A_v(j\omega) = \left(1 + \frac{R_2}{R_1}\right)\frac{z(j\omega)}{R_2 + z(j\omega)} = \left(1 + \frac{R_2}{R_1}\right)\frac{1}{1 + \dfrac{R_2}{z(j\omega)}} \tag{3-41}$$

Using Eq. (3-39) for the transimpedance of the amplifier in Eq. (3-41), and assuming that $z_o \gg R_2$ (generally true), yields

$$A_v(j\omega) = \frac{1 + R_2/R_1}{1 + j(\omega/\omega_a)} = \frac{A_{vo}}{1 + j(\omega/\omega_a)} \tag{3-42}$$

where A_{vo} is the low-frequency closed-loop gain $(1 + R_2/R_1)$ and ω_a is the frequency at which the closed-loop gain is down by 3 dB and is given by

$$\omega_a = \frac{z_o \omega_o}{R_2} \tag{3-43}$$

Note that the 3-dB bandwidth is a function only of the feedback resistance R_2; it is, to first order, independent of the closed-loop gain. Unlike the voltage-feedback amplifier, there is no gain-bandwidth trade-off. With the current-

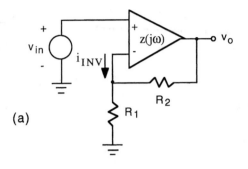

(a)

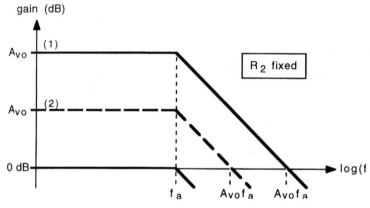

Figure 3-17 **(a) Noninverting current-feedback amplifier. (b) Gain-versus-frequency characteristics.**

feedback amplifier, the bandwidth is set by R_2 and the gain is set by R_1, illustrated for a fixed value of R_2 in the lower portion of Fig. 3-17.

For the unity-gain voltage buffer at the input of the current-feedback amplifier, consider the circuit in Fig. 3-18. Summing the voltage drops around the base-emitter loops of Q_1–Q_4 gives

$$V_i^+ - V_i^- = V_{be3} - V_{eb1} = V_{be2} - V_{eb4} \tag{3-44}$$

Assuming identical *NPN* and *PNP* transistors and neglecting base currents, the base-emitter voltages give

$$\frac{kT}{q} \ln\left(\frac{i_3}{I_S^{NPN}} \frac{I_S^{PNP}}{i_1}\right) = \frac{kT}{q} \ln\left(\frac{i_2}{I_S^{NPN}} \frac{I_S^{PNP}}{i_4}\right) \tag{3-45}$$

which, combined with $i_1 = i_2 = I_o$, yields

$$i_3 i_4 = I_o^2, \quad i_{INV} = i_3 - i_4 \tag{3-46}$$

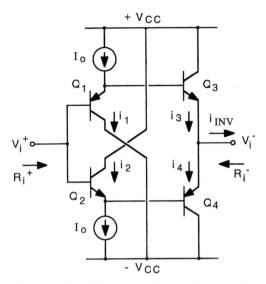

Figure 3-18 Unity-gain voltage buffer circuit.

Under quiescent conditions, $i_{INV} = 0$, $i_3 = i_4 = I_o$, and the input offset voltage from Eq. (3-44) is

$$V_{OS} = V_i^+ - V_i^- = \frac{kT}{q} \ln\left(\frac{I_S^{PNP}}{I_S^{NPN}}\right)$$ (3-47)

The input resistance at the noninverting input is

$$R_i^+ = \frac{\beta_{NPN}\beta_{PNP}}{2g_m}$$ (3-48)

and the input resistance at the inverting input is

$$R_i^- = \frac{1}{2g_m}$$ (3-49)

where $g_m = qI_o/kT$. The input resistance at the noninverting input is thus quite high, and at the inverting input, it is low.

The LH-4012 wideband buffer uses a circuit identical to that in Fig. 3-18 except that resistors are used in place of active bias current sources. The input to the buffer is taken at the noninverting terminal and the output is taken at the inverting terminal. It can provide $\pm 10\,V$ output into a 50Ω load and boasts a 3-dB bandwidth of $500\,MHz$, a slew rate of $12,000\,V/\mu s$, a risetime of $1.2\,ns$, and a phase linearity of $1°$.

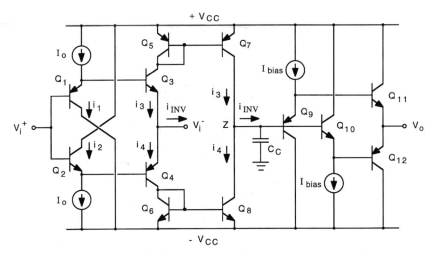

Figure 3-19   Circuit embodiment of a current-feedback amplifier.

A circuit embodiment of a current-feedback amplifier is shown in Fig. 3-19. Reference transistors Q_5 and Q_6, inserted in the inverting side of the unity-gain buffer, sense currents i_3 and i_4, which are mirrored in the current source transistors Q_7 and Q_8, respectively; the net current into node Z is thus equal to i_{INV}. The voltage presented to the output stage is then i_{INV} times the impedance at node Z.

Transimpedance

The impedance at node Z can be determined from the small-signal equivalent circuit for the amplifier depicted in Fig. 3-20. In the circuit, the compensation capacitance C_C usually dominates the response. Current sources i_3 and i_4 reflect the inverting currents from the input buffer, r_{o7} and r_{o8} are the output resistances of transistors Q_7 and Q_8. respectively, and r_{i9} and r_{i10} represent the input

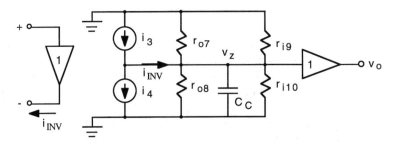

Figure 3-20   Small-signal equivalent circuit of the current-feedback amplifier.

resistances of the output stage looking into the bases of Q_9 and Q_{10}. respectively. From the equivalent circuit, the impedance at node Z is given by

$$z(j\omega) = \frac{z_o}{1 + j\omega z_o C_C} \tag{3-50}$$

where

$$z_o = r_{o7}||r_{o8}||r_{i9}||r_{i10} \tag{3-51}$$

Under worst-case conditions with a short circuit at the output,

$$r_{i9,10} = r_{\pi9,10} + \beta_{9,10}\, r_{\pi11,12} \tag{3-52}$$

$z(j\omega)$ represents the transimpedance of the current-feedback amplifier; its 3-dB frequency is thus

$$\omega_o = \frac{1}{z_o\, C_C} \tag{3-53}$$

The output voltage is then given by $v_o \approx v_z = i_{INV}\, z_o$.

Slew Rate

To first order, the slew rate of the current-feedback amplifier is not limited by internal bias currents in the circuit, as is the case for the voltage-feedback amplifier [see, for exampte, Eq. (3-25)]. Figure 3-21 depicts a first-order model to characterize the slew rate of the current-feedback amplifier. The slew rate is limited by the charging current of C_C,

$$\text{S.R.} = \frac{i_C}{C_C} \approx \frac{i_{INV}}{C_C} \tag{3-54}$$

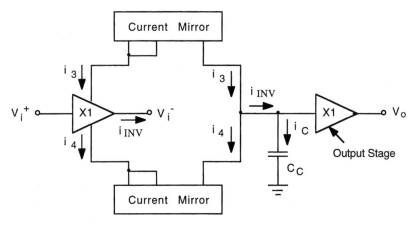

Figure 3-21   Slew rate model.

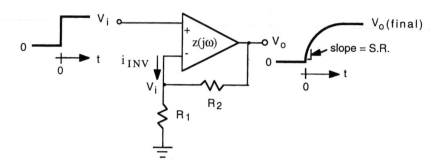

Figure 3-22   Slew rate for noninverting amplifier configuration.

i_{INV} is determined by the external circuit. Also, the required compensation capacitance is generally small for a current-feedback amplifier, thus the slew rate can be quite large.

Consider a noninverting amplifier configuration, as illustrated in Fig. 3-22. With a positive step voltage applied at the input, the output is initially zero. The inverting input current at $t = 0$ is

$$i_{\text{INV}}(0) = \frac{V_i}{R_1 \| R_2} = \frac{V_i}{R_2}\left(1 + \frac{R_2}{R_1}\right) = \frac{V_i A_{vo}}{R_2} \tag{3-55}$$

But, $V_i A_{vo}$ is the final value of the output voltage. Thus, the slew rate is given by

$$\text{S.R.} = \frac{V_o(\text{final})}{R_2 C_C} = \frac{\omega_o z_o}{R_2} V_o(\text{final}) = \omega_a V_o(\text{final}) \tag{3-56}$$

As an example, take $f_a = 100\,\text{MHz}$ and $V_o = 5\,\text{V}$: According to Eq. (3-56), the slew rate would be $3100\,\text{V}/\mu\text{s}$.

A simplified schematic of the OPA603 current-feedback amplifier is shown in Fig. 3-23. Here, instead of current mirrors, current sampling resistors are used in the collectors of the input buffer. Over a range in voltage gain of 1–10, this circuit exhibits a bandwidth of 100 MHz and a slew rate of 1000 V/μs.

3.3 Current-Differencing Amplifiers

A current-differencing amplifier (also referred to as a Norton amplifier) produces an output voltage that is proportional to the difference in the input currents; this is in contrast to the voltage-feedback amplifiers discussed in Section 3.1 wherein the output voltage of the amplifier is proportional to the difference in the input voltages. These amplifiers can be readily operated from

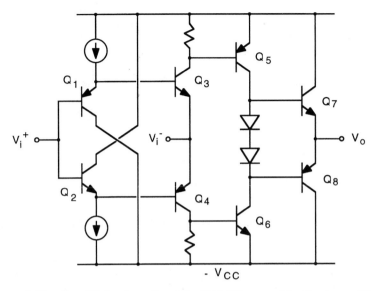

Figure 3-23 Simplified schematic of the OPA603 current-feedback amplifier.

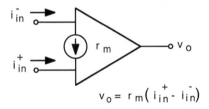

$$v_o = r_m (i_{in}^+ - i_{in}^-)$$

Figure 3-24 Idealized model for a current-differencing amplifier.

a single supply and, as such, find application in industrial and automotive control systems [5].

A model representation of the current-differencing amplifier is shown in Fig. 3-24. The output voltage is proportional to the difference in the input currents $(i_{in}^+ - i_{in}^-)$ through the *transresistance* parameter r_m. At the input of the amplifier is a current-differencing circuit, such as that illustrated in Fig. 3-25(a). This circuit is essentially a current mirror in which the noninverting input current, i_{in}^+, serves as the reference current, which is mirrored in the collector of Q_2. The output current is thus equal to the difference between i_{in}^+ and i_{in}^-.

The basic gain stage of the current-differencing amplifier derives from the circuit depicted in Fig. 3-25(b), which consists of a common-emitter (Q_1)–emitter follower (Q_2) cascade. The output current of the stage is approximately $-\beta_1 \beta_2 i_{in}$. Although this circuit can provide adequate gain, it requires a dc input

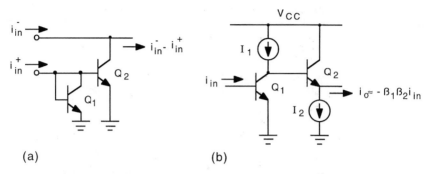

Figure 3-25   (a) Current differencing. (b) Basic gain stage.

current that is equal to the maximum output current divided by $\approx \beta^2$; the input current could be several microamperes for a peak output current of tens of milliamperes, for example. To further reduce the input current requirements, an additional buffer is added to the gain stage. Figure 3-26 shows a schematic of the complete current-differencing amplifier; the *pnp* emitter follower (Q_4) provides additional buffering for the gain stage. The small-signal output voltage is given by

$$v_o = \beta_3 \, \Delta i_{in} \, R_{i4} \| r_{o3} \tag{3-57}$$

where

$$\Delta i_{in} = i_{in}^+ - i_{in}^- \tag{3-58}$$

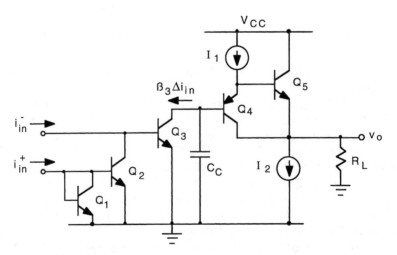

Figure 3-26   Schematic of a current-differencing (Norton) amplifier (MC-3301 type).

R_{i4} is the small-signal resistance seen looking into the base of Q_4 and is given by

$$R_{i4} = r_{\pi 4} + \beta_4 (r_{\pi 5} + \beta_5 R_L) = \beta_4 \left[\frac{kT}{qI_1} + \beta_5 \left(\frac{kT}{q(I_2 - I_1)} + R_L \right) \right] \quad (3\text{-}59)$$

r_{o3} is the output resistance of transistor Q_3 and is determined from

$$r_{o3} = \frac{\beta_4 V_{A3}}{I_1} \quad (3\text{-}60)$$

EXAMPLE. Determine the open-loop gain of the amplifier in Fig. 3-26. The circuit parameters are $I_1 = 200\ \mu\text{A}$, $I_2 = 1.2\ \text{mA}$, and $R_L = 5\ \text{k}\Omega$. The transistor parameters are $V_A^{NPN} = 100\ \text{V}$, $\beta_F^{NPN} = 100$, and $\beta_F^{PNP} = 40$. Assume room temperature. From Eq. (3-60),

$$r_{o3} = \frac{(40)(100\ \text{V})}{200\ \mu\text{A}} = 20\ \text{M}\Omega$$

Using the right-hand side of Eq. (3-59),

$$R_{i4} = (40) \left[\frac{26\ \text{mV}}{0.2\ \text{mA}} + (100) \left(\frac{26\ \text{mV}}{1.2\ \text{mA} - 0.2\ \text{mA}} + 5000\ \Omega \right) \right] = 20.1\ \text{M}\Omega$$

Thus,

$$v_o = (100)(20.1\ \text{M}\Omega \| 20\ \text{M}\Omega)\ \Delta i_{\text{in}} = 1 \times 10^9\ \Delta i_{\text{in}}$$

The transresistance is very large. In a closed-loop circuit, this large gain forces the difference between i_{in}^+ and i_{in}^- to be quite small, analogous to $v_i^+ \approx v_i^-$ in a voltage-difference amplifier.

Inverting Amplifier

To illustrate an application of a current-differencing amplifier, consider the inverting amplifier shown in Fig. 3-27. Note that, unlike a voltage-difference amplifier, the noninverting input cannot be grounded; the potential at this input is equal to V_{be}. Summing the currents at the inverting input gives

$$\frac{v_{\text{in}} - v_1}{R_1} + \frac{v_o - v_1}{R_2} = i_{\text{in}}^- \quad (3\text{-}61)$$

and at the noninverting input

$$v_2 = -i_{\text{in}}^+ R_3 = V_{\text{BE}}^+ \quad (3\text{-}62)$$

Noting that $v_1 = V_{\text{BE}}^-$ and that $V_{\text{BE}}^+ \approx V_{\text{BE}}^- = V_{\text{BE}}$, Eqs. (3-61) and (3-62) combine to give

$$v_o = \left[1 + R_2 \left(\frac{1}{R_1} - \frac{1}{R_3} \right) \right] V_{\text{BE}} - \frac{R_2}{R_1} v_{\text{in}} \quad (3\text{-}63)$$

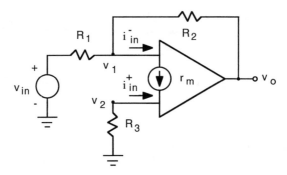

Figure 3-27   Inverting amplifier using a current-differencing op-amp.

If we set the value of R_3 to be equal to $R_1 \| R_2$, then the terms inside the square brackets in Eq. (3-63) cancel, giving

$$v_o = -\frac{R_2}{R_1} v_{in} \qquad (3\text{-}64)$$

A simplified schematic of the LM-3900 Norton op-amp is shown in Fig. 3-28. It differs from the circuit in Fig. 3-26 in that an additional *pnp* transistor (Q_6) is added to the gain stage. This transistor is normally off, but turns on under large-signal excursions to provide additional current sinking capability to improve the transient response (slew rate). Compensation is provided by

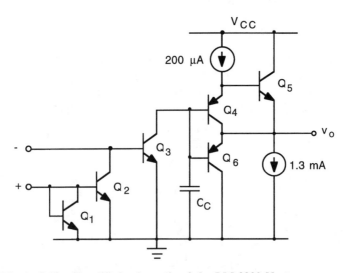

Figure 3-28   Simplified schematic of the LM-3900 Norton op-amp.

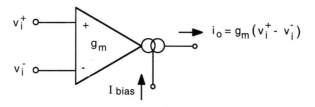

Figure 3-29   Idealized model for a transconductance amplifier.

capacitor C_C, which gives a single-pole response characteristic to the transresistance parameter

$$r(j\omega) = \frac{r_o}{1 + j(\omega/\omega_o)} \tag{3-65}$$

similar to that of the current-feedback amplifier.

3.4 Transconductance Amplifiers

A transconductance amplifier (also referred to as an operational transconductance amplifier, OTA) produces an output current that is proportional to the difference in input voltages; in this sense, the transconductance amplifier operates as a voltage-controlled current source. In addition, the proportionality between input voltage and output current is controlled by an external bias current. These amplifiers can be used in a variety of applications, including low-supply-voltage circuits [6] and active filter circuits [7].

A model representing the transconductance amplifier is shown in Fig. 3-29. The output current is proportional to the difference in input voltages $(v_i^+ - v_i^-)$ through the transconductance parameter g_m, which is controlled by an external bias current, I_{bias}. A basic configuration for a transconductance amplifier is shown in Fig. 3-30; superimposed on the circuit are the small-signal collector currents. At the input stage is a differential pair with current sources for loads. The output stage consists of a complementary pair of current sources driven by the input stage; the collector current in the differential-pair transistor Q_2 provides the reference current for the *pnp* current source, Q_7 and Q_8, whereas the collector current in the current-source transistor Q_4 provides the reference current for the *npn* current source Q_9 and Q_{10}. At the output,

$$i_o = g_m v_{in} \tag{3-66}$$

where

$$g_m = \frac{qI_{bias}}{2kT} \tag{3-67}$$

The external bias current (I_{bias}) is the reference current for the current source (Q_5 and Q_6) biasing the differential pair, thus setting the value of the transconductance.

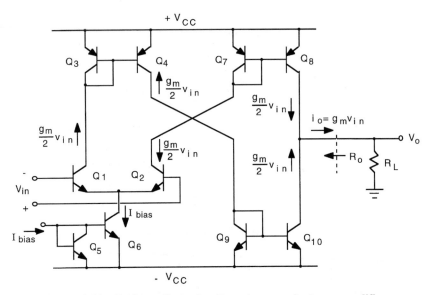

Figure 3-30   Basic configuration for a transconductance amplifier.

With reference to Fig. 3-30, some observations are worthy of note: (1) The output node is a high-impedance point with

$$R_o = r_{o8} || r_{o10} \tag{3-68}$$

Thus, for applications in which a large voltage gain is required, the external load resistance, R_L, must be large (some commercial transconductance amplifiers have output buffers to maintain a high output impedance at this node). (2) All the internal nodes are low-impedance points; they are connected to base-emitter junctions. Thus, the frequency response of the amplifier is determined by the capacitance at the output node. Also, as a result, internal compensation is usually not required.

A small-signal model representing the output of the transconductance amplifier is shown in Fig. 3-31. In the model, C_o represents the output capacitance of the amplifier itself and C_L is any external load capacitance. From the circuit, the small-signal voltage gain (v_o/v_{in}) is given by

$$A_v(j\omega) = \frac{g_m(R_o||R_L)}{1 + j\omega(R_o||R_L)(C_o + C_L)} = \frac{A_{vo}}{1 + j(\omega/\omega_o)} \tag{3-69}$$

where the -3-dB frequency is given by

$$\omega_o = \frac{1}{(R_o||R_L)(C_o + C_L)} \tag{3-70}$$

The low-frequency gain is determined by

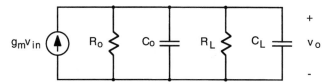

Figure 3-31   Small-signal model for the transconductance amplifier.

$$A_{vo} = \frac{qI_{\text{bias}}}{2kT} (R_o \| R_L) \qquad (3\text{-}71)$$

and is set by the value of the external bias current. This feature finds application in gain-controlled amplifiers. The unity-gain frequency is then given by

$$\omega_T = A_{vo}\,\omega_o = \frac{g_m}{(C_o + C_L)} = \frac{qI_{\text{bias}}}{2kT(C_o + C_L)} \qquad (3\text{-}72)$$

If the transconductance amplifier is operated with negative feedback, the closed-loop bandwidth is given by

$$f_o(\text{CL}) = \frac{A_{vo}}{A_{vo}(\text{CL})} f_o \qquad (3\text{-}73)$$

Because A_{vo} is controlled by I_{bias}, this makes the closed-loop bandwidth controllable by the external bias current; an application employing this feature is in active filters in which the bandwidth is electrically controlled [8]. The gain-bandwidth characteristics of the transconductance amplifier is illustrated in Fig. 3-32.

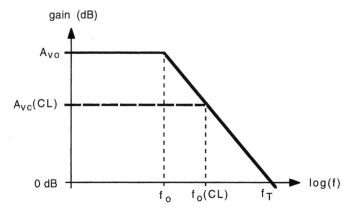

Figure 3-32   Gain-bandwidth characteristics of the transconductance amplifier. CL denotes the closed-loop behavior.

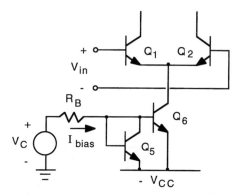

Figure 3-33 A simple circuit to externally control the bias current for the trans-conductance amplifier.

A simple method to set the bias current with an external control voltage is shown in Fig. 3-33. With this scheme, the bias current is determined by

$$I_{bias} = \frac{V_C + V_{CC} - V_{BE}}{R_B} \tag{3-74}$$

Unfortunately, with this circuit, the bias current is dependent on the supply voltage as well as V_{be} (which varies with the collector currents of Q_5 and Q_6). It will be left as a problem for the reader to design a bias control circuit to give I_{bias} as a function of V_C only.

To increase the output resistance of the transconductance amplifier (R_o) and to reduce current source errors, Wilson or cascode current sources are sometimes used in practice. The LM-3080 operational transconductance amplifier, illustrated in Fig. 3-34, utilizes Wilson current sources.

Linearization

Under open-loop operation, the input voltage (V_{in}) may not be small in comparison to the thermal voltage, kT/q. As a result, the transfer characteristic of the amplifier will be nonlinear (due to the exponential relation between the collector currents of the differential pair transistors and the input voltage). Two techniques that can be used to improve linearity are (1) emitter degeneration and (2) diode linearization.

Placing resistors (R_E) in each of the emitter legs of the differential-pair transistors (see Fig. 3-11) increases the linear range of the input by approximately $I_{bias} R_E$ volts. Doing so, however, reduces the gain of the amplifier to the extent

$$i_o = \frac{g_m}{1 + g_m R_E} v_{in} \tag{3-75}$$

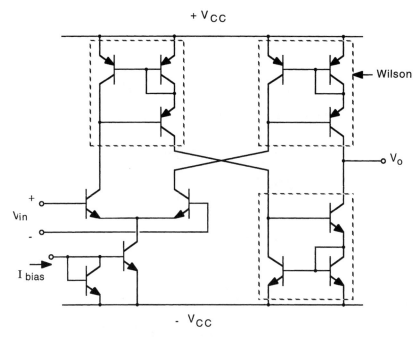

Figure 3-34   Simplified schematic of the LM-3080 operational transconductance amplifier.

A more profitable approach is to place diodes at the inputs of the differential pair, as illustrated in Fig. 3-35; here, the voltages across forward-biased diodes D_1 and D_2 are used to counteract the exponential base-emitter characteristics of transistors Q_1 and Q_2. With reference to Fig. 3-35, the transistor pair currents are

$$i_1 = \frac{I_{\text{bias}}}{1 + e^{-qV_b/kT}} \quad \text{and} \quad i_2 = \frac{I_{\text{bias}}}{1 + e^{qV_b/kT}} \tag{3-76}$$

where the voltage at the base of Q_1 (V_b) is

$$V_b = V_{\text{D2}} - V_{\text{D1}} = \frac{kT}{q} \ln\left(\frac{I_{\text{D2}}}{I_{\text{D1}}}\right) \tag{3-77}$$

Neglecting the base currents in Q_1 and Q_2, the diode currents are $I_{\text{D1}} = (I_D - i_s)$ and $I_{\text{D2}} = (I_D + i_s)$. Thus,

$$V_b = \frac{kT}{q} \ln\left(\frac{I_D - i_s}{I_D + i_s}\right) \tag{3-78}$$

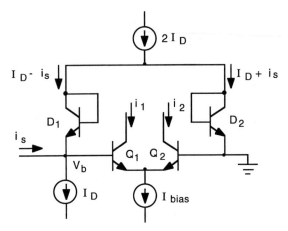

Figure 3-35 **Diode linearization scheme for the input stage of a transconductance amplifier.**

Using Eq. (3-78) in Eq. (3-76), the transistor currents become

$$i_1 = \frac{I_{\text{bias}}(I_D - i_s)}{2I_D} \quad \text{and} \quad i_2 = \frac{I_{\text{bias}}(I_D + i_s)}{2I_D} \tag{3-79}$$

The output current is

$$i_o = i_2 - i_1 = \frac{I_{\text{bias}}}{I_D} i_s \tag{3-80}$$

which is seen to be linear with respect to the input source current, i_s.

This type of diode linearization is employed in many commercial transconductance amplifiers; Figure 3-36 shows a simplified schematic of the LM-13600 operational transconductance amplifier. With this amplifier, g_m is adjustable over six decades in bias current, ranging from 0.1 μA to 1 mA, with good linearity. It has an open-loop bandwidth of 2 MHz and a unity-gain compensated slew rate of 50 V/μs. An optional Darlington buffer is also included.

Applications

Several applications utilizing transconductance amplifiers will now be illustrated: (1) Figure 3-37 illustrates a sample-and-hold circuit; during the *sample* interval, the hold capacitor is charged to voltage $V_{\text{in}} + 2V_{\text{BE}}$. During the *hold* interval, the amplifier is cutoff and the output is equal to the value of the input

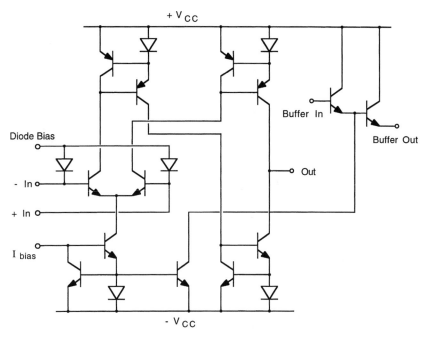

Figure 3-36 Simplified schematic of the LM-13600 operational transconductance amplifier.

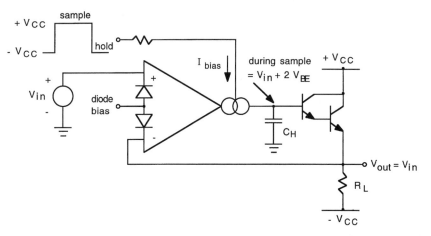

Figure 3-37 Application of a transconductance amplifier in a sample-and-hold circuit.

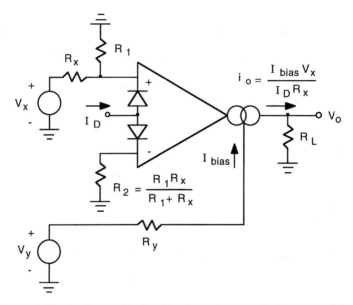

Figure 3-38   Analog multi circuit using a transconductance amplifier.

signal and the end of the previous sample interval. (2) Figure 3-38 shows an
analog multiplier circuit; the y input is used to control the bias current which
sets the gain of the transconductance amplifier in response to the x input. For
a Wilson current source (as in Fig. 3-36), the bias current is given as

$$I_{\text{bias}} = \frac{V_y + V_{\text{CC}} - 2V_{\text{BE}}}{R_y} \qquad (3\text{-}81)$$

which, combined at the output, gives

$$V_o = \frac{R_L}{I_D R_x R_y}[V_x V_y + V_x(V_{\text{CC}} - 2V_{\text{BE}})] \qquad (3\text{-}82)$$

Normally, one would modify the bias current control circuit to give I_{bias} directly
proportional to V_y and thereby eliminate the V_x offset in Eq. (3-82). (3) A
voltage-controlled low-pass filter is illustrated in Fig. 3-39; the 3-dB bandwidth of the filter is given by

$$\omega_o = \frac{g_m R_1}{(R_1 + R_2)C} = \frac{q I_{\text{bias}} R_1}{2kT(R_1 + R_2)C} \qquad (3\text{-}83)$$

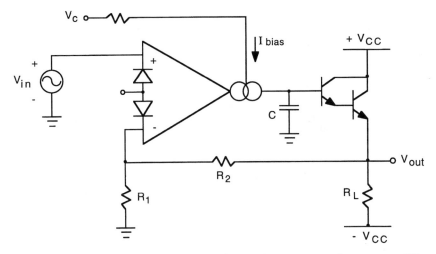

Figure 3-39 **Voltage-controlled low-pass filter using a transconductance amplifier.**

CMOS Transconductance Amplifier

Figure 3-40 illustrates a transconductance amplifier using CMOS transistors. Like the bipolar counterpart, an external bias current sets the transconductance of the differential-pair input stage, which is reflected in the output current: In the circuit, i_2 is the reference current for the current source comprising transistors M_4 and M_6; then, neglecting channel-length modulation and assuming that all PMOS transistors are identical (and that all NMOS transistors are likewise identical), $i_6 = i_2$. Likewise, i_1 is the reference current for the current source comprising transistors M_3 and M_5; thus, $i_5 = i_1$. Also, i_5 is the reference current for the current source comprising transistors M_7 and M_8; thus, $i_8 = i_5$. The output current is then

$$i_o = i_6 - i_8 = i_2 - i_1 \qquad (3\text{-}84)$$

and is equal to the difference in currents in the differential pair M_1 and M_2. Thus,

$$i_o = g_m v_{in} \qquad (3\text{-}85)$$

where

$$g_m = \sqrt{\mu_n C'_{ox} (W/L)_N I_{bias}} \qquad (3\text{-}86)$$

In practice, owing to the effects of channel-length modulation, the effective transconductance of the amplifier will differ somewhat from that calculated by

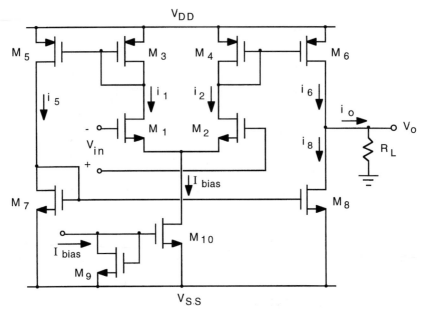

Figure 3-40   CMOS transconductance amplifier.

Eq. (3-86). Also of note: In the CMOS amplifier, the transconductance varies as the *square root* of the bias current, compared to a linear variation in the bipolar amplifier [see Eq. (3-67)]. The output resistance of the amplifier can be increased by using cascode pairs for transistors M_6 and M_8 [9].

Linearization

Figure 3-41 illustrates a scheme by which the linear range of a MOSFET transconductance amplifier can be increased [10]. This technique utilizes two transistors, M_3 and M_4, connected between the sources of the differential pair. These transistors, operating in the triode region, act as voltage-controlled source-degeneration resistances. With reference to the circuit: At node (a) we have $I_1 = I_o + I_3 - I_4$, and at node (b) we have $I_2 = I_o - I_3 + I_4$. For M_3 and M_4 operating in the triode region, we have

$$I_3 = \mu_n C_{ox}' (W/L)* \left[(V_i - V_b - V_{TH}) V_{ab} - \frac{1}{2} V_{ab}^2 \right] \qquad (3-87)$$

and

$$I_4 = \mu_n C_{ox}' (W/L)* \left[(0 - V_a - V_{TH}) V_{ba} - \frac{1}{2} V_{ba}^2 \right] \qquad (3-88)$$

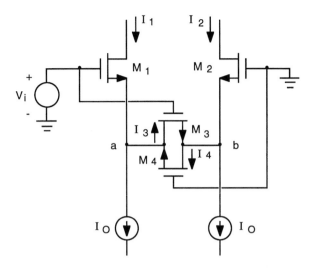

Figure 3-41   Linearization scheme for a MOSFET transconductance amplifier.

where the asterisk is used to denote the channel width/length ratio for the linearization transistors M_3 and M_4 (which is different than that of the differential-pair transistors M_1 and M_2). The node potentials are given by

$$V_a = V_i - V_{GS1} = V_i - V_{TH} - \sqrt{\frac{2I_1}{\mu_n C'_{ox}(W/L)}} \qquad (3\text{-}89)$$

and

$$V_b = -V_{GS2} = -V_{TH} - \sqrt{\frac{2I_2}{\mu_n C'_{ox}(W/L)}} \qquad (3\text{-}90)$$

Defining the output current as $I_1 - I_2 = 2(I_3 - I_4)$, and noting that $V_{ba} = -V_{ab}$, we find

$$I_3 - I_4 = \frac{(W/L)(W/L)^*}{(W/L) + 4(W/L)^*} \sqrt{\frac{2\mu_n C'_{ox}}{(W/L)}} (\sqrt{I_1} + \sqrt{I_2})V_i \qquad (3\text{-}91)$$

Substituting for I_1 and I_2 in terms of I_O, I_3, and I_4, and solving the resulting quadratic equation, we obtain

$$I_1 - I_2 = \frac{4(W/L)^*}{1 + \frac{4(W/L)^*}{(W/L)}} \sqrt{\frac{2\mu_n C'_{ox} I_O}{(W/L)}} V_i \qquad (3\text{-}92)$$

which is linear in V_i. For a given bias current, I_O, there is a relation between the channel width/length ratios which optimizes the linear range; typically this in a range $(W/L) \div (W/L)^*$ of about 3–7.

Problems

For all problems assume room temperature, $kT/q = 26\,\text{mV}$.
Note: Where required, use the following device parameters unless otherwise specified:

NPN: $\beta_F = 100$ $I_S = 2 \times 10^{-16}\,\text{A}$ $V_A = 75\,\text{V}$

PNP: $\beta_F = 50$ $I_S = 5 \times 10^{-17}\,\text{A}$ $V_A = 75\,\text{V}$

NMOS: $W/L = 10$ $\mu_n C'_{ox} = 30\,\mu\text{A}/\text{V}^2$ $V_{TH} = 1\,\text{V}$ $\lambda = 0.02\,\text{V}^{-1}$

PMOS: $W/L = 30$ $\mu_p C'_{ox} = 10\,\mu\text{A}/\text{V}^2$ $V_{TH} = -1\,\text{V}$ $\lambda = 0.02\,\text{V}^{-1}$

3.1 Verify text Eqs (3-6) through (3-8) for the single-stage op-amp model shown in Fig. 3-3.

3.2 For the folded-cascode differential amplifier stage shown in Fig. 3-42 determine:
(a) The low-frequency, small-signal voltage gain, v_{out}/v_{in}, for V_{in} near zero.
(b) The maximum and minimum values for V_{out}. You may assume $|V_{CE(sat)}| = 0.2\,\text{V}$.

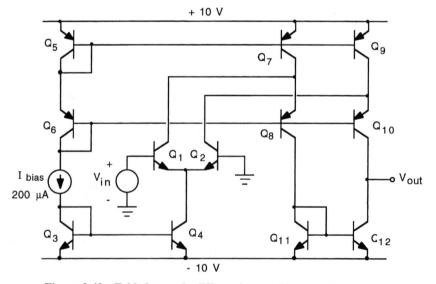

Figure 3-42   Folded-cascode differential amplifier for Problem 3.2.

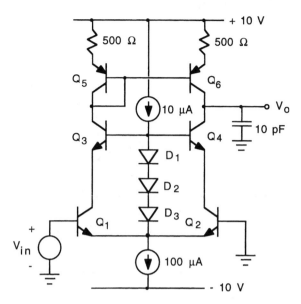

Figure 3-43   Cascode differential amplifier for Problem 3.3.

3.3 (a) For the cascode differential amplifier stage shown in Fig. 3-43 determine the low-frequency small-signal voltage gain A_{vo}. The diodes are fabricated from *NPN* transistors.

(b) The frequency response of the circuit is dominated by the 10-pF load capacitance. Determine the -3-dB frequency for the amplifier stage.

(c) Use SPICE to simulate the circuit to check your results above. Specifically, (1) plot the dc transfer characteristic for V_{in} ranging from -5 mV to $+5$ mV, and (2) plot the small-signal voltage gain versus frequency (log-log plot) for frequency ranging from 1 Hz to 100 MHz.

3.4 For the two-stage voltage op-amp shown in Fig. 3-44, compensation can be achieved either by placing C_C as a feedback capacitor across the second gain stage (a) or as a shunt capacitance at the input of the second stage (b). In either case, C_C dominates the response. For this problem, the current sources can be assumed to be ideal and the output resistances of the transistors can be neglected.

(a) Find the low-frequency voltage gain, A_{vo} and, for the feedback compensation connection, the slew rate, S.R., the unity-gain bandwidth, f_T, and the -3-dB frequency, f_o.

(b) For the shunt compensation connection, find S.R., f_T, and f_o.

3.5 Derive an expression for the low-frequency voltage gain, v_o/v_{in}, for the single-stage op-amp shown in Fig. 3-45. Express your result in terms of

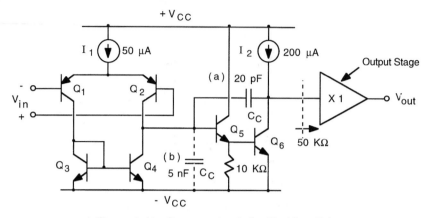

Figure 3-44   Op-amp circuit for Problem 3.4.

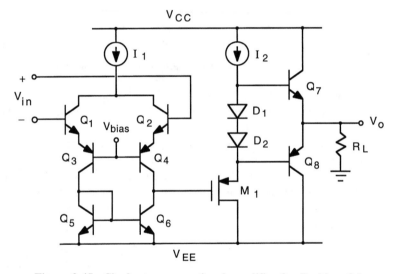

Figure 3-45   Single-stage operational amplifier for Problem 3.5.

the Early voltages of the bipolar transistors and other parameters as needed.

3.6 A two-stage BiCMOS operational amplifier is shown in Fig. 3-46.

(a) Determine an expression for the low-frequency, open-loop voltage gain for V_o near zero. Assume that both output transistors, Q_4 and Q_5, are conducting in this calculation.

(b) Calculate the voltage gain, taking $I_1 = 100\,\mu A$, $I_2 = 200\mu A$, and

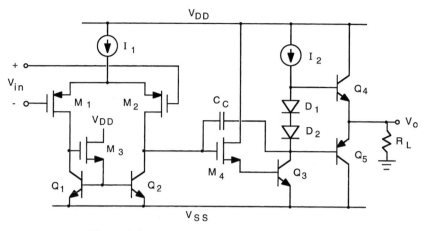

Figure 3-46   BiCMOS op-amp for Problem 3.6.

$R_L = 1 \text{ k}\Omega$. Diode D_1 is fashioned from an *NPN* transistor and diode D_2 is fashioned from a *PNP* transistor.

(c) Determine the common-mode input range for the amplifier.

3.7 The high-speed buffer circuit of Fig. 3-47 is relatively insensitive to the load current in R_L due to the current absorbing capability of Q_9, controlled by feedback through Q_6.

(a) Describe the operation of the circuit, showing that $V_o = V_{in}$, and that this result is maintained under a varying load current.

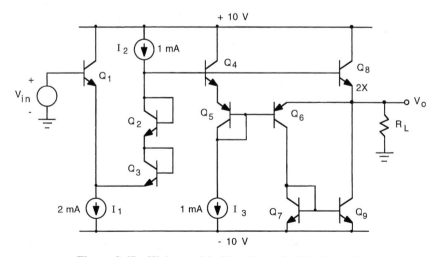

Figure 3-47   High-speed buffer circuit for Problem 3.7.

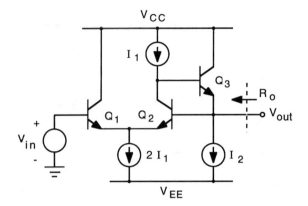

Figure 3-48   Closed-loop buffer circuit for Problem 3.8.

(b) Simulate the circuit using SPICE for values of R_L of $2\,k\Omega$, $5\,k\Omega$, and $20\,k\Omega$, to show V_o versus V_{in} for V_{in} ranging from $-10\,V$ to $+10\,V$. Q_8 is identical to the other *NPN* transistors except for its emitter area which is twice the size.

(c) Show that the input offset voltage (for $V_o = 0$) is given by

$$V_{OS} = \frac{kT}{q} \ln\left(\frac{I_{C1}\,I_{C8}}{2I_{C2}^2}\right)$$

Calculate V_{OS} and compare with that determined from your simulation.

3.8 Figure 3-48 shows a closed-loop unity-gain buffer circuit in which the feedback loop comprising Q_2 and Q_3 provides a low output resistance.
(a) Show that $V_o \approx V_i$, and $R_o \approx 2/\beta_F g_{m2}$.
(b) Show that the input offset voltage is given by

$$V_{OS} = \frac{kT}{q} \ln\left(\frac{I_1 + I_2/\beta_F}{I_1 - I_2/\beta_F}\right)$$

(c) Calculate R_o and V_{OS}, given that $I_1 = I_2 = 500\,\mu A$.

3.9 (a) Calculate the low-frequency value of the transimpedance, z_o, for the current-feedback amplifier depicted in Fig. 3-19. Take $I_o = 1\,mA$, $I_{bias} = 2\,mA$, and assume a near short-circuit load at the output.
(b) The capacitance C_C comprises primarily the base-collector junction capacitance of transistors Q_7 though Q_{10}. If the capacitance of each transistor is $0.05\,pF$, determine the open-loop, -3-dB frequency, f_o, for the amplifier.
(c) Repeat (a) and (b) for a 5-$k\Omega$ load at the output instead of a short circuit; assume that V_o is still near zero for this calculation.

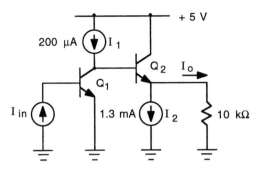

Figure 3-49 Norton gain stage for Problem 3.11.

3.10 For the inverting amplifier shown in Fig. 3-27 with a transresistance parameter $r(j\omega)$ given by Eq. (3-65), show that for $R_3 = R_1 \| R_2$, the closed-loop voltage gain is given by

$$A(j\omega) = \frac{A_{vo}}{1 + j(\omega/\omega_a)}$$

where $A_{vo} = -R_2/R_1$ and $\omega_a = R_2/\omega_o r_o$, assuming that $r_o \gg R_2$.

3.11 (a) For the Norton amplifier gain stage in Fig. 3-49 show that the small-signal output current is given by $i_o \approx -\beta_F^2 i_{in}$, where Q_1 and Q_2 are identical transistors.

(b) Simulate the circuit using SPICE, showing I_o versus I_{in}, for I_{in} ranging from 2 to 5 μA. From the simulation, verify the result in (a). Take $I_S = 2 \times 10^{-15}$ A and $\beta_F = 50$.

3.12 In Fig. 3-50, a transconductance amplifier is used as an inverting amplifier. Show that the small-signal voltage gain is given by

$$\frac{v_o}{v_i} = \frac{1 - g_m R_2}{1 + g_m R_1}$$

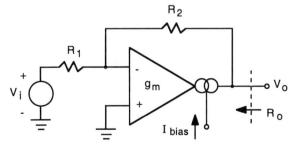

Figure 3-50 Transconductance amplifier circuit for Problem 3.12.

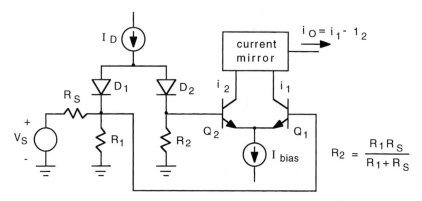

Figure 3-51   Diode-compensated transconductance amplifier circuit for Problem 3.13.

and that the output resistance is given by

$$R_o = \frac{R_1 + R_2}{1 + g_m R_1}$$

3.13 In the diode-compensated transconductance amplifier shown in Fig. 3-51, show that

$$i_o = \frac{I_{\text{bias}} V_S}{I_D R_S}$$

You may neglect base currents and assume that ΔV_{BE} is small relative to V_S.

3.14 For the multiplier circuit using the diode-linearized transconductance amplifier in Fig. 3-52, design a circuit that gives for the multiplier $V_o = K V_x V_y$, where K is a constant. Do **not** use op-amps in your part of the circuit.

3.15 (a) Show that the open-loop, low-frequency voltage gain of the CMOS transconductance amplifier in Fig. 3-40 is given by

$$A_{vo} = \frac{2R_L \sqrt{\mu_n C'_{\text{ox}} (W/L)_N I_{\text{bias}}}}{2 + I_{\text{bias}} R_L (\lambda_N + \lambda_P)}$$

(b) Calculate A_{vo} and the -3-dB frequency for this amplifier operating at a bias current of $100\,\mu\text{A}$ and $R_L = 100\,\text{k}\Omega$ if its unity-gain frequency is $50\,\text{MHz}$.

(c) Show that the optimum bias current which maximizes the voltage gain is given by

$$I_{\text{bias}} (\text{opt}) = \frac{2}{R_L (\lambda_N + \lambda_P)}$$

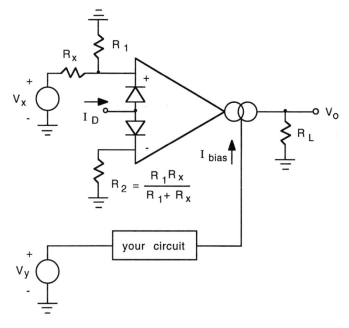

Figure 3-52   Analog multiplier circuit for Problem 3-14.

3.16 Carry through the analysis using Eqs. (3-87), (3-88), and (3-91) to obtain Eq. (3-92) for the linearized MOSFET transconductance amplifier.

References

1. J.E. Soloman, "The Monolithic Op Amp: A Tutorial Study," *IEEE J. Solid-State Circuits*, SC-*9*, 314–332 (Dec. 1974).

2. J.H. Huijsing and D. Linebarger, "Low-Voltage Operational Amplifier with Rail-to-Rail Input and Output Ranges," *IEEE J. Solid-State Circuits*, SC-*20*, 1144–1150 (Dec. 1985).

3. P.R. Gray and R.G. Meyer, "MOS Operational Amplifier Design—A Tutorial Overview," *IEEE J. Solid-State Circuits*, SC-*17*, 969–982 (Dec. 1982).

4. P.E. Allen and M.B. Terry, "The Use of Current Amplifiers for High-Performance Voltage Applications," *IEEE J. Solid-State Circuits*, SC-*15*, 155–162 (Apr. 1980).

5. T.M. Frederiksen, W.F. Davis, and D.W. Zobel, "A New Current-Differencing Single-Supply Operational Amplifier," *IEEE J. Solid-State Circuits*, SC-6, 340–347 (Dec. 1971).

6. O.H. Schade, Jr. and E.J. Kramer, "A Low-Voltage BiMOS Op Amp," *IEEE J. Solid-State Circuits*, SC-*16*, 661–668 (Dec. 1981).

7. R.L. Geiger and E. Sánchez-Sinencio, "Active Filter Design Using Operational Transconductance Amplifiers: A Tutorial," *IEEE Circuits Devices Mag.*, *1-1*, 20–32 (Mar. 1985).

8. K. Fukahori, "A Bipolar Voltage-Controlled Tunable Filter," *IEEE J. Solid-State Circuits*, SC-*16*, 729–737 (Dec. 1981).

9. E.A. Vittoz, "The Design of High-Performance Analog Circuits on Digital CMOS Chips," *IEEE J. Solid-State Circuits*, SC-*20*, 657–665 (Jun. 1985).

10. F. Krummenacher and N. Joehl, "4-MHz CMOS Continuous-Time Filter with On-Chip Automatic Tuning," *IEEE J. Solid-State Circuits*, SC-*23*, 750–758 (Jun. 1988).

Chapter 4

Feedback and Compensation of Feedback Amplifiers

Feedback, whereby a portion of the signal at the output of a circuit is deliberately applied to its input, is used in many analog circuits. Negative feedback is widely used in amplifier circuits to alter their behavioral characteristics. Among them are: (1) a stabilization of the gain with respect to changes in circuit element and device parameter values, variations in supply voltage and temperature, (2) a reduction in distortion and noise effects, (3) an increased bandwidth, and (4) an alteration of the amplifier's input and output impedances.

Amplifiers employing negative feedback may produce self-oscillation if the gain is sufficiently high and the feedback signal is in phase with the input at some frequency; these amplifiers require compensation to stabilize them against self-oscillation.

In this chapter, we examine negative feedback as it applies to amplifier circuits and present a systematic classification and analysis procedure for various feedback configurations. Stability considerations and methods for compensation of feedback amplifiers are also discussed.

4.1 Basic Feedback Concepts

Figure 4-1 shows a block diagram of a general feedback amplifier system. The basic amplifier is characterized by a forward gain a and the feedback network is characterized by its reverse transmission f. The input x_i and output x_o signals may be voltages or currents. The signal is sampled at the output of the amplifier and applied to the right-hand port of the feedback network. At the left-hand port, the feedback signal fx_o is mixed with the input signal, giving a signal equal to $x_i - fx_o$ at the input to the amplifier. The output is then

$$x_o = a(x_i - fx_o) \tag{4-1}$$

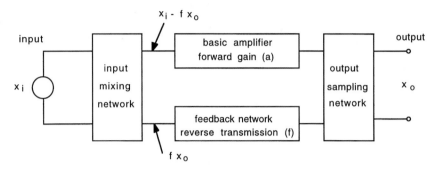

Figure 4-1   Block diagram of a general feedback amplifier system.

The overall gain of the amplifier with feedback is

$$\frac{x_o}{x_i} = A = \frac{a}{1 + af} \tag{4-2}$$

The product of a and f represents the net gain in the signal traversing forward through the amplifier and back through the feedback network; it is referred to as the loop gain T ($= af$) and thereby Eq. (4-2) can be expressed as

$$\frac{x_o}{x_i} = A = \frac{a}{1 + T} \tag{4-3}$$

Equation (4-3) is a fundamental relation for negative feedback which expresses the closed-loop gain (with feedback applied) A in terms of the open-loop gain of the amplifier (without feedback) a and the loop gain T. The system gain is thus reduced by a factor $1 + T$. It is to be noted that if $T \gg 1$, then

$$A \approx \frac{a}{T} = \frac{1}{f} \tag{4-4}$$

and is independent of the gain of the basic amplifier. Because the feedback network is often composed of stable, passive elements, the closed-loop gain is well controlled.

Gain Stabilization

In practice, the gain of the basic amplifier, a, is not well controlled; it is influenced by variations in integrated-circuit processing, changes in transistor device parameters, variations in operating bias, and variations in temperature. Negative feedback reduces the sensitivity of the overall gain A to variations in a. To see this, we differentiate Eq. (4-2), giving

$$\frac{dA}{da} = \frac{1}{(1 + af)^2} = \frac{1}{(1 + T)^2} \tag{4-5}$$

Thus, if a changes by an amount Δa, then A changes by an amount

$$\Delta A = \frac{\Delta a}{(1 + T)^2}$$

Expressed as a fractional change,

$$\frac{\Delta A}{A} = \frac{\Delta a}{A(1 + T)^2} = \frac{1}{1 + T}\frac{\Delta a}{a} \qquad (4\text{-}6)$$

As expressed by Eq. (4-6), the fractional change in the overall closed-loop gain A is a factor of $1 + T$ smaller than the fractional change in a. As an example, if the gain a of an amplifier with $T = 49$ changes by 10%, then the closed-loop gain A changes by $10\%/(1 + 49) = 0.2\%$.

Reduction in Distortion

Nonlinearities in the basic amplifier give rise to distortion in the output signal, especially if the signals in the amplifier are relatively large in magnitude. Such conditions are often encountered, for example, in the output stage of an amplifier where the output voltage has a large swing. Negative feedback applied to such an amplifier causes the distortion components of the output signal (also referred to as distortion products) to be fed back into the input of the amplifier where they subtract from themselves, resulting in a decrease in the overall distortion. The following discussion will demonstrate this process.

Consider the feedback amplifier system depicted in Fig. 4-1. Let the input to the basic amplifier be denoted x_ε; with feedback, this is equal to the difference in the input signal x_i and the feedback signal fx_o. In this context, x_ε is referred to as the *error signal*. Without feedback, the output of the amplifier x_o is equal to ax_ε. To see the reduction in distortion by feedback, it is simpler to view the process in reverse [1]. Instead of viewing a pure input producing a distorted output, we determine what predistortion is required at the input to produce a pure undistorted output. In this case, we relate the input as a function of the output, say in terms of a power series:

$$x_\varepsilon = \alpha_1 x_o + \alpha_2 x_o^2 + \alpha_3 x_o^3 + \cdots \qquad (4\text{-}7)$$

where $\alpha_1, \alpha_2, \alpha_3, \ldots$ are constants. For a linear amplifier (no distortion), all constants but α_1 would be zero. Normalizing with respect to the linear term, we obtain

$$x_\varepsilon = \alpha_1\left(x_o + \frac{\alpha_2 x_o^2}{\alpha_1} + \frac{\alpha_3 x_o^3}{\alpha_1} + \cdots\right) \qquad (4\text{-}8)$$

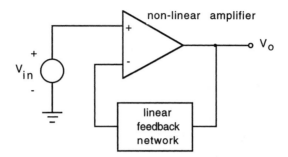

Figure 4-2   Nonlinear amplifier with negative feedback.

The higher-order terms (x_o^2, x_o^3, ...) are a measure of the distortion products in the signal. With feedback applied, a signal $-fx_o$ is added to the input, giving

$$x_\varepsilon = fx_o + \alpha_1 x_o + \alpha_2 x_o^2 + \alpha_3 x_o^3 + \cdots \qquad (4\text{-}9)$$

Again, normalizing with respect to the linear term,

$$x_\varepsilon = (\alpha_1 + f)\left(x_o + \frac{\alpha_2 x_o^2}{\alpha_1 + f} + \frac{\alpha_3 x_o^3}{\alpha_1 + f} + \cdots\right) \qquad (4\text{-}10)$$

Noting that $\alpha_1 \approx 1/a$, we have

$$\frac{\alpha_1}{\alpha_1 + f} = \frac{1}{1 + af} = \frac{1}{1 + T} \qquad (4\text{-}11)$$

Comparing Eqs. (4-8) and (4-10), we see that the distortion terms with feedback are reduced by a factor of $1 + T$. In actuality, the nonlinear components are reduced relative to the linear components.

To demonstrate the reduction in distortion with negative feedback, a nonlinear amplifier, depicted in Fig. 4-2, is simulated. The large-signal, voltage transfer characteristic of the amplifier with and without feedback is shown in Fig. 4-3; the improvement in linearity with feedback is evident. The price paid is, of course, the lower closed-loop gain with feedback.

Increased Bandwidth

To illustrate the increase in the bandwidth of an amplifier operated with negative feedback, consider the basic amplifier to have a single pole in its transfer characteristic such that

$$a(j\omega) = \frac{a_o}{1 + j(\omega/\omega_o)} \qquad (4\text{-}12)$$

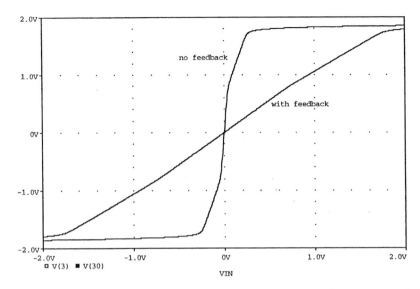

Figure 4-3 Voltage transfer characteristic of a nonlinear amplifier with and without negative feedback.

where ω_o is the frequency at which the open-loop gain of the basic amplifier in down by 3 dB from the gain at low frequency a_o. Further, assume that the feedback network is purely resistive such that the feedback factor f is a constant. From Eq. (4-2), the closed-loop gain is then

$$A(j\omega) = \frac{a(j\omega)}{1 + a(j\omega)f} = \frac{a(j\omega)}{1 + T(j\omega)} \tag{4-13}$$

which, using Eq. (4-12), results in

$$A(j\omega) = \frac{\dfrac{a_o}{1 + j(\omega/\omega_o)}}{1 + \dfrac{a_o f}{1 + j(\omega/\omega_o)}} = \frac{a_o}{1 + a_o f + j(\omega/\omega_o)} = \frac{a_o}{(1 + a_o f)\left(1 + j\left[\dfrac{\omega}{\omega_o(1 + a_o f)}\right]\right)} \tag{4-14}$$

Noting that the low-frequency closed-loop gain, A_o, is

$$A_o = \frac{a_o}{1 + a_o f} \tag{4-15}$$

Eq. (4-14) can be expressed as

$$A(j\omega) = \frac{A_o}{1 + j\left[\dfrac{\omega}{\omega_o(1 + T_o)}\right]} \tag{4-16}$$

where $T_o = a_o f$ and is the low-frequency loop gain.

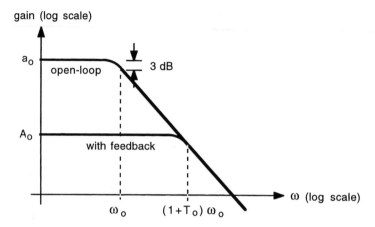

Figure 4-4   Gain versus frequency for a feedback amplifier.

The closed-loop gain $A(j\omega)$ also has a single-pole response; its frequency is larger than that of the basic amplifier by a factor of $1 + T_o$. Feedback has thus increased the -3-dB bandwidth of the amplifier from ω_o to $(1 + T_o)\omega_o$, as illustrated in Fig. 4-4. This increase in bandwidth is accompanied by a decrease in gain by the same factor $(1 + T_o)$.

4.2 Feedback Circuit Example

The simple circuit of Fig. 4-5 will serve as an example to illustrate the analysis of a feedback amplifier. In this circuit, a single transistor is connected as a common-emitter *transresistance* amplifier; it develops an output voltage V_o proportional to an input current signal I_s. Feedback is provided by resistor R_F which samples the voltage at the output node and feeds a current that is proportional

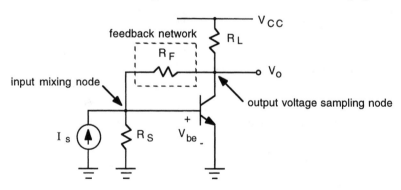

Figure 4-5   Feedback amplifier circuit.

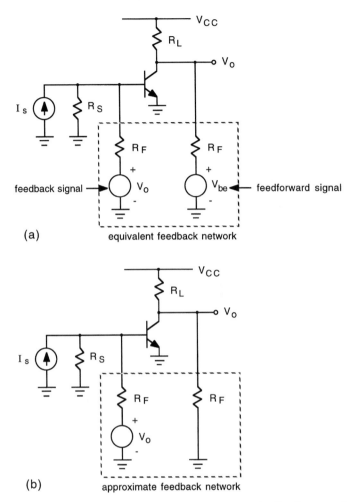

Figure 4-6 (a) Equivalent circuit represention of the feedback network for the amplifier of Fig. 4-5. (b) Neglecting the feedforward signal in the feedback network.

to the output voltage back to the input where it is mixed with the input signal. To see that this is negative feedback, consider that the output voltage increases: An increase in V_o results in an increase in the signal fed back to the base of the transistor, resulting in an increased collector current; the increased collector current results in a decrease in collector-to-emitter voltage, and hence a decrease in V_o.

The feedback network may be replaced by the equivalent circuit shown in Fig. 4-6(a); this circuit produces the same feedforward and feedback signals as the

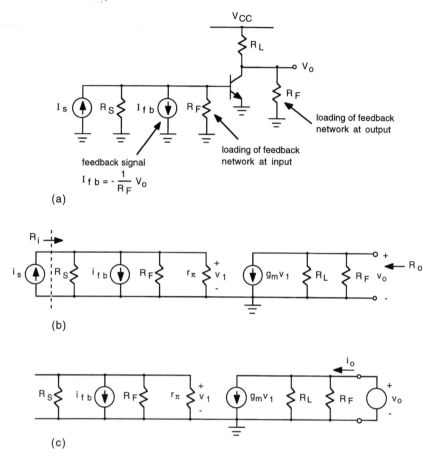

Figure 4-7   (a) Representing the feedback signal as a current. (b) Small-signal equivalent circuit of the feedback amplifier. (c) Small-signal circuit for calculating the output resistance.

original feedback network of Fig. 4-5. The signal fed forward through the feedback network is normally much smaller than the signal fed forward through the basic amplifier and can thus be neglected, resulting in the approximate equivalent circuit of the feedback network shown in Fig. 4-6(b). In Fig. 4-7(a), the feedback voltage source is replaced by its Norton equivalent, a current source of value $-V_o/R_F$ in parallel with the resistance R_F; this current source, I_{fb}, is directed opposite to the input signal, I_s, to emphasize the negative feedback. In this equivalent circuit, the feedback resistance R_F appears as a shunt at both the input and output of the amplifier and represents the loading of the basic amplifier by the feedback network.

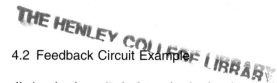
The closed-loop, small-signal gain, v_o/i_s, is determined using the small-signal equivalent circuit of the feedback amplifier shown in Fig. 4-7(b). At the output,

$$v_o = -g_m v_1 (R_L \| R_F) = -g_m v_1 R_{oo} \tag{4-17}$$

where we have introduced the parameter R_{oo}, which equals $R_L \| R_F$; the reason for using this parameter will become evident later. At the input,

$$v_1 = (i_s - i_{fb})(R_S \| R_F \| r_\pi) = \left(i_s + \frac{v_o}{R_F}\right) R_{io} \tag{4-18}$$

On the right-hand side of Eq. (4-18) we have substituted for the feedback current $i_{fb} = -v_o/R_F$, and have introduced the parameter R_{io}, which equals $R_S \| R_F \| r_\pi$. Substituting for v_1 from Eq. (4-18) into Eq. (4-17) yields

$$\frac{v_o}{i_s} = \frac{-g_m R_{io} R_{oo}}{1 + g_m R_{io} R_{oo}/R_F} \tag{4-19}$$

This is the closed-loop gain of the amplifier with feedback.

If the feedback signal is removed (i.e., make $i_{fb} = 0$), the gain of the amplifier can be easily shown to be

$$\left.\frac{v_o}{i_s}\right|_{i_{fb}=0} = -g_m R_{io} R_{oo} \equiv a \tag{4-20}$$

In this context, a is the gain of the basic amplifier without feedback. Further, it is profitable to define the feedback factor

$$f = -\frac{1}{R_F} \tag{4-21}$$

such that the feedback signal is

$$i_{fb} = f v_o \tag{4-22}$$

Using these parameters, Eq. (4-19) can be expressed in the form

$$\frac{v_o}{i_s} = \frac{a}{1 + af} \tag{4-23}$$

which is the fundamental feedback equation.

Input Resistance

With reference to Fig. 4-7(b), the input resistance of the amplifier with feedback is

$$R_i = \frac{v_1}{i_s} \tag{4-24}$$

where from Eq. (4-17)

$$v_1 = \frac{-v_o}{g_m R_{oo}}$$

Thus,

$$R_i = \frac{-1}{g_m R_{oo}} \frac{v_o}{i_s} \tag{4-25}$$

which, using Eq. (4-19), results in

$$R_i = \frac{R_{io}}{1 + g_m R_{io} R_{oo}/R_F} = \frac{R_{io}}{1 + af} = \frac{R_{io}}{1 + T} \tag{4-26}$$

It is to be noted that if the feedback signal i_{fb} is removed, the input resistance would be

$$R_i \bigg|_{i_{fb} = 0} = R_S \| R_F \| r_\pi = R_{io} \tag{4-27}$$

The input resistance of this amplifier is thus reduced by a factor of $1 + T$ by the feedback.

Output Resistance

The test circuit of Fig. 4-7(c) is used to calculate the output resistance of the feedback amplifier. Formally,

$$R_o = \frac{v_o}{i_o} \bigg|_{i_s = 0} \tag{4-28}$$

where in Fig. 4-7(c), v_o is a test voltage source.

At the output,

$$i_o = \frac{v_o}{R_L} + \frac{v_o}{R_F} + g_m v_1 = \frac{v_o}{R_{oo}} + g_m v_1 \tag{4-29}$$

At the input,

$$v_1 = -i_{fb}(R_S \| R_F \| r_\pi) = -i_{fb} R_{io} \tag{4-30}$$

Now,

$$i_{fb} = \frac{-v_o}{R_F}$$

so

$$v_1 = \frac{R_{io}}{R_F} v_o$$

which, upon substitution into Eq. (4-29), gives

$$R_o = \frac{R_{oo}}{1 + g_m R_{io} R_{oo}/R_F} = \frac{R_{oo}}{1 + af} = \frac{R_{oo}}{1 + T} \qquad (4\text{-}31)$$

It is also noted that if the feedback is removed, the output resistance would be

$$R_o \bigg|_{i_{fb} = 0} = R_L \| R_F = R_{oo} \qquad (4\text{-}32)$$

The output resistance of this amplifier is thus reduced by a factor of $1 + T$ by the feedback.

4.3 Feedback Configurations

In a feedback amplifier, the output signal, which may be either a voltage or a current, is sampled and a feedback signal, again either a voltage or a current, which is proportional to the output signal is mixed at the input of the amplifier. Accordingly, four basic feedback configurations can be identified [2, 3]. These are illustrated in Fig. 4-8.

In Figs. 4-8(a) and 4-8(b), the feedback network samples the output *voltage*; these two amplifiers are said to have *voltage feedback*. In Figs. 4-8(c) and 4-8(d), the feedback network samples the output *current*; these two amplifiers are said to have *current feedback*. If the feedback signal is a voltage, it is combined in series with the input signal (a voltage) at the input of the amplifier; this is referred to as *series* mixing. If the feedback signal is a current, it is combined in parallel with the input signal (a current) at the input of the amplifier, this is referred to as *shunt* mixing.

In the feedback arrangement depicted in Fig. 4-8(a), the feedback network produces a feedback voltage, v_{fb}, which is proportional to the output voltage and is equal to $f v_o$. The input to the basic amplifier (which in this case is a voltage amplifier), v_i, is thus reduced by the feedback voltage. This feedback configuration is called *series voltage*, referring to the fact that feedback signal is mixed in *series* with the input and its value derives from the output *voltage*. Unfortunately, this terminology is not universal; another commonly used term for this configuration is *series–shunt*, referring to feedback network being in *series* with the input and in *shunt* across the output.

In Fig. 4-8(b), the feedback network produces a feedback current, i_{fb}, which is proportional to the output voltage and is equal to $f v_o$. The input to the basic amplifier (in this case a transresistance amplifier), i_i, is thus reduced by the feedback current. This feedback configuration is called *shunt voltage*, referring to the fact that the feedback signal is mixed in *shunt* with the input signal; the

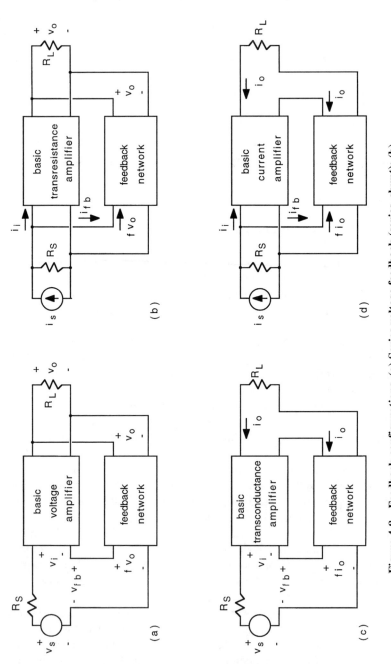

Figure 4-8 Feedback configurations. (a) Series voltage feedback (series–shunt); (b) shunt voltage feedback (shunt–shunt); (c) series current feedback (series–series); (d) shunt current feedback (shunt–series).

other terminology used for this configuration is shunt–shunt, referring to the feedback network which shunts both the input and output.

In Fig. 4-8(c), the feedback network produces a feedback voltage, v_{fb}, which is proportional to the output current and is equal to fi_o. The input to the basic amplifier (in this case a transconductance amplifier), v_i, is thus reduced by the feedback voltage. This feedback configuration is called *series current*, referring to the fact that the feedback signal is mixed in *series* with the input signal; the other terminology used for this configuration is series–series, referring to the feedback network which is in series with both the input and output.

In Fig. 4-8(d), the feedback network produces a feedback current, i_{fb}, which is proportional to the output current and is equal to fi_o. The input to the basic amplifier (in this case a current amplifier), i_i, is thus reduced by the feedback current. This feedback configuration is called *shunt current*, referring to the fact that the feedback signal is mixed in *shunt* with the input signal; the other terminology used for this configuration is shunt–series, referring to the feedback network which shunts the input and is in series with the output. In the following sections, each of these feedback configurations are discussed in detail.

Series Voltage

In the *series voltage* feedback configuration, repeated in Fig. 4-9(a), the output voltage v_o is sampled by the feedback network and a feedback voltage fv_o is mixed in series at the input. The effect of the feedback network on the amplifier can be seen by the circuit transformation depicted in Fig. 4-9(b). As far as the feedback network is concerned, it sees a current i_s at its input and a voltage v_o at its output; it is appropriate, therefore, to represent the input side of the feedback network by its Thevenin equivalent and the output side by its Norton equivalent. The Thevenin equivalent at the input consists of resistance r_{if} in series with the open-circuit voltage v_{oc}; r_{if} is the equivalent resistance at the input port of the feedback network, evaluated with v_o set to zero (output short circuited), and v_{oc} is the voltage at the input of the feedback network with i_s set to zero (input open circuited). v_{oc} is the feedback signal, equal to fv_o. The Norton equivalent at the output consists of resistance r_{of} in parallel with the short-circuit current i_{sc}; r_{of} is the equivalent resistance at the output port of the feedback network, evaluated with i_s set to zero (input open circuited), and i_{sc} is the current at the output of the feedback network with v_o set to zero (output short circuited). i_{sc} is the feedforward signal. Because the feedback network is passive, this feedforward signal is usually much smaller than the signal fed forward through the basic amplifier; i_{sc} can thus be neglected, resulting in the approximate equivalent circuit for the feedback network shown in the bottom panel of Fig. 4-9(b).

The basic voltage amplifier is represented by the equivalent circuit shown in the upper portion of Fig. 4-10(a); here r_{ia} represents the input resistance of the

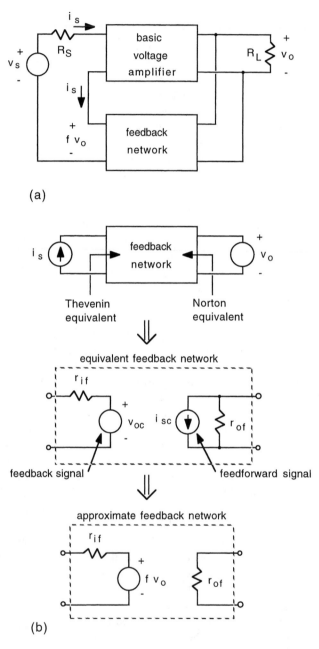

(a)

(b)

Figure 4-9   (a) Series voltage feedback amplifier. (b) Transformation of feedback network.

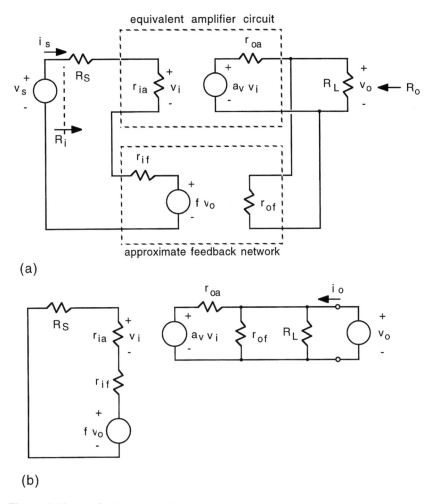

(a)

(b)

Figure 4-10   (a) Series voltage feedback configuration using an equivalent circuit for the basic amplifier. (b) Circuit for calculating the output resistance.

basic voltage amplifier and r_{oa} its output resistance. The feedback network is replaced by its approximate equivalent circuit. From the circuit in Fig. 4-10(a) we have for the input current

$$i_s = \frac{v_s - fv_o}{R_S + r_{ia} + r_{if}} = \frac{v_s - fv_o}{R_{io}} \tag{4-33}$$

where

$$R_{io} \equiv R_S + r_{ia} + r_{if} \qquad (4\text{-}34)$$

and represents the input resistance of the amplifier without feedback ($f = 0$).
    At the output,

$$v_o = \frac{R_L \| r_{of}}{R_L \| r_{of} + r_{oa}} a_v v_i = \frac{R_{oo}}{r_{oa}} a_v v_i \qquad (4\text{-}35)$$

where

$$R_{oo} \equiv r_{oa} \| r_{of} \| R_L \qquad (4\text{-}36)$$

and represents the output resistance of the amplifier without feedback.
    The input voltage to the basic amplifier v_i is equal to $i_s\, r_{ia}$, which combined with
Eqs. (4-33) and (4-35) yields

$$v_o = \frac{R_{oo}}{r_{oa}} a_v \frac{r_{ia}}{R_{io}} (v_s - f v_o) \qquad (4\text{-}37)$$

which gives for the voltage gain

$$\frac{v_o}{v_s} = \frac{\dfrac{a_v r_{ia} R_{oo}}{r_{oa} R_{io}}}{1 + \dfrac{a_v r_{ia} R_{oo}}{r_{oa} R_{io}} f} \qquad (4\text{-}38)$$

It is to be noted that if the feedback signal is removed,

$$\left. \frac{v_o}{v_s} \right|_{f=0} = \frac{a_v r_{ia} R_{oo}}{r_{oa} R_{io}} \equiv a \qquad (4\text{-}39)$$

In this context, a represents the gain of the amplifier without feedback. Equation
(4-38) can thus be expressed in terms of the fundamental feedback equation:

$$\frac{v_o}{v_s} = \frac{a}{1 + af} = \frac{a}{1 + T} \qquad (4\text{-}40)$$

Input Resistance

With reference to Fig. 4-10(a), the input resistance of the amplifier with feedback is

$$R_i = \frac{v_s}{i_s} \qquad (4\text{-}41)$$

where, using Eqs. (4-33) and (4-40),

$$i_s = \frac{v_s - fv_o}{R_{io}} = \left(1 - \frac{af}{1 + af}\right)\frac{v_s}{R_{io}} \tag{4-42}$$

Thus,

$$R_i = (1 + af)R_{io} = (1 + T)R_{io} \tag{4-43}$$

The input resistance of the amplifier with *series* feedback is *increased* by a factor $1 + T$. The reason for this is that the feedback voltage fv_o subtracts from the input voltage v_s, giving a smaller net input voltage to the amplifier and thereby a smaller input current, i_s.

Output Resistance

To determine the output resistance of the amplifier with feedback, we set the input signal source, v_s, to zero and apply a test source at the output; using a test voltage v_o, the circuit is shown in Fig. 4-10(b). The output current resulting from the test voltage is

$$i_o = \frac{v_o}{R_L} + \frac{v_o}{r_{of}} + \frac{v_o - a_v v_i}{r_{oa}} \tag{4-44}$$

At the input,

$$v_i = -\frac{r_{ia}}{R_S + r_{ia} + r_{if}}fv_o = -\frac{r_{ia}fv_o}{R_{io}} \tag{4-45}$$

Substituting for v_i in Eq. (4-44) gives

$$i_o = \left(\frac{1}{R_L} + \frac{1}{r_{of}} + \frac{1}{r_{oa}} + \frac{a_v r_{ia}f}{r_{oa}R_{io}}\right)v_o = \left(\frac{1}{R_{oo}} + \frac{a_v r_{ia}f}{r_{oa}R_{io}}\right)v_o$$

$$i_o = \left(1 + \frac{a_v r_{ia}R_{oo}f}{r_{oa}R_{io}}\right)\frac{v_o}{R_{oo}} = (1 + af)\frac{v_o}{R_{oo}}$$

$$\tag{4-46}$$

Thus,

$$R_o = \frac{v_o}{i_o} = \frac{R_{oo}}{1 + af} = \frac{R_{oo}}{1 + T} \tag{4-47}$$

The output resistance of the amplifier with *voltage* feedback is reduced by a factor $1 + T$. The physical reason why voltage sampling by the feedback network lowers the output resistance can be seen by examining Fig. 4-10(b). Due to the negative feedback signal, the dependent voltage source $a_v v_i$ in the equivalent amplifier circuit will be a negative voltage, giving an increased current in r_{oa}, thereby increasing the output current i_o from what it would be without feedback;

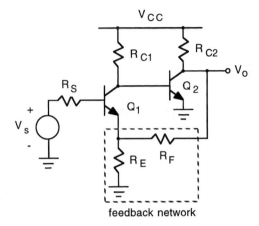

Figure 4-11   Two-stage series voltage feedback amplifier.

the output resistance is thereby reduced. It should be remarked that this will be the case regardless of how the feedback signal is mixed at the input; the shunt voltage feedback configuration will also have a reduced output resistance.

Series Voltage Feedback Example

A simple two-stage amplifier employing series voltage feedback is shown in Fig. 4-11. In the circuit, the feedback network samples the output voltage, and a feedback voltage, proportional to V_o, is applied in series with the input. To see this, envision that the output voltage is increasing: This increases the voltage at the emitter of Q_1, thereby lowering its base-emitter voltage; the resulting decrease in the collector current of Q_1 increases the voltage at its collector and also thereby the base-emitter voltage of Q_2. Q_2 conducts more heavily, lowering the output voltage.

The procedure for calculating the equivalent circuit of the feedback network is illustrated in Fig. 4-12. As shown in Fig. 4-12(a), we **open-circuit** the input side of the feedback network to calculate the feedback voltage

$$V_{fb} = \frac{R_E}{R_E + R_F} V_o = fV_o \qquad (4\text{-}48)$$

and the output resistance

$$r_{of} = R_E + R_F \qquad (4\text{-}49)$$

As shown in Fig. 4-12(b), we **short-circuit** the output side of the feedback network to calculate the input resistance

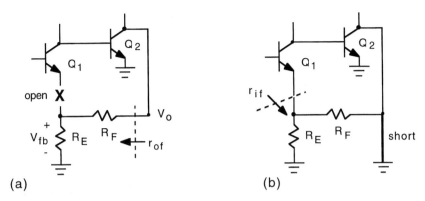

Figure 4-12 (a) Procedure for calculating feedback voltage and equivalent output resistance of the feedback network. (b) Procedure for calculating the equivalent input resistance of the feedback network.

$$r_{if} = R_E \| R_F \qquad (4\text{-}50)$$

The equivalent circuit of the feedback network (neglecting its feedforward signal) is added to the basic amplifier, as shown in Fig. 4-13(a). Here, the feedback voltage, v_{fb}, and the equivalent input resistance of the feedback network, r_{if}, appear in series with the base-emitter input circuit of the amplifier, and the equivalent output resistance of the feedback network, r_{of}, appears in parallel (shunt) with the output of the amplifier. The equivalent circuit of the feedback amplifier shown in Fig. 4-13(a) can be analyzed directly for the closed-loop voltage gain and the input and output resistances. Alternately, the circuit could be analyzed with the feedback signal removed, giving the open-loop gain, a, and the input and output resistances, R_{io} and R_{oo} respectively; the standard feedback formulas can then be used to determine the closed-loop response. This later procedure is usually simpler than a direct analysis of the circuit with the feedback signal applied. The small-signal equivalent circuit of the feedback amplifier with the feedback signal removed is shown in Fig. 4-13(b).

From Fig. 4-13(b),

$$v_1 = \frac{r_{\pi 1}}{R_S + r_{\pi 1} + (\beta_{FI} + 1)(R_E \| R_F)} v_s \qquad (4\text{-}51)$$

so

$$v_2 = -g_{m1} v_1 (R_{C1} \| r_{\pi 2}) = -\frac{\beta_{FI}(R_{C1} \| r_{\pi 2})}{R_S + r_{\pi 1} + (\beta_{FI} + 1)(R_E \| R_F)} v_s \qquad (4\text{-}52)$$

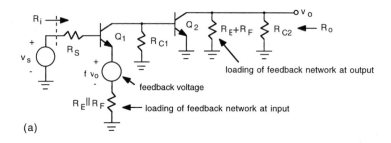

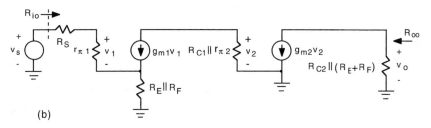

Figure 4-13 **(a) AC equivalent circuit of the series voltage feedback amplifier. (b) Small-signal equivalent circuit without feedback.**

where in the right-hand term of Eq. (4-52) we have used $g_{m1} r_{\pi 1} = \beta_{F1}$. The output voltage is

$$v_o = - g_{m2} v_2 [R_{C2}||(R_E + R_F)]$$ (4-53)

which, after combining with Eq. (4-52), yields

$$\left.\frac{v_o}{v_s}\right|_{f=0} = a = \frac{\beta_{F1}\beta_{F2}R_{C1}[R_{C2}||(R_E + R_F)]}{(r_{\pi 2} + R_{C1})[R_S + r_{\pi 1} + (\beta_{F1} + 1)(R_E||R_F)]}$$ (4-54)

where we have used $g_{m2} r_{\pi 2} = \beta_{F2}$.

The closed-loop gain with feedback is then

$$\frac{v_o}{v_s} = \frac{a}{1 + af} = \frac{a}{1 + T}$$ (4-55)

where

$$T = af = \frac{aR_E}{R_E + R_F}$$ (4-56)

The input resistance without feedback [see Fig. 4-12(b)] is

$$R_{io} = R_S + r_{\pi 1} + (\beta_{F1} + 1)(R_E||R_F)$$ (4-57)

The input resistance with feedback is then

$$R_i = (1 + T) R_{io} = (1 + T) [R_S + r_{\pi 1} + (\beta_{F1} + 1) (R_E || R_F)] \qquad (4\text{-}58)$$

The output resistance without feedback [see Fig. 4-12(b)] is

$$R_{oo} = R_{C2} || (R_E + R_F) \qquad (4\text{-}59)$$

The output resistance with feedback is then

$$R_o = \frac{R_{oo}}{1 + T} = \frac{R_{C2} || (R_E + R_F)}{1 + T} \qquad (4\text{-}60)$$

Shunt Voltage

In the *shunt voltage* feedback configuration, repeated in Fig. 4-14(a), the output voltage v_o is sampled by the feedback network and a feedback current fv_o is mixed in parallel at the input. The effect of the feedback network on the amplifier is illustrated in the circuit transformation depicted in Fig. 4-14(b). As far as the feedback network is concerned, it sees a voltage v_i, the voltage at the input to the basic amplifier, at its input and a voltage v_o at its output; it is appropriate, therefore, to represent the input and output sides of the feedback network by their Norton equivalents. The Norton equivalent at the input consists of resistance r_{if} in parallel with the short-circuit current i_{sc}; r_{if} is the equivalent resistance at the input port of the feedback, evaluated with v_o set to zero (output short circuited), and i_{sc} is the current at the input of the feedback network with v_i set to zero (input short circuited). i_{sc} is the feedback signal, equal to fv_o. The Norton equivalent at the output consists of resistance r_{of} in parallel with the short-circuit feedforward current, which is neglected in comparison with the feedforward signal through the basic amplifier. r_{of} is the equivalent resistance at the output port of the feedback network, evaluated with v_i set to zero (input short circuited). The resulting approximate equivalent circuit for the feedback network is shown in the bottom panel of Fig. 4-14(b).

The basic transresistance amplifier is represented by the equivalent circuit shown in the upper portion of Fig. 4-15(a); here, r_{ia} represents the input resistance of the basic transresistance amplifier and r_{oa} its output resistance. The feedback network is represented by its approximate equivalent circuit. From the circuit in Fig. 4-15(a), the output voltage is

$$v_o = \frac{r_{of} || R_L}{r_{oa} + r_{of} || R_L} r_m i_i = \frac{R_{oo}}{r_{oa}} r_m i_i \qquad (4\text{-}61)$$

where

$$R_{oo} \equiv r_{oa} || r_{of} || R_L \qquad (4\text{-}62)$$

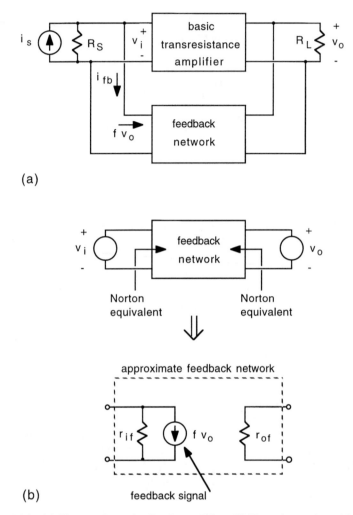

(a)

(b)   feedback signal

Figure 4-14   (a) Shunt voltage feedback amplifier. (b) Transformation of feedback network.

and represents the output resistance of the amplifier without feedback ($f = 0$).
   At the input,

$$v_i = (i_s - fv_o)(R_S || r_{if} || r_{ia}) = (i_s - fv_o) R_{io} \qquad (4\text{-}63)$$

where

$$R_{io} \equiv R_S || r_{if} || r_{ia} \qquad (4\text{-}64)$$

and represents the input resistance of the amplifier without feedback.

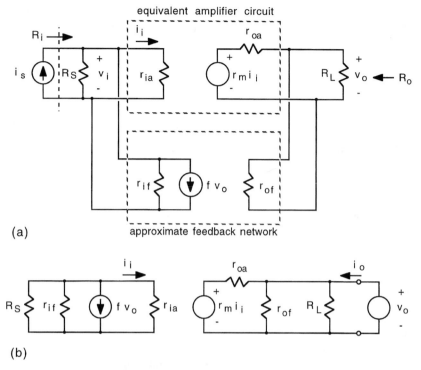

(a)

(b)

Figure 4-15   (a) Shunt voltage feedback configuration using an equivalent circuit for the basic amplifier. (b) Circuit for calculating the output resistance.

The input current to the basic amplifier i_i is equal to v_s/r_{ia}, which, combined with Eqs. (4-61) and (4-63), yields

$$v_o = \frac{R_{oo}}{r_{oa}} r_m \frac{R_{io}}{r_{ia}} (i_s - fv_o) \qquad (4\text{-}65)$$

which gives for the gain

$$\frac{v_o}{i_s} = \frac{\dfrac{r_m R_{io} R_{oo}}{r_{ia} r_{oa}}}{1 + \dfrac{r_m R_{io} R_{oo}}{r_{ia} r_{oa}} f} \qquad (4\text{-}66)$$

It is to be noted that for this amplifier the feedback factor f has units of amps/volt. Further, it is noted that if the feedback signal is removed,

$$\left. \frac{v_o}{i_s} \right|_{f=0} = \frac{r_m R_{io} R_{oo}}{r_{ia} r_{oa}} \equiv a \qquad (4\text{-}67)$$

In this context, a (which has units of volts/amp) represents the gain of the amplifier without feedback. Thus, Eq. (4-66) can be expressed in terms of the fundamental feedback equation

$$\frac{v_o}{i_s} = \frac{a}{1 + af} = \frac{a}{1 + T} \tag{4-68}$$

Input Resistance

With reference to Fig. 4-15(a), the input resistance with feedback is

$$R_i = \frac{v_i}{i_s} \tag{4-69}$$

where, using Eqs. (4-63) and (4-68),

$$v_i = (i_s - fv_o)R_{io} = \left(1 - \frac{af}{1 + af}\right)i_s R_{io} \tag{4-70}$$

Thus,

$$R_i = \frac{R_{io}}{1 + af} = \frac{R_{io}}{1 + T} \tag{4-71}$$

The input resistance with *shunt* feedback is *reduced* by a factor $1 + T$. The reason for this reduction can be seen by examining Fig. 4-15(a): To maintain the same output with feedback, the input current i_s has to be increased because the feedback current fv_o subtracts from the input current to the amplifier i_i.

Output Resistance

The test circuit shown in Fig. 4-15(b) is used to calculate the output resistance of the shunt voltage feedback amplifier. The output current resulting from the test voltage is

$$i_o = \frac{v_o}{R_L} + \frac{v_o}{r_{of}} + \frac{v_o - r_m i_i}{r_{oa}} = \frac{v_o}{R_{oo}} - \frac{r_m i_i}{r_{oa}} \tag{4-72}$$

At the input,

$$i_i = -\frac{R_S\|r_{if}}{R_S\|r_{if} + r_{ia}}fv_o = -\frac{R_{io}}{r_{ia}}fv_o \tag{4-73}$$

Substituting into Eq. (4-72) gives

$$i_o = \frac{v_o}{R_{oo}} + \frac{r_m}{r_{oa}}\frac{R_{io}}{r_{ia}}fv_o = \frac{v_o}{R_{oo}} + \frac{afv_o}{R_{oo}} \tag{4-74}$$

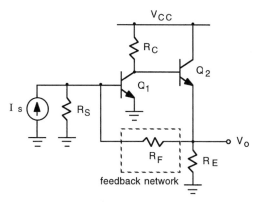

Figure 4-16 Shunt voltage feedback amplifier.

where in the last term we have used Eq. (4-67). The output resistance is then

$$R_o = \frac{v_o}{i_o} = \frac{R_{oo}}{1 + af} = \frac{R_{oo}}{1 + T} \tag{4-75}$$

Voltage feedback *reduces* the output resistance by a factor of $1 + T$.

Shunt Voltage Feedback Example.

Figure 4-16 illustrates a shunt voltage feedback amplifier employing a common-emitter gain stage followed by an emitter follower output stage. In the circuit, the feedback network samples the output voltage and a feedback current, proportional to V_o, is applied in shunt with the input. To show that this circuit constitutes negative feedback, visualize the output voltage increasing: An increase in V_o increases the current flowing through the feedback resistance R_F to the input node; this increases the base current of Q_1, causing it to conduct more heavily, lowering the voltage at its collector. The output voltage of the emitter follower transistor Q_2 follows this drop in voltage.

The procedure for calculating the equivalent circuit of the feedback network is illustrated in Fig. 4-17. As shown in Fig. 4-17(a), we **short-circuit** the input side of the feedback network to calculate the feedback current

$$I_{fb} = -\frac{V_o}{R_F} = fV_o \tag{4-76}$$

and the output resistance

$$r_{of} = R_F \tag{4-77}$$

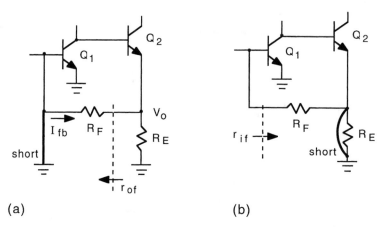

(a)   (b)

Figure 4-17 (a) Procedure for calculating feedback current and equivalent output resistance of the feedback network. (b) Procedure for calculating the equivalent input resistance of the feedback network.

As shown in Fig. 4-17(b), we short-circuit the output side of the feedback to calculate the input resistance

$$r_{if} = R_F \tag{4-78}$$

The equivalent circuit of the feedback network (neglecting its feedforward signal) is added to the basic amplifier, as shown in Fig. 4-18(a). Here, the feedback current, i_{fb}, and the equivalent input resistance of the feedback network, r_{if}, appear in parallel (shunt) with the input of the amplifier, and the equivalent output resistance of the feedback network appears in parallel (shunt) with the output of the amplifier.

The small-signal equivalent circuit of the amplifier without feedback ($f = 0$) is shown in Fig. 4-18(b); we use this circuit to calculate the open-loop parameters, a, R_{io}, and R_{oo}, of the feedback amplifier. Summing the currents at the output node gives

$$\frac{v_2}{r_{\pi 2}} + g_{m2} v_2 = \frac{\beta_{F2} + 1}{r_{\pi 2}} v_2 = \frac{v_o}{R_F \| R_E} \tag{4-79}$$

where in the second term we have used $g_{m2} r_{\pi 2} = \beta_{F2}$. Summing the currents at the collector of Q_1 gives

$$g_{m1} v_1 + \frac{v_2 + v_o}{R_C} + \frac{v_2}{r_{\pi 2}} = 0 \tag{4-80}$$

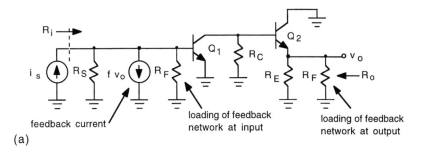

(a)

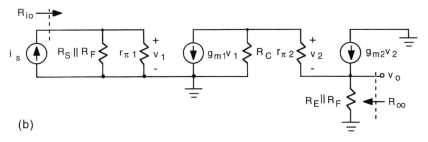

(b)

Figure 4-18 **(a) AC equivalent circuit of the shunt voltage feedback amplifier. (b) Small-signal equivalent circuit without feedback.**

which, solved for v_2 and substituted into Eq. (4-79), yields

$$v_o = -\frac{g_{m1}R_C(\beta_{F2}+1)(R_F\|R_E)}{(\beta_{F2}+1)(R_F\|R_E)+R_C+r_{\pi2}}v_1 \qquad (4\text{-}81)$$

At the input node,

$$i_s = \frac{v_1}{R_S\|R_F}+\frac{v_1}{r_{\pi1}} \qquad (4\text{-}82)$$

which, solved for v_1 and substituted into Eq. (4-81), gives for the open-loop gain

$$\left.\frac{v_o}{i_s}\right|_{f=0} = a = -\frac{\beta_{F1}(\beta_{F2}+1)R_C(R_S\|R_F)(R_F\|R_E)}{(R_S\|R_F+r_{\pi1})[(\beta_{F2}+1)(R_F\|R_E)+R_C+r_{\pi2}]} \qquad (4\text{-}83)$$

where we have used $g_{m1}r_{\pi1}=\beta_{F1}$.

The closed-loop gain with feedback is then

$$\frac{v_o}{i_s} = \frac{a}{1+af} = \frac{a}{1+T} \qquad (4\text{-}84)$$

where

$$T = af = -\frac{a}{R_F} \tag{4-85}$$

The input resistance without feedback [see Fig. 4-18(b)] is

$$R_{io} = \frac{(R_S || R_F)\, r_{\pi 1}}{R_S || R_F + r_{\pi 1}} \tag{4-86}$$

The input resistance with feedback is then

$$R_i = \frac{R_{io}}{1 + T} = \frac{\dfrac{(R_S || R_F)\, r_{\pi 1}}{R_S || R_F + r_{\pi 1}}}{1 + T} \tag{4-87}$$

The output resistance without feedback [see Fig. 4-18(b)] is calculated by reflecting $R_C + r_{\pi 2}$ into the emitter circuit of Q_2 and combining in parallel with the resistance, $R_F || R_E$. This gives

$$R_{oo} = \frac{(R_F || R_E)(R_C + r_{\pi 2})}{(\beta_{F2} + 1)(R_F || R_E) + R_C + r_{\pi 2}} \tag{4-88}$$

The output resistance with feedback is then

$$R_o = \frac{R_{oo}}{1 + T} = \frac{\dfrac{(R_F || R_E)(R_C + r_{\pi 2})}{(\beta_{F2} + 1)(R_F || R_E) + R_C + r_{\pi 2}}}{1 + T} \tag{4-89}$$

Series Current

In the *series current* feedback configuration, repeated in Fig. 4-19(a), the output current i_o is sampled by the feedback network and a feedback voltage fi_o is mixed in series at the input. The effect of the feedback network on the amplifier can be seen by the circuit transformation depicted in Fig. 4-19(b). As far as the feedback network is concerned, it sees a current i_s at its input and a current i_o at its output; it is appropriate, therefore, to represent both the input side and the output side of the feedback network by its Thevenin equivalent. The Thevenin equivalent at the input consists of resistance r_{if} in series with the open-circuit voltage v_{oc}; r_{if} is the equivalent resistance at the input port of the feedback network, evaluated with i_o set to zero (output open circuited), and v_{oc} is the voltage at the input of the feedback network with i_s set to zero (input open circuited). v_{oc} is the feedback signal, equal to fi_o. The Thevenin equivalent at the output consists of resistance r_{of} in series with the open-circuit feedforward voltage, which is neglected in comparison with the

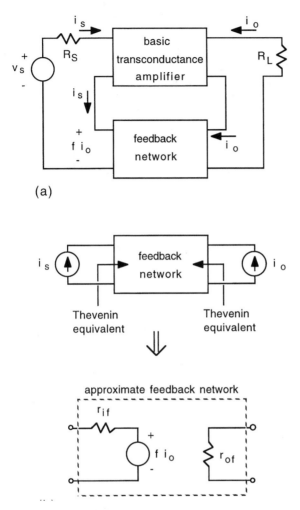

Figure 4-19 **(a) Series current feedback amplifier. (b) Transformation of feedback network.**

feedforward signal through the basic amplifier. r_{of} is the equivalent resistance at the output port of the feedback network, evaluated with i_s set to zero (input open circuited). The resulting approximate equivalent circuit for the feedback network is shown in the bottom panel of Fig. 4-19(b).

The basic transconductance amplifier is represented by the equivalent circuit shown in the upper portion of Fig. 4-20(a); here, r_{ia} represents the input resistance of the basic transconductance amplifier and r_{oa} its output resistance.

equivalent amplifier circuit

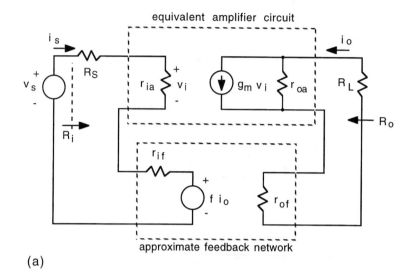

(a)

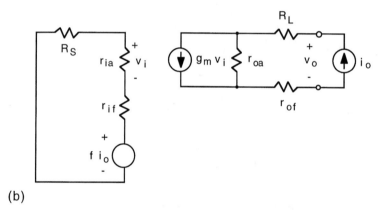

(b)

Figure 4-20   (a) Series current feedback configuration using an equivalent circuit for the basic amplifier. (b) Circuit for calculating the output resistance.

The feedback network is represented by its approximate equivalent circuit. From the circuit in Fig. 4-20(a), the output current is

$$i_o = \frac{r_{oa}}{r_{oa} + r_{of} + R_L} g_m v_i = \frac{r_{oa}}{R_{oo}} g_m v_i \tag{4-90}$$

where

$$R_{oo} = r_{oa} + r_{of} + R_L \tag{4-91}$$

and represents the output resistance of the amplifier without feedback ($f = 0$).

At the input,

$$i_s = \frac{v_s - f i_o}{R_S + r_{ia} + r_{if}} = \frac{v_s - f i_o}{R_{io}} \tag{4-92}$$

where

$$R_{io} = R_S + r_{ia} + r_{if} \tag{4-93}$$

and represents the input resistance of the amplifier without feedback.

The input voltage to the basic amplifier v_i is equal to $i_s r_{ia}$, which, substituted into Eq. (4-90) and combined with Eq. (4-92), yields the gain

$$\frac{i_o}{v_s} = \frac{\dfrac{g_m r_{ia} r_{oa}}{R_{io} R_{oo}}}{1 + \dfrac{g_m r_{ia} r_{oa}}{R_{io} R_{oo}} f} \tag{4-94}$$

It is noted that for this amplifier the feedback factor f has units of volts/amp. If the feedback signal is removed,

$$\left. \frac{i_o}{v_s} \right|_{f=0} = \frac{g_m r_{ia} r_{oa}}{R_{io} R_{oo}} \equiv a \tag{4-95}$$

Here, a (which has units of amps/volt) represents the gain of the amplifier without feedback. Thus, Eq. (4-94) can be expressed in terms of the fundamental feedback equation

$$\frac{i_o}{v_s} = \frac{a}{1 + af} = \frac{a}{1 + T} \tag{4-96}$$

Input Resistance

With reference to Fig. 4-20(a), the input resistance of the amplifier with feedback is

$$R_i = \frac{v_s}{i_s} \tag{4-97}$$

where, using Eqs. (4-92) and (4-96),

$$i_s = \frac{v_s - f i_o}{R_{io}} = \left(1 - \frac{af}{1 + af} \right) \frac{v_s}{R_{io}} \tag{4-98}$$

Thus,

$$R_i = (1 + af) R_{io} = (1 + T) R_{io} \tag{4-99}$$

As expected, the input resistance of the amplifier is increased by the series feedback.

Output Resistance

In the series current feedback amplifier, the output signal is a current (i_o). The output resistance is determined by breaking the series output circuit and applying a test current as shown in Fig. 4-20(b). The output voltage resulting from the test current is

$$v_o = i_o R_L + (i_o - g_m v_i) r_{oa} + i_o r_{of} = i_o R_{oo} - g_m r_{oa} v_i \qquad (4\text{-}100)$$

At the input,

$$v_i = -\frac{r_{ia}}{R_S + r_{ia} + r_{if}} f i_o = -\frac{r_{ia} f i_o}{R_{io}} \qquad (4\text{-}101)$$

Substituting for v_i into Eq. (4-100) gives

$$v_o = i_o R_{oo} + \frac{g_m r_{ia} f i_o}{R_{io}} = i_o R_{oo} (1 + af) \qquad (4\text{-}102)$$

Thus,

$$R_o = \frac{v_o}{i_o} = (1 + af) R_{oo} = (1 + T) R_{oo} \qquad (4\text{-}103)$$

The output resistance of the amplifier with *current* feedback is *increased* by a factor $1 + T$. The reason why current sampling by the feedback network raises the output resistance can be seen by examining Fig. 4-20(b). Due to the negative feedback signal, the dependent current source $g_m v_i$ in the amplifier circuit will be a negative current, giving an increased current in r_{oa}, thereby increasing the output voltage v_o from what it would be without feedback; the output resistance is thereby increased. This will be the case regardless of how the feedback signal is mixed at the input; the shunt current feedback configuration will also have an increased output resistance.

Series Current Feedback Example

A series triple amplifier employing series current feedback is shown in Fig. 4-21. This circuit is useful as a wideband amplifier [4]; the MC 1553 integrated analog amplifier is based on this circuit configuration. In the circuit of Fig. 4-21, the feedback network samples the emitter current of Q_3, which is equal to I_o / α_{F3}, and is thus proportional to the output current. The voltage developed across R_{E2} is sampled by the voltage divider comprising R_{E1} and R_F, producing the feedback voltage across R_{E1}; this feedback voltage is in series with the base-emitter input circuit of Q_1.

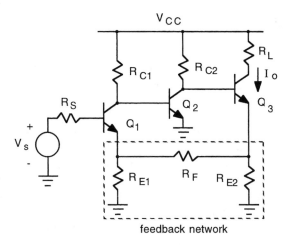

Figure 4-21 Series current feedback triple.

The procedure for calculating the equivalent circuit of the feedback network is illustrated in Fig. 4-22. As shown in Fig. 4-22(a), we **open-circuit** the input side of the feedback network to calculate the feedback voltage. The voltage developed across R_{E2} is

$$V_{RE2} = \frac{(R_{E1} + R_F)\,R_{E2}}{R_{E1} + R_F + R_{E2}} \frac{I_o}{\alpha_{F3}} \tag{4-104}$$

Thus,

$$V_{fb} = \frac{R_{E1}}{R_{E1} + R_F} V_{E2} = \frac{R_{E1}\,R_{E2}}{\alpha_{F3}\,(R_{E1} + R_F + R_{E2})} I_o = fI_o \tag{4-105}$$

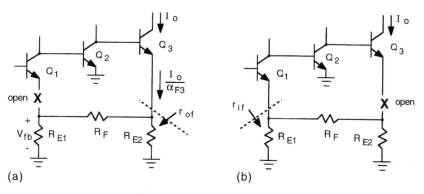

(a)   (b)

Figure 4-22   (a) Procedure for calculating the feedback voltage and the equivalent output resistance of the feedback network. (b) Procedure for calculating the equivalent input resistance of the feedback network.

The output resistance of the feedback network is

$$r_{of} = R_{E2} || (R_F + R_{E1}) \tag{4-106}$$

As shown in Fig. 4-22(b), we **open-circuit** the output side of the feedback network to calculate the input resistance

$$r_{if} = R_{E1} || (R_F + R_{E2}) \tag{4-107}$$

The equivalent circuit of the feedback network (neglecting its feedforward signal) is added to the basic amplifier, as shown in Fig. 4-23(a). Here, the feedback voltage, v_{fb}, and the equivalent input resistance of the feedback network, r_{if}, appear in series with the base-emitter input circuit of the amplifier, and the equivalent output resistance of the feedback network, r_{of}, appears in series with the output circuit of the amplifier.

The small-signal equivalent circuit of the amplifier without feedback ($f = 0$) is shown in Fig. 4-23(b); we use this circuit to calculate the open-loop gain, a. In analyzing this circuit, we will make use of the results for the series voltage feedback example of Fig. 4-13. Here, the first two stages of Fig. 4-23 correspond to the series voltage circuit in which $R_E || R_F$ in Fig. 4-13 corresponds to $R_{E1} || (R_F + R_{E2})$ in Fig. 4-23 and $R_{C2} || (R_E + R_F)$ in Fig. 4-13 corresponds to $R_{C2} || R_{eq3}$ in Fig. 4-23 where R_{eq3} represents the input resistance of the third stage (Q_3), given by

$$R_{eq3} = r_{\pi3} + (\beta_{F3} + 1) [R_{E2} || (R_F + R_{E1})] \tag{4-108}$$

Making these substitutions into Eq. (4-54) results in

$$\frac{v_{o2}}{v_s} = \frac{\beta_{F1} \beta_{F2} R_{C1} (R_{C2} || R_{eq3})}{(r_{\pi2} + R_{C1})(R_S + R_{eq1})} \tag{4-109}$$

where

$$R_{eq1} = r_{\pi1} + (\beta_{F1} + 1) [R_{E1} || (R_F + R_{E2})] \tag{4-110}$$

From Fig. 4-23(b),

$$i_o = g_{m3} v_3 \tag{4-111}$$

where

$$v_3 = \frac{r_{\pi3}}{r_{\pi3} + (\beta_{F3} + 1) [R_{E2} || (R_F + R_{E1})]} v_{o2} = \frac{r_{\pi3}}{R_{eq3}} v_{o2} \tag{4-112}$$

Substituting for v_{o2} from Eq. (4-105) then gives

$$\left. \frac{i_o}{v_s} \right|_{f=0} = a = \frac{\beta_{F1} \beta_{F2} \beta_{F3} R_{C1} R_{C2}}{(R_{C2} + R_{eq3})(r_{\pi2} + R_{C1})(R_S + R_{eq1})} \tag{4-113}$$

where we have used $g_{m3} r_{\pi3} = \beta_{F3}$.

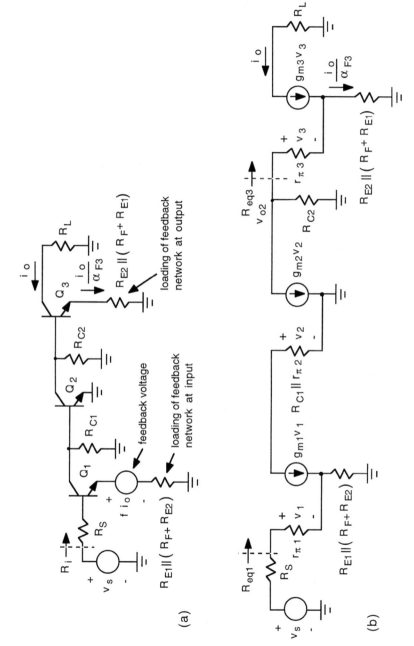

Figure 4-23 (a) AC equivalent circuit of the series current triple. (b) Small-signal equivalent circuit without feedback.

The closed-loop gain with feedback is then

$$\frac{i_o}{v_s} = \frac{a}{1 + af} = \frac{a}{1 + T} \tag{4-114}$$

where

$$T = af = \frac{aR_{E1}R_{E2}}{\alpha_{F3}(R_{E1} + R_F + R_{E2})} \tag{4-115}$$

Typically, the open-loop gain for the series current triple is very large (a numerical example follows). The loop gain T will, therefore, usually be much larger than unity, giving

$$\frac{i_o}{v_s} \approx \frac{1}{f} = \frac{\alpha_{F3}(R_{E1} + R_F + R_{E2})}{R_{E1}R_{E2}} \tag{4-116}$$

The gain is thus set principally by the resistance values of the feedback network.

EXAMPLE. Determine a, T, the closed-loop gain i_o/v_s, and R_i for the series current triple amplifier of Fig. 4-21. The circuit elements are $R_S = 600\,\Omega$, $R_{C1} = 5\,k\Omega$, $R_{C2} = 3\,k\Omega$, $R_{E1} = 200\,\Omega$, $R_{E2} = 100\,\Omega$, and $R_F = 1\,k\Omega$. The bias collector currents are $I_{C1} = 500\,\mu A$, $I_{C2} = 1\,mA$, and $I_{C3} = 2\,mA$. In addition, $\beta_{F1} = \beta_{F2} = \beta_{F3} = 100$. Take room temperature.

These bias currents give $r_{\pi1} = 5.2\,k\Omega$, $r_{\pi2} = 2.6\,k\Omega$, and $r_{\pi3} = 1.3\,k\Omega$. Using Eqs. (4-110) and (4-108),

$$R_{eq1} = 5.2\,k\Omega + (101)[0.2\,k\Omega\|(1\,k\Omega + 0.1\,k\Omega)] = 5.37\,k\Omega$$

and

$$R_{eq3} = 1.3\,k\Omega + (101)[0.1\,k\Omega\|(1\,k\Omega + 0.2\,k\Omega)] = 1.39\,k\Omega$$

From Eq. (4-113),

$$a = \frac{(100)(100)(100)(5\,k\Omega)(3\,k\Omega)}{(10\,k\Omega + 1.39\,k\Omega)(2.6\,k\Omega + 5\,k\Omega)(0.6\,k\Omega + 5.37\,k\Omega)} = 29{,}025\,mA/V$$

Using Eq. (4-105), the feedback factor is

$$f = \frac{(0.2\,k\Omega)(0.1\,k\Omega)}{(0.99)(0.2\,k\Omega + 1\,k\Omega + 0.1\,k\Omega)} = 0.0155\,V/mA$$

Thus, the loop gain is

$$T = (29{,}025\,mA/V)(0.0155\,V/mA) = 450$$

which indeed is much larger than unity. Hence, the closed-loop gain is

$$\frac{i_o}{v_s} \approx \frac{1}{f} = 64.5\,\text{mA}/\text{V}$$

For the input resistance

$$R_{io} = R_S + R_{\text{eq1}} = 0.6\,\text{k}\Omega + 5.37\,\text{k}\Omega = 5.97\,\text{k}\Omega$$

Thus,

$$R_i = (1 + T)\,R_{io} = (451)\,(5.97\,\text{k}\Omega) = 2.69\,\text{M}\Omega$$

which is large.

Shunt Current

In the *shunt current* feedback configuration, repeated in Fig. 4-24(a), the output current i_o is sampled by the feedback network and a feedback current $f i_o$ is mixed in parallel at the input. The effect of the feedback network on the amplifier can be seen by the circuit transformation depicted in Fig. 4-24(b). As far as the feedback network is concerned, it sees a voltage v_i, the voltage at the input to the basic amplifier, at its input and a current i_o at its output; it is appropriate, therefore, to represent the input side of the feedback network by its Norton equivalent and the output side of the feedback network by its Thevenin equivalent. The Norton equivalent at the input consists of resistance r_{if} in parallel with the short-circuit current i_{sc}; r_{if} is the equivalent resistance at the input port of the feedback network, evaluated with i_o set to zero (output open circuited), and i_{sc} is the current at the input of the feedback network with v_i set to zero (input short circuited). i_{sc} is the feedback signal, equal to $f i_o$. The Thevenin equivalent at the output consists of resistance r_{of} in series with the open-circuit feedforward voltage, which is neglected in comparison with the feedforward signal through the basic amplifier. r_{of} is the equivalent resistance at the output port of the feedback network, evaluated with v_i set to zero (input short circuited). The resulting approximate equivalent circuit for the feedback network is shown in the bottom panel of Fig. 4-24(b).

The basic current amplifier is represented by the equivalent circuit shown in the upper portion of Fig. 4-25(a); here, r_{ia} represents the input resistance of the basic current amplifier and r_{oa} its output resistance. The feedback network is represented by its approximate equivalent circuit. From the circuit in Fig. 4-25(a), the output current is

$$i_o = \frac{r_{oa}}{r_{oa} + r_{of} + R_L}\, a_i i_i = \frac{r_{oa}}{R_{oo}}\, a_i i_i \tag{4-117}$$

where

$$R_{oo} = r_{oa} + r_{of} + R_L \tag{4-118}$$

and represents the output resistance of the amplifier without feedback $(f = 0)$.

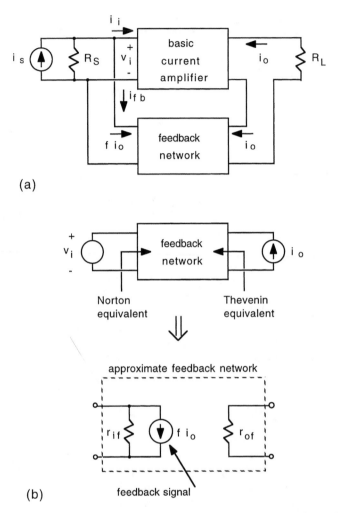

Figure 4-24   (a) Shunt current feedback amplifier. (b) Transformation of feedback network.

Summing the currents at the input gives

$$i_s = \frac{v_i}{R_S} + \frac{v_i}{r_{ia}} + \frac{v_i}{r_{if}} + fi_o = \frac{v_i}{R_{io}} + fi_o \qquad (4\text{-}119)$$

where

$$R_{io} = R_S \| r_{ia} \| r_{if} \qquad (4\text{-}120)$$

and represents the input resistance of the amplifier without feedback.

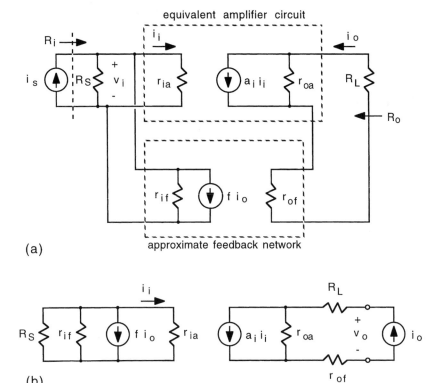

(a)

(b)

Figure 4-25 (a) Shunt current feedback configuration using an equivalent circuit for the basic amplifier. (b) Circuit for calculating the output resistance.

The input current to the basic amplifier is equal to v_i/r_{ia}, which, substituted into Eq. (4-117) and combined with Eq. (4-119), gives the gain

$$\frac{i_o}{i_s} = \frac{\dfrac{a_i r_{oa} R_{io}}{r_{ia} R_{oo}}}{1 + \dfrac{a_i r_{oa} R_{io}}{r_{ia} R_{oo}} f} \qquad (4\text{-}121)$$

It is noted that for this amplifier the feedback factor f has units of amps/amp. If the feedback signal is removed,

$$\left.\frac{i_o}{i_s}\right|_{f=0} = a = \frac{a_i r_{oa} R_{io}}{r_{ia} R_{oo}} \qquad (4\text{-}122)$$

Here, a (which has units of amps/amp) represents the gain of the amplifier without feedback. Thus, Eq. (4-121) can be expressed in terms of the fundamental feedback equation

$$\frac{i_o}{i_s} = \frac{a}{1 + af} = \frac{a}{1 + T} \tag{4-123}$$

Input Resistance

With reference to Fig. 4-25(a), the input resistance of the amplifier with feedback is

$$R_i = \frac{v_i}{i_s} \tag{4-124}$$

where, using Eqs. (4-119) and (4-123),

$$v_i = (i_s - fi_o) R_{io} = \left(1 - \frac{af}{1 + af}\right) i_s R_{io} \tag{4-125}$$

Thus,

$$R_i = \frac{R_{io}}{1 + af} = \frac{R_{io}}{1 + T} \tag{4-126}$$

The input resistance with *shunt* feedback is *reduced* by a factor $1 + T$.

Output Resistance

The output resistance is determined by breaking the series output circuit and applying a test current as shown in Fig. 4-25(b). The output voltage resulting from the test current is

$$v_o = i_o R_L + (i_o - a_i i_i) r_{oa} + i_o r_{of} = i_o R_{oo} - a_i r_{oa} i_i \tag{4-127}$$

At the input,

$$i_i = -\frac{R_S \| r_{if}}{R_S \| r_{if} + r_{ia}} fi_o = -\frac{R_{io} fi_o}{r_{ia}} \tag{4-128}$$

Substituting for i_i into Eq. (4-127) gives

$$v_o = i_o R_{oo} + \frac{a_i r_{oa} R_{io} fi_o}{r_{ia}} = i_o R_{oo} (1 + af) \tag{4-129}$$

Thus,

$$R_o = \frac{v_o}{i_o} = (1 + af) R_{oo} = (1 + T) R_{oo} \tag{4-130}$$

The output resistance of the amplifier with *current* feedback is *increased* by a factor $1 + T$.

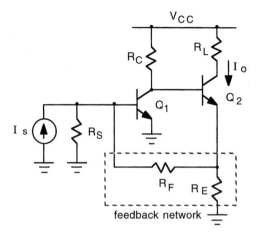

Figure 4-26 **Shunt current feedback example.**

Shunt Current Feedback Example

Figure 4-26 illustrates a shunt current feedback amplifier employing two common-emitter gain stages. In the circuit, the feedback network samples the output current and a feedback current, proportional to I_o, is applied in shunt with the input. To show that this circuit constitutes negative feedback, visualize the output current increasing: An increase in I_o increases the voltage across R_E which increases the current flowing through the feedback resistance R_F to the input node; this increases the base current of Q_1, causing it to conduct more heavily, lowering the voltage at its collector. Q_2 conducts less, lowering its collector current I_o.

The procedure for calculating the equivalent circuit of the feedback network is illustrated in Fig. 4-27. As shown in Fig. 4-27(a), we **short-circuit** the input side of the feedback network to calculate the feedback current

$$I_{\text{fb}} = -\frac{R_E}{R_F + R_E}\frac{I_o}{\alpha_{F2}} = fI_o \qquad (4\text{-}131)$$

and the output resistance

$$r_{of} = R_F \| R_E \qquad (4\text{-}132)$$

As shown in Fig. 4-27(b), we **open-circuit** the output side of the feedback to calculate the input resistance

$$r_{if} = R_F + R_E \qquad (4\text{-}133)$$

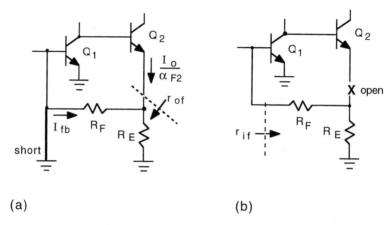

(a)   (b)

Figure 4-27   (a) Procedure for calculating feedback current and equivalent output resistance of the feedback network. (b) Procedure for calculating the equivalent input resistance of the feedback network.

The equivalent circuit of the feedback network (neglecting its feedforward signal) is added to the basic amplifier, as shown in Fig. 4-28(a). Here, the feedback current, i_{fb}, and the equivalent input resistance of the feedback network, r_{if}, appear in parallel (shunt) with the input of the amplifier and the equivalent output resistance of the feedback network appears in series with the output circuit of the amplifier.

The small-signal equivalent circuit of the amplifier without feedback ($f = 0$) is shown in Fig. 4-28(b). It is left as an exercise to show that the open-loop gain is given by

$$\left. \frac{i_o}{i_s} \right|_{f=0} = a = - \frac{\beta_{F1} \beta_{F2} R_C [R_S || (R_F + R_E)]}{[r_{\pi 1} + R_S || (R_F + R_E)] [R_C + r_{\pi 2} + (\beta_{F2} + 1)(R_F || R_E)]}$$

(4-134)

4.4 Dual-Loop Feedback

Amplifiers may simultaneously employ both shunt and series feedback; such amplifiers are termed dual-loop feedback amplifiers in that two separate feedback paths exist. Dual-loop feedback allows a more independent control of the amplifier's closed-loop input and output impedances; this is useful, for example, if the amplifier is to interface with specified source and load impedances [5].

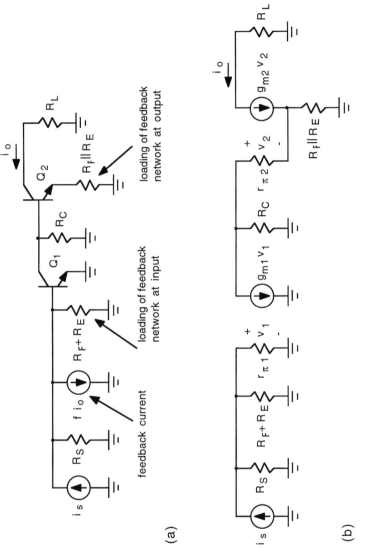

Figure 4-28 (a) AC equivalent circuit of the shunt current feedback amplifier. (b) Small-signal equivalent circuit without feedback.

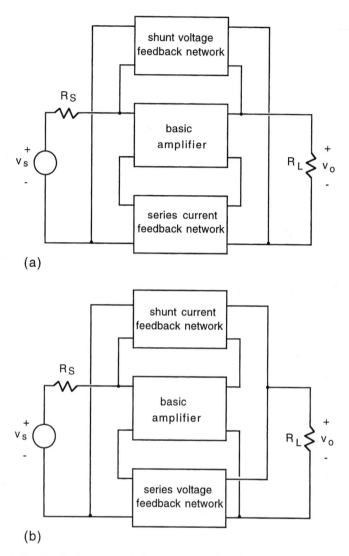

Figure 4-29 **(a) Series current–shunt voltage dual-loop feedback amplifier. (b) Series voltage–shunt current dual-loop feedback amplifier.**

Figure 4-29 illustrates the two possible global dual-loop configurations employing shunt and series feedback. In Fig. 4-29(a), a *series current–shunt voltage* feedback amplifier is depicted, and in Fig. 4-29(b), a *series voltage–shunt current* feedback amplifier is shown. Each of these will be considered in the sections that follow.

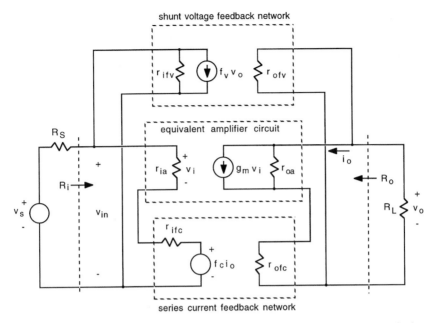

Figure 4-30   Dual-loop series current–shunt voltage feedback using an equivalent circuit for the basic amplifier.

Series Current–Shunt Voltage

Figure 4-30 shows a dual-loop series current and shunt voltage feedback amplifier using a transconductance equivalent circuit model for the basic amplifier. Any of the four equivalent circuit representations for the basic amplifier could be used; the transconductance model is a convenient and familiar form. Parameters representing the equivalent circuit of the series current feedback network are denoted with the subscript c (for current) and those representing the shunt voltage feedback network are denoted with the subscript v (for voltage). We analyze this circuit for the closed-loop voltage gain, v_o/v_s.

At the output, the voltage across the output resistance of the amplifier r_{oa} is

$$v_{r_{oa}} = -g_m v_i r_{oa} || [r_{ofc} + (r_{ofv} || R_L)] = -\frac{g_m v_i r_{oa} [r_{ofc} + (r_{ofv} || R_L)]}{r_{oa} + r_{ofc} + (r_{ofv} || R_L)} \qquad (4\text{-}135)$$

The output voltage, using the voltage–divider relation, is

$$v_o = \frac{r_{ofv} || R_L}{(r_{ofv} || R_L + r_{ofc})} v_{r_{oa}} \qquad (4\text{-}136)$$

Then, using Eq. (4-135),

$$v_o = - \frac{g_m v_i r_{oa} (r_{ofv} || R_L)}{r_{oa} + r_{ofc} + (r_{ofv} || R_L)} \qquad (4\text{-}137)$$

which can be manipulated into the following form:

$$v_o = - \frac{g_m r_{oa} (R_{oo} || R_L)}{r_{oa} + r_{ofc}} v_i \qquad (4\text{-}138)$$

where

$$R_{oo} = r_{ofv} || (r_{oa} + r_{ofc}) = \frac{r_{ofv} (r_{oa} + r_{ofc})}{r_{ofv} + r_{oa} + r_{ofc}} \qquad (4\text{-}139)$$

and represents the output resistance of the amplifier without feedback and excluding the external load, R_L.

Summing the currents at the input gives

$$\frac{v_s - v_{in}}{R_S} = \frac{v_{in}}{r_{ifv}} + f_v v_o + \frac{v_{in} - f_c i_o}{r_{ia} + r_{ifc}} \qquad (4\text{-}140)$$

where, from the output,

$$i_o = - \frac{v_o}{r_{ofv} || R_L} = - \frac{r_{ofv} + R_L}{r_{ofv} R_L} v_o \qquad (4\text{-}141)$$

and upon substitution into Eq. (4-140) gives

$$v_{in} = \frac{R_{io}}{R_S + R_{io}} v_s - \frac{R_S R_{io}}{R_S + R_{io}} \left[f_v + \frac{(r_{ofv} + R_L) f_c}{r_{ofv} R_L (r_{ia} + r_{ifc})} \right] v_o \qquad (4\text{-}142)$$

where

$$R_{io} = r_{ifv} || (r_{ia} + r_{ifc}) = \frac{r_{ifv} (r_{ia} + r_{ifc})}{r_{ifv} + r_{ia} + r_{ifc}} \qquad (4\text{-}143)$$

and represents the input resistance of the amplifier without feedback, excluding the source resistance, R_s. Applying the voltage-divider relation at the input gives

$$v_i = \frac{r_{ia}}{r_{ia} + r_{ifc}} (v_{in} - f_c i_o) = \frac{r_{ia}}{r_{ia} + r_{ifc}} \left[v_{in} + \frac{(r_{ofv} + R_L) f_c}{r_{ofv} R_L} v_o \right] \qquad (4\text{-}144)$$

which, after using Eq. (4-142), yields

$$v_i = \frac{r_{ia} R_{io}}{(r_{ia} + r_{ifc})(R_S + R_{io})} \left\{ v_s - \left[R_S f_v - \left(1 + \frac{R_S}{r_{ifv}} \right) \left(1 + \frac{R_L}{r_{ofv}} \right) \frac{f_c}{R_L} v_o \right] \right\}$$

$$(4\text{-}145)$$

Substituting Eq. (4-145) into Eq. (4-138) then gives

$$v_o = -\frac{g_m r_{ia} r_{oa} R_{io} (R_{oo} \| R_L)}{(r_{ia} + r_{ifc})(r_{oa} + r_{ofc})(R_S + R_{io})}\left\{v_s - \left[R_S f_v - \left(1 + \frac{R_S}{r_{ifv}}\right)\left(1 + \frac{R_L}{r_{ofv}}\right)\frac{f_c}{R_L}v_o\right]\right\}$$

$$(4\text{-}146)$$

Equation (4-146) is in the form

$$v_o = a v_s - a f v_o \tag{4-147}$$

where

$$a = -\frac{g_m r_{ia} r_{oa} R_{io} R_{oo} R_L}{(r_{ia} + r_{ifc})(r_{oa} + r_{ofc})(R_S + R_{io})(R_{oo} + R_L)} \tag{4-148}$$

and

$$f = R_S f_v - \left(1 + \frac{R_S}{r_{ifv}}\right)\left(1 + \frac{R_L}{r_{ofv}}\right)\frac{f_c}{R_L} \tag{4-149}$$

The closed-loop gain is then

$$\frac{v_o}{v_s} = \frac{a}{1 + af} \tag{4-150}$$

Here, f represents the net feedback factor combining both the series and shunt feedback paths. If the loop gain, af, is much greater than unity, the closed-loop gain is approximately

$$\frac{v_o}{v_s} \approx \frac{1}{f} = \frac{1}{R_S f_v - \left(1 + \dfrac{R_S}{r_{ifv}}\right)\left(1 + \dfrac{R_L}{r_{ofv}}\right)\dfrac{f_c}{R_L}} \tag{4-151}$$

Input Resistance

To calculate the input resistance, excluding the source resistance, we place a test source at the input of the feedback amplifier, as indicated in Fig. 4-31 (a). The input current resulting from the test voltage is

$$i_{in} = \frac{v_{in}}{r_{ifv}} + f_v v_o + \frac{v_{in} - f_c i_o}{r_{ia} + r_{ifc}} \tag{4-152}$$

which, after substituting for i_o from Eq. (4-141), yields

$$i_{in} R_{io} = v_{in} + \left[R_{io} f_v + \left(1 - \frac{R_{io}}{r_{ifv}}\right)\left(1 + \frac{R_L}{r_{ofv}}\right)\frac{f_c}{R_L}\right]v_o \tag{4-153}$$

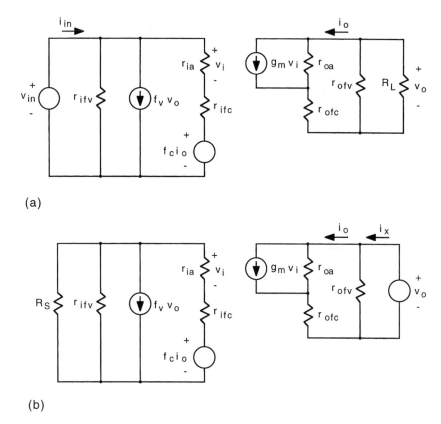

(a)

(b)

Figure 4-31 (a) Circuit for calculating the input resistance. (b) Circuit for calculating the output resistance.

Combining Eqs. (4-138) and (4-144) gives

$$v_o = \frac{a\left(1 + \dfrac{R_S}{R_{io}}\right)}{1 - a\left(1 + \dfrac{R_S}{R_{io}}\right)\left(1 + \dfrac{R_L}{r_{ofv}}\right)\dfrac{f_c}{R_L}} v_{in} \tag{4-154}$$

which, after substituting into Eq. (4-153), yields

$$i_{in} R_{io} = \frac{1 + a(R_S + R_{io})\left[f_v - \left(1 + \dfrac{R_L}{r_{ofv}}\right)\dfrac{f_c}{r_{ifv} R_L}\right]}{1 - a\left(1 + \dfrac{R_S}{R_{io}}\right)\left(1 + \dfrac{R_L}{r_{ofv}}\right)\dfrac{f_c}{R_L}} v_{in} \tag{4-155}$$

The input resistance is then

$$R_i = \frac{v_{in}}{i_{in}} = \frac{1 - a\left(1 + \dfrac{R_S}{R_{io}}\right)\left(1 + \dfrac{R_L}{r_{ofv}}\right)\dfrac{f_c}{R_L}}{1 + a\,(R_S + R_{io})\left[f_v - \left(1 + \dfrac{R_L}{r_{ofv}}\right)\dfrac{f_c}{r_{ifv}\,R_L}\right]}\,R_{io} \qquad (4\text{-}156)$$

The numerator of Eq. (4-156) represents the increase in input resistance due to the series feedback path and the denominator represents the decrease in resistance due to the shunt feedback path.

If the series and shunt loop gains $a(\ )$ are much larger than unity, then the input resistance is approximately

$$R_i \approx \frac{\left(1 + \dfrac{R_L}{r_{ofv}}\right)\dfrac{f_c}{R_L}}{\left(1 + \dfrac{R_L}{r_{ofv}}\right)\dfrac{f_c}{r_{ifv}\,R_L} - f_v} \qquad (4\text{-}157)$$

Output Resistance

To calculate the output resistance, excluding the load resistance, we place a test source at the output of the feedback amplifier, as indicated in Fig. 4-31(b). The output resistance is calculated from

$$R_o = \frac{v_o}{i_x} \qquad (4\text{-}158)$$

where, from the output,

$$i_x = \frac{v_o}{r_{ofv}} + i_o \qquad (4\text{-}159)$$

Also,

$$v_o = (i_o - g_m v_i)\,r_{oa} + i_o\,r_{ofc} \qquad (4\text{-}160)$$

which gives

$$i_o = \frac{v_o}{r_{oa} + r_{ofc}} + \frac{g_m\,r_{oa}\,v_i}{r_{oa} + r_{ofc}} \qquad (4\text{-}161)$$

which, substituted into Eq. (4-159), yields

$$i_x = \frac{v_o}{R_{oo}} + \frac{g_m\,r_{oa}\,v_i}{r_{oa} + r_{ofc}} \qquad (4\text{-}162)$$

Summing the currents at the input, denoting the voltage across the parallel combination of resistors R_S and r_{ifv} as v_{in}, gives

$$\frac{v_{in}}{R_S \| r_{ifv}} + f_v v_o + \frac{v_{in} - f_c i_o}{r_{ia} + r_{ifc}} = 0 \qquad (4\text{-}163)$$

which leads to

$$v_{\text{in}} = \frac{R_S R_{io}}{R_S + R_{io}} \left(\frac{f_c i_o}{r_{ia} + r_{ifc}} - f_v v_o \right) \tag{4-164}$$

Applying the voltage–divider relation at the input provides

$$v_i = \frac{r_{ia}}{r_{ia} + r_{ifc}} (v_{\text{in}} - f_c i_o) \tag{4-165}$$

which, solved for v_{in} and substituted into Eq. (4-164), gives

$$v_i = \frac{r_{ia}}{r_{ia} + r_{ifc}} \left[\frac{R_S R_{io}}{R_S + R_{io}} \left(\frac{f_c i_o}{r_{ia} + r_{ifc}} - f_v v_o \right) - f_c i_o \right] \tag{4-166}$$

Then, using Eq. (4-159), we have

$$v_i = \frac{r_{ia}}{r_{ia} + r_{ifc}} \left\{ - \frac{R_{io}(R_S + r_{ifv})}{r_{ifv}(R_S + R_{io})} f_c i_x + \left[\frac{R_{io}(R_S + r_{ifv})}{r_{ifv}(R_S + R_{io})} \frac{f_c}{r_{ofv}} + \frac{R_S R_{io}}{R_S + R_{io}} f_v \right] v_o \right\} \tag{4-167}$$

Finally, combining Eq. (4-167) with Eq. (4-162), and noting Eq. (4-148), yields

$$i_x \left[1 - a \left(1 + \frac{R_S}{r_{ifv}} \right) \left(1 + \frac{R_L}{R_{oo}} \right) \frac{f_c}{R_L} \right] = \frac{v_o}{R_{oo}} \left\{ 1 + a \left(1 + \frac{R_{oo}}{R_L} \right) \left[R_S f_v - \left(1 + \frac{R_S}{r_{ifv}} \right) \frac{f_c}{r_{ofv}} \right] \right\} \tag{4-168}$$

Thus,

$$R_o = \frac{1 - a \left(1 + \dfrac{R_S}{r_{ifv}} \right) \left(1 + \dfrac{R_L}{R_{oo}} \right) \dfrac{f_c}{R_L}}{1 + a \left(1 + \dfrac{R_{oo}}{R_L} \right) \left[R_S f_v - \left(1 + \dfrac{R_S}{r_{ifv}} \right) \dfrac{f_c}{r_{ofv}} \right]} R_{oo} \tag{4-169}$$

The numerator of Eq. (4-169) represents the increase in output resistance due to the series feedback path and the denominator represents the decrease in resistance due to the shunt feedback path.

If the series and shunt loop gains $a(\ )$ are much larger than unity, then the output resistance is approximately

$$R_o \approx \frac{\left(1 + \dfrac{R_S}{r_{ifv}} \right) f_c}{\left(1 + \dfrac{R_S}{r_{ifv}} \right) \dfrac{f_c}{r_{ofv}} - R_S f_v} \tag{4-170}$$

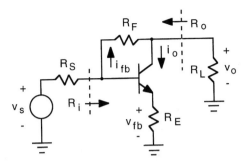

Figure 4-32   Dual-loop series current–shunt voltage feedback amplifier using local feedback.

Series Current–Shunt Voltage Feedback Example 1

Figure 4-32 shows a dual-loop feedback employing local series current and shunt voltage feedback; emitter-degeneration resistor R_E provides the series feedback for the single-transistor amplifier, and resistor R_F provides shunt feedback between collector and base. In this circuit, $r_{ifc} = r_{ofc} = R_E$ and $r_{ifv} = r_{ofv} = R_F$.

The series feedback voltage (neglecting base current) is

$$v_{\text{fb}} = i_o R_E = f_c i_o \tag{4-171}$$

so

$$f_c = R_E \tag{4-172}$$

The shunt feedback current (determined by shorting the input to the amplifier) is

$$i_{\text{fb}} = -\frac{v_o}{R_F} = f_v v_o \tag{4-173}$$

so

$$f_v = -\frac{1}{R_F} \tag{4-174}$$

In this amplifier, $r_{ia} = r_\pi$, $R_{io} = R_F \| (r_\pi + R_E)$, and $R_{oo} = R_F$, neglecting $r_{oa} = r_o$. Using Eq. (4-148), the open-loop gain, assuming that $r_{oa} \gg r_{ofc}$ (i.e., $r_o \gg R_E$), is

$$a = -\frac{\beta_F R_F^2 R_L}{[(r_\pi + R_E)(R_S + R_F) + R_S R_F](R_F + R_L)} \tag{4-175}$$

where we have substituted $\beta_F = g_m r_\pi$.

From Eq. (4-149), the combined feedback factor is

$$f = -\frac{R_S}{R_F} - \left(1 + \frac{R_S}{R_F}\right)\left(1 + \frac{R_L}{R_F}\right)\frac{R_E}{R_L} \tag{4-176}$$

The loop gain is then

$$T = af = \frac{\beta_F [R_S R_F R_L + R_E (R_S + R_F)(R_F + R_L)]}{[(r_\pi + R_E)(R_S + R_F) + R_S R_F](R_F + R_L)} \tag{4-177}$$

If the value of the loop gain is considerably larger than unity (for this amplifier, this is achieved by making $g_m R_E \gg 1$), then the closed-loop gain of the amplifier can be approximated as

$$\frac{v_o}{v_s} \approx \frac{1}{f} = -\frac{1}{\dfrac{R_S}{R_F} + \left(1 + \dfrac{R_S}{R_F}\right)\left(1 + \dfrac{R_L}{R_F}\right)\dfrac{R_E}{R_L}} \tag{4-178}$$

Further, if the shunt feedback resistance R_F is much larger than both the source (R_S) and load (R_L) resistances, then the gain is

$$\frac{v_o}{v_s} \approx -\frac{1}{\dfrac{R_S}{R_F} + \dfrac{R_E}{R_L}} \tag{4-179}$$

The first term on the right-hand side of Eq. (4-179) represents the contribution to the closed-loop gain resulting from the shunt feedback path, and the second term represents the contribution to the gain from the series feedback path.

Also, for the loop gain much larger than unity, the input resistance (excluding R_S) from Eq. (4-157) is

$$R_i \approx \frac{\left(1 + \dfrac{R_L}{R_F}\right)\dfrac{R_E}{R_L}}{\left(1 + \dfrac{R_L}{R_F}\right)\dfrac{R_E}{R_F R_L} + \dfrac{1}{R_F}} = \frac{R_E R_F (R_F + R_L)}{R_F R_L + R_E (R_F + R_L)} \tag{4-180}$$

Likewise, from Eq. (4-170), the output resistance (excluding R_L) is

$$R_o \approx \frac{\left(1 + \dfrac{R_S}{R_F}\right)R_E}{\left(1 + \dfrac{R_S}{R_F}\right)\dfrac{R_E}{R_F} + \dfrac{R_S}{R_F}} = \frac{R_E R_F (R_F + R_S)}{R_F R_S + R_E (R_F + R_S)} \tag{4-181}$$

Note the symmetry in Eqs. (4-180) and (4-181) as they relate to the source and load resistances.

As a further example, assume this amplifier is to match its input resistance to R_S and its output resistance to R_L. Additionally, take $R_F \gg R_L$, R_S, and R_E (which is normally the case). The matched input and output resistances are then

$$R_i \approx \frac{R_E R_F}{R_E + R_L} = R_S \tag{4-182}$$

and

$$R_o \approx \frac{R_E R_F}{R_E + R_S} = R_L \tag{4-183}$$

As evidenced by Eqs. (4-182) and (4-183), a simultaneous match at both the input and output requires that $R_S = R_L$. With this match, the series and shunt feedback resistances are related through

$$R_E (R_F - R) \approx R_E R_F = R^2 \tag{4-184}$$

where $R = R_S = R_L$.

From Eq. (4-179), the voltage gain is

$$\frac{v_o}{v_s} = A_v \approx -\frac{1}{\dfrac{R}{R_F} + \dfrac{R_E}{R}} = -\frac{R_F R}{R^2 + R_E R_F} \tag{4-185}$$

which, using Eq. (4-184), gives

$$A_v \approx -\frac{R_F}{2R} = -\frac{1}{2}\sqrt{\frac{R_F}{R_E}} \tag{4-186}$$

To design for a specific closed-loop gain under matched conditions, the feedback resistances are then given by

$$R_F = -2A_v R \tag{4-187}$$

and

$$R_E = -\frac{R}{2A_v} \tag{4-188}$$

Series Current–Shunt Voltage Feedback Amplifier Example 2

Figure 4-33(a) shows a series triple amplifier employing series current and shunt voltage feedback; the feedback network comprising resistors R_{E1}, R_{F1}, and R_{E2} samples the output current and applies a feedback voltage in series at the input, and resistor R_{F2} provides shunt voltage feedback from the output to the input of the amplifier.

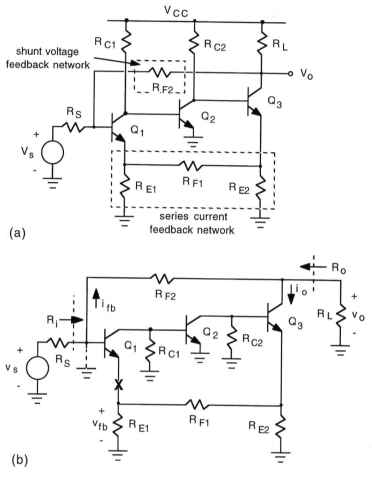

Figure 4-33 **(a) Dual-loop series current–shunt voltage feedback amplifier. (b) AC circuit for calculating feedback parameters.**

The ac circuit for calculating the feedback parameters is illustrated in Fig. 4-33(b). With the input shorted, the shunt feedback current is

$$i_{\text{fb}} = -\frac{v_o}{R_{F2}} = f_v v_o \tag{4-189}$$

so

$$f_v = -\frac{1}{R_{F2}} \tag{4-190}$$

Also, $r_{ifv} = r_{ofv} = R_{F2}$.

With the emitter of Q_1 open-circuited, the voltage at the emitter of Q_3 is

$$v_{E3} = R_{E2} || (R_{E1} + R_{F1}) \frac{i_o}{\alpha_{F3}} \approx R_{E2} || (R_{E1} + R_{F1}) i_o \qquad (4\text{-}191)$$

where in the rightmost term we have taken α_{F3} to be unity. The series feedback voltage is then

$$v_{\text{fb}} = \frac{R_{E1}}{R_{E1} + R_{F1}} v_{E3} = \frac{R_{E1} R_{E2}}{R_{E1} + R_{F1} + R_{E2}} i_o = f_c i_o \qquad (4\text{-}192)$$

so

$$f_c = \frac{R_{E1} R_{E2}}{R_{E1} + R_{F1} + R_{E2}} \qquad (4\text{-}193)$$

From Eq. (4-149), the combined feedback factor is

$$f = -\frac{R_S}{R_{F2}} - \left(1 + \frac{R_S}{R_{F2}}\right)\left(1 + \frac{R_L}{R_{F2}}\right) \frac{R_{E1} R_{E2}}{(R_{E1} + R_{F1} + R_{E2}) R_L} \qquad (4\text{-}194)$$

The series triple amplifier has a large open-loop gain, a. Therefore, it is expected that the loop gain with feedback, af, will be much larger than unity. Thus, the closed-loop gain is approximately

$$\frac{v_o}{v_s} \approx \frac{1}{f} = -\frac{R_{F2} R_L (R_{E1} + R_{F1} + R_{E2})}{R_S R_L (R_{E1} + R_{F1} + R_{E2}) + R_{E1} R_{E2} R_{F2}} \qquad (4\text{-}195)$$

In arriving at Eq. (4-195), we have assumed that $R_{F2} \gg R_S$ and R_L. Likewise, the input resistance (excluding R_S) is, from Eq. (4-157),

$$R_i \approx \frac{f_c}{\dfrac{f_c}{r_{ifv}} - R_L f_v} = \frac{R_{E1} R_{E2} R_{F2}}{R_{E1} R_{E2} + R_L (R_{E1} + R_{F1} + R_{E2})} \qquad (4\text{-}196)$$

From Eq. (4-170), the output resistance (excluding R_L) is

$$R_o \approx \frac{f_c}{\dfrac{f_c}{r_{ofv}} - R_S f_v} = \frac{R_{E1} R_{E2} R_{F2}}{R_{E1} R_{E2} + R_S (R_{E1} + R_{F1} + R_{E2})} \qquad (4\text{-}197)$$

As with the previous example, a simultaneous match at both the input and output requires that $R_S = R_L$, giving

$$R_{E1} R_{E2} (R_{F2} - R) = (R_{E1} + R_{F1} + R_{E2}) R^2 \qquad (4\text{-}198)$$

where $R = R_S = R_L$.

For $R_{F2} \gg R$, this simplifies to

$$\frac{R_{E1} R_{E2} R_{F2}}{R_{E1} + R_{F1} + R_{E2}} \approx R^2 \tag{4-199}$$

From Eq. (4-195), the corresponding voltage gain is

$$A_v = -\frac{R_{F2} R (R_{E1} + R_{F1} + R_{E2})}{R^2 (R_{E1} + R_{F1} + R_{E2}) + R_{E1} R_{E2} R_{F2}} \tag{4-200}$$

which, using Eq. (4-199), gives

$$A_v \approx -\frac{R_{F2}}{2R} = -\frac{1}{2}\sqrt{\frac{R_{F2} (R_{E1} + R_{F1} + R_{E2})}{R_{E1} R_{E2}}} \tag{4-201}$$

Series Voltage–Shunt Current

The dual-loop series voltage and shunt current feedback amplifier, also using a transconductance equivalent circuit model for the basic amplifier, is shown in Fig. 4-34. Analysis of this circuit proceeds in a fashion similar to that

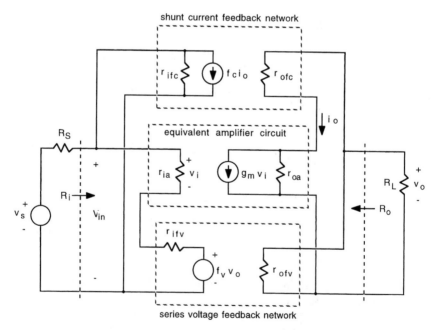

Figure 4-34 Dual-loop series voltage–shunt current feedback using an equivalent circuit for the basic amplifier.

carried out for the series current–shunt voltage configuration. Again, the closed-loop voltage gain can be expressed as

$$\frac{v_o}{v_s} = \frac{a}{1 + af}$$

(4-202)

with

$$a = -\frac{g_m r_{ia} r_{oa} R_{io} R_{oo} R_L}{(r_{ia} + r_{ifv})(r_{oa} + r_{ofc})(R_S + R_{io})(R_{oo} + R_L)}$$

(4-203)

and

$$f = \left(1 + \frac{R_S}{r_{ifc}}\right) f_v - \left(1 + \frac{R_L}{r_{ofv}}\right) \frac{R_S}{R_L} f_c$$

(4-204)

Here,

$$R_{io} = r_{ifc} \| (r_{ia} + r_{ifv}) = \frac{r_{ifc}(r_{ia} + r_{ifv})}{r_{ifc} + r_{ia} + r_{ifv}}$$

(4-205)

and

$$R_{oo} = r_{ofv} \| (r_{ofc} + r_{oa}) = \frac{r_{ofv}(r_{ofc} + r_{oa})}{r_{ofv} + r_{ofc} + r_{oa}}$$

(4-206)

If the loop gain, af, is much greater than unity, the closed-loop gain is given approximately by

$$\frac{v_o}{v_s} \approx \frac{1}{f} = \frac{1}{\left(1 + \frac{R_S}{r_{ifc}}\right) f_v - \left(1 + \frac{R_L}{r_{ofv}}\right) \frac{R_S}{R_L} f_c}$$

(4-207)

Input Resistance

The circuit in Fig. 4-35(a) is used to calculate the closed-loop input resistance; R_i is equal to v_{in}/i_{in}, and results in

$$R_i = \frac{1 + a\left(1 + \frac{R_S}{R_{io}}\right) f_v}{1 - a(R_S + R_{io})\left[\left(1 + \frac{R_L}{r_{ofv}}\right) \frac{f_c}{R_L} - \frac{f_v}{r_{ifc}}\right]} R_{io}$$

(4-208)

The numerator of Eq. (4-208) represents the increase in input resistance due to the series feedback path and the denominator represents the decrease in resistance due to the shunt feedback path.

For large loop gain,

$$R_i \approx \frac{f_v}{\frac{f_v}{r_{ifc}} - \left(1 + \frac{R_L}{r_{ofv}}\right) \frac{f_c}{R_L}}$$

(4-209)

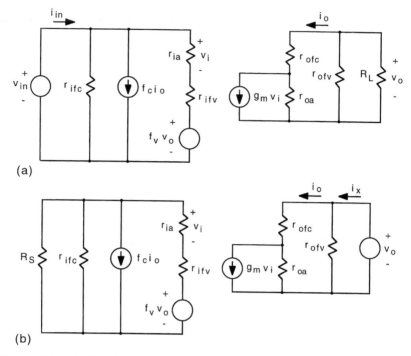

(a)

(b)

Figure 4-35 (a) Circuit for calculating the input resistance. (b) Circuit for calculating the output resistance.

Output Resistance

The test circuit in Fig. 4-35(b) is used to calculate the closed-loop output resistance; R_o is equal to v_o/i_o, and results in

$$R_o = \frac{1 - a\left(1 + \dfrac{R_{oo}}{R_L}\right)\dfrac{R_S}{R_{oo}}f_c}{1 + a\left(1 + \dfrac{R_{oo}}{R_L}\right)\left[\left(1 + \dfrac{R_S}{r_{ifc}}\right)f_c - \dfrac{R_S}{r_{ofv}}f_c\right]}R_{oo} \qquad (4\text{-}210)$$

The numerator of Eq. (4-210) represents the increase in output resistance due to the series feedback path and the denominator represents the decrease in resistance due to the shunt feedback path.

If the loop gain is much larger than unity, the output resistance is approximately

$$R_o \approx \frac{R_S f_c}{\dfrac{R_S}{r_{ofv}}f_c - \left(1 + \dfrac{R_S}{r_{ifc}}\right)f_v} \qquad (4\text{-}211)$$

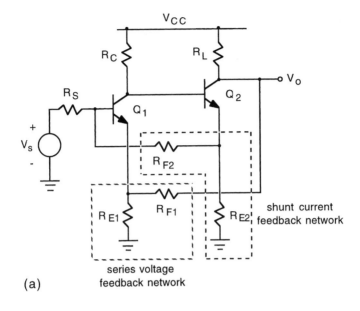

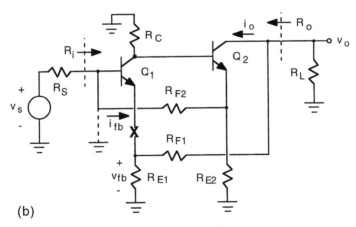

Figure 4-36 (a) **Dual-loop series voltage–shunt current feedback amplifier. (b) AC circuit for calculating feedback parameters.**

Series Voltage–Shunt Current Feedback Amplifier Example

Figure 4-36(a) shows a two-stage amplifier employing series voltage and shunt current feedback; the voltage divider comprising resistors R_{E1} and R_{F1} provide the feedback voltage and the current divider comprising resistors R_{E2} and R_{F2} provide the feedback current.

The ac circuit for calculating the feedback parameters is illustrated in Fig. 4-36(b). With the input shorted, the shunt feedback current is

$$i_{fb} = -\frac{R_{E2}}{R_{E2} + R_{F2}}\frac{i_o}{\alpha_{F3}} \approx -\frac{R_{E2}}{R_{E2} + R_{F2}}i_o = f_c i_o \qquad (4\text{-}212)$$

so

$$f_c = -\frac{R_{E2}}{R_{E2} + R_{F2}} \qquad (4\text{-}213)$$

Also,

$$r_{ifc} = R_{F2} + R_{E2} \qquad (4\text{-}214)$$

With the emitter of Q_1 open-circuited, the series feedback voltage is

$$v_{fb} = \frac{R_{E1}}{R_{E1} + R_{F1}}v_o = f_v v_o \qquad (4\text{-}215)$$

so

$$f_v = \frac{R_{E1}}{R_{E1} + R_{F1}} \qquad (4\text{-}216)$$

Also,

$$r_{ofv} = R_{F1} + R_{E1} \qquad (4\text{-}217)$$

From Eq. (4-204), the combined feedback factor is

$$f = \left(1 + \frac{R_S}{R_{F2} + R_{E2}}\right)\left(\frac{R_{E1}}{R_{E1} + R_{F1}}\right) + \left(1 + \frac{R_L}{R_{F1} + R_{E1}}\right)\frac{R_S R_{E2}}{R_L (R_{E2} + R_{F2})} \qquad (4\text{-}218)$$

Typically, the feedback resistances R_{F1} and R_{F2} will be considerably larger than the source, R_S, and load, R_L, resistances. If this is the case, then Eq. (4-218) simplifies to

$$f \approx \frac{R_{E1}}{R_{E1} + R_{F1}} + \frac{R_S R_{E2}}{R_L (R_{E2} + R_{F2})} \qquad (4\text{-}219)$$

And for large loop gain, the closed-loop gain is then

$$\frac{v_o}{v_s} \approx \frac{1}{f} = \frac{(R_{E1} + R_{F1})(R_{E2} + R_{F2}) R_L}{R_S R_{E2} (R_{E1} + R_{F1}) + R_{E1} R_L (R_{E2} + R_{F2})} \qquad (4\text{-}220)$$

From Eqs. (4-209) and (4-211), the approximate input and output resistances are

$$R_i \approx \frac{R_{E1} R_L (R_{E2} + R_{F2})}{R_{E1} R_L + R_{E2} (R_{E1} + R_{F1} + R_L)} \tag{4-221}$$

and

$$R_o \approx \frac{R_S R_{E2} (R_{E1} + R_{F1})}{R_S R_{E2} + R_{E1} (R_S + R_{E2} + R_{F2})} \tag{4-222}$$

EXERCISE. Assuming that the current gain (β_F) of the transistors are much larger than unity, show that the open-loop gain of the dual-loop feedback amplifier in Fig. 4-36(a) is given by

$$a \approx \frac{g_{m1} \beta_{F2} R_C (R_{F2} + R_{E2}) [R_L || (R_{F1} + R_{E1})]}{(R_S + R_{F2} + R_{E2})[1 + g_{m1}(R_{E1} || R_{F1})] \{R_C + r_{\pi 2}[1 + g_{m2}(R_{E2} || R_{F2})]\}}$$

Figure 4-37 shows the schematic diagram of a commercial wideband amplifier employing the basic dual-loop feedback pair of Fig. 4-36(a). This amplifier is designed to drive a 50-Ω load with a gain of about 20 dB and exhibits a -3-dB bandwidth of 700 MHz using transistors with unity-gain frequencies

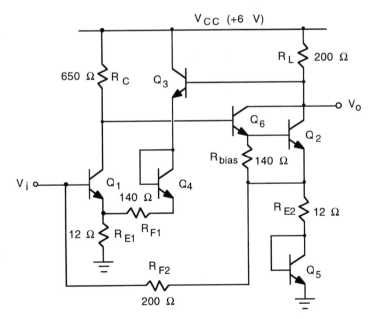

Figure 4-37 NE5205 wideband amplifier employing series voltage and shunt current feedback.

(f_T) of about 2 GHz [6]. In the circuit, the Darlington pair comprising transistors Q_2 and Q_6 are used in place of the single second gain transistor Q_2 in Fig. 4-36(a); this provides additional buffering at the output. Transistor Q_3 buffers the feedback loading of R_{F1} at the output, and the diodes formed by Q_4 and Q_5 provide dc level shifting.

4.5 Stability of Feedback Amplifiers

A feedback amplifier is normally operated with negative feedback: The feedback signal presented to the input of the amplifier is 180° out of phase with respect to the input signal, thereby reducing the net input to the amplifier. The phase of the feedback signal derives from the phase of the signal propagating forward through the amplifier and back through the feedback network. The phase shift of the amplifier generally increases with frequency; if at some frequency the phase of the feedback signal were to increase by 180°, then at that frequency the feedback signal would be in phase with the input to the amplifier, resulting in the amplifier operating with *positive* feedback. If the magnitude of the loop gain $T(j\omega)$ at that frequency (see Fig. 4-38) is greater than unity, then the output of the amplifier would continue to build, even in the absence of an external input signal. The amplifier at this point would become unstable and would likely oscillate at some frequency where the magnitude and phase of the loop gain leads to positive feedback. The closed-loop gain of the feedback amplifier depicted in Fig. 4-38 can be expressed as

$$A(j\omega) = \frac{v_o}{v_i} = \frac{a(j\omega)}{1 + |T(j\omega)| e^{j\phi(\omega)}} \qquad (4\text{-}223)$$

It is clear that for $|T(j\omega)| = 1$ and $\phi = -180°$, the gain [from Eq. (4-223)] would become infinite. The conditions for stability can be stated: If the magnitude of the loop gain is equal to or greater than unity at some frequency where the phase of the loop gain is $-180°$, then the amplifier is unstable. Stated mathematically,

$$|T(j\omega)| \geq 1 \quad \text{at } \omega \text{ where } \angle T(j\omega) = -180° \qquad (4\text{-}224)$$

Gain and Phase Relationship

Both the gain and phase are affected by feedback. Consider the feedback system depicted in Fig. 4-38 in which the feedback network is independent of frequency—such as would be for a feedback network fashioned from passive resistive elements. As there is no phase shift associated with the feedback network, the closed-loop phase derives solely from the amplifier. Denoting the

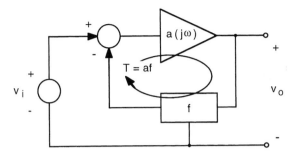

Figure 4-38   Feedback amplifier configuration.

phase shift of the amplifier by θ, the closed-loop gain can be expressed in the form

$$A(j\omega) = \frac{v_o}{v_i} = \frac{|a(j\omega)| \angle \theta}{1 + |T(j\omega)| \angle \theta} = \left| \frac{a(j\omega)}{1 + T(j\omega)} \right| \angle \phi \qquad (4\text{-}225)$$

where ϕ is the phase with feedback and is determined by

$$\phi = -\tan^{-1} \left[\frac{\tan(\theta)}{1 + |T(j\omega)|\sqrt{1 + \tan^2(\theta)}} \right] \qquad (4\text{-}226)$$

The denominator in Eq. (2-226) is larger than unity, giving $\phi < \theta$. Thus, the phase is reduced with negative feedback.

To illustrate the gain and phase relationship with feedback, consider first an amplifier with a single pole at frequency p_1. The open-loop gain of the amplifier is then

$$a(j\omega) = \frac{a_o}{1 + j\omega/|p_1|} \qquad (4\text{-}227)$$

which has a gain magnitude of

$$|a(j\omega)| = \frac{a_o}{\sqrt{1 + (\omega/p_1)^2}} \qquad (4\text{-}228)$$

and phase

$$\angle a(j\omega) = -\tan^{-1}\left(\frac{\omega}{|p_1|}\right) \qquad (4\text{-}229)$$

With feedback

$$A(j\omega) = \frac{\dfrac{a_o}{1 + \dfrac{j\omega}{|p_1|}}}{1 + \dfrac{a_o f}{1 + j\omega/|p_1|}} = \frac{A_o}{1 + j\omega/(1 + T_o)|p_1|} \qquad (4\text{-}230)$$

where $T_o = a_o f$ and $A_o = a_o/(1 + T_o)$.

In terms of gain magnitude and phase,

$$|A(j\omega)| = \frac{A_o}{\sqrt{1 + [\omega/(1 + T_o)p_1]^2}} \qquad (4\text{-}231)$$

and

$$\angle A(j\omega) = -\tan^{-1}\left[\frac{\omega}{(1 + T_o)|p_1|}\right] \qquad (4\text{-}232)$$

The effect of feedback is to move the open-loop pole of the amplifier at p_1 to higher frequency $(1 + T_o)$ times p_1. This is illustrated in the gain and phase plots (Bode plot) of Fig. 4-39. Because the maximum phase is $-90°$, this feedback amplifier is stable for all closed-loop gains.

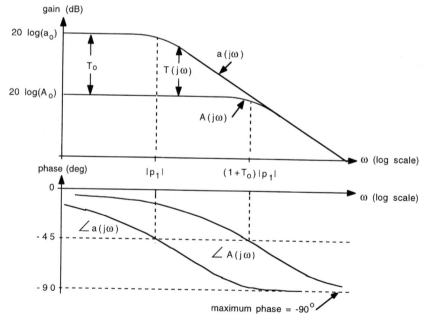

Figure 4-39   Gain and phase characteristics of a single-pole feedback amplifier.

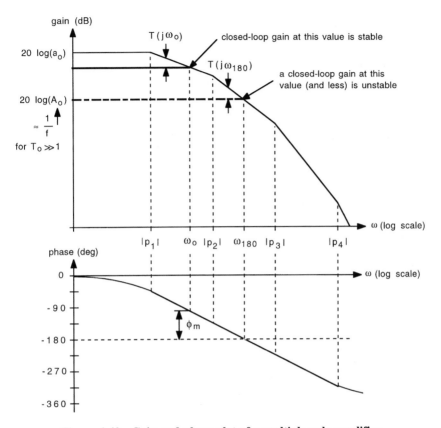

Figure 4-40   Gain and phase plot of a multiple-pole amplifier.

Consider now an amplifier with multiple poles (more than two) such that

$$a(j\omega) = \frac{a_o}{\left(1 + \dfrac{j\omega}{|p_1|}\right)\left(1 + \dfrac{j\omega}{|p_2|}\right)\left(1 + \dfrac{j\omega}{|p_3|}\right)\cdots} \qquad (4\text{-}233)$$

and

$$-\angle a(j\omega) = \tan^{-1}\left(\frac{\omega}{|p_1|}\right) + \tan^{-1}\left(\frac{\omega}{|p_2|}\right) + \tan^{-1}\left(\frac{\omega}{|p_3|}\right) + \cdots \qquad (4\text{-}234)$$

The gain and phase characteristics of this amplifier are illustrated in Fig. 4-40. The phase shift for an amplifier with three or more poles can exceed 180°, so the potential for instability exists with feedback applied. If the magnitude of the loop gain $T(j\omega)$ is greater than or equal to unity at the frequency at which its phase is $-180°$, then the amplifier will be unstable; the frequency at the $180°$ phase point is denoted ω_{180} and marks the boundary between stable and unstable operation: As illustrated in Fig. 4-40, a feedback amplifier with a closed-loop gain equal to or smaller than that given for $|T(j\omega)| = 1$ at $\omega = \omega_{180}$ is unstable—closed-loop gains larger than this value are stable and have a phase less than $-180°$. The difference between this phase and the $180°$ line is the phase margin, denoted ϕ_m. At $\omega = \omega_{180}$, the amplifier's open-loop phase is

$$- \angle a\,(j\omega_{180}) = \tan^{-1}\left(\frac{\omega_{180}}{|p_1|}\right) + \tan^{-1}\left(\frac{\omega_{180}}{|p_2|}\right) + \tan^{-1}\left(\frac{\omega_{180}}{|p_3|}\right) + \cdots = 180° \tag{4-235}$$

The poles in most amplifiers are usually widely separated in frequency. Thus, poles beyond the third contribute little to the total phase shift of the amplifier. In addition, one pole is usually dominant, meaning it is at a frequency that is perhaps 5 or 10 times lower than the frequency of the next pole. If this is the case, then the first dominant pole, say p_1, will contribute nearly $90°$ to the phase shift of the amplifier. Thus,

$$\tan^{-1}\left(\frac{\omega_{180}}{|p_2|}\right) + \tan^{-1}\left(\frac{\omega_{180}}{|p_3|}\right) \approx 90° \tag{4-236}$$

so

$$\tan^{-1}\left(\frac{\omega_{180}}{|p_2|}\right) \approx 90° - \tan^{-1}\left(\frac{\omega_{180}}{|p_3|}\right) = \tan^{-1}\left(\frac{|p_3|}{\omega_{180}}\right) \tag{4-237}$$

where a trigonometric identity has been used for the middle terms in Eq. (4-237). Thus, the ω_{180} frequency is approximated by

$$\omega_{180} \approx \sqrt{p_2 p_3} \tag{4-238}$$

Effect of Phase Margin on Closed-Loop Response

From the standpoint of stability, it is desired to have a certain degree of phase margin to allow for variations in the transfer characteristics of the amplifier due to changes in circuit element values, temperature, power supply, etc. The amount of phase margin also affects the closed-loop response of the amplifier.

Consider a feedback amplifier with a phase margin ϕ_m and denote the frequency at which the magnitude of the loop gain is unity as ω_o. Then at this frequency

$$T(j\omega_o) = 1e^{j(-180 + \phi_m)} = -1e^{j\phi_m} \tag{4-239}$$

For a feedback network in which the feedback factor f is constant, independent of frequency,

$$|T(j\omega_o)| = |a(j\omega_o)f| = 1 \tag{4-240}$$

from which

$$|a(j\omega_o)| = \frac{1}{f} \tag{4-241}$$

The magnitude of the closed-loop gain at ω_o is

$$|A(j\omega_o)| = \left| \frac{1}{f(1 - e^{j\phi_m})} \right| \tag{4-242}$$

If the low-frequency loop gain $T_o = a_o f$ is much greater than unity, then $1/f \approx A_o$, and the gain at ω_o relative to the gain at low frequency becomes

$$\left| \frac{A(j\omega_o)}{A_o} \right| = \left| \frac{1}{1 - e^{j\phi_m}} \right| = \frac{1}{\sqrt{(1 - \cos\phi_m)^2 + \sin^2\phi_m}} \tag{4-243}$$

The relative gain at ω_o for various values of phase margin is listed in Table 4-1. A phase margin of 90° is achievable only for amplifiers containing a single pole. At a 60° phase margin, the response is flat at ω_o. Smaller values of phase margin give rise to gain peaking. In practice, amplifiers are designed for phase margins in excess of 30° to minimize peaking of the response.

Table 4-1   Relative Gain for Various Values of Phase Margin

ϕ_m	$\left\| A\dfrac{(j\omega_o)}{A_o} \right\|$		
90°	0.707	(-3 dB)	Single pole only
60°	1	(0 dB)	
45°	1.31	($+2.3$ dB)	Gain peaking
30°	1.92	($+5.7$ dB)	Gain peaking
15°	3.83	($+11.7$ dB)	Gain peaking
0°	∞		Oscillating

Figure 4-41 shows the simulated gain and phase response of a feedback amplifier containing three poles, at $-10\,\text{kHz}$, $-100\,\text{kHz}$, and $-1\,\text{MHz}$. Without feedback, the open-loop gain is 60 dB. Various amounts of feedback are applied to give closed-loop gains of 40, 30, and 20 dB. Both gain peaking and the steepness of the phase shift increase with increased feedback, f. At 40 dB gain, the phase margin is 58° with a gain peaking of 0.3 dB. At 30 dB, the phase margin is 26° with a gain peaking of 6.8 dB, and at 20 dB, the phase margin is 14° with a gain peaking of 12 dB.

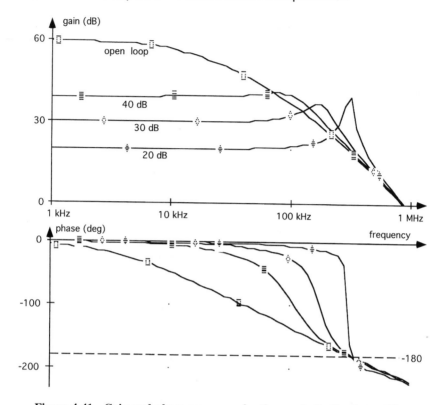

Figure 4-41   Gain and phase response of a three-pole feedback amplifier.

4.6 Compensation of Feedback Amplifiers

Generally, compensation involves altering the open-loop transfer function $a(j\omega)$ of the amplifier such that, with feedback, the amplifier is stable for all values of closed-loop gain. To illustrate various compensation schemes, we will consider an amplifier with three poles, such that

$$a(j\omega) = \frac{a_o}{\left(1 + \dfrac{j\omega}{|p_1|}\right)\left(1 + \dfrac{j\omega}{|p_2|}\right)\left(1 + \dfrac{j\omega}{|p_3|}\right)} \qquad (4\text{-}244)$$

The gain and phase characteristics of this amplifier are sketched in Fig. 4-42. The maximum phase shift is 270°, which can lead to instability if the amplifier is operated with sufficient feedback such that phase shift is 180° at a frequency where the magnitude of the loop gain is unity. For unconditional stability, that

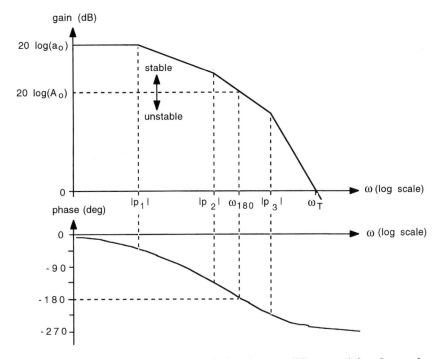

Figure 4-42 Gain and phase characteristics of an amplifier containing three poles.

is for all closed-loop gains, we compensate the amplifier so that it is stable down to unity gain ($f = 1$) with some phase margin, ϕ_m.

Compensation Methods

(1) Add an Additional Dominant Pole

A simple brute-force method of compensation is to add an additional pole to the amplifier at a frequency low enough so that it dominates the response. This illustrated in Fig. 4-43, which shows a Bode plot of the feedback amplifier with and without the added compensation pole. The added pole (p_A) shifts the gain and phase response to a much lower frequency such that phase shift at the compensated unity-gain frequency ω_{TC} is less than 180°. Implicit in this illustration is that the added pole does not appreciably alter the location of the original poles of the amplifier; this is not generally true, but is close for many amplifiers. Additionally, if we make $\omega_{TC} = |p_1|$, the compensated amplifier will have a phase margin of about 45°. The chief drawback to this type of compensation is that it requires a relatively large value of capacitance, as the following example illustrates.

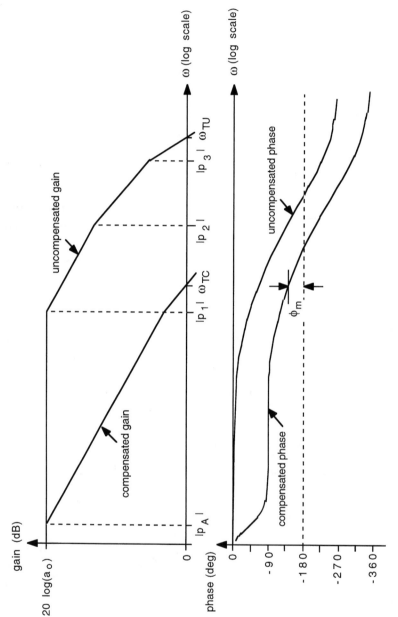

Figure 4-43 Compensation by adding a dominant pole.

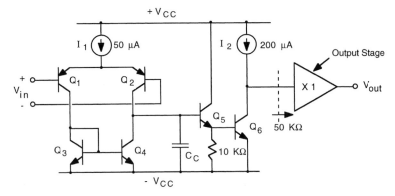

Figure 4-44   Two-stage op-amp using added-pole compensation.

Added-Pole Compensation Example

A simplified schematic of a two-stage op-amp is shown in Fig. 4-44. Compensation capacitance C_C adds a dominant pole; prior to compensation, the amplifier has three negative real poles at $f_{p1} = -1\,\text{MHz}$, $f_{p2} = -6\,\text{MHz}$, and $f_{p3} = -40\,\text{MHz}$. Setting the frequency of the added pole $f_{pA} = f_{p1}/a_o$ gives a phase margin of 45°. Neglecting the output resistance of the transistors, the open-loop low-frequency gain a_o is about 2×10^5. Thus,

$$f_{pA} = \frac{-1\,\text{MHz}}{2 \times 10^5} = -5\,\text{Hz}$$

which indeed is at a frequency much lower than the original dominant pole (1 MHz) of the amplifier. The resistance in parallel with C_C sets the added-pole frequency:

$$|P_A| = 2\pi|f_{pA}| = 31.4\ \text{rads/s} = \frac{1}{(R_{o1}||R_{i2})\,C_C}$$

where R_{o1} is the output resistance of the differential input stage (neglected in this example) and R_{i2} is the input resistance of the second gain stage (Q_5 and Q_6) and is equal to approximately $600\,\text{k}\Omega$. The value of the compensation capacitance is then

$$C_C = \frac{1}{(31.4\ \text{rads/s})(600\,\text{k}\Omega)} = 53\,\text{nF}$$

which is rather large.

(2) Move Dominant Pole to a Lower Frequency

A more commonly used method of compensation is to shift the dominant pole of the amplifier to a lower frequency such that the phase shift at the new unity-gain frequency (ω_{TC}) is less than 180°; this is illustrated in the Bode plot of Fig. 4-45.

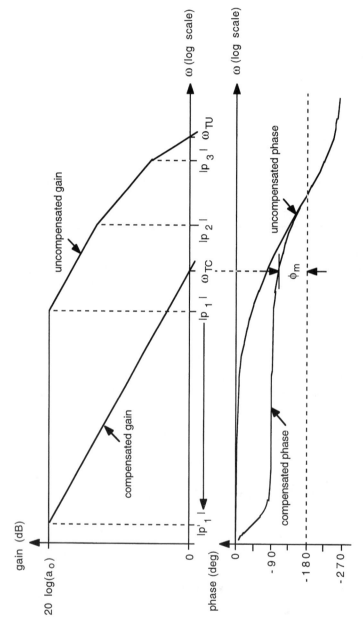

Figure 4-45 Compensation by moving the dominant pole of the amplifier to a lower frequency.

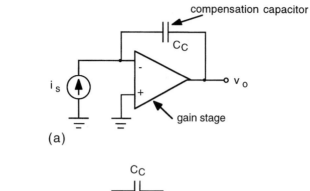

(a)

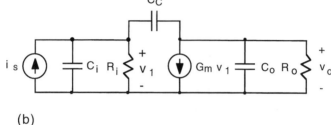

(b)

Figure 4-46 (a) **Pole-splitting compensation capacitance added to amplifier gain stage.** (b) **Equivalent circuit of gain stage with compensation capacitance.**

This approach yields a much larger bandwidth than with the added dominant pole method because ω_{TC} is now near p_2, which may be 5–10 times the frequency of p_1. Also, the required value of the compensation capacitance is much lower, making it integratable on-chip.

Moving the dominant pole is achieved by *Miller multiplication*, in which the compensation capacitor is connected as a feedback element across the second-gain stage. This is illustrated in Fig. 4-46(a). In Fig. 4-46(b), the gain stage is modeled in terms of the total resistance R_i and capacitance C_i at its input, the total resistance R_o and capacitance C_o at its output, and the effective transconductance G_m of the stage. Compensation capacitance C_C is connected between the input and output of the stage.

Consider first the response of the stage without the compensation capacitor. It is easy to show that

$$\frac{v_o}{i_s} = -\frac{G_m R_i R_o}{(1 + sR_i C_i)(1 + sR_o C_o)} = \frac{a_o}{(1 - s/p_1)(1 - s/p_2)} \tag{4-245}$$

where $a_o = -G_m R_i R_o$. The stage has two poles at

$$p_1 = -\frac{1}{R_i C_i} \quad \text{and} \quad p_2 = -\frac{1}{R_o C_o} \tag{4-246}$$

Consider now the circuit with the compensation capacitor. Summing the currents at the input node in Fig. 4-46 gives

$$i_s = \frac{v_1}{R_i} + sC_i v_1 + sC_C(v_1 - v_o) \tag{4-247}$$

At the output node

$$sC_C(v_1 - v_o) = G_m v_1 + sC_o v_o + \frac{v_o}{R_o} \tag{4-248}$$

Combining Eqs. (4-247) and (4-248) gives, for the response of the stage,

$$\frac{v_o}{i_s} = \frac{-R_i R_o (G_m - sC_C)}{1 + s[R_i(C_i + C_C) + R_o(C_o + C_C) + G_m R_i R_o] + s^2 R_i R_o [C_i C_o + C_C(C_i + C_o)]} \tag{4-249}$$

The response has two poles and a zero; the zero is at a frequency G_m/C_C. The compensation capacitance C_C is generally small. Thus, if the transconductance G_m of the stage is reasonably large, then the zero will be at a much higher frequency than those of the poles. The zero will have a negligible effect on the response and can be neglected. In addition, the term $G_m R_i R_o$ is generally much larger than the first two terms multiplying s in the denominator of Eq. (4-249). Thus, Eq. (2-249) becomes approximately

$$\frac{v_o}{i_s} \approx \frac{a_o}{1 + sG_m R_i R_o + s^2 R_i R_o [C_i C_o + C_C(C_i + C_o)]} \tag{4-250}$$

which can be written as

$$\frac{v_o}{i_s} = \frac{a_o}{(1 - s/p_1')(1 - s/p_2')} = \frac{a_o}{1 - s(1/p_1' + 1/p_2') + s^2(1/p_1' p_2')} \tag{4-251}$$

where p_1' and p_2' are the new pole frequencies of the gain stage. Normally, one of the poles will be dominant, say p_1'. Hence,

$$\frac{v_o}{i_s} \approx \frac{a_o}{1 - s/p_1' + s^2(1/p_1' p_2')} \tag{4-252}$$

Equating the coefficients of s in the denominator of Eqs. (4-250) and (4-252) gives

$$p_1' = -\frac{1}{G_m R_i R_o C_C} \tag{4-253}$$

Equating the coefficients of s^2 in the denominator of Eqs. (4-250) and (4-252) and substituting for p_1' from Eq. (4-253) gives

$$p_2' = -\frac{G_m C_C}{C_i C_o + C_C(C_i + C_o)} \tag{4-254}$$

If the value of the compensation capacitance is considerably larger than the capacitance at the output of the stage, then p_2' simplifies to

$$p_2' = -\frac{G_m}{C_i + C_o} \qquad (4\text{-}255)$$

for $C_C \gg C_o$.

As a result of the Miller multiplication, the original poles of the stage have been split further apart: p_1 is reduced to a lower frequency, and p_2 increases to a higher frequency. This *pole splitting* actually enhances the compensation process because the phase shift due to the second pole is moved to a higher frequency.

Move Dominant-Pole Compensation Example

The same two-stage op-amp used in the previous added-pole compensation example is repeated in Fig. 4-47; R_i and C_i denote respectively the resistance and capacitance at the input to the gain stage, and R_o and C_o denote respectively the resistance and capacitance at the output of the stage. The effective trans-conductance of the stage is denoted G_m. Pole-splitting compensation capacitance C_C is connected between the input and output of the stage. R_i is again $600 \, \text{k}\Omega$, so for p_1 at $-1 \, \text{MHz}$, $C_i = -1/R_i p_1 = 0.265 \, \text{pF}$. R_o is $50 \, \text{k}\Omega$, so for p_2 at $-6 \, \text{MHz}$, $C_o = -1/R_o p_2 = 0.53 \, \text{pF}$. In addition,

$$G_m = \frac{g_{m5} g_{m6}}{g_{m5} + g_{m6}/\beta_{F6}} = 7.5 \, \text{mA}/\text{V}$$

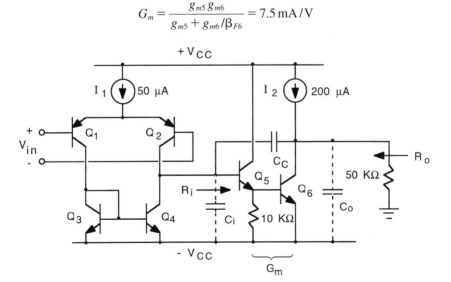

Figure 4-47   **Two-stage op-amp using pole-splitting compensation.**

Setting $\omega_{TC} = \omega_{p2}$ gives a phase margin of 45°. Thus,

$$\omega'_{p1} = \frac{\omega_{p2}}{a_o} = -189 \text{ rads/s} \quad (-30 \text{ Hz})$$

This frequency is six times larger than the 5 Hz obtained in the previous example. The required value for the compensation capacitance is from Eq. (4-253):

$$C_C = -\frac{1}{G_m R_i R_o p'_1} = \frac{1}{(7.5 \text{ mA/V})(600 \text{ k}\Omega)(50 \times 10^3 \text{ }\Omega)(174 \text{ rads/s})} = 25 \text{ pF}$$

which is considerably smaller than the 58 nF required in the previous example. The second pole (originally at -6 MHz) has been moved out [using Eq. (4-255)] to

$$p'_2 = -\frac{G_m}{C_i + C_o} = -\frac{7.5 \times 10^{-3}}{(0.265 + 0.53) \times 10^{-12}} = -9.43 \times 10^9 \text{ rads/s} \quad (-1.5 \text{ GHz})$$

which is now truly nondominant. The third pole of this amplifier at -40 MHz now becomes the second most dominant pole.

Pole-Splitting Compensation with MOSFET Gain Stages

If MOSFETs are used in the second gain stage, the value of G_m will be considerably lower (perhaps a factor of 10) than for a bipolar stage. The transfer function of the stage is still given by Eq. (4-249); however, due to the lower value of G_m, the frequency of the zero may not (in fact, probably not) be much higher than that of the poles. Consequently, the effect of the zero cannot be ignored; the zero tends to flatten the gain at high frequencies due to its $+20$ dB/decade contribution to the amplitude response. In addition, this positive real zero contributes $-90°$ to the phase shift, giving a negative phase margin at the unity-gain frequency. As a result, the compensation will not be effective in stabilizing the amplifier.

Two techniques, illustrated in Fig. 4-48, have been developed to eliminate the effect of this low-frequency zero. At high frequencies, the feedforward signal through the feedback network (C_C) is not negligible with respect to the feedforward gain of the amplifier stage; in Fig. 4-48(a), a unity-gain buffer inserted in the feedback path eliminates the feedforward signal through C_C [7]. Although this technique works well, it does require additional devices and adds to the circuit complexity. A simpler method is to insert a nulling resistor, R_Z, in series with the compensation capacitance, as illustrated in Fig. 4-48(b) [8]. With this resistor, the frequency of the zero is given by

$$z = \frac{1}{(1/G_m - R_Z)C_C} \tag{4-256}$$

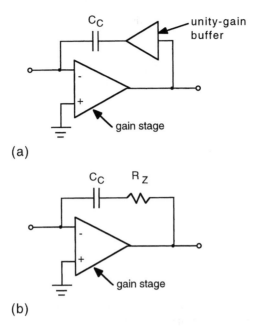

(a)

(b)

Figure 4-48 Compensation schemes for MOSFET gain stages: (a) using a buffer to eliminate the feedforward signal through the compensation capacitor; (b) using a resistor to alter the location of the zero.

As evidenced by Eq. (4-256), the zero can be eliminated by making R_Z equal to $1/G_m$. Increasing R_Z beyond this value moves the zero to a negative frequency which can improve the phase margin.

(3) Add a Feedback Zero

A third method of compensation is to alter the transmission characteristics of the feedback network; adding a zero in the feedback path can alter the pole response of the basic amplifier. Generally, this technique is applied to fixed-gain amplifiers. To illustrate the process, consider an amplifier with three poles such that

$$a(s) = \frac{a_o}{(1 - s/p_1)(1 - s/p_2)(1 - s/p_3)} \qquad (4\text{-}257)$$

where $|p_3| > |p_2| > |p_1|$.

This amplifier is connected to a feedback network which contains a single zero such that

$$f(s) = f_o\left(1 - \frac{s}{z_1}\right) \qquad (4\text{-}258)$$

For the special case in which the frequency of the zero is set equal to that of the dominant pole p_1, the loop gain becomes

$$T(s) = a(s)f(s) = \frac{a_o f_o}{(1 - s/p_2)(1 - s/p_3)} = \frac{T_o}{(1 - s/p_2)(1 - s/p_3)} \quad (4\text{-}259)$$

The closed-loop gain is then

$$A(s) = \frac{a(s)}{1 + T(s)} = \frac{\dfrac{a_o}{(1 - s/p_1)(1 - s/p_2)(1 - s/p_3)}}{1 + \dfrac{T_o}{(1 - s/p_2)(1 - s/p_3)}} \quad (4\text{-}260)$$

which can be manipulated in the following fashion:

$$A(s) = \frac{a_o}{1 + T_o} \frac{1}{\dfrac{(1 - s/p_1)(1 - s/p_2)(1 - s/p_3)}{1 + T_o} + \dfrac{T_o}{1 + T_o}(1 - s/p_1)} \quad (4\text{-}261)$$

The term $a_o/(1 + T_o)$ is recognized as the low-frequency, closed-loop gain A_o and the factor $T_o/(1 + T_o)$ in the last term in the denominator is approximately equal to unity. Thus, Eq. (4-260) is approximately

$$A(s) \approx \frac{A_o}{\left(1 - \dfrac{s}{p_1}\right)\left[1 + \dfrac{1}{1 + T_o}\left(1 - \dfrac{s}{p_2}\right)\left(1 - \dfrac{s}{p_3}\right)\right]}$$

$$= \frac{A_o}{\left(1 - \dfrac{s}{p_1}\right)\left[1 + \dfrac{1}{1 + T_o} - \dfrac{s}{1 + T_o}\left(\dfrac{1}{p_2} + \dfrac{1}{p_3}\right) + \dfrac{s^2}{(1 + T_o)p_2 p_3}\right]} \quad (4\text{-}262)$$

In the denominator of Eq. (4-262), the term $1/(1 + T_o)$ can be neglected with respect to 1. In addition, if p_3 is much larger than p_2, then the term $1/p_3$ may be neglected with respect to the $1/p_2$ term in the denominator. Consequently, Eq. (4-262) becomes approximately

$$A(s) \approx \frac{A_o}{\left(1 - \dfrac{s}{p_1}\right)\left[1 - \dfrac{s}{(1 + T_o)p_2} + \dfrac{s^2}{(1 + T_o)p_2 p_3}\right]} \quad (4\text{-}263)$$

which, for $|p_3| \gg |p_2|$, can be expressed in the form

$$A(s) \approx \frac{A_o}{\left(1 - \dfrac{s}{p_1}\right)\left(1 - \dfrac{s}{[1 + T_o]p_2}\right)\left(1 + \dfrac{s}{p_3}\right)} \quad (4\text{-}264)$$

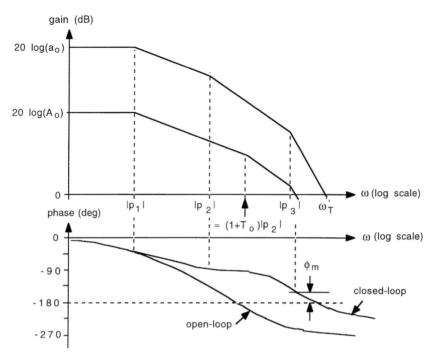

Figure 4-49 Compensation by adding a feedback zero.

As seen by Eq. (4-264), the effect of a feedback zero at p_1 is to move the secondmost dominant pole p_2 out to a higher frequency, by a factor of approximately $1 + T_o$. In practice, both p_2 and p_3 will be moved by the feedback; however, for $|p_3| \gg |p_2|$, the shift will be primarily in p_2. The phase is shifted to a higher frequency, resulting in a positive phase margin for the amplifier, as illustrated in Fig. 4-49.

Feedback Zero Compensation Example

Figure 4-50(a) shows the ac schematic of a fixed-gain series voltage amplifier employing a zero in the feedback network. With the emitter of Q_1 open-circuited, the feedback voltage is

$$v_{fb} = \frac{R_E}{R_E + \dfrac{R_F}{1 + sR_F C_F}} v_o = \frac{R_E}{R_E + R_F} \frac{1 + sR_F C_F}{1 + s(R_E \| R_F)} v_o = f(s) v_o$$

The feedback function has a zero at

$$z_{F1} = -\frac{1}{R_F C_F}$$

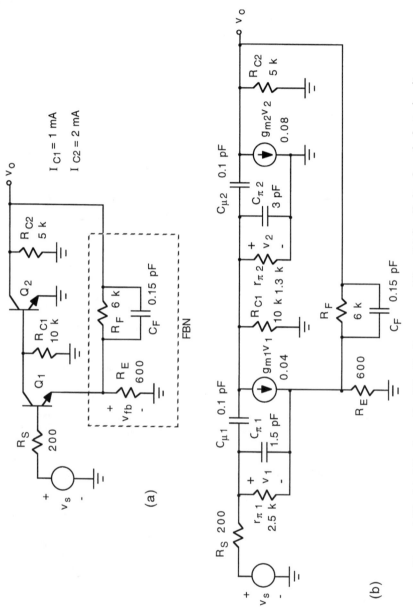

Figure 4-50 (a) AC schematic of feedback zero amplifier. (b) Small-signal equivalent circuit.

and a pole at

$$p_{F1} = -\frac{1}{(R_E \| R_F)\, C_F}$$

Because $R_F \gg R_E$, the feedback zero is dominant and p_{F1} can be neglected, giving

$$f(s) \approx f_o \left(1 - \frac{s}{z_{F1}}\right)$$

where

$$f_o = \frac{R_E}{R_E + R_F}$$

At a bias current of 1 mA, $g_{m1} \approx 40 \, \text{mA/V}$ for Q_1, and $g_{m2} \approx 80 \, \text{mA/V}$ for Q_2 biased at 2 mA; for $\beta_F = 100$, $r_{\pi1} = 2.5 \, \text{k}\Omega$ for Q_1, and $r_{\pi2} = 1.3 \, \text{k}\Omega$ for Q_2. For the transistors, C_{jE} and C_{jC} are taken as 0.3 pF and 0.1 pF, respectively, and τ_F is given as 30 ps. This gives $C_{\pi1} = 1.5 \, \text{pF}$ and $C_{\pi2} \approx 3 \, \text{pF}$. The small-signal equivalent circuit for the feedback amplifier is shown in Fig. 4-50(b).

Figure 4-51 shows the simulated gain and phase response for the feedback amplifier of Fig. 4-50(b). Two sets of characteristics are shown: one without the feedback zero ($C_F = 0$), and one with 0.15 pF of feedback capacitance. Without the feedback zero, the amplifier is unstable; with the zero, the amplifier has a phase margin of about 75°.

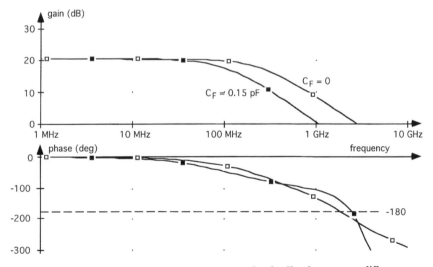

Figure 4-51   Gain and phase response of a feedback zero amplifier.

Problems

For all problems assume room temperature, $kT/q = 26\,\text{mV}$.
Note: Where required, use the following device parameters unless otherwise specified:

NPN: $\beta_F = 100$	$I_S = 2 \times 10^{-16}\,\text{A}$	$V_A = 75\,\text{V}$
PNP: $\beta_F = 50$	$I_S = 5 \times 10^{-17}\,\text{A}$	$V_A = 75\,\text{V}$
NMOS: $W/L = 10$	$\mu_n C'_{ox} = 30\,\mu\text{A}/\text{V}^2$	$V_{TH} = 1\,\text{V} \qquad \lambda = 0.02\,\text{V}^{-1}$
PMOS: $W/L = 30$	$\mu_p C'_{ox} = 10\,\mu\text{A}/\text{V}^2$	$V_{TH} = -1\,\text{V} \qquad \lambda = 0.02\,\text{V}^{-1}$

4.1 An amplifier has a measured gain of 2000. After adding negative feedback, the gain is reduced to 50.
(a) Find the loop gain, T, and the feedback factor, f.
(b) The gain of the basic amplifier has a sensitivity to temperature of 10%. What is the sensitivity of the closed-loop gain (with feedback) to temperature?

4.2 A feedback amplifier is to have a closed-loop gain of 30 dB and a sensitivity of 2% with respect to gain variations in the basic amplifier. What open-loop gain, a, of the basic amplifier is required? Determine the loop gain, T.

4.3 A feedback amplifier has a low-frequency open-loop gain, a_o, of 10^4 and an open-loop unity-gain frequency, f_T, of 100 MHz. The basic amplifier can be characterized by a single-pole response. With feedback, the amplifier is to have a -3-dB bandwidth of 2 MHz. Determine the required feedback factor, f, and the resulting low-frequency, closed-loop gain, A_o, of the amplifier.

4.4 In the feedback amplifier of Fig. 4-52, the transistor bias currents are $I_{C1} = 500\,\mu\text{A}$ and $I_{C2} = 1.2\,\text{mA}$. Determine the closed-loop gain, v_o/v_i, and the

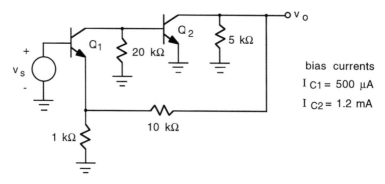

Figure 4-52   Feedback amplifier for Problem 4.4.

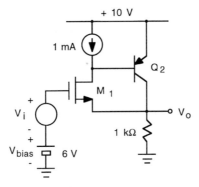

Figure 4-53 **BiCMOS buffer for Problem 4.5.**

closed-loop input, R_i, and output, R_o, resistances. Neglect the Early effect for both transistors.

4.5 The BiCMOS buffer of Fig. 4-53 has a low output resistance due to the feedback provided by the 1-kΩ resistance.

(a) Determine the quiescent bias drain current of M_1, the collector current of Q_2, and the output voltage, V_O. For M_1, $W/L = 50$. The 1-mA bias current source may be assumed to be ideal and the Early effect for both transistors can be neglected.

(b) Determine the closed-loop, small-signal, low-frequency voltage gain, v_o/v_i, and the output resistance of the buffer.

4.6 In the buffered feedback amplifier of Fig. 4-54, Q_3 removes feedback loading at the output. Show that

$$\frac{v_o}{v_s} = \frac{-R_F}{R_S} \frac{1}{1 + R_F/G_M R^* R_L}$$

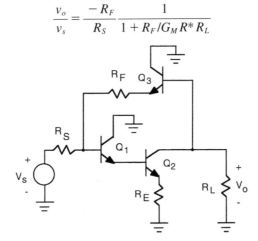

Figure 4-54 **Buffered feedback amplifier for Problem 4.6.**

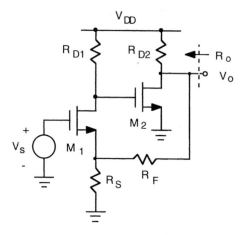

Figure 4-55   NMOS feedback amplifier for Problem 4.7.

where

$$G_M = \frac{g_{m2}}{2 + g_{m2} R_E}$$

and

$$R^* = R_S \| R_F \| [\beta_1 (2 r_{\pi 2} + \beta_2 R_E)]$$

4.7 In the feedback amplifier of Fig. 4-55, determine expressions for the open-loop gain, a, the closed-loop gain, v_o/v_s, and the output resistance, R_o. Assume the MOSFETs are operating in saturation and neglect r_o.

4.8 For the feedback amplifier shown in Fig. 4-56, calculate the closed-loop gain, v_o/v_s, the loop gain, T, and the input and output resistance. For the

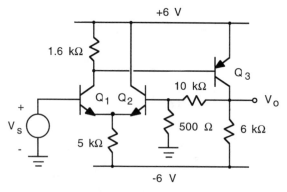

Figure 4-56   Feedback amplifier for Problem 4.8.

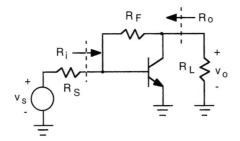

Figure 4-57   Amplifier circuit for Problem 4.10.

transistors, take $|V_{BE(on)}| = 0.8$ V and $V_A = \infty$. Assume the quiescent output voltage is zero.

4.9 Show that the open-loop gain of the amplifier in Fig. 4-26 is given by Eq. (4-134).

4.10 In the analysis of the feedback amplifier of Fig. 4-57, r_o of the transistor may be neglected.

(a) Show that the open-loop gain is given by

$$a = \frac{v_o}{v_s} = -\frac{g_m(R_F||r_\pi)(R_F||R_L)}{R_S + (R_F||r_\pi)}$$

(b) Excluding the source and load resistances, show that the closed-loop input and output resistances are given by

$$R_i = \frac{R_{io}}{1 + a(1 + R_{io}/R_S)f}$$

and

$$R_o = \frac{R_{oo}}{1 + a(1 + R_{oo}/R_L)f}$$

where

$$R_{io} = (R_F||r_\pi), \qquad R_{oo} = R_F, \qquad \text{and} \qquad f = -\frac{R_S}{R_F}$$

4.11 A transimpedance amplifier employing shunt-current feedback is shown in Fig. 4-58.

(a) Determine the quiescent ($I_s = 0$) collector currents for the transistors and the output voltage, V_O. For the transistors, take $V_{BE(on)} = 0.75$ V and neglect the Early effect.

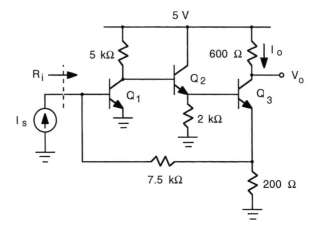

Figure 4-58   Transimpedance amplifier for Problem 4.11.

(b) Determine the open-loop gain $a = i_o/i_s$, the closed-loop gain v_o/i_s, and the closed-loop input resistance, R_i.

(c) Check your results in (b) using SPICE (or similar) circuit simulation.

4.12 For the CMOS feedback amplifier shown in Fig. 4-59, determine the open-loop gain, $a = v_o/v_s$, the closed-loop voltage gain, and the closed-loop output resistance. Use the transistor parameters given at the beginning of the problem section except for M_7, which has a channel width/length ratio $W/L = 60$.

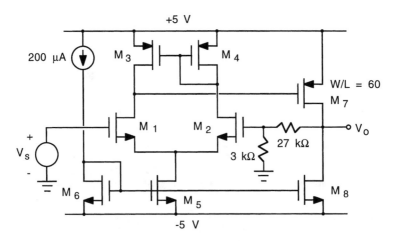

Figure 4-59   CMOS amplifier for Problem 4.12.

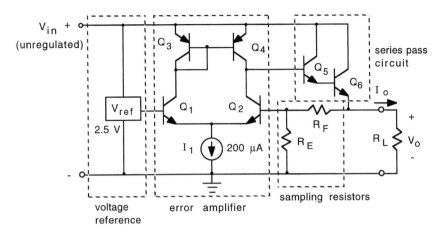

Figure 4-60   Voltage regulator circuit for Problem 4.13.

4.13 Figure 4-60 shows a voltage regulator circuit; its purpose is to deliver a constant (regulated) voltage from a power supply which may vary in value. Additionally, the output voltage, V_o, should remain constant with changes in the load, R_L. The circuit functions as a feedback amplifier which forces the voltage at the base of Q_2 (the inverting input of the differential amplifier) to be equal to the reference voltage connected at the noninverting input of the amplifier. The voltage divider provided by the feedback sampling resistors then gives $V_o = (1 + R_F/R_E) V_{ref}$.

(a) The loading of the feedback network may be neglected in comparison with R_L. Show that the open-loop gain, depicting the gain between the base of Q_2 and the output, is given approximately by

$$a = \frac{qI_1}{2kT} \left(\frac{2}{I_1} \frac{V_{A2} V_{A4}}{V_{A2} + V_{A4}} \middle\| \frac{\beta_{F5} \beta_{F6} V_o}{I_o} \right)$$

(b) To maintain good regulation with respect to changes in the load, the regulator should have a very low output resistance. Again neglecting the loading effect of the feedback network, and assuming that the loop gain T is much larger than unity, show that the closed-loop output resistance of the regulator, including R_L, is given by

$$R_o = \frac{r_{oa} V_o}{a V_{ref} (1 + r_{oa} I_o / V_o)}$$

where r_{oa} is the open-loop output resistance of the amplifier, given by

$$r_{oa} = \frac{2 V_{A2} V_{A4}}{\beta_{F5} \beta_{F6} I_1 (V_{A2} + V_{A4})} + \frac{2kT}{qI_o}$$

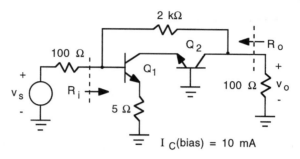

Figure 4-61   Cascode feedback amplifier for Problem 4.14.

(c) The change in output voltage resulting from a change in load current is determined by $\Delta V_o = \Delta I_o R_o$. The load regulation is defined as

$$\text{Load regulation} = \frac{\Delta V_o}{V_o} = \frac{R_o}{V_o} \Delta I_o$$

Determine the load regulation for the circuit of Fig. 4-60 for a change in output current of 100 mA in which $V_o = 10\,\text{V}$ and $I_o = 10\,\text{mA}$.

4.14 Determine the closed-loop voltage gain, input resistance, and output resistance of the cascode feedback amplifier shown in Fig. 4-61. The transistors are each biased at 10 mA and their output resistances, r_o, may be neglected.

4.15 Figure 4-62 shows the NE5205 used as a high-frequency amplifier. The dc blocking capacitors, C_S and C_L, may be assumed large such that they have zero impedance at the frequencies used by the amplifier.
(a) Calculate the quiescent bias collector currents of all transistors in the amplifier as well as the quiescent voltage at the collectors of Q_2 and Q_6. You may neglect the Early voltage for the transistors and take $V_{BE\,(on)} = 0.75\,\text{V}$.
(b) Determine the closed-loop voltage gain, v_o/v_s, as well as the input (R_i) and output (R_o) resistances, as indicated in the figure.
(c) Check your results in (a) and (b) using SPICE circuit simulation.

4.16 Verify Eq. (4-226) for the closed-loop phase of a feedback amplifier.

4.17 An amplifier has a low-frequency gain of 60 dB (1000) and a frequency response with three negative real poles at $-100\,\text{kHz}$, $-1\,\text{MHz}$, and $-10\,\text{MHz}$.
(a) This amplifier is to be connected in a feedback loop with $f = \text{constant}$ and a low-frequency closed-loop gain of 40 dB (100). Determine the bandwidth f_o, the phase margin ϕ_m, and the amount of gain peaking at f_o.
(b) Repeat (a) for a closed-loop gain of 20 dB (10).

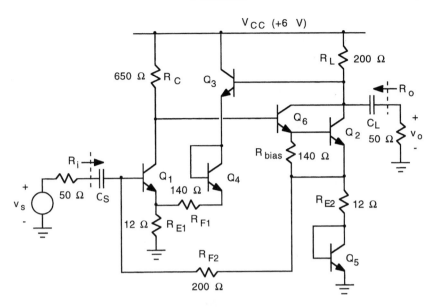

Figure 4-62 NE5205 amplifier circuit for Problem 4.15.

4.18 The amplifier of Problem 4.17 is to be unity-gain compensated with a phase margin of 45°.

(a) If compensation is to be achieved by adding a dominant-pole, calculate the required dominant-pole frequency p_A and the resulting bandwidth f_{TC}, assuming that the original poles of the amplifier remain fixed.

(b) If compensation is to be achieved by moving the dominant pole of the amplifier to a lower frequency, calculate the new dominant pole frequency p_1' and the bandwidth f_{TC} assuming that the other two amplifier poles remain fixed.

4.19 The operational amplifier shown in Fig. 4-63 is to be compensated using a pole-splitting capacitor C_C. Before compensation, the gain response has three negative real poles at -1 MHz, -4 MHz, and -12 MHz. As a result of pole splitting, the second pole (at -4 MHz) is moved out well beyond -200 MHz so as to make it negligible. Assume that the third pole (at -12 MHz) is unaffected by the compensation.

Determine the value of compensation capacitance required to achieve a phase margin of 55° in a unity-gain feedback connection. Calculate also the unity-gain bandwidth f_{TC}. The low-frequency, open-loop gain of the amplifier is 80 dB (10,000). The resistance measured at the input to the second gain stage (Q_5, Q_6) is 100 kΩ, and the resistance measured at its output is 50 kΩ.

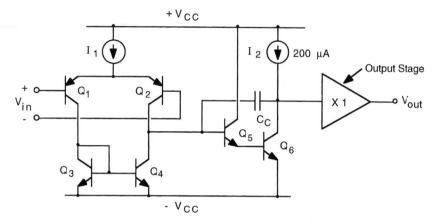

Figure 4-63   Operational amplifier circuit for Problem 4.19.

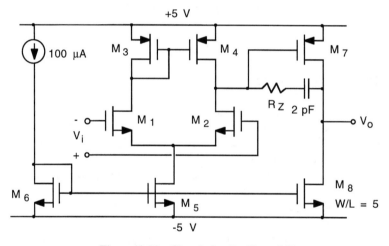

Figure 4-64   Circuit for Problem 4.20.

4.20 In the CMOS operational amplifier shown in Fig. 4-64, resistor R_Z is used in conjunction with the 2-pF compensation capacitor to move the zero to infinity. The amplifier itself can be characterized as having a capacitance of 0.5 pF at the output of the input stage (from the drain of M_2 to ground) and a capacitance of 0.5 pF at the output (from the drain of M_7 to ground). (a) Determine the value of the resistance R_Z needed to move the zero to infinity. Use the transistor parameters given at the beginning of the problem section except for M_8 which has a channel width/length ratio $W/L = 5$.

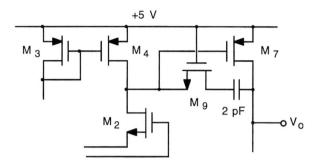

Figure 4-65   MOSFET resistor for Problem 4.22.

(b) Calculate the open-loop voltage gain a, the -3-dB bandwidth f_o, and the unity-gain frequency f_{TC}.

(c) Compare your results in (b) with a SPICE circuit simulation. Also, simulate the circuit with R_Z set to zero to show the effect of the zero on the phase margin of the amplifier.

4.21 In the CMOS amplifier of Fig. 4-64, a load capacitance C_L is connected at the output.

(a) Determine the largest value for C_L for which the amplifier maintains a phase margin of 45°. Assume that the conditions stated in Problem 4.20 apply.

(b) Using the value for C_L determined in (a), simulate the circuit using SPICE to verify the phase margin.

4.22 In Fig. 4-65 (which shows a portion of the CMOS amplifier of Fig. 4-64), transistor M_9 is used in place of the zero compensation resistor R_Z. Determine the required channel width/length ratio $(W/L)_9$ of M_9 such that its resistance is equal to that required to move the zero to infinity.

4.23 The ac schematic of a fixed-gain feedback amplifier is given in Fig. 4-66.

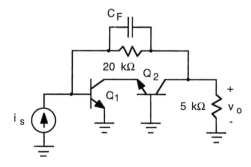

Figure 4-66   Fixed-gain amplifier circuit for Problem 4.23.

Determine the value of the feedback capacitance C_F needed to cancel the dominant pole of the amplifier. The transistors are biased at collector currents of 1 mA, which gives a value for C_π of 2 pF for each transistor. The value of C_μ is small such that it can be neglected. Additionally, r_o may be neglected. Determine the closed-loop gain, v_o/i_s, of the amplifier as well as the -3 dB bandwidth with the value of C_F determined above.

References

1. F.D. Waldhauer, *Feedback*, Wiley–Interscience, New York, 1982, Chap. 1.

2. A.S. Sedra and K.C. Smith, *Microelectronic Circuits*, 2nd ed., Holt, Rinehart and Winston, New York, 1987, Chap. 12.

3. P.R. Gray and R.G. Meyer, *Analysis and Design of Analog Integrated Circuits*, 3rd ed., Wiley, New York, 1993, Chap. 8.

4. J.E. Solomon and G.R. Wilson, "A Highly Densensitized Wideband Monolithic Amplifier," *IEEE J. Solid-State Circuits*, SC-1, 19–28 (Sept. 1966).

5. A.B. Grebene, *Bipolar and MOS Analog Integrated Circuit Design*, Wiley–Interscience, New York, 1984, Chap. 8.

6. R.G. Meyer and R.A. Blauschild, "A Four-Terminal Wideband Monolithic Amplifier," *IEEE J. Solid-State Circuits*, SC-17, 634–638 (Dec. 1981).

7. Y.P. Tsividis and P.R. Gray, "An Integrated NMOS Operational Amplifier with Internal Compensation," *IEEE J. Solid-State Circuits, SC-11*, 748–754 (Dec. 1976).

8. P.R. Gray and R.G. Meyer, *Analysis and Design of Analog Integrated Circuits*, 3rd ed., Wiley, New York, 1993, pp. 621–623.

Chapter 5

Translinear Circuits

Translinear circuits form a class of circuits which exploit the *linear* relationship between the *trans*conductance of a transistor and its voltage or current. These circuits were originally developed with integrated bipolar transistors [1], but more recently, have included integrated MOSFET devices as well [2]. Applications of translinear circuits include (1) wideband current amplifiers, (2) analog multiplier/divider circuits, (3) root-mean-square (rms) conversion circuits, (4) sine/cosine generation circuits, and (5) other signal processing circuits, to name a few.

In this chapter, we present the translinear circuit principle as it applies to bipolar and MOS circuits. Several types of translinear circuits are also discussed.

5.1 Translinear Circuit Classes

There are two classes of translinear circuits which relate the transconductance of a transistor to either its current or voltage:

Transconductance Linear with Current

A transistor whose transconductance varies linearly with its current has

$$g_m = \frac{dI}{dV} = aI \tag{5-1}$$

where a is a constant (with respect to I or V). Integrating gives

$$I = be^{aV} \tag{5-2}$$

where b is another constant.

Equation (5-2) describes the I_C–V_{BE} characteristic for a bipolar transistor. It is observed that the transconductance of a bipolar transistor varies linearly with

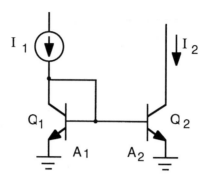

Figure 5-1   Simple translinear circuit.

its collector current and that this relationship is maintained over a wide range
(many orders of magnitude) in current. This property, as we shall see, when
applied to circuits containing loops of base-emitter junctions and which have
inputs and outputs consisting of currents allows precise linear and nonlinear
signal processing functions to be implemented.

An example of a simple translinear circuit is shown in Fig. 5-1; the reader
will recognize this circuit as a basic current mirror. Here, however, we will
view the circuit in a slightly different context. The base-emitter voltages of
the two transistors are

$$V_{be1} = \frac{kT}{q} \ln\left(\frac{I_{c1}}{J_{S1} A_1}\right) \approx \frac{kT}{q} \ln\left(\frac{I_1}{J_{S1} A_1}\right) \tag{5-3}$$

and

$$V_{be2} = \frac{kT}{q} \ln\left(\frac{I_2}{J_{S2} A_2}\right) \tag{5-4}$$

where $J_{S1,2}$ and $A_{1,2}$ are the saturation current densities and emitter areas of transistors Q_1 and Q_2, respectively. In the right-hand term of Eq. (5-3), we have
neglected base currents and approximated I_{c1} by the current source I_1. Assuming
identical transistors (except for emitter areas), $J_{S1} = J_{S2}$, and noting that $V_{be1} = V_{be2}$,
Eqs. (5-3) and (5-4) give

$$I_2 = \frac{A_2}{A_1} I_1 \tag{5-5}$$

The remarkable thing is that this relationship is independent of temperature,
and the specific values of J_S, I_1, and I_2 over the range in which the transconductance (g_m) remains linear with current; for a bipolar transistor, this covers about

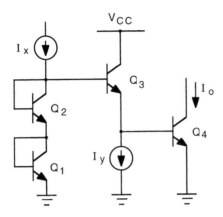

Figure 5-2   Two-input translinear circuit.

six decades in current and several hundred degrees Celsius. In the circuit of Fig. 5-1, current source I_1 may be viewed as an input signal and I_2 as an output; this circuit functions then as a current amplifier, with a gain equal to A_2/A_1.

Figure 5-2 shows another translinear circuit; here I_x and I_y are input currents and the output is taken as the collector current of Q_4, I_o. We will neglect base currents and assume that the four transistors are identical. Summing the base-emitter voltages around the closed-loop containing Q_1, Q_2, Q_3, and Q_4 gives

$$V_{be1} + V_{be2} = V_{be3} + V_{be4} \tag{5-6}$$

Substituting for the base-emitter voltages yields

$$2\frac{kT}{q}\ln\left(\frac{I_x}{I_S}\right) = \frac{kT}{q}\ln\left(\frac{I_y}{I_S}\right) + \frac{kT}{q}\ln\left(\frac{I_o}{I_S}\right) \tag{5-7}$$

from which

$$I_o = \frac{I_x^2}{I_y} \tag{5-8}$$

which again, over a wide range, is independent of temperature, the value of I_S, or the magnitudes of signals I_x and I_y.

Translinear Circuit Principle

Consider a closed-loop containing an even number of forward-biased base-emitter junctions, half arranged with clockwise polarities and half arranged with counterclockwise polarities, such as illustrated in Fig. 5-3. Arbitrary

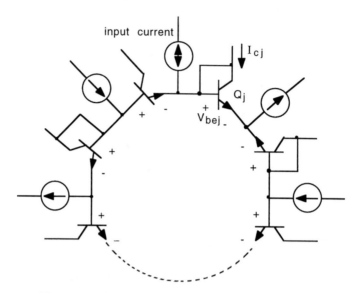

Figure 5-3   Translinear loop containing bipolar transistors.

current sources are shown connected as inputs and outputs are taken as collector currents. Summing the base-emitter voltages around the loop gives

$$\sum_{j=1}^{N} V_{bej} = 0 \quad \text{or} \quad \sum_{CW} V_{bej} = \sum_{CCW} V_{bej} \tag{5-9}$$

where

$$V_{bej} = \frac{kT}{q} \ln\left(\frac{I_{cj}}{A_j J_S}\right) \tag{5-10}$$

Substituting Eq. (5-10) into Eq. (5-9) and assuming identical transistors, except for emitter areas, yields

$$\sum_{CW} \frac{kT}{q} \ln\left(\frac{I_{cj}}{A_j}\right) = \sum_{CCW} \frac{kT}{q} \ln\left(\frac{I_{cj}}{A_j}\right) \tag{5-11}$$

which can be written as

$$\prod_{CW} \left(\frac{I_{cj}}{A_j}\right) = \prod_{CCW} \left(\frac{I_{cj}}{A_j}\right) \tag{5-12}$$

Noting that I_{cj}/A_j equals the collector-current density, Eq. (5-12) expresses the *translinear circuit principle* for bipolar transistors: The *product of the current densities in a clockwise direction* equals *the product of current densities in a counterclockwise direction* [1].

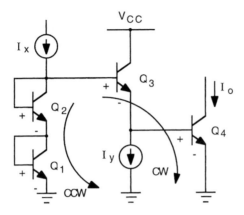

Figure 5-4 Translinear circuit illustrating clockwise and counterclockwise polarities.

The translinear circuit of Fig. 5-2 is repeated in Fig. 5-4 to illustrate analysis using the translinear circuit principle. Transistors Q_3 and Q_4 have clockwise base-emitter polarities and transistors Q_1 and Q_2 have counterclockwise polarities. With identical emitter areas, we have

$$I_y I_o = I_x I_x \implies I_o = \frac{I_x^2}{I_y} \tag{5-13}$$

Figure 5-5 shows another example of a translinear circuit having two inputs; the bidirectional arrow on the I_x input current indicates that it may flow in

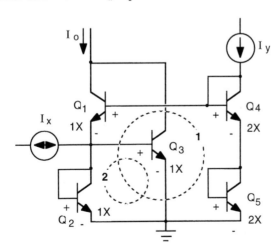

Figure 5-5 Another example of a translinear circuit.

either direction. Input I_y may flow only in the direction indicated. The 1X and 2X notations indicate relative emitter areas for the transistors. Applying the translinear principle to loop 1 containing transistors Q_1, Q_2, Q_4, and Q_5 yields

$$\frac{I_{c1}}{1} \frac{I_{c2}}{1} = \frac{I_y}{2} \frac{I_y}{2} \tag{5-14}$$

and for loop 2 comprising Q_1 and Q_3,

$$\frac{I_{c1}}{1} = \frac{I_{c3}}{1} \tag{5-15}$$

Taking I_x to be a positive quantity when flowing into the circuit, summing the currents at the x input (neglecting base currents) gives

$$I_{c1} = I_{c2} + I_x \tag{5-16}$$

At the output,

$$I_o = I_{c2} + I_{c3} \tag{5-17}$$

Substituting Eq. (5-15) into Eq. (5-17) and combining with Eq. (5-16) yields

$$I_{c1} = \frac{I_o + I_x}{2} \quad \text{and} \quad I_{c2} = \frac{I_o - I_x}{2} \tag{5-18}$$

which, using Eq. (5-14), gives

$$I_o = \sqrt{I_x^2 + I_y^2} \tag{5-19}$$

This circuit forms a vector magnitude.

Gilbert [1] classifies translinear loops according to the arrangement of base-emitter junctions. In Fig. 5-6(a), the translinear loop contains junctions arranged with alternating polarities, and in Fig. 5-6(b), the arrangement is balanced. Both circuits have the same translinear response, namely

$$\frac{I_2}{A_2} \frac{I_4}{A_4} = \frac{I_1}{A_1} \frac{I_3}{A_3} \tag{5-20}$$

There is a difference, however, with respect to β_F sensitivity as it relates to base current. Consider currents I_1 and I_2 to be inputs and the collector currents of Q_3 and Q_4 to be outputs. Then for equal emitter areas,

$$\frac{I_4}{I_3} = \frac{I_1}{I_2} \tag{5-21}$$

In the balanced arrangement, the base currents of Q_3 and Q_4 are dependent on the emitter currents of Q_1 and Q_2, and hence on the input currents I_1 and I_2. The relationship in Eq. (5-21) is thereby sensitive to β_F. In the alternate arrange-

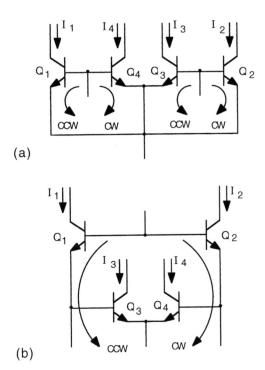

(a)

(b)

Figure 5-6 (a) Translinear loop with alternating polarities. (b) Loop in which the polarities are balanced.

ment, the base currents of Q_3 and Q_4 are not dependent on I_1 and I_2 and thus the relationship is, to first order, independent of β_F.

Translinear Loops with Voltage Sources

Consider a translinear circuit with a voltage source V_s inserted into the loop. Taking V_s to be positive for a clockwise sense, summation of the voltages around the loop gives

$$\sum_{CW} V_{bej} + V_s = \sum_{CCW} V_{bej} \tag{5-22}$$

Substituting for V_{be} gives

$$\ln \prod_{CW} \left(\frac{I_{cj}}{A_j J_S} \right) + \frac{qV_s}{kT} = \ln \prod_{CCW} \left(\frac{I_{cj}}{A_j J_S} \right) \tag{5-23}$$

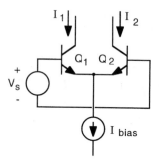

Figure 5-7   Differential pair as a translinear loop.

from which

$$\frac{\prod_{CW}\left(\dfrac{I_{cj}}{A_j}\right)}{\prod_{CCW}\left(\dfrac{I_{cj}}{A_j}\right)} = e^{-qV_s/kT} \qquad (5\text{-}24)$$

The differential pair shown in Fig. 5-7 may be analyzed as a translinear loop containing a voltage source. From Eq. (5-24), we have directly

$$\frac{I_1}{I_2} = e^{qV_s/kT} \qquad (5\text{-}25)$$

Transconductance Linear with Voltage

A transistor whose transconductance varies linearly with its voltage has

$$g_m = \frac{dI}{dV} = aV \qquad (5\text{-}26)$$

where a is a constant (with respect to I or V).

Integrating gives

$$I = \frac{1}{2}aV^2 + b \qquad (5\text{-}27)$$

where b is another constant.

Equation (5-27) describes the $I_D - V_{GS}$ characteristic for a MOSFET operating in saturation. Like the bipolar counterpart, circuits containing loops of gate-source junctions of MOSFETs operate in a translinear fashion. The range in current over which the transconductance remains linear with voltage is considerably less than with bipolar transistors. None the less, useful MOSFET translinear circuits have been produced.

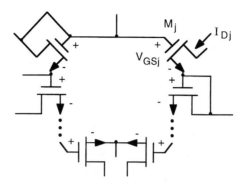

Figure 5-8   Translinear loop containing MOS transistors.

Translinear Circuit Principle

Figure 5-8 illustrates a loop of MOSFET junctions comprising an equal number of clockwise and counterclockwise polarities. Summing the gate-source voltages around the loop gives

$$\sum_{CW} V_{gsj} = \sum_{CCW} V_{gsj} \qquad (5\text{-}28)$$

with

$$V_{gsj} = V_{TH} + \sqrt{\frac{I_{dj}}{K_j(W/L)_j}} \qquad (5\text{-}29)$$

where

$$K_j = \frac{\mu C_{ox}'}{2}$$

Thus,

$$\sum_{CW}\left(V_{THj} + \sqrt{\frac{I_{dj}}{K_j(W/L)_j}}\right) = \sum_{CCW}\left(V_{THj} + \sqrt{\frac{I_{dj}}{K_j(W/L)_j}}\right) \qquad (5\text{-}30)$$

For matched devices, the threshold voltage terms cancel, and thereby the K_j terms. The translinear principle for MOSFETs then becomes

$$\sum_{CW}\sqrt{\frac{I_{dj}}{(W/L)_j}} = \sum_{CCW}\sqrt{\frac{I_{dj}}{(W/L)_j}} \qquad (5\text{-}31)$$

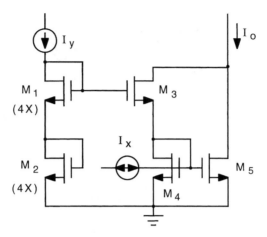

Figure 5-9   Translinear MOSFET circuit.

which states: *The sum of the square-root currents per unit aspect ratio in a clockwise direction equals the sum of the square-root currents per unit aspect ratio in a counterclockwise direction* [2].

A MOSFET translinear circuit is shown in Fig. 5-9; the (4X) notation on transistors M_1 and M_2 indicate that their channel/length ratios (W/L) are four times that of the other transistors. Application of Eq. (5-31) to the loop containing transistors M_1, M_2, M_3, and M_4 yields

$$\sqrt{\frac{I_{d1}}{4}} + \sqrt{\frac{I_{d2}}{4}} = \sqrt{\frac{I_{d3}}{1}} + \sqrt{\frac{I_{d4}}{1}} \tag{5-32}$$

Here, $I_{d1} = I_{d2} = I_y$. Also, $I_{d4} = I_{d3} + I_x = I_{d5}$, and $I_o = I_{d3} + I_{d5}$. Combining these relations into Eq. (5-32) results in

$$2\sqrt{\frac{I_y}{4}} = \sqrt{\frac{I_o + I_x}{2}} + \sqrt{\frac{I_o - I_x}{2}} \tag{5-33}$$

which solved for I_o yields

$$I_o = \frac{I_x^2 + I_y^2}{2I_y} \tag{5-34}$$

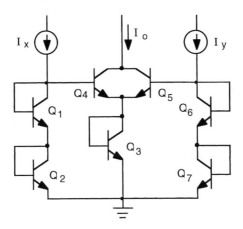

Figure 5-10   Vector magnitude circuit.

5.2 Analog Functions with Translinear Circuits

In this section, several translinear circuits used to implement analog functions are presented. These circuits have application in a variety of signal processing systems.

Vector Magnitude

Figure 5-10 shows a bipolar translinear circuit which implements a vector magnitude function. This version is preferred over the circuit illustrated in Fig. 5-5 in that the circuit symmetry tends to cancel degradations caused by parasitic base and emitter resistances of the transistors [3]. The translinear principle applied to the loop containing transistors Q_1, Q_2, Q_3, and Q_4 gives

$$I_{c3} I_{c4} = I_{c1} I_{c2} = I_x^2 \tag{5-35}$$

where $I_{c3} = I_o$.

For the loop containing Q_3, Q_5, Q_6, and Q_7,

$$I_{c3} I_{c5} = I_{c6} I_{c7} = I_y^2 \tag{5-36}$$

For Q_4 and Q_5,

$$I_{c4} + I_{c5} = I_o \tag{5-37}$$

Combining Eqs. (5-35) and (5-36) into Eq. (5-37) then gives

$$I_o = \sqrt{I_x^2 + I_y^2} \tag{5-38}$$

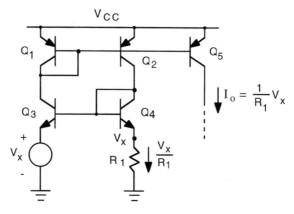

Figure 5-11   Voltage-to-current converter circuit.

The vector magnitude circuit of Fig. 5-10 operates in a current mode; input signals, as well as the output, are currents. For the circuit to operate with voltage signals, voltage-to-current converter circuits can be placed at the inputs and a current-to-voltage converter circuit can be placed at the output.

Figure 5-11 illustrates a circuit that functions well as a voltage-to-current converter. In the circuit, Q_1 and Q_2 form a current mirror which, due to their equal base-emitter voltages, have the same collector currents. These current are reflected in the collector currents of Q_3 and Q_4, causing them to have the same base-emitter voltages; the voltage at the emitter of Q_4 is thereby equal to the input voltage V_x at the emitter of Q_3. The emitter current of Q_4 is thus equal to V_x/R_1, which is then (neglecting base currents) equal to the collector current of Q_2. This current is mirrored by Q_5 giving an output current that is proportional to the input voltage. This circuit derives from a general form of this configuration called a *current conveyor* [4].

The circuit of Fig. 5-10, combined with voltage/current converter circuits, results in the voltage-mode vector magnitude circuit shown in Fig. 5-12. In the circuit, the current mirror provided by Q_1 and Q_2 converts the output current to an output voltage $V_o = R_2 I_o$. Thus,

$$V_o = \frac{R_2}{R_1} \sqrt{V_x^2 + V_y^2} \;\Rightarrow\; \sqrt{V_x^2 + V_y^2} \quad \text{for} \quad R_1 = R_2 \qquad (5\text{-}39)$$

Two-Quadrant Squarer

Circuits that provide an output proportional to the square of the input find application in power measurement and high-frequency, radio-frequency (RF)

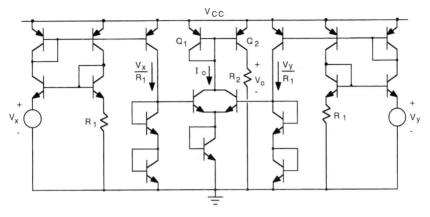

Figure 5-12   Practical embodiment of a voltage-mode vector magnitude circuit.

detection. Figure 5-13 shows a translinear circuit that functions as a two-quadrant squarer. From the loop containing transistors Q_1, Q_2, Q_4, and Q_5,

$$\frac{I_{c1}}{1} \frac{I_{c2}}{1} = \frac{I_{c4}}{2} \frac{I_{c5}}{2} \tag{5-40}$$

Neglecting base currents and taking I_x positive entering the input node,

$$I_{c1} = I_x + I_{c2} = I_{c3} \quad \text{and} \quad I_{c2} = I_{bias} - I_{c3} \tag{5-41}$$

which combine to give

$$I_{c1} = \frac{I_{bias} + I_x}{2} \quad \text{and} \quad I_{c2} = \frac{I_{bias} - I_x}{2} \tag{5-42}$$

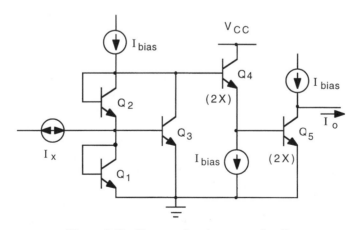

Figure 5-13   Two-quadrant squarer circuit.

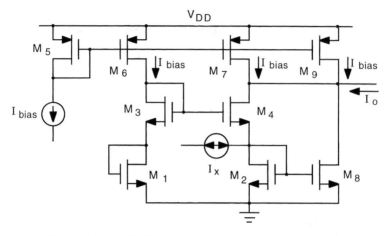

Figure 5-14   CMOS version of the two-quadrant squarer.

Now, $I_{c4} = I_{bias}$ and $I_{c5} = I_{bias} - I_o$. These relations, combined with Eq. (5-42) into Eq. (5-40), yields

$$I_o = \frac{I_x^2}{I_{bias}} \tag{5-43}$$

A CMOS version of the two-quadrant squarer is shown in Fig. 5-14; transistors M_5, M_6, M_7, and M_9 implement the I_{bias} sources. It is left as an exercise for the reader to show that this circuit gives

$$I_o = \frac{I_x^2}{8\,I_{bias}} \tag{5-44}$$

Absolute Value

Circuits which provide an output that is proportional to the absolute value of an input signal find application as RF detectors. The vector magnitude circuit of Fig. 5-5 would function as an absolute-value circuit if signal I_y is made zero; transistors Q_4 and Q_5 would thereby not be needed. Such a circuit, although functional, would suffer from errors caused by base current.

An improved absolute-value circuit is shown in Fig. 5-15. In this circuit, the current source comprising transistors Q_6 and Q_7 forward biases the two series diodes, formed by Q_8 and Q_9; the voltage at the base of Q_4 is then equal to $2V_{be}$. As a consequence of this bias arrangement, the Darlington pair, transistors Q_2, Q_4, and transistor Q_1 will not conduct at the same time. For I_x positive (entering the circuit), the Darlington pair is off and current I_x flows through transistor

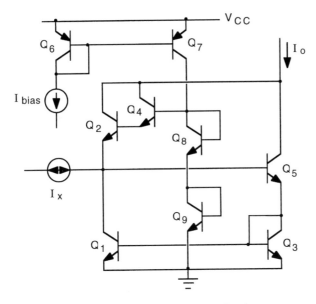

Figure 5-15   Absolute-value circuit.

Q_1, which is part of a Wilson current source comprising transistors Q_1, Q_3, and Q_5. The output current is then given from Eq. (2-24) as

$$I_o = I_x \left[1 - \frac{2}{\beta_F^2 + 2\beta_F + 2} \right] \approx I_x \left(1 - \frac{2}{\beta_F^2} \right) \tag{5-45}$$

For I_x negative, the Wilson current source is off and the output current flows through transistors Q_2 and Q_4. It is easily shown that

$$I_o = I_x \left[1 - \frac{1}{\beta_F^2 + 2\beta_F + 2} \right] \approx I_x \left(1 - \frac{1}{\beta_F^2} \right) \tag{5-46}$$

To a high degree of accuracy, the circuit gives

$$I_o = |I_x| \tag{5-47}$$

The only real problem with this circuit is the switching on and off of the transistors as I_x changes polarity; thus, I_o is not continuous as I_x crosses zero. This can induce switching noise in the circuit. Nonetheless, the circuit functions well, as illustrated by the simulation shown in Fig. 5-16.

Analog Multipliers

Analog muitiplier circuits produce an output that is proportional to the product of two input signals; they find wide application in communications circuits,

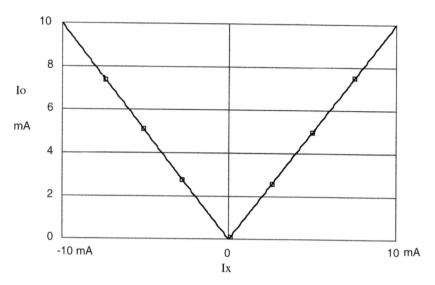

Figure 5-16   Simulation of the absolute-value circuit.

such as mixers, balanced modulators, and phase detectors. The Gilbert multiplier cell, illustrated in Fig. 5-17, forms the basis of many multiplier circuits [5].

The Gilbert cell consists of two cross-coupled differential pairs (Q_1, Q_2 and Q_3, Q_4), fed serially by a third differential pair (Q_5, Q_6); the x-input signal is

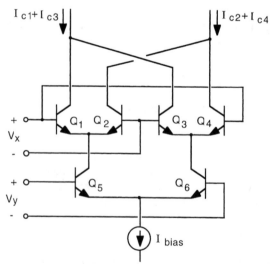

Figure 5-17   Gilbert multiplier cell.

applied to the upper differential pairs and the y-input signal is applied to the lower differential pair. The output is taken differentially at the collectors of the cross-coupled pairs, expressed as

$$I_o = (I_{c1} + I_{c3}) - (I_{c2} + I_{c4}) = (I_{c1} - I_{c2}) - (I_{c4} - I_{c3}) \qquad (5\text{-}48)$$

As expressed by the right-hand term in Eq. (5-48), the output is equal to the difference in the differential collector currents of the two upper differential pairs. The differential output current of a single pair is given by Eq. (2-233)

$$I_{c1} - I_{c2} = I_{EE} \tanh\left(\frac{qV_{12}}{2kT}\right) \qquad (5\text{-}49)$$

where base currents have been neglected; V_{12} is the differential input voltage. Applying Eq. (5-49) to Eq. (5-48) gives

$$I_o = (I_{c5} - I_{c6}) \tanh\left(\frac{qV_x}{2kT}\right) \qquad (5\text{-}50)$$

Substituting for the differential current of the lower differential pair, Eq. (5-50) becomes

$$I_o = I_{\text{bias}} \tanh\left(\frac{qV_y}{2kT}\right) \tanh\left(\frac{qV_x}{2kT}\right) \qquad (5\text{-}51)$$

The product is nonlinear in V_x and V_y. If, however, the amplitudes of the signals are much smaller than the thermal voltage, kT/q, then the tanh functions are approximately linear, giving

$$I_o \approx \left(\frac{q}{2kT}\right)^2 I_{\text{bias}}\, V_x\, V_y \qquad (5\text{-}52)$$

To remove this restriction on the signal amplitudes, the input signals can be preprocessed to compensate for the tanh nonlinearity. In this regard, consider the circuit shown in Fig. 5-18. Here, the modulation parameter x in the current

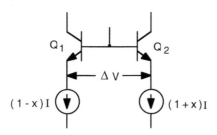

Figure 5-18   Inverse hyperbolic tangent conversion.

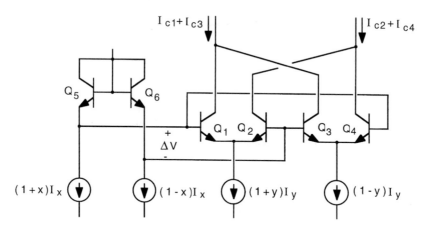

Figure 5-19   Linearized multiplier.

sources represents an input signal; its value can vary between -1 and $+1$. The voltage difference between the emitters of the two transistors is given by

$$\Delta V = V_{be2} - V_{be1} = \frac{kT}{q} \ln\left(\frac{1+x}{1-x}\right) \tag{5-53}$$

Applying the trigonometric identity

$$\tanh^{-1} x = \frac{1}{2} \ln\left(\frac{1+x}{1-x}\right) \tag{5-54}$$

shows that the circuit in Fig. 5-18 can be used to compensate for the *tanh* nonlinearity of the differential pairs in the multiplier circuit. This compensation needs to be applied only to the x input; because (Fig. 5-17) $I_{c5} - I_{c6}$ varies as tanh(V_y), the lower differential pair (Q_5, Q_6) can be eliminated if the y inputs are supplied as currents. Such a linearized multiplier circuit is shown in Fig. 5-19. In the circuit, the x and y signals are proportional to the input voltage signals: $x = K_x V_x$ and $y = K_y V_y$. The output current $(I_{c1} + I_{c3}) - (I_{c2} + I_{c4})$ is given by

$$I_o = [(1+y)I_y - (1-y)I_y] \tanh\left(\frac{q\Delta V}{2kT}\right) \tag{5-55}$$

which, using Eqs. (5-53) and (5-54), results in

$$I_o = 2I_y xy = (2K_x K_y I_y) V_x V_y \tag{5-56}$$

For the multiplier to function with voltage signals, a differential voltage-to-current converter is needed at the inputs. Two methods are commonly employed: diode linearization and emitter degeneration.

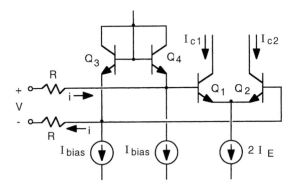

Figure 5-20   Diode linearization.

Diode Linearization

Connecting forward-biased diodes at the inputs of a differential pair results in currents that are linearly proportional to input voltages, similar to that employed in the transconductance amplifier (see Fig. 3-35). Consider the circuit shown in Fig. 5-20. The translinear loop comprising transistors Q_1–Q_4 provides

$$I_{c1} I_{c4} = I_{c2} I_{c3} \tag{5-57}$$

Neglecting base currents, we have

$$I_{c1} + I_{c2} = 2I_E, \qquad I_{c3} = I_{bias} + i, \quad \text{and} \quad I_{c4} = I_{bias} - i \tag{5-58}$$

Combining Eqs. (5-57) and (5-58) gives

$$I_{c1} = \left(1 + \frac{i}{I_{bias}}\right) I_E$$

and

$$I_{c2} = \left(1 - \frac{i}{I_{bias}}\right) I_E \tag{5-59}$$

Summing the voltages at the input,

$$V = iR + V_{be1} - V_{be2} + iR \tag{5-60}$$

Now, if $I_{bias} R \gg kT/q$, then the differences in the base-emitter voltages of transistors Q_1 and Q_2 will be small in comparison to iR, giving $i \approx v/2R$. Thus,

$$I_{c1} = \left(1 + \frac{V}{2I_{bias} R}\right) I_E = (1 + x) I_E$$

and

$$I_{c2} = \left(1 - \frac{V}{2I_{bias} R}\right) I_E = (1 - x) I_E \tag{5-61}$$

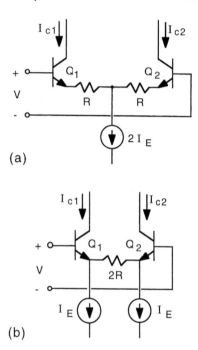

Figure 5-21 Two forms of linearization by emitter degeneration.

where $x = V/2I_{bias}R$. The two collector currents are now linearly proportional to the input voltage V.

Emitter Degeneration

Placing resistors in the emitter circuit of a differential pair can linearize the response; the resistors provide emitter degeneration and two alternate forms are shown in Fig. 5-21. For the circuit in Fig. 5-21(a), summing the voltages around the base-emitter loop yields

$$V = V_{be1} + I_{c1}R - I_{c2}R - V_{be2} \qquad (5\text{-}62)$$

where base currents have been neglected. If $I_E R \gg kT/q$, then the two base-emitter voltages in Eq. (5-62) can be assumed to be approximately equal; they thereby cancel, giving $I_{c1} - I_{c2} = V/R$. Also, $I_{c1} + I_{c2} = 2I_E$. Combining these relations with Eq. (5-62) gives

$$I_{c1} = \left(1 + \frac{V}{2I_E R}\right)I_E = 1 + x$$

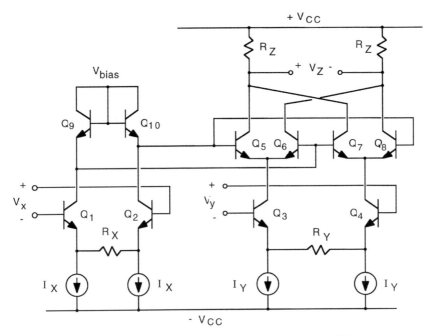

Figure 5-22   Four-quadrant analog multiplier (MC-1495 type).

and

$$I_{c2} = \left(1 - \frac{V}{2I_E R}\right) I_E = 1 - x \tag{5-63}$$

where $x = V/2I_E R$.

The version shown in Fig. 5-21(b) gives the same result [Eq. (5-63)]; however, it has a voltage range that is about $2V_{be}$ less than that using the version in Fig. 5-21(a).

A simplified schematic of a commercial four-quadrant analog multiplier circuit is shown in Fig. 5-22; it utilizes the second version of emitter degeneration [Fig. 5-21(b)] for linearization. The output voltage $V_Z = I_o R_Z = 2I_Y R_Z xy$, which, using Eqs. (5-52) and (5-63), results in

$$V_Z = \frac{2R_Z}{I_X R_X R_Y} V_x V_y \tag{5-64}$$

Resistors R_X, R_Y, and R_Z are connected externally, usually chosen such that $2R_Z/I_X R_X R_Y = 0.1$, giving $V_Z = 0.1\, V_x V_y$. With ± 15-V power supplies, this allows inputs in excess of ± 10 V to be used. Simulation of the circuit in Fig. 5-22

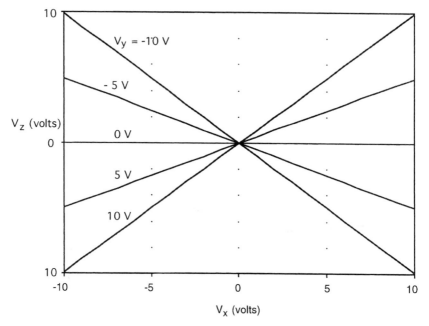

Figure 5-23 **Simulation of the multiplier circuit of Fig. 5-22.**

is shown in Fig. 5-23. In the circuit, $I_X = I_Y = 1\,\text{mA}$, $R_X = R_Y = 15\,\text{k}\Omega$, and $R_Z = 11.25\,\text{k}\Omega$.

MOS Four-Quadrant Multiplier

The MOS version of the Gilbert multiplier cell is shown in Fig. 5-24 [6]. As with the bipolar transistor version, the output is taken differentially as

$$I_o = (I_{d1} + I_{d3}) - (I_{d2} + I_{d4}) = (I_{d1} - I_{d2}) - (I_{d4} - I_{d3}) \tag{5-65}$$

The differential output current of a single differential pair is given by Eq. (2-243),

$$I_{d1} - I_{d2} = K\left(\frac{W}{L}\right)V_{12}\sqrt{\frac{2I_{ss}}{K(W/L)} - V_{12}^2} \tag{5-66}$$

where $K = \mu_n C'_{ox}/2$ and V_{12} is the differential input voltage, with a range given by

$$-\sqrt{\frac{I_{ss}}{K(W/L)}} < V_{12} < \sqrt{\frac{I_{ss}}{K(W/L)}} \tag{5-67}$$

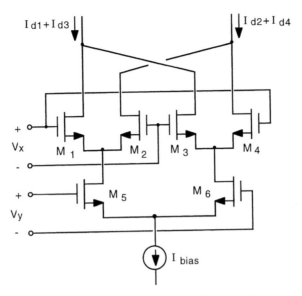

Figure 5-24 MOS Gilbert multiplier cell.

The output current is thus

$$I_o = K\left(\frac{W}{L}\right)V_x\sqrt{\frac{2I_{d5}}{K(W/L)} - V_x^2} - K\left(\frac{W}{L}\right)V_x\sqrt{\frac{2I_{d6}}{K(W/L)} - V_x^2} \qquad (5\text{-}68)$$

Substituting for I_{d5} and I_{d6} gives

$$I_o = K\left(\frac{W}{L}\right)V_x\left[\sqrt{\frac{I_{bias}}{K(W/L)} + V_y\sqrt{\frac{2I_{bias}}{K(W/L)} - V_y^2} - V_x^2}\right.$$

$$\left. - \sqrt{\frac{I_{bias}}{K(W/L)} - V_y\sqrt{\frac{2I_{bias}}{K(W/L)} - V_y^2} - V_x^2}\right] \qquad (5\text{-}69)$$

which, after some manipulation, can be rewritten in the following form:

$$I_o = K\left(\frac{W}{L}\right)V_x\left[\sqrt{\left(\sqrt{\frac{I_{bias}}{K(W/L)} - \frac{V_y^2}{2}} + \frac{V_y}{\sqrt{2}}\right)^2 - V_x^2}\right.$$

$$\left. - \sqrt{\left(\sqrt{\frac{I_{bias}}{K(W/L)} - \frac{V_y^2}{2}} - V_y\sqrt{2}\right)^2 - V_x^2}\right] \qquad (5\text{-}70)$$

Here, the output current is nonlinear in V_x and V_y, in which both inputs interact. Thus, the inputs cannot be predistorted to compensate for the nonlinearity as was done with the bipolar multiplier circuit. However, if the magnitudes of the inputs are kept small with respect to $\sqrt{I_{\text{bias}} K(W/L)}$, Eq. (5-70) simplifies to

$$I_o = K\left(\frac{W}{L}\right)V_x\left[\sqrt{\frac{I_{\text{bias}}}{K(W/L)} - \frac{V_y^2}{2}} + \frac{V_y}{\sqrt{2}} - \left(\sqrt{\frac{I_{\text{bias}}}{K(W/L)} - \frac{V_y^2}{2}} - \frac{V_y}{\sqrt{2}}\right)\right]$$

$$= \sqrt{2} K\left(\frac{W}{L}\right)V_x V_y \qquad\qquad\qquad (5\text{-}71)$$

which is linear in V_x and V_y; typically, the inputs are limited to about ± 0.5 V before significant nonlinearity appears.

Linearization

Consider the differential pair shown in Fig. 5-25 wherein a component proportional to the square of the differential input voltage is added to the common-source bias current. Here,

$$I_{d1} = \frac{I_{\text{bias}}}{2} + \frac{K(W/L)}{2} V \sqrt{\frac{2I_{\text{bias}}}{K(W/L)}}$$

and

$$I_{d2} = \frac{I_{\text{bias}}}{2} - \frac{K(W/L)}{2} V \sqrt{\frac{2I_{\text{bias}}}{K(W/L)}} \qquad\qquad (5\text{-}72)$$

Thus,

$$I_{d1} - I_{d2} = K\left(\frac{W}{L}\right)V\sqrt{\frac{2I_{\text{bias}}}{K(W/L)}} = \sqrt{2K\left(\frac{W}{L}\right)I_{\text{bias}}}\, V \qquad (5\text{-}73)$$

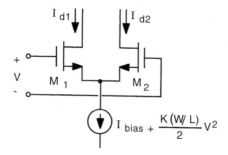

Figure 5-25   MOSFET linearization.

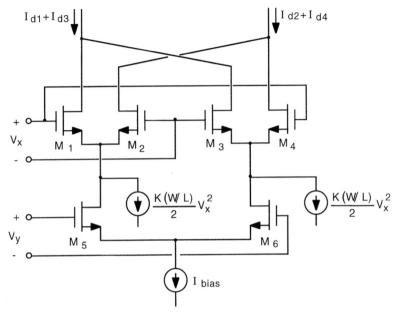

Figure 5-26   Linearized MOS Gilbert multiplier cell.

The differential output current is thus linearly proportional to V. This lineariz-ation applied to the MOS Gilbert cell in Fig. 5-26 gives

$$I_o = K\left(\frac{W}{L}\right)V_x\left[\sqrt{\frac{I_{bias}}{K(W/L)} - \frac{V_y^2}{2}} + \frac{V_y}{\sqrt{2}} - \left(\sqrt{\frac{I_{bias}}{K(W/L)} - \frac{V_y^2}{2}} - \frac{V_y}{\sqrt{2}}\right)\right]$$

$$= \sqrt{2}\,K\left(\frac{W}{L}\right)V_x V_y \tag{5-74}$$

The linear range has now been increased to

$$-\sqrt{\frac{I_{bias}}{K(W/L)}} < V_{x,y} < \sqrt{\frac{I_{bias}}{K(W/L)}} \tag{5-75}$$

which implies that a small channel width–channel length ratio (W/L) is desired for a large input range; V_{Dsat} is equal to this range, however. Thus, V_x needs to have a large common-mode component relative to the differential-mode com-ponent to keep transistors M_1–M_2 and M_3–M_4 operating in the saturation region.

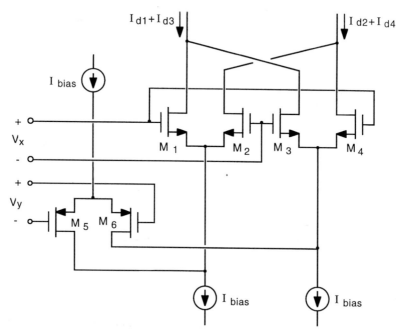

Figure 5-27   Folded CMOS Gilbert cell.

Using a folded CMOS Gilbert cell structure, shown in Fig. 5-27, allows a smaller common-mode voltage to be used. For this circuit,

$$I_o = K_N \left(\frac{W}{L}\right)_N V_x \left[\sqrt{\frac{2(I_{\text{bias}} - I_{d5})}{K_N(W/L)_N} - V_x^2} - \sqrt{\frac{2(I_{\text{bias}} - I_{d6})}{K_N(W/L)_N} - V_x^2}\right] \quad (5\text{-}76)$$

where

$$I_{d5} = \frac{I_{\text{bias}}}{2} - \frac{K_P(W/L)_P}{2} V_y \sqrt{\frac{2I_{\text{bias}}}{K_P(W/L)_P} - V_y^2}$$

and

$$I_{d6} = \frac{I_{\text{bias}}}{2} + \frac{K_P(W/L)_P}{2} V_y \sqrt{\frac{2I_{\text{bias}}}{K_P(W/L)_P} - V_y^2} \quad (5\text{-}77)$$

Substituting for I_{d5} and I_{d6} into Eq. (5-76) results in

$$I_o = K_N \left(\frac{W}{L}\right)_N V_x \left[\sqrt{\frac{K_P(W/L)_P}{K_N(W/L)_N}\left(\sqrt{\frac{I_{\text{bias}}}{K_P(W/L)_P} - \frac{V_y^2}{2}} + \frac{V_y}{\sqrt{2}}\right)^2 - V_x^2}\right.$$

$$\left. - \sqrt{\frac{K_P(W/L)_P}{K_N(W/L)_N}\left(\sqrt{\frac{I_{\text{bias}}}{K_P(W/L)_P} - \frac{V_y^2}{2}} - \frac{V_y}{\sqrt{2}}\right)^2 - V_x^2}\right] \quad (5\text{-}78)$$

V_x can now have a smaller common-mode component relative to its differential-mode component. The V_x^2 nonlinearity can be removed by adding a component $K_N(W/L)_N V_x^2/2$ to the x-input differential-pair bias currents, as was done in Fig. 5-26, giving

$$I_o = \sqrt{2K_N(W/L)_N K_P(W/L)_P}\; V_x V_y \qquad (5\text{-}79)$$

Linearization Implementation

The two circuits shown in Fig. 5-28 can be used to implement the MOS linearization scheme. Consider first the circuit of Fig. 5-28(a), in which input V_x contains a common-mode component V_{cx}. The output current is

$$I_o = I_{d1} + I_{d2} = K_N\left(\frac{W}{L}\right)_N\left(V_{cx} + \frac{V_x}{2} - V_{TN}\right)^2 + K_N\left(\frac{W}{L}\right)_N\left(V_{cx} - \frac{V_x}{2} - V_{TN}\right)^2$$

$$= 2K_N\left(\frac{W}{L}\right)_N(V_{cx} - V_{TN})^2 + \frac{K_N(W/L)_N}{2}V_x^2 \qquad (5\text{-}80)$$

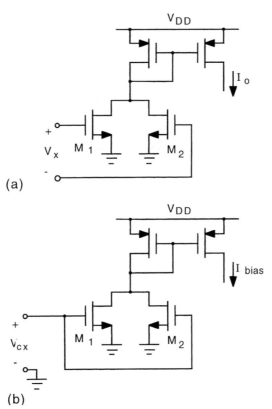

(a)

(b)

Figure 5-28   Linearization circuits for the MOS multiplier.

The first term on the right-hand side of Eq. (5-80) represents the bias current due to the common-mode voltage, V_{cx}, and the second term represents the linearization component. The common-mode component can be implemented by the circuit of Fig. 5-28(b) in which

$$I_{\text{bias}} = I_{d1} + I_{d2} = 2K_N(WL)_N(V_{cx} - V_{TN})^2 \tag{5-81}$$

A complete analog CMOS multiplier circuit using the linearization circuits of Fig. 5-28 is shown in Fig. 5-29. Transistors M_1–M_6 comprise the folded multiplier cell in which the bias current of the y-input differential pair (M_5, M_6) is biased by the common-mode voltage. This current, mirrored in M_{13} and M_{14}, is also used to bias the two source follower transistors, M_{17} and M_{18}, used to level shift the x input. The output voltage is developed across the load resistors, resulting in

$$V_o = \sqrt{2K_N(W/L)_N K_P(WL)_P} \, R_D V_x V_y \tag{5-82}$$

5.3 Trigonometric Functions with Translinear Circuits

Circuits which implement trigonometric functions, that is circuits which produce an output proportional to a trigonometric function of an input, find application in signal processing, servo-control systems, and signal generation. Among the most useful are circuits which generate sine and cosine functions.

Consider the translinear circuit shown in Fig. 5-30. The translinear principle applied to the base-emitter loop gives

$$I_{c2} I_{c4} I_{c6} = I_{c1} I_{c3} I_{c5} \tag{5-83}$$

Then ignoring base currents,

$$[(1-x)I_{\text{bias}}]^2 I_{c2} = [(1+x)I_{\text{bias}}]^2 I_{c1} \tag{5-84}$$

Combining Eq. (5-84) with $I_{c1} + I_{c2} = 2I_{\text{bias}}$ gives

$$I_{c1} = \frac{(1-x)^2}{1+x^2} I_{\text{bias}} \quad \text{and} \quad I_{c2} = \frac{(1+x)^2}{1+x^2} I_{\text{bias}} \tag{5-85}$$

Taking the output as $I_o = (I_{c2} + I_{c6}) - (I_{c1} + I_{c5}) = (I_{c2} - I_{c1}) + (I_{c6} - I_{c5})$ then yields

$$I_o = 2x\left(\frac{1-x^2}{1+x^2}\right) I_{\text{bias}} \tag{5-86}$$

Equation (5-86) is an approximation to a sine function for $-1 < x < 1$,

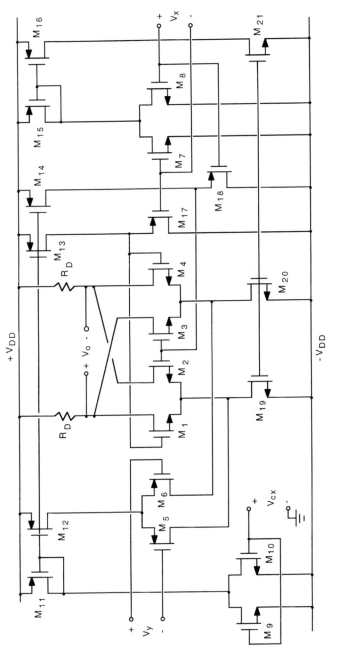

Figure 5-29   Linearized CMOS multiplier circuit.

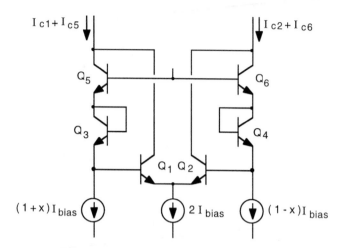

Figure 5-30   Translinear sine function circuit.

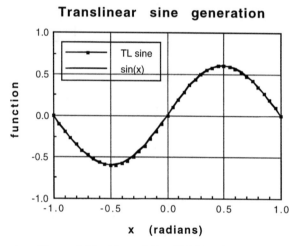

Figure 5-31   Plots of Eq. (5-86) and sin (x).

which corresponds to an angle $-\pi < \theta < \pi$ radians, and is plotted in Fig. 5-31 along with the trigonometric sine function. The maximum error in the two curves is about 3%.

A more accurate synthesis of the sine function can be obtained with the circuit shown in Fig. 5-32 [7]. In this circuit, the inner transistor bases (Q_2 and Q_3) are biased at a potential $I_{BB}R$ more positive than the outer transistor bases (Q_1 and Q_4); here, the voltage drop $I_{BB}R$ controls the angle scaling factor. The

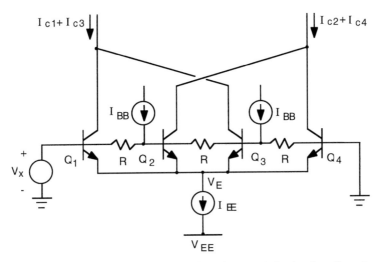

Figure 5-32   A more accurate version of a trigonometric sine function circuit.

input signal V_x controls the equivalent angle of the sine function, and for one
cycle of the function $(-1 < x < 1)$

$$x = \frac{\pi V_x}{3 I_{BB} R} \tag{5-87}$$

When $V_x = 0$, the circuit is balanced with $I_{c1} = I_{c4}$ and $I_{c2} = I_{c3}$. Taking the output
differentially as

$$I_o = (I_{c2} + I_{c4}) - (I_{c1} + I_{c3}) \tag{5-88}$$

then has $I_o = 0$. When V_x is made positive, the circuit symmetry is unbalanced
with $I_{c1} > I_{c4}$ and $I_{c2} > I_{c3}$, resulting in a positive output; for V_x negative, $I_{c4} > I_{c1}$
and $I_{c3} > I_{c2}$, giving a negative output. As V_x is varied from $-3 I_{BB} R / \pi$ to
$+ 3 I_{BB} R / \pi$, the output traces one cycle of the function.

Denoting the voltages at the base nodes of transistors Q_2 and Q_3 as V_2 and V_3,
respectively, and summing the currents at these nodes (neglecting base currents) yields

$$\text{Node base } Q_2: \quad \frac{V_x - V_2}{R} + I_{BB} = \frac{V_2 - V_3}{R}$$

$$\text{Node base } Q_3: \quad \frac{V_2 - V_3}{R} + I_{BB} = \frac{V_3}{R} \tag{5-89}$$

Solving for the node voltages,

$$V_2 = \frac{2}{3} V_x + I_{BB} R \quad \text{and} \quad V_3 = \frac{1}{3} V_x + I_{BB} R \qquad (5\text{-}90)$$

The transistor collector currents are

$$I_{c1} = I_S \exp\left[\frac{q}{kT}(V_x - V_E)\right] = I_S \exp\left(-\frac{qV_E}{kT}\right) \exp\left(\frac{qV_x}{kT}\right) = I_{c4} \exp\left(\frac{qV_x}{kT}\right)$$

$$I_{c2} = I_S \exp\left[\frac{q}{kT}(V_2 - V_E)\right] = I_{c4} \exp\left[\frac{q}{kT}\left(\frac{2}{3} V_x + I_{BB} R\right)\right]$$

$$I_{c3} = I_S \exp\left[\frac{q}{kT}(V_3 - V_E)\right] = I_{c4} \exp\left[\frac{q}{kT}\left(\frac{1}{3} V_x + I_{BB} R\right)\right]$$

with

$$I_{c4} = I_S \exp\left(-\frac{qV_E}{kT}\right) \qquad (5\text{-}91)$$

Summing the currents at the common-emitter node gives

$$I_{c1} + I_{c2} + I_{c3} + I_{c4} = I_{EE} \qquad (5\text{-}92)$$

Combining Eqs. (5-91) and (5-92) and substituting into Eq. (5-88) yields

$$\frac{I_o}{I_{EE}} = \frac{1 - e^{qV_x/kT} + e^{qI_{BB}R/kT}(e^{2qV_x/3kT} - e^{qV_x/3kT})}{1 + e^{qV_x/kT} + e^{qI_{BB}R/kT}(e^{2qV_x/kT} + e^{qV_x/3kT})} \qquad (5\text{-}93)$$

It is profitable to let $\alpha = qI_{BB} R/kT$; then from Eq. (5-87), $qV_x/3kT = \alpha\pi/x$. This allows Eq. (5-93) to be cast in the following form:

$$\frac{I_o}{I_{EE}} = \frac{1 - e^{(3\alpha/\pi)x} + e^{\alpha}(e^{(2\alpha/\pi)x} - e^{(\alpha/\pi)x})}{1 + e^{(3\alpha/\pi)x} + e^{\alpha}(e^{(2\alpha/\pi)x} + e^{(\alpha/\pi)x})} \qquad (5\text{-}94)$$

In this form, x represents the angle of the function, ranging from $-\pi$ to $+\pi$ radians. A plot of Eq. (5-94) presents a very close approximation of a sine function, with a maximum error of about 0.2% for α set to a value of 3.

A simulation of the circuit in Fig. 5-32 is shown in Fig. 5-33, where $R = 1\,k\Omega$ and $I_{BB} = 75\,\mu A$ were used. A simulation at three temperatures is shown. The input range is from $-200\,mV$ to $+200\,mV$ for the angle ranging from $-180°$ to $+180°$, and is virtually independent of temperature. Only the amplitude of the sine function is appreciably sensitive to temperature. As described in Ref. 7, the angular range can be increased by π radians by adding an additional transistor to the circuit; a six-transistor circuit would have a range of $\pm 360°$.

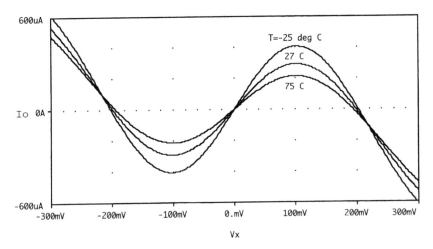

Figure 5-33 Simulation of the circuit in Fig. 5-32 at various temperatures.

5.4 Gilbert Gain Cell

An interesting translinear circuit is shown in Fig. 5-34; if x is taken as an input signal, then it is reused by combining it at the output, taken at the collectors of Q_1 and Q_4. This configuration is referred to as a Gilbert gain cell and can be used as a controlled-gain current-mode amplifier [3]. This circuit can be viewed as a differential cascode amplifier with a current gain larger than unity. Applying the translinear principle to the base-emitter loop gives

$$I_{c1} I_{c2} = I_{c3} I_{c4} \tag{5-95}$$

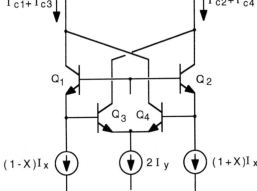

Figure 5-34 Gilbert gain cell.

where, neglecting base currents, $I_{c1} = (1 - x)I_x$ and $I_{c4} = (1 + x)I_{c4}$. Additionally, $I_{c2} + I_{c3} = 2I_y$ (neglecting base currents), which, combined with Eq. (5-95), gives

$$I_{c2} = (1 + x)I_y \quad \text{and} \quad I_{c3} = (1 - x)I_y \qquad (5\text{-}96)$$

Taking the output differentially at the collectors of Q_1, Q_3 and Q_2, Q_4, we obtain

$$I_o = (I_{c2} + I_{c4}) - (I_{c1} - I_{c3}) = 2x(I_x + I_y) \qquad (5\text{-}97)$$

Likewise, taking the input differentially at the emitters of Q_1 and Q_4,

$$I_{in} = (1 + x)I_x - (1 - x)I_x = 2xI_x \qquad (5\text{-}98)$$

The gain of this amplifier is then expressed as

$$\text{Gain} = \frac{I_o}{I_{in}} = 1 + \frac{I_y}{I_x} \qquad (5\text{-}99)$$

where the ratio of the bias currents I_x and I_y sets the gain. The minimum gain is unity and the maximum gain is limited to about 10 or so due to errors due to finite base currents; the base currents of transistors Q_2 and Q_3 add to the output via transistors Q_1 and Q_4, which are out of phase. It is left as an exercise for the reader to show that if base currents are taken into account, the gain is given approximately by

$$\frac{I_o}{I_{in}} = \frac{\beta_F}{\beta_F + 1}\left(1 + \frac{\beta_F}{\beta_F + 1}\frac{I_y}{I_x}\right) \qquad (5\text{-}100)$$

Several cells can be cascaded together to form an amplifier with larger gain, as illustrated in Fig. 5-35. The total gain is now

$$\text{Gain} = 1 + \frac{I_1}{I_i} + \frac{I_2}{I_i} + \cdots + \frac{I_n}{I_i} \qquad (5\text{-}101)$$

The gain of each stage is limited to a maximum of about 10 and can be independently controlled by its bias current, I_n. Used as a current-mode amplifier, this circuit achieves a large bandwidth.

Problems

For all problems assume room temperature, $kT/q = 26\,\text{mV}$.
Note: Where required, use the following device parameters unless otherwise specified:

NPN: $\beta_F = 100$	$I_S = 2 \times 10^{-16}\,\text{A}$	$V_A = 75\,\text{V}$
PNP: $\beta_F = 50$	$I_S = 5 \times 10^{-17}\,\text{A}$	$V_A = 75\,\text{V}$

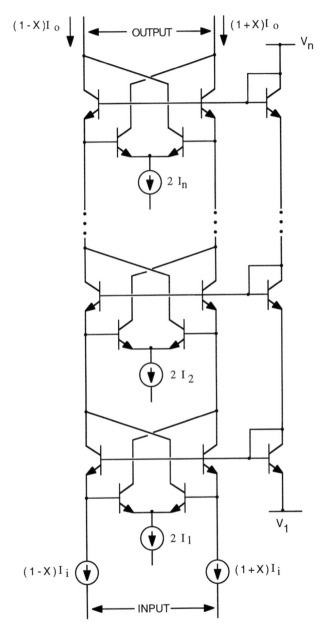

Figure 5-35 Current-mode amplifier using cascaded gain cells.

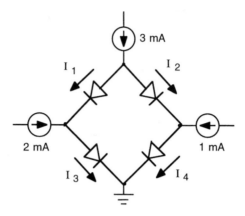

Figure 5-36   Diode ring for Problem 5.1.

NMOS: $W/L = 10$ $\mu_n C'_{ox} = 30\,\mu A/V^2$ $V_{TH} = 1\,V$ $\lambda = 0.02\,V^{-1}$

PMOS: $W/L = 30$ $\mu_p C'_{ox} = 10\,\mu A/V^2$ $V_{TH} = -1\,V$ $\lambda = 0.02\,V^{-1}$

5.1 Using the translinear circuit principle, determine the currents I_1–I_4 in the diode ring in Fig. 5-36.

5.2 Using four bipolar transistors and a bias current source, design a translinear circuit that gives

$$I_o = \sqrt{\frac{A_3 A}{A_1 A_2}}\, I_{bias}$$

where $A_{1,2,3,4}$ are the emitter areas of the transistors. Base currents may be neglected.

5.3 Using three MOS transistors and a bias current source, design a translinear circuit that gives

$$I_o = \frac{(W/L)_3}{(W/L)_1 + (W/L)_2}\, I_{bias}$$

where $(W/L)_{1,2,3}$ are the channel width/length dimensions of the transistors.

5.4 Treating the MOSFET differential pair in Fig. 5-37 as a translinear loop containing a voltage source, show that

$$I_o = I_{d1} - I_{d2} = K\left(\frac{W}{L}\right) V_s \sqrt{\frac{2 I_{bias}}{K(W/L)} - V_s^2}$$

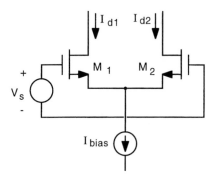

Figure 5-37   MOSFET differential pair for Problem 5.4.

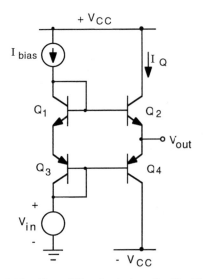

Figure 5-38   Class AB output stage for Problem 5.5.

5.5 The Class AB output stage shown in Fig. 5-38 may be viewed as a translinear circuit. Neglecting base currents, show that for $V_{\text{out}} = 0$, the quiescent bias current of the output transistors is given by

$$I_Q = \sqrt{\frac{A_2 A_4}{A_1 A_3}}\, I_{\text{bias}}$$

where A_{1-4} are the emitter areas of transistors Q_{1-4}, respectively.

5.6 Simulate, using SPICE, the two-quadrant squarer circuit of Fig. 5-13. Take $V_{CC} = 5\,\text{V}$, $I_{\text{bias}} = 1\,\text{mA}$, and neglect V_A in the transistor model. Connect the I_{bias}

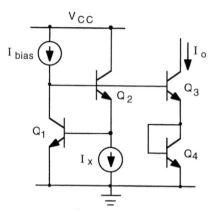

Figure 5-39   Circuit for Problem 5.8.

sources for transistors Q_2 and Q_5 to V_{CC} and connect a second 5-V source to
the collector of Q_5 to measure the output current I_o. In the simulation, vary
I_x from $-1\,mA$ to $+1\,mA$, and plot the *square root* of I_o versus I_x to show
the squarer relationship. Simulate the circuit first with β_F set to 10,000 and
then with β_F set to 100 to show the effects of base current on the circuit
performance. Comment on it.

5.7 Verify that the output current of the two-quadrant CMOS squarer circuit
in Fig. 5-14 is given by Eq. (5-44).

5.8 In the translinear circuit shown in Fig. 5-39, all transistors are identical.
Determine the output current I_o, neglecting base currents.

5.9 In the translinear circuit shown in Fig. 5-40, all transistors are identical,

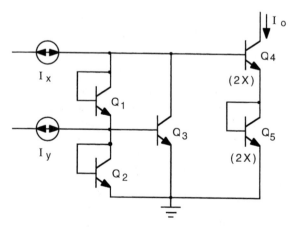

Figure 5-40   Circuit for Problem 5.9.

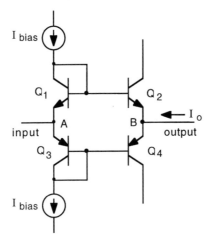

Figure 5-41   Translinear loop circuit for Problem 5.10.

except for emitter areas as noted. Determine the output current I_o, neglecting base currents.

5.10 Show that the offset voltage V_{BA} in the translinear loop circuit shown in Fig. 5-41 is given approximately by

$$V_{BA} = \frac{kT}{2qI_{bias}} I_o$$

Base currents may be neglected and you may assume that the output current I_o is much smaller than $2I_{bias}$.

5.11 The Gilbert cell shown in Fig. 5-42 may be used as a four-quadrant

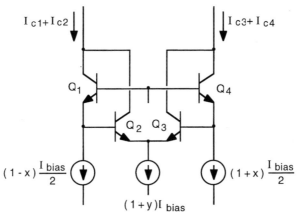

Figure 5-42   Gilbert cell used as a four-quadrant multiplier for Problem 5.11.

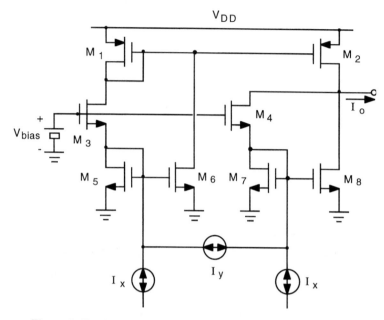

Figure 5-43   CMOS four-quadrant multiplier for Problem 5.12.

multiplier. Assuming identical devices and neglecting base currents, derive an expression for the output current I_o, taking it as $(I_{c1} + I_{c2}) - (I_{c3} + I_{c4})$.

5.12 Figure 5-43 shows another version of a CMOS four-quadrant multiplier. The NMOS transistors are identical, as are the PMOS transistors. Show that the output current is given by

$$I_o = \frac{2I_x I_y}{K_N (W/L)_N (V_{\text{bias}} - 2V_{TN})^2}$$

5.13 Figure 5-44 shows an analog function circuit in which input signal x varies from -1 to $+1$. Determine the output function, taken as $I_o = (I_{c2} + I_{c8}) - (I_{c1} + I_{c7})$, expressing it as a function of x; base currents may be neglected. Plot your result, normalized to I_{bias}, for x varying from -1 to $+1$.

5.14 Show that the gain of the Gilbert gain cell shown in Fig. 5.34 is given by Eq. (5-100).

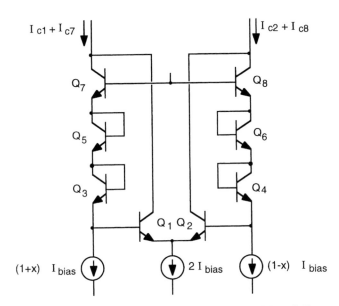

Figure 5-44   Analog function circuit for Problem 5.13.

References

1. B. Gilbert, "Translinear Circuits: A Proposed Classification," *Electron. Lett.*, *11*, 14–16 (1975).

2. E. Seevinck and R.J. Wiegerink, "Generalized Translinear Circuit Principle," *IEEE J. Solid-State Circuits*, *26*, 1098–1102 (Aug. 1991).

3. B. Gilbert, "Current-Mode Circuits from a Translinear Viewpoint: A Tutorial," *Analogue IC Design: The Current-Mode Approach*, C. Toumazou, F.J. Lidgey, and D.G. Haigh, Eds., Peter Peregrinus, London, 1990, Chap. 2.

4. A.S. Sedra and G.W. Roberts, "Current Conveyor Theory and Practice," *Analogue IC Design: The Current-Mode Approach*, C. Toumazou, F.J. Lidgey, and D.G. Haigh, Eds., Peter Peregrinus, London, 1990, Chap. 3.

5. B. Gilbert, "A Precise Four-Quadrant Multiplier with Subnanosecond Response," *IEEE J. Solid-State Circuits*, SC–3, 365–373 (Dec. 1968).

6. J.N. Babanezhad and G.C. Temes, "A 20-V Four-Quadrant CMOS Analog Multiplier," *IEEE J. Solid-State Circuits*, vol. SC–20, 1158–1168 (Dec. 1985).

7. B. Gilbert, "A Monolithic Microsystem for Analog Synthesis of Trigonometric Functions and Their Inverses," *IEEE J. Solid-State Circuits*, SC–17, 1179–1191, (Dec. 1982).

Index